一寸光阴

All Things Considered ★

事事关心 ★

哑巴 吃 饺子，心里有数
yǎ ba

有情饮水饱，
无情食饭饥。

现代汉语高级读本

An Advanced Reader of Modern Chinese

概不外

Princeton Language Program: Modern Chinese

Princeton University Press is proud to publish the Princeton Language Program in Modern Chinese. Based on courses taught through Princeton University Department of East Asian Studies and the Princeton in Beijing Program, this comprehensive series is designed for university students who wish to learn or improve upon their knowledge of Mandarin Chinese.

Students begin with either *Chinese Primer* or *Oh, China!* depending on their previous exposure to the language. After the first year, any combination of texts at a given level can be used. While all of the intermediate and advanced texts focus on modern life in China, and especially on the media, texts marked with an asterisk (*) in the chart below compare China to the United States and are particularly appropriate for American students.

PROGRAM OVERVIEW			
FIRST YEAR	SECOND YEAR	THIRD YEAR	ADVANCED
Chinese Primer (For beginners with no previous knowledge of Chinese)	*A New China*	*A Kaleidoscope of China*	*Anything Goes*
OR	*A Trip to China*	*All Things Considered*	*China's Own Critics*
Oh, China! (For students who speak and understand some Chinese, especially "heritage" students who speak the language at home.)	*An Intermediate Reader of Modern Chinese**	*Newspaper Readings**	*China's Peril and Promise*
			Literature and Society
			Readings in Contemporary Chinese Cinema

All Things Considered

事事关心

现代汉语高级读本

An Advanced Reader of Modern Chinese

Revised Edition

周质平

Chih-p'ing Chou

夏 岩　　　吴妙慧

Yan Xia　　Meow Hui Goh

Princeton University Press

Princeton and Oxford

Published by Princeton University Press
41 William Street, Princeton, New Jersey 08540

In the United Kingdom: Princeton University Press
6 Oxford Street, Woodstock, Oxfordshire OX20 1TW

press.princeton.edu

Library of Congress Control Number: 2011925521

ISBN 978-0-691-15310-0

British Library Cataloging-in-Publication Data is available

This book has been composed in STKaiti, Simsun, and Times New Roman

The publisher would like to acknowledge the authors of this volume for
providing the camera-ready copy from which this book was printed.

Printed on acid-free paper. ∞

Printed in the United States of America

7 9 10 8 6

事事关心
All Things Considered

目 录
Table of Contents

（一）会话篇

（二）读报篇

修订版序

《事事关心》是 2001 年出版的。过去 10 年来，许多学校采用作为教材。在使用的过程中，我们发现了一些错误和不足，在这次修订时做了改正和增补。

这次修订主要集中在版面的重新安排上。初版的设计是课文繁简字两页互见，而将生词置于课文之后。新版则采简体字课文与生词同页互见，繁体字课文置于每课之末。这一改变为学生学习提供了进一步的方便，同时也反映了简化字在国际汉语教学中发展的趋势。

修订版在内容上有增无减，但由于版面及字体大小的改动，在篇幅上减轻了初版的厚重，更便于翻阅和携带。

这次修订由杨玖老师主其事，对生词及词语例句部分进行增补。Ms. Cara Healey 校看全稿英文部分，并提出许多宝贵意见。我们在此对两位深致谢忱。当然，书中如有任何错误，都由作者负责。

周质平
夏　岩
吴妙慧
2010 年 12 月 31 日

Preface to the Revised Edition

All Things Considered was first published in 2001 and has been adopted by many institutions. In the process of using this book, we discovered a few errors and a few insufficient explanations, which we have now taken the opportunity to correct and append in this revised edition.

The main focus of this revision has been rearranging and reformatting the layout of each page. Originally, traditional and simplified character texts were juxtaposed on adjacent pages, with vocabulary words following. The revised edition juxtaposes the simplified character text and vocabulary words on adjacent pages and includes the traditional character text at the end of each lesson. This change makes it much more convenient for students to prepare the lesson, while at the same time it reflects the growing trend of using simplified characters in international Chinese language education.

Although we have actually increased the number of vocabulary words and example sentences in the revised edition, due to changes in formatting and font size, this edition actually has fewer pages than the last, making the book easier to flip through and carry.

Ms. Joanne Chiang undertook the revision of this book, coordinating the supplementation of vocabulary words and example sentences. Ms. Cara Healey proofread the entire English portion of the manuscript and also provided many valuable suggestions. To them we extend our sincere thanks. Of course, any errors in the final manuscript are the authors' own.

Chih-p'ing Chou
Yan Xia
Meow Hui Goh
December 31, 2010

序
xù
preface

　　过去十年来，普林斯顿大学对外汉语教研室的同仁共同编写了一系列的教科书。这些教科书除了供普大及普林斯顿北京汉语培训班使用外，美、加及其他地区也有不少学校用作教材。从多年教学实践中，我们感到：从中级到高级教材之间，跨越的幅度过大，在衔接上有一定的困难。这一衔接的"断层"现象也不独普大教材为然，坊间一般的教材在不同的程度上都有这个问题。

　　初级和中级的教材是特别为学习汉语的学生所写的。在词汇和句型的安排上都做了一定的控制。但三年级以上的材料则是选自现当代作家的作品，在文体上包括报刊、散文、小说和短剧等。在时间上则横跨自五四以来的八十年。

　　美国对外汉语教学界所说的"高级汉语"，其实，是很不"高级"的，是指学过两年以上现代汉语的学生而言。一般来说，在汉字的掌握上，一年级的学生约在五、六百字之间，二年级的学生约在一千二百字左右。但实际的使用能力则远低于此数。如用近年来为许多学校所采用的"口语能力测定标准"，学过两年汉语的学生至多能达到"一级上"到"中级下"之间，也就是勉强能用汉语作些日常生活的会话，谈谈身边琐事，有点购物和问路的能力，如此而已。换句话说，使用"高级"教材的学生其语言能力是很有限的，是连"文字初通"都谈不上的。

　　但是现有的坊间高级对外汉语教材却不少是选自鲁迅、胡适、巴金、茅盾等现代作家的作品。试问一个仅仅学了两年（实际上是两学年，约60个星期，每星期约四、五小时）汉语的美国学生，如何有能力看鲁迅这样风格特殊的白话文。这些二十年代作家所写的白话文虽是现代汉语的典范作品，但这种书面语和口语的距离是很大的。

要在这些作品之中选出一篇真能"上口"的文字真是少之又少。 被许多学校选为高级读本的鲁迅小说选，对美国学生来说，哪里是"现代汉语"。在他们的日常生活中既听不到也看不到类似这样的句子：

但心又不竟堕下去而至于断绝，他只是很重很重地堕着、堕着。

（鲁迅《野草·风筝》）

这样的句子，对一个对外汉语教师而言，既不是"现代汉语"，也不是"古代汉语"，它简直就是病句！

鲁迅是现代中国文学的宗师巨匠，他可以写这样的"病句"，但我们却不能用这样的"病句"作为"样板"来教外国学生。

我看了不少学校用鲁迅的小说来教学了两年汉语的美国学生。可怜！那些学生何尝"读"过鲁迅的小说，他们只是在死记每个故事的"生字表"，透过死记硬背，将故事的情节寻出一个大概来。因为故事的深刻和动人，学生也都一致叫好。 但若细细分析他们到底学到了多少现代汉语，那真是少得可怜了。

我们有鉴于现行高级汉语读本在语言难度上远远超过学生的能力，在经过几次讨论以后，决定另编一本在现有中级和高级读本之间的读物。在内容上仍以讨论与日常生活有关的问题为主。第一部分是对话。有些话题在一本教科书上出现，也许有人会觉得不甚得体，但我们觉得，只要是日常生活中使用的语言都不妨教给学生。至于雅俗或格调之高下，则见仁见智，不必勉强求同。 我们平心静气地想想，在日常生活之中的话题是否都是得体而又高雅的。一定程度的"不得体"正是真实和生动之所自来。我们力求对话生动有趣并富争议性，以便在上课时进行讨论。

除了编写的会话以外，我们从最近两年国内的报纸上选了20篇新闻报道或短评，从日常生活到国家大事，无所不谈，反映了一个在快速变动中的中国社会。有些对话的题材是从新闻中脱胎而来，所用的词汇大同小异，可以收复习强化的功效。

本书课文是由周质平编写的。对报刊原文做了必要的增删，以便教学。对话部分的生词和词语例句是吴妙慧编的。读报部分和全部的练习是夏岩编的。

　　《事事关心》初稿成于 2000 年春季。我们在普林斯顿大学暑期北京培训班和普大东亚系试用了一年，极受学生欢迎。有些学校也已将此书作为教材。

　　本书每课课文采繁简并列方式。课文之后有生词解释和词语例句，并备有配合课文和生词的录音带。

　　在编写的最后阶段，普大的杨玖老师和王晶玉老师校看书稿，为我们提供了许多宝贵的意见。Mr. David Carini 为我们做了一部分例句的翻译，并校看了生词的英语注释。我们在此向他们深致谢忱。当然，书中如有任何错误，都应该由我们负责。

周质平

夏岩

吴妙慧

2001 年 2 月 15 日

Preface

All Things Considered is a modern Chinese language textbook designed to bridge the gap between intermediate and advanced Chinese. It is targeted at students who have completed intermediate courses but are not yet prepared for the complexity of advanced Chinese.

The textbook consists of two parts. Part One contains twelve dialogues; Part two is a selection of Chinese newspaper articles from 1999 to 2000. The articles offer an introduction to contemporary Chinese society.

A new feature in *All Things Considered* is that several topics appear in both dialogue and essay forms. By covering the same topic twice, students will be able to not only learn the vocabulary and grammatical structures better, but also to see clearly the difference between speaking and writing in Chinese. And by keeping a portion of the textbook in dialogue form we emphasize speaking and reading equally; many advanced books, by contrast, assume that students already speak Chinese well enough and therefore ignore the spoken part of the language altogether. The overall proficiency level required for this textbook is lower than that for the previous advanced textbooks published by the Princeton University Press. We believe such a textbook is badly needed in the field.

The articles that we have selected are all related to contemporary issues in China, and their focus is on everyday life rather than the weighty political and social essays often seen in other advanced textbooks. Some of the topics are controversial; we believe this will evoke students' interest and increase their participation in class discussions. Following the tradition of our earlier textbooks, the text is arranged in both simplified and traditional characters, and vocabulary and sentence patterns accompany the text. Each lesson also contains a series of exercises that teachers will find useful for in-class work or homework assignments.

The draft of *All Things Considered* was written in the spring of 2000 and field-tested over the following year in Princeton Chinese language classes and the Princeton in Beijing summer program. Students consistently gave it high marks in their end-of-year evaluations.

We would like to express our sincere gratitude to Ms. Joanne Chiang and Ms. Jingyu Wang, who have taken pains to proofread the manuscript and have made valuable suggestions for the final version. We are deeply indebted to Mr. David Carini, who has not only translated part of the glossary and sentence patterns into English but also edited all of the English in the book. However, any errors are strictly the responsibility of the authors.

Chih-p'ing Chou
Yan Xia
Meow Hui Goh
February 15, 2001

List of Abbreviations

adj. = adjective

adv. = adverb

aux. = auxiliary

AN = Measure Word

conj. = conjunction

idm. = idiom

int. = interjection

n. = noun

num. = number

o. = object

part. = particle

phr. = phrase

prefix = prefix

prep. = preposition

pron. = pronoun

s. = subject

suffix = suffix

v. = verb

v.-c. = verb-complement

v.-o. = verb-object

* 轻声字注音不标调号，但在注音前加一个圆点，如"桌子"：zhuō.zi。一般轻读，有时重读的字，在注音上标调号，注音前再加一个圆点。如"因为"：yīn.wèi。两字之间可插入其他成分时，加 //，如："理发"：lǐ//fà。各词条的注音都依据商务印书馆出版的《现代汉语词典》。

Characters pronounced with a neutral tone are transcribed not with a tone marker on top of the main vowel, as ordinary characters are, but with a dot before the initial consonant, such as "桌子": zhuō.zi. Characters usually pronounced with a neutral tone but occasionally with a stress are transcribed with both a tone marker and a dot before the initial consonant, such as "因为": yīn.wèi, where 为 is usually pronounced with a neutral tone but sometimes with a falling tone (the fourth tone). When there can be an insertion between two characters, a // is added, such as "理发": lǐ//fà. The phonetic notation for all entries is based on *Xiandai Hanyu Cidian* published by The Commercial Press.

All Things Considered

事事关心

第一课　　刚到中国

甲：你是哪一天到北京的啊？

乙：我是三天以前到的。

甲：你是从纽约直飞北京的吗？

乙：不是。据我所知(1)，从纽约没有直飞北京的飞机。我是从纽约直飞东京，在东京转机再飞北京的。

甲：一路上都很顺利吧？

乙：很顺利，就是(2)在东京转机等了三个多小时。东京的机场很小，人又多，这三个小时比从纽约到东京还(3)累！

甲：你以前来过中国没有？

乙：小时候跟着父母来过一次。

甲：那是什么时候的事啊？

乙：那是我上小学的时候。父亲到上海去谈生意，我跟着他和母亲来了一趟中国。都快(4)十年前的事了。

甲：十年前的事还有印象吗？

乙：虽然快十年了，但是对许多事都还印象深刻呢！

甲：你最难忘的是什么事啊？

乙：我最难忘的是去参观长城和故宫。

刚	剛	gāng	*adv.*	just
北京		Běijīng	*n.*	Beijing, capital of China
直飞	直飛	zhífēi	*v.*	fly directly 直飞北京/直飞美国
据	據	jù	*prep.*	according to; on the grounds of
东京	東京	Dōngjīng	*n.*	Tokyo, Japan
转机	轉機	zhuǎn//jī	*v.-o.*	change flights
再		zài	*adv.*	then (indicates that an action occurs after the previous one is concluded) 吃了饭再看电视/做完功课再出去/先去东京再去北京
一路上		yílù.shàng	*adv.*	on one's way (to a place)
顺利	順利	shùnlì	*adj.*	smooth; successful; without a hitch
等		děng	*v.*	wait
机场	機場	jīchǎng	*n.*	airport
还	還	hái	*adv.*	更；even more
小时候	小時候	xiǎo shí.hou		when one was little; when one was a kid
上海		Shànghǎi	*n.*	Shanghai, China
谈	談	tán	*v.*	talk; negotiate
生意		shēng.yi	*n.*	business
跟		gēn	*v.*	follow
趟		tàng	*AN*	measure word for trip
印象		yìnxiàng	*n.*	impression
深刻		shēnkè	*adj.*	deep; profound
难忘	難忘	nánwàng	*adj.*	memorable; difficult to forget
参观	參觀	cānguān	*v.*	visit (a place, such as a tourist spot) 参观学校/参观有名的景点
长城	長城	Chángchéng	*n.*	the Great Wall
故宫		Gùgōng	*n.*	the Imperial Palace

甲：在美国没见过这么古老的建筑吧？

乙：我对这两个地方印象特别深刻，倒不是因为建筑古老，而是(5)因为我不懂为什么中国人两千年来要把自己围在城墙里头。而且一个皇帝竟然(6)住那么大的房子。在中国当皇帝太舒服了！

甲：那是古代的中国，现代的中国可不一样了。

乙：噢，是吗！？

甲：这次你到中国来计划做些什么事啊？
    jì huà

乙：我想学习中文，也想体验一下中国人的生活。上次来中国跟着父母住在大旅馆里，完全没有机会跟中国人打交道。这种观光客式的参观旅游，对一个地方的了解都是很肤浅的。这次来，
    fū qiǎn
    我想用中文多和中国人谈谈。吃他们吃的饭，坐他们坐的车，我要把自己的生活尽量(7)"中国化"。

古老		gǔlǎo	*adj.*	ancient; old
建筑	建築	jiànzhù	*n.*	building; structure; architecture
懂		dǒng	*v.*	understand
千		qiān	*n.*	thousand
				两千块钱/三千个学生
围	圍	wéi	*v.*	surround; enclose
墙	牆	qiáng	*n.*	wall
				城墙: city wall
皇帝		huángdì	*n.*	emperor
竟然		jìngrán	*adv.*	unexpectedly; to one's surprise
住		zhù	*v.*	live in; reside

房子		fáng.zi	*n.*	house
舒服		shū.fu	*adj.*	comfortable
古代		gǔdài	*n.*	ancient times
现代	現代	xiàndài	*n.*	modern times
噢		ō	*int.*	Oh! (expressing sudden realization)
计划	計劃	jìhuà	*v./n.*	plan to, plan
学习	學習	xuéxí	*v.*	learn; study
体验	體驗	tǐyàn	*v.*	learn through one's personal experience; experience (life)
生活		shēnghuó	*n.*	life; livelihood
父母		fùmǔ	*n.*	parent; 父亲跟母亲
旅馆	旅館	lǚguǎn	*n.*	hotel
完全		wánquán	*adv.*	completely
机会	機會	jīhuì	*n.*	opportunity; chance
打交道		dǎ jiāodào	*v.-o.*	make contact with 他常跟外国人打交道。
观光客	觀光客	guān guāng kè	*n.*	tourist
——式		shì	*suffix*	type; style 中国式的家具
旅游	旅遊	lǚyóu	*n./v.*	tourism; tour
了解		liǎojiě	*v./n.*	understand; comprehend, understanding
肤浅	膚淺	fūqiǎn	*adj.*	(of one's understanding of a subject or issue) superficial; shallow
尽量	儘量	jǐnliàng	*adv.*	to the fullest (amount, degree, etc.) 尽量早点儿来/尽量少花钱
——化		huà	*suffix*	- ize; -ify
中国化	中國化	Zhōngguó huà	*v.*	"sinicize"; become Chinese; be like a Chinese person

甲：许多美国人都跟我说过同样的话。他们总把体验中国人的生活想成和初中学生"野外求生"差不多，又刺激又好玩儿。其实你只要在摄氏三十六度的天气里过一天没有空调的生活，你就(8)不想体验中国人的生活了。

乙：你也未免(9)把我说得太禁不起考验了。下个周末我就打算坐硬卧去西安呢！

同样	同樣	tóngyàng	*adj.*	same 用同样的方法/上同样的学校
总	總	zǒng	*adv.*	always; invariably
初中		chūzhōng	*n.*	junior high school
野外求生		yěwài qiúshēng	*n.*	outdoor education 野外：wildness 求生：seek to survive
差不多		chà.buduō	*adj.*	about the same; similar 我的看法和他的差不多。
刺激		cìjī	*adj.*	exciting
好玩儿		hǎowánr	*adj.*	fun; amusing; interesting
其实	其實	qíshí	*adv.*	actually; in fact
只要		zhǐyào	*conj.*	so long as
摄氏	攝氏	Shèshì	*n.*	Celsius 华氏：Fahrenheit
度		dù	*n.*	degree for temperature
天气	天氣	tiānqì	*n.*	weather

空调	空調	kōngtiáo	n.	air conditioning; air conditioner
未免		wèimiǎn	adv.	(of something that one finds has gone too far) rather; a bit too
禁不起		jīn.buqǐ	v.-c.	unable to stand (a test, trial, etc.) 禁得起: able to stand
考验	考驗	kǎoyàn	n.	test; trial
周末	週末	zhōumò	n.	weekend
打算		dǎsuàn	v.	plan to; intend to
硬卧	硬臥	yìngwò	n.	"hard sleeper;" (There are two kinds of seats in the trains in China, the "hard sleeper" and the "soft sleeper 软卧."
西安		Xī'ān	n.	Xi'an, China

词语例句

(1) 据我所知，…：According to what I know, ...

◆ 据我所知，从纽约没有直飞北京的飞机。

    According to what I know, there is no direct flight from New York to Beijing.

  1. A：他以前来过中国吗?

     B：据我所知，这是他第一次来中国。

     A：Has he come to China before?

     B：According to what I know, this is the first time that he's been in China.

  2. 他说中国的火车只有硬卧，但是据我所知，还有软卧。

    He said that the trains in China only have "hard sleepers," but according to what I know, there are also "soft" ones.

(2) S. 都…，就是……: everything is … , except…

◆ 一路上都很顺利，就是在东京转机等了三个多小时。

Everything was going smoothly, except I waited in Tokyo more than three hours while changing flights.

1. 这次旅游什么都很好，就是天气太热了。

This tour was wonderful, except the weather was just too hot.

2. 这家饭馆的菜和服务都很好，就是价钱太贵了。

The food and service of this restaurant are good, but it's too expensive.

(3) A 比 B 还 adj. : A is even more adj. than B

◆ 这三个小时比从纽约到东京还累！

These three hours were even more tiresome than flying from New York to Tokyo.

1. 中文很难学，没想到日文比中文还难学。

Chinese is hard to learn; surprisingly Japanese is even harder.

2. 坐汽车比骑自行车还慢，你还是骑车去吧！

It is even slower by bus than by bicycle. You'd better go by bicycle.

(4) 都快…了: It is almost … already.

◆ 都快十年前的事了。

It has been almost ten years already.

1. 都快八点了，你怎么还不走？

It's almost eight o'clock already. Why don't you get a move on?

2. 他都快 90 岁了，身体还很健康。

He is almost 90 years old already but still in good shape.

(5) 不是 A，而是 B: it's not A, but B

◆ 我对这两个地方印象特别深刻倒不是因为建筑古老，而是因为我不懂为什么中国人两千年来要把自己围在城墙里头。

The reason that I remember these two places especially well is not because the buildings there are old, but because I don't understand why the Chinese kept themselves secluded within the walls for two thousand years.

1. 想买房子的不是我，而是他。

It is him and not me who wants to buy a house.

2. 我父亲到中国不是去观光的，而是去谈生意的。

My father did not go to China for sight seeing, but to do business.

3. 我不了解中国人不是因为我不想了解他们，而是因为我没有机

8

会跟他们打交道。

The reason that I do not understand the Chinese people is not because I do not
wish to do so, but because I have not had the chance to make contact with them.

(6) 竟然: unexpectedly; to one's surprise

◆ 一个皇帝竟然住那么大的房子。

I can't believe that an emperor lived in such a big house!

1. 我没想到东京的机场竟然这么小！

I didn't expect Tokyo's airport to be so small!

2. 那已经是十年前的事了，你竟然还没忘记啊？

That was something that happened ten years ago, and you still haven't forgotten
it?

(7) 尽量: to the fullest (amount, degree, etc.)

◆ 我要把自己的生活尽量"中国化"。

I want to make my life as "Chinese" as possible.

1. 今天的菜那么多，你们要尽量吃。

There are so many dishes today; please eat to your heart's content.

2. 我来了中国，一定要尽量多跟中国人打交道。

Now that I'm in China I must do my best to interact more with Chinese people.

(8) 只要…就…: so long as …; as long as

◆ 其实你只要在摄氏三十六度的天气里过一天没有空调的生活，你
就不想体验中国人的生活了。

In fact, if you live just one day without air-conditioning when the temperature is
36°C, you will not want to experience the Chinese way of life anymore.

1. A：跟中国人做生意真难！

   B：其实只要你能"中国化"一点儿，就能顺利地跟他们做生意
      了。

   A：It is so difficult to do business with the Chinese!

   B：Actually, if only you could be a little more "Chinese," you could do
      business with them smoothly.

2. 只要那个地方是我参观过的，我就会有印象。

   As long as I have been to a place, I'll remember it.

(9) 未免: (of something that one finds has gone too far) rather; a bit too

9

◆ 你也未免把我说得太禁不起考验了。

What you have said makes it seem as if I'm incapable of standing up to trials!

1. 转一次飞机要等两天，未免太过分了吧！

Having to wait two days to change a flight is a bit too much!

2. 吃过中国人的饭，坐过中国人的火车，就算是体验过中国

人的生活了吗？这种想法未免太肤浅了。

Can you say you have experienced the Chinese way of life just by eating Chinese food and taking a train in China? This is but a rather shallow thought.

练习

I. Choose the correct answer.

1. 我没想到这么大的一个旅馆里头 _____ 没有空调。

　　a. 虽然　　b. 竟然　　c. 当然

2. A: 你还记得不记得十年以前的事？

　B: _____。

　　a. 十年以前的事对我完全没有印象了。

　　b. 我对十年以前的事情完全没有印象了。

　　c. 对我十年以前的事情完全没有印象了。

3. 你 _____ 多跟中国人打交道，_____ 能了解他们的生活。

　　a. 只有…就　　b. 只要…才　　c. 只要…就

II. Choose the most appropriate word for each blank and fill in with its Chinese equivalent.

to the fullest	smooth	deep	rather/a bit too
superficial	make contact with	Americanize	memorable

1. 据我所知，他并不是一个 _____ 的人。他对历史、政治都有很

_____ 的看法。

2. 你去哪儿你的父母都要跟着你，他们对你 _____ 太不放心了。

3. 为了让教室里所有的学生都听懂，她 _____ 说得很慢，说得很清楚。

4. 在美国住了二十年，他的生活已经完全 _____ 了。

5. 他爸爸在日本做生意，常常跟日本人 <u>打交道</u>。

III. Choose the phrase that is closest in meaning to the underlined phrase in the sentence.

1. 中国的公共交通非常方便，<u>尤其</u>是北京和上海。
   (a.)特别 b. 由于 c.有些

2. 人好看不好看无所谓，最<u>要紧</u>的是性情好。
   a. 严重 (b.)重要 c. 紧张

3. 她<u>计划</u>周末坐硬卧去上海。
   (a.)打算 b. 决定 c. 愿意

IV. Complete the following dialogue between a Chinese person and an American student using the expressions provided .

中国人：你不是中国人吧？这次到中国来计划做些什么事啊？
美国留学生：除了学习以外，我还想体验"中国化"，要尽量跟中国大学生打交道。
   （除了…以外，体验，尽量，跟…打交道）

中国人：我很想到纽约去旅游，可是我该怎么去呢？
美国留学生：据我所知，从北京到纽约很累，应该在东京转机。
   （据我所知，转机，直飞，从…到…，累）

V. Composition

 一次难忘的旅行

繁体字课文

甲：你是哪一天到北京的啊？

乙：我是三天以前到的。

甲：你是從紐約直飛北京的嗎？

乙：不是。據我所知(1)，從紐約沒有直飛北京的飛機。我是從紐約直飛東京，在東京轉機再飛北京的。

甲：一路上都很順利吧？

乙：很順利，就是(2)在東京轉機等了三個多小時。東京的機場很小，人又多，這三個小時比從紐約到東京還(3)累！

甲：你以前來過中國沒有？

乙：小時候跟著父母來過一次。

甲：那是什麼時候的事啊？

乙：那是我上小學的時候。父親到上海去談生意，我跟著他和母親來了一趟中國。都快(4)十年前的事了。

甲：十年前的事還有印象嗎？

乙：雖然快十年了，但是對許多事都還印象深刻呢！

甲：你最難忘的是什麼事啊？

乙：我最難忘的是去參觀長城和故宮。

甲：在美國沒見過這麼古老的建築吧？

乙：我對這兩個地方印象特別深刻，倒不是因為建築古老，而是(5)因為我不懂為什麼中國人兩千年來要把自己圍在城牆裏頭。而且一個皇帝竟然(6)住那麼大的房子。在中國當皇帝太舒服了！

甲：那是古代的中國，現代的中國可不一樣了。

乙：噢，是嗎！？

甲：這次你到中國來計劃做些什麼事啊？

乙：我想學習中文，也想體驗一下中國人的生活。上次來中國跟著
　　父母住在大旅館裏，完全沒有機會跟中國人打交道。這種觀光
　　客式的參觀旅遊，對一個地方的了解都是很膚淺的。這次來，
　　我想用中文多和中國人談談。吃他們吃的飯，坐他們坐的車，
　　我要把自己的生活儘量(7)"中國化"。

甲：許多美國人都跟我說過同樣的話。他們總把體驗中國人的生活想
　　成和初中學生"野外求生"差不多，又刺激又好玩儿。其實你只
　　要在攝氏三十六度的天氣裏過一天沒有空調的生活，你就(8)不
　　想體驗中國人的生活了。

乙：你也未免(9)把我說得太禁不起考驗了。下個週末我就打算坐硬
　　臥去西安呢！

第二课　　租自行车

甲：昨天我想坐公共汽车去天坛，等了几班车，都上不去。

乙：为什么上不去呢？

甲：因为我排队，不想跟别人抢着(1)上车。

乙：那可不成，别人都抢，你也得抢。

甲：可我从小就(2)习惯排队。

乙：要是大家都不排队，你就得抢。要是你怕挤，怕抢，也许(3)坐地铁好些(4)，地铁比公共汽车快多了(5)。

甲：地铁站离学校太远，走到最近的地铁站也得二十分钟。

乙：你既然不想浪费时间，为什么(6)不坐出租车呢？

甲：出租车太贵了，坐趟车比吃顿饭还贵呢！

乙：公交车太挤，地铁太远。出租车又太贵，我看你只好(7)骑自行车了。

甲：自行车好是好，就是(8)比较危险。北京的交通规则我不熟，万

租		zū	*v.*	rent
自行车	自行車	zìxíngchē	*n.*	bicycle; bike
公共汽车	公共汽車	gōnggòng qìchē	*n.*	public bus
天坛	天壇	Tiāntán	*n.*	Temple of Heaven
班		bān	*AN*	measure word for scheduled transport vehicles or planes

14

排队	排隊	pái//duì	v.-o.	stand in line; form a line
抢	搶	qiǎng	v.	scramble for
上车	上車	shàng//chē	v.-o.	board a bus
				下车：get off a bus
不成		bùchéng	v.	won't do
从小	從小	cóngxiǎo	adv.	since one was very young; from one's childhood
习惯	習慣	xíguàn	v.	be accustomed to; be used to
怕		pà	v.	be afraid of; fear
挤	擠	jǐ	v./adj.	jostle; push against, crowded
也许	也許	yěxǔ	adv.	perhaps; probably
地铁	地鐵	dìtiě	n.	subway
地铁站	地鐵站	dìtiě zhàn	n.	subway station
离	離	lí	v.	apart from
远	遠	yuǎn	adj.	far
近		jìn	adj.	near; close
分钟	分鐘	fēnzhōng	AN	measure word for time; minute
既然		jìrán	conj.	since; as; now that
浪费	浪費	làngfèi	v.	waste
出租车	出租車	chūzūchē	n.	cab; taxi
顿	頓	dùn	AN	measure word for meal
				一天吃三顿饭
公交车	公交車	gōngjiāo chē	n.	public bus; 公共汽车
只好		zhǐhǎo	adv.	have to; be forced to
骑	騎	qí	v.	ride (a bicycle, a horse, etc.)
比较	比較	bǐjiào	adv.	relatively; fairly
危险	危險	wēixiǎn	adj.	dangerous
交通		jiāotōng	n.	traffic
规则	規則	guīzé	n.	rule; regulation
熟		shú	adj.	familiar

一(9)出了事儿，可就糟了。

乙：北京骑车的人多得很，你跟着大家骑，靠边儿走，保证(10)安全。

甲：我在北京只待两个月，买辆新车划不来(11)。

乙：你不想买新车，可以租一辆。

甲：噢？自行车还能租吗？

乙：当然能啦！新的、旧的、贵的、便宜的(12)，各种式样的都有。你想租辆什么样的车啊？

甲：我想租辆不新不旧(13)的中档车。每天在街上骑骑，又省钱，又省时间，还(14)可以锻炼身体。住在宿舍里什么运动都没有，才(15)来了两个星期就胖了好几公斤，一定得想个法子运动运动。

乙：北京人大多骑车上班，这不但解决了交通问题，也锻炼了身体，真是一举两得。

甲：这真是个好主意！我明天就去租辆自行车。

万一	萬一	wànyī	*conj.*	if by any chance; just in case
出事儿		chū//shìr	*v.-o.*	meet with a mishap; have an accident
糟		zāo	*adj.*	terrible; in a mess
靠		kào	*prep.*	keep to; get near 靠右边走/靠墙站着
边儿	邊儿	biānr	*n.*	side; edge
保证	保證	bǎozhèng	*v.*	guarantee
安全		ānquán	*adj.*	safe

待		dāi	v.	stay
辆	輛	liàng	AN	measure word for vehicles
划不来	划不來	huá.bùlái	v.-c.	not worth it
				划得来: worth it
当然	當然	dāngrán	adv.	certainly; of course
旧	舊	jiù	adj.	old; used; worn
便宜		pián.yi	adj.	cheap
各种	各種	gèzhǒng	adj.	various kinds
式样	式樣	shìyàng	n.	style; type; model
中档	中檔	zhōngdàng	adj.	(of the quality of things) second rate
				中: middle
				档: grade of consumer goods
街		jiē	n.	street
省		shěng	v.	save
锻炼	鍛煉	duànliàn	v.	exercise (the body)
身体	身體	shēntǐ	n.	body; health
宿舍		sùshè	n.	dormitory
运动	運動	yùndòng	n.	physical exercise
才		cái	adv.	(here) only; 只
胖		pàng	adj./v.	fat, get fat; put on weight
公斤		gōngjīn	AN	measure word for weight; kilograms
法子		fá.zi	n.	means; way
大多		dàduō	adv.	mostly
上班		shàng//bān	v.-o.	go to work
				下班: come off duty
解决	解決	jiějué	v.	resolve
问题	問題	wèntí	n.	problem; question; matter
一举两得	一舉兩得	yì jǔ liǎng dé	idm.	"one act two gains," - kill two birds with one stone
主意		zhú.yì	n.	idea

（在租车店里）

甲：师傅，你们租自行车吗？

乙：我们卖自行车也租自行车。你想租辆什么样的车？

甲：我想租辆不新不旧的中档车。

乙：这两天暑期班刚开学，来租车的人特别多，好车都租出去了，
　　只剩下这几辆了，你看看吧！

甲：我想试试⒃这辆。能骑一下吗？

乙：行啊！别走远了，就在店门口骑两圈儿。

甲：好，好。

（过了一会儿）

甲：这车怎么租啊？一个月多少钱？

乙：我们这儿租车不论月，论⒄天数。一天五块钱。

甲：一天五块钱，一个月就得一百五十块钱，两个月租下来⒅，
　　不是和买辆车差不多了吗？

乙：三百块钱可买不到这样的车。

甲：好吧，好吧，我先租两个星期试试。

乙：除了租金，你还得付押金。押金一百块。

甲：我还想买个安全帽。你们有没有安全帽？

乙：骑自行车戴什么安全帽⒆？在北京你见过骑车的人戴安全帽

吗？

甲：见倒是没见过，可是……

乙：放心，在北京骑车，没事儿！

店		diàn	*n.*	shop; store
师傅	師傅	shī.fu	*n.*	a respectful form of address for a service worker
暑期班		shǔqībān	*n.*	summer school 暑期：summer session 班：class
开学	開學	kāi//xué	*v.-o.*	start school; begin a term
特别		tèbié	*adv.*	especially
剩下	剩下	shèng.xià	*v.*	be left (over); remain
试		shì	*v.*	try
门口	門口	ménkǒu	*n.*	doorway; entrance
圈儿	圈儿	quānr	*AN*	measure word for rounds
论	論	lùn	*prep.*	by; regarding; in terms of 这儿的房子都论月租。
天数	天數	tiānshù	*n.*	number of days
租金		zūjīn	*n.*	rental fee; rent
付		fù	*v.*	pay
押金		yājīn	*n.*	deposit
安全帽		ānquán mào	*n.*	safety helmet
戴		dài	*v.*	wear (a cap, a watch, etc.)
放心	放心	fàng//xīn	*v.-o.*	set one's mind at rest; feel relieved
没事儿	沒事儿	méishìr	*phr.*	it's nothing; no problem

词语例句

(1) 抢着 v. : scramble for; vie for

◆ 我排队，不想跟别人抢着上车。

　I always stand in line; I don't want to vie with others to get on the bus.

　1. 在饭馆儿里，中国人有抢着付帐的习惯。

　　In a restaurant, Chinese are used to vying for the bill.

　2. 下课的时间一到，学生们就抢着跑出教室去。

　　As soon as the class was over, the students scrambled to run out of the classroom.

(2) 从小就 v. : have v.-ed from childhood; have v.-ed since one was very young

◆ 我从小就习惯排队。

　I have been used to lining up since I was very young.

　1. 他从小就住在外国。

　　He has lived in foreign country since he was very young.

　2. 你从小就会骑自行车，在北京骑车应该没问题。

　　You are used to riding a bicycle from childhood; you should have no problem riding a bicycle in Beijing.

(3) 要是…，也许…: If ..., perhaps ...

◆ 要是你怕挤，怕抢，也许坐地铁好些。

　If you're afraid to squeeze in and to fight (for a seat), perhaps it's better that you take the subway.

　1. 要是你觉得直飞太累，也许你可以先到东京住两天。

　　If you think that flying there directly will make you too tired, maybe you can stop over in Tokyo for two days.

　2. 要是新车太贵，那我们也许得租辆中档的。

　　If the new car is too expensive, then we might have to rent a second-rate one.

(4) adj. 些: more adj.

◆ 坐地铁好些。

　1. 住在宿舍里虽然挤，可是方便些。

　　Although the dormitory is crowded, it's more convenient to stay there (than in some other place.)

　2. 坐软卧很贵，但舒服些。

It's very expensive to travel on the "soft sleepers," but it's more comfortable that way.

(5) A 比 B adj. 多了: A is much more adj. then B

◆ 地铁比公共汽车快多了。

　　The subway is much faster then the buses.

　　1. 我们还是坐公车吧！公车站比地铁站近多了。

　　　Let's take a bus! The bus station is much closer than the subway station.

　　2. 他只学了几个月的中文，可是却说得比我好多了。

　　　He has studied Chinese for only a few months, but he speaks much better than I do.

(6) 既然…，为什么不/还…呢？: Since (it's the case that)…, why not/still…?

◆ 你既然不想浪费时间，为什么不坐出租车呢？

　　Since you don't want to waste your time, why don't you take a cab?

　　1. 你既然来了北京，为什么不去参观长城和故宫呢？

　　　Since you're here in Beijing, why don't you visit the Great Wall and the Imperial Palace?

　　2. 既然他那么怕跟中国人打交道，为什么还要来中国呢？

　　　Since he's so afraid of making contact with Chinese people, why did he come to China?

(7) 只好: have to; be forced to

◆ 我看你只好骑自行车了。

　　I think that you'll just have to ride a bicycle.

　　1. 大家都抢着上车，我只好跟着抢了。

　　　Everyone is jostling to get on the bus. I have no choice but to follow suit.

　　2. 你这个菜也不吃，那个菜也不吃，我看你只好吃白米饭了。

　　　You won't eat this dish, and you won't eat that one either. I think that you'll be left with only white rice to eat.

(8) adj. 是 adj.，就是…: It is indeed adj., but it's just that …

◆ 自行车好是好，就是比较危险。

　　（Riding a）bicycle is good, but it's just more dangerous.

　　1. 坐公共汽车便宜是便宜，就是太浪费时间了。

　　　Taking a bus is indeed cheap, but it's just too time consuming.

　　2. 这么做可以是可以，就是怕会出事儿。

Doing it this way is fine, but I'm just worried that something might go wrong.

(9) 万一: if by any chance; just in case

◆ 北京的交通规则我不熟，万一出了事儿，可就糟了。

I'm not familiar with the traffic regulations in Beijing. If something goes wrong, it will be terrible.

1. 这辆车那么旧，万一在路上坏了，怎么办呢?

This car is so old, what if it breaks down on the road?

2. 你少做一点儿菜，万一他们不来，也不浪费。

Don't cook so much. If by some chance they do not show up, nothing will be wasted.

(10) 保证: to guarantee

◆ 北京骑车的人多得很，你跟着大家骑，靠边儿走，保证安全。

There are many bike riders in Beijing, so just follow the crowd and keep to the side. I guarantee you'll be safe.

1. 这种安全帽好得很，戴了保证又舒服又安全又好看!

This kind of safety helmet is just great! I guarantee you'll be comfortable, safe, and good-looking wearing it!

2. 我想的这个主意保证能解决你的问题。

I guarantee that this idea of mine will solve your problems.

(11) 划得来/划不来: worth it/not worth it

◆ 我在北京只待两个月，买辆新车划不来。

I'll only be staying in Beijing for two months, so buying a new bicycle is not worth it.

1. 出去吃顿饭得挤公车，到了饭馆还得排队等，真划不来!

You will have to squeeze into a bus to go out for a meal, and when you get to the restaurant you'll still have to wait in line. It's really not worth it!

2. 你想开一家店? 除了租金，还得先付押金，到底划不划得来?

You're thinking of opening a store? In addition to the rental fee, you'll also have to pay a deposit in advance. Is it really worth it?

(12) A 的、B 的、C 的: A ones, B ones, C ones

◆ 新的、旧的、贵的、便宜的，各种式样的都有。

There are different types: new ones, old ones, expensive ones, and cheaper ones.

1. 我这儿的衣服很多，无论是长的、短的，还是大的、小的，我都有。

I have all different types of clothes: long ones, short ones, big ones, and small ones – I have everything.

2. 我不喜欢看小说。 无论是现代的还是古代的，是讲社会的还是个人生活的，我都不看。

I do not like to read novels. No matter if they are modern or classic, and no matter if they are about society as a whole or the life of an individual, I simply do not read them.

(13) 不 A 不 B : not A not B; neither A nor B

◆ 我想租辆不新不旧的中档车。

I want to rent a mid-range (price/quality) bicycle that is neither (too) new nor (too) old.

1. 这个房子不大不小，刚好！

This house is neither too big nor too small. It's just right!

2. 这个电影不好不坏，没什么特别的。

This movie is not good, but it's not bad either. There is nothing special about it.

(14) 又···，又···，还···: both ... and ..., in addition, ...

◆ 每天在街上骑骑，又省钱，又省时间，还可以锻炼身体。

Ride it on the streets everyday, and you'll save time and money; in addition, you can also get some exercise.

1. 那个地铁站又小，人又多，去那儿还得走二十分钟，我还是坐出租车吧！

That subway station is not only small but also crowded. Moreover, it takes twenty minutes to walk there. I would rather take a cab!

2. 这种东西又好吃，又吃不胖，还很便宜，我得多买一点儿。

This stuff tastes good and doesn't make you fat. What's more, it's cheap. I have to buy more of it.

(15) 才: only

◆ 住在宿舍里什么运动都没有，才来了两个星期就胖了好几公斤。

Staying in the dormitory, I do not get any exercise; as a result I've gained quite a few kilos in just two weeks.

1. 你才过了一天没有空调的生活就受不了了，还说禁得起考验！

After just one day without air-conditioning you can't stand it, yet you claimed you could stand up to the test!

2. 租辆车一个月才一百五十块，便宜得很。

It costs only one hundred and fifty dollars to rent a car for a month. That's very cheap.

(16) 试试: to give it a try

◆ 我想试试这辆。

I would like to try this one.

1. 这个电脑我还没有试用过，不知道好不好。

I have not tried using this computer, so I'm not sure if it's good or not.

2. 这儿的安全帽都一样，你不用试了。

The safety helmets here are all the same, you don't need to try one on.

(17) 不论 A, 论 B : do not go by A, but rather B

◆ 我们这儿租车不论月，论天数。

At our shop, we don't rent out a bicycle by months. We do it by days.

1. 中国人不论磅，论公斤。

Chinese people do not measure weight by pounds; they go by kilograms.

2. 我交朋友不论他有没有钱，只论他人好不好。

When I make friends, I don't care if he's rich; I only care if he's a good person.

(18) Time duration + v. 下来: after v.-ing for …

◆ 两个月租下来，不是和买辆车差不多了吗？

After renting for two months, doesn't it cost the same as buying one?

1. 在北京两年住下来，你的中文肯定会进步很多。

After living in Beijing for two years, your Chinese will definitely improve a lot.

2. 在这儿一个月住下来，我对交通规则已经很熟了。

I am quite familiar with the traffic rules after living here for one month.

(19) v. 什么 o. : (rhetorical question) why would one v. + o. ?

◆ 骑自行车戴什么安全帽？

Why would anyone wear a safety helmet when riding a bicycle?

1. 排什么队？我从来没看过上厕所还要排队！

Why would you line up? I've never seen that one has to line up for the restroom!

2. 在北京吃什么麦当劳？你应该吃当地的小吃！

Why do you want to go to McDonald's in Beijing? You should try the local refreshments!

练习

I. Choose the correct answer.

1. 我本来有 100 块钱，买书用了 30 块，买酒用了 20 块钱，我还 _____ ？
      a. 剩下多少钱　b. 多少钱剩下了　c. 离开多少钱

2. 这条马路有点儿危险，你最好 _____ 。
      a. 向边儿走　b. 靠边儿走　c. 跟边儿靠

3. 中国改革开放 _____ 二十年， _____ 发生了这么大的变化。
      a. 才，就　b. 就，才　c. 已经，竟然

4. 我对这张 CD 很有兴趣，我可以不可以 _____ 一下？
      a. 听试试　b. 试听　c. 听听试

5. 在这儿租车不 _____ 小时。
      a. 用　b. 论　c. 据

6. _____ 你要体验中国人的生活， _____ 还住在这么贵的饭店里？
      a. 因为，为什么　b. 虽然，但是　c. 既然，为什么

II. Choose the most appropriate word for each blank and fill in with its Chinese equivalent.

familiar	fear	guarantee	save
follow	scramble for	waste	if by any chance

1. 我在这儿住了二十年，对所有的地方都 _____ 得很。只要你 _____ 我，我 _____ 你找得到要去的地方。

2. 住在宿舍里，虽然人有点儿多，可是离什么地方都很近，可以 _____ 很多时间。

3. 中国人在饭馆儿吃饭的时候，常常 _____ 付钱。

4. 虽然校园里很安全，可是你一个女孩子，也不要这么晚一个人走路， _____ 出了什么事，可就麻烦了。

III. Choose the phrase that is closest in meaning to the underlined phrase in the sentence.

1. 放心，在北京骑车，<u>没事儿</u>。
      a. 别出事　b. 没有工作　c. 不会有问题

2. 天气这么热，<u>你还戴什么帽子</u>！
    a. 你戴什么式样的帽子
    b. 你戴什么牌子的帽子
    c. 你不必戴帽子

3. 昨天我的皮包<u>给</u>一个男人偷了。
    a. 把   b. 被   c. 要

4. 其实去北京学中文真的很<u>划得来</u>，因为不但可以很快地提高中文水平，还可以比较深刻地了解中国文化。
    a. 省钱   b. 值得   c. 有用

IV. Composition

1. 你的朋友刚到北京，请你告诉他在北京坐地铁、公共汽车、骑自行车、坐出租车，各有什么好处、坏处。
  尽量用以下的生词：抢、挤、排队、糟、熟、省、浪费、
                  危险、尽量、一举两得
  尽量用以下的句型：万一、要是…也许…、划不来、
                 A 比 B adj. 多了、adj. 些

2. 大学旁边有一家租车店，租自行车也卖自行车，可是生意一直不好。现在请你为这家店写一个广告 (guǎnggào:advertisement) 来吸引 (xīyǐn: to attract) 顾客(gùkè: customer) 租自行车。
  这个广告的内容(nèiróng: content) 应该有：
    a. 租车店的名字、地址（dìzhǐ: address）、电话
    b. 这家店的自行车是什么样的?
    c. 租金、押金的情况

繁体字课文

甲：昨天我想坐公共汽車去天壇，等了幾班車，都上不去。

乙：為什麼上不去呢？

甲：因為我排隊，不想跟別人搶著⑴上車。

乙：那可不成，別人都搶，你也得搶。

甲：可我從小就⑵習慣排隊。

乙：要是大家都不排隊，你就得搶。要是你怕擠，怕搶，也許⑶坐地鐵好些⑷，地鐵比公共汽車快多了⑸。

甲：地鐵站離學校太遠，走到最近的地鐵站也得二十分鐘。

乙：你既然不想浪費時間，為什麼⑹不坐出租車呢？

甲：出租車太貴了，坐趟車比吃頓飯還貴呢！

乙：公車太擠，地鐵太遠，出租車又太貴，我看你只好⑺騎自行車了。

甲：自行車好是好，就是⑻比較危險。北京的交通規則我不熟，萬一⑼出了事ㄦ，可就糟了。

乙：北京騎車的人多得很，你跟著大家騎，靠邊ㄦ走，保證⑽安全。

甲：我在北京只待兩個月，買輛新車划不來⑾。

乙：你不想買新車，可以租一輛。

甲：噢？自行車還能租嗎？

乙：當然能啦！新的、舊的、貴的、便宜的⑿，各種式樣的都有。你想租輛什麼樣的車啊？

甲：我想租輛不新不舊(13)的中檔車。每天在街上騎騎，又省錢，又省時間，還(14)可以鍛煉身體。住在宿舍裏什麼運動都沒有，才(15)來了兩個星期就胖了好幾公斤，一定得想個法子運動運動。

乙：北京人大多騎車上班，這不但解決了交通問題，也鍛煉了身體，真是一舉兩得。

甲：這真是個好主意！我明天就去租輛自行車。

（在租車店裏）

甲：師傅，你們租自行車嗎？

乙：我們賣自行車也租自行車。你想租輛什麼樣的車？

甲：我想租輛不新不舊的中檔車。

乙：這兩天暑期班剛開學，來租車的人特別多，好車都租出去了，只剩下這幾輛了，你看看吧！

甲：我想試試(16)這輛。能騎一下嗎？

乙：行啊！別走遠了，就在店門口騎兩圈兒。

甲：好，好。

（過了一會兒）

甲：這車怎麼租啊？一個月多少錢？

乙：我們這兒租車不論月，論(17)天數。一天五塊錢。

甲：一天五塊錢，一個月就得一百五十塊錢，兩個月租下來(18)，不是和買輛車差不多了嗎？

乙：三百塊錢可買不到這樣的車。

甲：好吧，好吧，我先租兩個星期試試。

乙：除了租金，你還得付押金。押金一百塊。

甲：我還想買個安全帽。你們有沒有安全帽？

乙：騎自行車戴什麼安全帽⑲？在北京你見過騎車的人戴安全帽嗎？

甲：見倒是沒見過，可是……

乙：放心，在北京騎車，沒事儿！

第三课　　出了车祸

甲：妈，我昨天出了个车祸。

乙：什么？出了车祸！受伤了没有？

甲：受了一点儿小伤，不是太严重。我现在是在医院病房里给您打电话。

乙：你住院了啊？伤得一定不轻吧？

甲：腿上骨头给撞折了。

乙：怎么回事儿啊？

甲：昨天我去学校附近一家饭馆儿吃饭，过马路的时候，我看是绿灯就过街了，没看到一辆右转的车，就给撞上了。好在那辆车开得不是太快，要不然(1)大概连命都没有了。

乙：警察来了没有？

甲：交通警察来得倒挺快，救护车也来了。可是他们都说是我不对，我应该让汽车先走！

乙：行人让汽车，汽车不让行人，这不是太危险了吗？那个司机有保险吗？他应该负责(2)医疗费用。

车祸	車禍	chēhuò	n.	car accident
出车祸	出車禍	chū//chēhuò	v.-o.	get into a car accident
受伤	受傷	shòu//shāng	v.-o.	be injured

严重	嚴重	yánzhòng	*adj.*	(of a state or problem) serious
医院	醫院	yīyuàn	*n.*	hospital
病房		bìngfáng	*n.*	"sickroom," ward (of a hospital)
住院		zhù//yuàn	*v.-o.*	be hospitalized
轻	輕	qīng	*adj.*	slight; not serious; light 他病得不轻。 这把椅子很轻。
腿		tuǐ	*n.*	leg
骨头	骨頭	gǔ.tou	*n.*	bone
给	給	gěi	*prep.*	(here) passive marker, same as 被
撞		zhuàng	*v.*	hit (by a car); collide; bump against
折		shé	*v.*	break; become broken
绿灯	綠燈	lǜdēng	*n.*	green light
过	過	guò	*v.*	cross; pass
右转	右轉	yòuzhuǎn	*v.*	make a right turn; turn to the right 左转： turn to the left
好在		hǎozài	*adv.*	luckily; fortunately
要不然		yào.burán	*conj.*	otherwise; or else
大概		dàgài	*adv.*	probably
命		mìng	*n.*	one's life
警察	警察	jǐngchá	*n.*	police; policeman
挺		tǐng	*adv.*	quite
救护车	救護車	jiùhùchē	*n.*	ambulance
让	讓	ràng	*v.*	yield; allow
行人		xíngrén	*n.*	pedestrian
司机	司機	sījī	*n.*	driver
保险	保險	bǎoxiǎn	*n.*	insurance
负责	負責	fùzé	*v.*	be responsible for; be in charge of
医疗	醫療	yīliáo	*n.*	medical treatment
费用	費用	fèiyòng	*n.*	expense; cost

甲：他是个个体的出租车司机。据他说(3)没买保险，加上(4)是我不对，医疗费得我自己出。

乙：你在中国出了事儿，不知道美国的保险能不能付钱。明天让你爸爸给保险公司打个电话问问。

甲：医生说我得住四五天院，出院以后还得用轮椅。我担心功课要被耽误(5)了。

乙：耽误功课无所谓，最要紧的是(6)身体。医院里设备好不好啊？

甲：我住的是普通病房，一间四五个人，没有电视也没有空调，很不舒服。

乙：你越说我越担心。要不要我飞去北京照顾你啊？

甲：除了腿受伤，没什么其他问题。您放心，不必(7)为这件事儿飞到北京来。我自己会照顾自己。过两天再给您打电话吧！

乙：以后走路可千万(8)得小心啊！

个体	個體	gètǐ	*n.*	individual
据说	據說	jùshuō	*v.*	it is said
				据 sb. 说：according to sb.
加上		jiāshàng	*conj.*	moreover; in addition
出		chū	*v.*	pay; contribute (money)
公司		gōngsī	*n.*	company
出院		chū//yuàn	*v.-o.*	be discharged from the hospital
轮椅	輪椅	lúnyǐ	*n.*	wheelchair
担心	擔心	dānxīn	*v.*	worry; feel anxious
耽误	耽誤	dānwù	*v.*	delay; hold up
无所谓	無所謂	wúsuǒwèi	*v.*	doesn't matter
要紧	要緊	yàojǐn	*adj.*	important; urgent
设备	設備	shèbèi	*n.*	equipment; facilities
普通		pǔtōng	*adj.*	common; ordinary
间	間	jiān	*AN*	measure word for rooms
照顾	照顧	zhàogù	*v.*	look after; care for
其他		qítā	*adj.*	other
不必		búbì	*adv.*	need not
为	為	wèi	*prep.*	for
走路		zǒu//lù	*v.-o.*	walk; go on foot
				我常常走路到学校去。
千万	千萬	qiānwàn	*adv.*	be sure to; must
小心		xiǎoxīn	*v.*	be careful

词语例句

(1) 好在…，要不然… : luckily…, otherwise…

◆ 好在那辆车开得不是太快，要不然大概连命都没有了。

Luckily that car wasn't going too fast; otherwise I probably would have lost my life.

1. 好在我来中国以前已经学了一年的中文，要不然连吃饭都会有问题。

Luckily I had already learned a year of Chinese before I came to China; if not I would have problems even with getting a meal.

2. 好在你买了保险，要不然怎么付得起这么贵的医疗费呢？

Luckily you have insurance; otherwise how could you afford such expensive medical fees?

(2) 负责: be responsible for; be in charge of

◆ 他应该负责医疗费用。

He should be responsible for the medical charges.

1. 张先生负责外国学生的事儿，你有问题可以问他。

Mr. Zhang is in charge of foreign students' affairs. You can go to see him if you have problems.

2. 生了孩子，就要负责照顾他。

After giving birth to a child, one must be responsible for its care.

(3) 据 sb. 说: according to sb.

◆ 据他说，没买保险，…

According to him he has no insurance, ...

1. 据我的朋友说，在这儿是人让车，不是车让人。

According to my friend, here it's pedestrians who should yield to cars and not vice versa.

2. 据说这儿的出租车司机大多是个体户。

It is said that most of the drivers here are self-employed individuals.

(4) …，加上…: …, in addition, …

◆ 据他说，没买保险，加上是我不对，医疗费得我自己出。

He said that he has no insurance; in addition, I'm at fault, so I have to pay for the medical charges myself.

1. 我吃得多了，加上没运动，所以胖了好几公斤。

I've been eating more lately and haven't been exercising, so I've gained quite a few kilos.

2. 这家医院有好的医生，再加上有好的设备，所以很有名。

This hospital has good doctors as well as good equipment. That's why it's well known.

(5) 耽误: to delay; to hold up

◆ 我担心功课要被耽误了。

I'm worried that my studies will be held up.

1. 你别在这儿耽误我的时间了，快回去吧！

Don't stay here and waste my time – go back quickly!

2. 我因为出了车祸，所以把整个出国的计划都耽误了。

My whole plan of going abroad was delayed because I got into an accident.

(6) ……无所谓，最要紧的是…: It doesn't matter that …, what's most important is …

◆ 耽误功课无所谓，最要紧的是身体。

It doesn't matter that your studies have been delayed; what's most important is your health.

1. 我来中国学不好中文无所谓，最要紧的是好好地玩儿。

Coming to China but not learning Chinese well doesn't bother me; what's most important is to have a lot of fun.

2. A：您想租一辆什么样的自行车？

　　B：我想租一辆中档的车。好不好看无所谓，最要紧的是安全。

A：What kind of bicycle are you looking for (to rent)?

B：I want something second rate. It doesn't matter if it looks good; what's most important is that it's safe.

(7) 不必: need not

◆ 你不必为这件事飞到北京来。

You don't have to fly over to Beijing for this matter.

(Please remember that 不必 does not have a positive form; therefore, never use 必 when something is necessary. To say "must," or "need to," use "得" or "必须.")

1. 我会好好地照顾自己，你们不必担心。

I will take good care of myself. You don't have to worry.

2. 在美国，开车的人一定得买保险，可是在中国却不必。

In the United States, a person who drives has to buy insurance, but in China, one does not have to do that.

(8) 千万: be sure to; must

◆ 以后走路可千万得小心啊!

From now on you must be cautious when you walk (on the street).

1. 你一个人在北京，千万要照顾好身体，别让我担心。

Now that you're in Beijing by yourself, you must take good care of your health. Don't make me worried.

2. 那家店的自行车你千万别租，都是坏的。

Make sure you don't rent any bikes from that shop; they're all bad.

练习

I. Complete the following dialogue using the expressions provided.

在路上，一辆出租车出了事，交通警察马上来了。

警察：怎么回事儿啊？撞伤了一个学生，是不是你开得太快了？

司机：真对不起，我开得是有一点儿快，＿＿＿＿＿＿＿＿＿＿。

（好在，要不然）

警察：我看，你得负责医疗费用。

司机：＿＿＿＿＿＿＿＿＿＿。 （…无所谓，最要紧的是…）

警察：你为什么那么不小心？为什么不开得慢一点儿呢？

司机：我的孩子病了，我要送他去医院。＿＿＿＿＿＿＿＿＿。

（耽误，要是，怕）

警察：＿＿＿＿＿＿＿＿＿＿＿＿＿＿＿＿＿＿。 （千万）

司机：是，是，我记住了。我以后再也不开得这么快了。

36

II. Answer the question using as many new words that you've learned as possible.

1. 你认为应该是行人让车还是车让行人？出了车祸，行人完全没有责任（zérèn, responsibility）吗？ 在美国，行人是不是被宠坏 (chǒnghuài: spoiled) 了？

2. 你出过车祸吗？要是你出了车祸，应该怎么办？

3. 在北京，你过马路的时候有困难吗？在北京过马路跟在美国有什么不同？

4. 要是你在北京病了而且住院了，你要不要母亲从美国飞到北京来照顾你？为什么？

5. 什么样的医院是好医院？有没有电视和空调很要紧吗？

III. Complete the following dialogues using the expressions provided.

1. 什么？你出了车祸？那么你还能出国吗？
    （好在，要不然，耽误，严重）

2. 你为什么不买一辆高档的自行车呢？ （加上）

3. 今天是星期天，没什么事。我们去参观故宫，好不好？
    （据 sb. 说，排队）

4. 我想到美国去留学，你认为我应该注意什么？ （千万）

IV. Composition

Rewrite the dialogue of Lesson 3 into an essay.

繁体字课文

甲：媽，我昨天出了個車禍。

乙：什麼？出了車禍！受傷了沒有？

甲：受了一點ㄦ小傷，不是太嚴重。我現在是在醫院病房裏給您打電話。

乙：你住院了啊？傷得一定不輕吧？

甲：腿上骨頭給撞折了。

乙：怎麼回事ㄦ啊？

甲：昨天我去學校附近一家飯館ㄦ吃飯，過馬路的時候，我看是綠燈就過街了，沒看到一輛右轉的車，就給撞上了。好在那輛車開得不是太快，要不然(1)大概連命都沒有了。

乙：警察來了沒有？

甲：交通警察來得倒挺快，救護車也來了。可是他們都說是我不對，我應該讓汽車先走！

乙：行人讓汽車，汽車不讓行人，這不是太危險了嗎？那個司機有保險嗎？他應該負責(2)醫療費用。

甲：他是個個體的出租車司機。據他說(3)沒買保險，加上(4)是我不對，醫療費得我自己出。

乙：你在中國出了事ㄦ，不知道美國的保險能不能付錢。明天讓你爸爸給保險公司打個電話問問。

甲：醫生說我得住四五天院，出院以後還得用輪椅。我擔心功課要被耽誤(5)了。

乙：耽誤功課無所謂，最要緊的是(6)身體。醫院裏設備好不好啊？

甲：我住的是普通病房，一間四五個人，沒有電視也沒有空調，很
　　不舒服。

乙：你越說我越擔心。要不要我飛去北京照顧你啊？

甲：除了腿受傷，沒什麽其他問題。您放心，不必(7)爲這件事儿飛到
　　北京來。我自己會照顧自己。過兩天再給您打電話吧！

乙：以後走路可千萬(8)得小心啊！

第四课　旗袍和筷子

甲：这件衣服真漂亮，是在哪儿买的啊？

乙：不是买的，是定做的。现成的也有，可是没这么合身。

甲：这是什么衣服啊？

乙：这是旗袍，据说是清朝女人穿的衣服，可是民国以后穿的人还是很多。

甲：可是我在中国怎么从来没见过(1)女人穿旗袍？

乙：因为穿了旗袍，行动工作都不方便，所以大家都不穿了。

甲：印度人一般(2)都穿他们自己的服装。中国人在穿着上好像(3)不太坚持自己的传统。

乙：穿衣服是天天都得做的事儿，最要紧的是方便和实用。如果(4)为了坚持传统，每天穿着旗袍上课、工作，那就太不方便了。这样的传统是不值得(5)坚持的。

甲：中国人在穿着上完全接受(6)了西方的影响，但是在饮食上好像就比较保守了。一般来说(7)中国人都用筷子吃饭。在中国我还没见过用刀叉吃饭的中国人。

乙：不用刀叉吃饭，倒不一定是为了维持传统。用筷子又简单又方

| 旗袍 | qípáo | n. | qipao, ("long gown"), a traditional Chinese costume for women |

筷子		kuài.zi	*n.*	chopsticks
漂亮		piào.liang	*adj.*	beautiful
定做		dìngzuò	*v.*	have sth. made to order; tailored 我定做了一件衣服。
现成	現成	xiànchéng	*adj.*	ready-made
合身		héshēn	*adj.*	(of clothes) fitting
清朝		Qīng Cháo	*n.*	the Qing Dynasty (1644-1911)
民国	民國	Mínguó	*n.*	the Republic of China (1912-present, moved to Taiwan in 1949)
行动	行動	xíngdòng	*v.*	move; get about
印度人		Yìndùrén	*n.*	Indian (person from India)
一般		yìbān	*adv.*/*adj.*	usually; commonly, general; ordinary; common
服装	服裝	fúzhuāng	*n.*	clothing; costume
穿着	穿著	chuānzhuó	*n.*	dress; attire
好像	好像	hǎoxiàng	*v.*	seem to be
坚持	堅持	jiānchí	*v.*	persist in; insist on 他总是坚持自己的看法。
传统	傳統	chuántǒng	*n.*	tradition
实用	實用	shíyòng	*adj.*	practical; pragmatic, functional
值得		zhí.dé	*v.*	deserve; be worth
接受		jiēshòu	*v.*	accept; receive (influence, etc.)
西方		Xīfāng	*n.*	the West
影响	影響	yǐngxiǎng	*n.*	influence
饮食	飲食	yǐnshí	*n.*	food and drink; diet
保守		bǎoshǒu	*adj.*	conservative
一般来说	一般來說	yìbān lái shuō		generally speaking
刀叉		dāochā	*n.*	knife and fork
维持	維持	wéichí	*v.*	keep; maintain; preserve
简单	簡單	jiǎndān	*adj.*	simple; uncomplicated

便，没什么**理由**把筷子**淘汰**掉(8)。我认为两种文化交流的时候，用什么和不用什么的**标准**只是实用，和维持传统是没有关系的。

甲：筷子方便是方便，但是我觉得不太**卫生**。大家一桌吃饭，都把筷子伸到盘子里去夹菜。要是有人感冒，就很容易传染。

乙：这个我同意。尤其是(9)喝汤的时候，大家都用汤勺儿在汤碗里舀来舀去(10)，然后再放进嘴里喝，还有人用筷子往汤碗里夹东西吃，简直(11)像在汤里洗筷子，看了让我觉得恶心。

甲：现在比较高档的饭馆儿都有公筷和公勺儿，大家已经不用自己的筷子和汤勺儿去夹菜舀汤了。

乙：你指出了一个很有趣的问题。虽然这只是一件小事儿，但是却可以说明(12)一个文化交流的现象。中西文化交流的时候，并不一定是西方的取代(13)中国的，或者中国的取代西方的。有时中国

理由		lǐyóu	n.	reason; grounds; justification
淘汰		táotài	v.	eliminate through selection or competition
认为	認爲	rènwéi	v.	think that; believe that
文化		wénhuà	n.	culture
交流		jiāoliú	v.	exchange (each other's experiences, view, etc.)
标准	標準	biāozhǔn	n.	standard; criterion
卫生	衛生	wèishēng	adj./n.	hygienic, hygiene; sanitation

伸		shēn	*v.*	extend; stretch
盘子	盤子	pán.zi	*n.*	plate; tray
夹	夾	jiā	*v.*	press from both sides; (here) pick up (with chopsticks)
感冒		gǎnmào	*v./n.*	catch cold, cold
容易		róngyì	*adv.*	easily; likely
传染	傳染	chuánrǎn	*v.*	spread (a disease); infect
同意		tóngyì	*v.*	agree
尤其		yóuqí	*adv.*	especially
喝		hē	*v.*	drink
汤	湯	tāng	*n.*	soup
勺儿		sháor	*n.*	spoon
碗		wǎn	*n.*	bowl
舀		yǎo	*v.*	spoon out; scoop up
嘴		zuǐ	*n.*	mouth
往		wǎng	*prep.*	toward; in the direction of
简直	簡直	jiǎnzhí	*adv.*	simply; virtually
洗		xǐ	*v.*	wash
恶心	噁心	ěxīn	*adj.*	disgusting; feel like vomiting
高档	高檔	gāodàng	*adj.*	(of the quality of things) first rate; high-class
公筷		gōngkuài	*n.*	a pair of chopsticks that is shared by all for the purpose of picking up food from the main platter
公勺儿		gōngsháor		serving spoon
指出		zhǐchū	*v.*	point out
有趣		yǒuqù	*adj.*	interesting
却	卻	què	*adv.*	but; yet
说明	說明	shuōmíng	*v.*	show; illustrate, explain
现象	現象	xiànxiàng	*n.*	phenomenon
取代		qǔdài	*v.*	replace; supersede

受了西方的影响，开始有了变化，用公筷、公勺儿就是一个最好的例子，这叫"改良"。有时西方也受中国的影响，就像最近豆腐成了美国超级市场上一种日常食品，这就是中美文化交流的结果(14)。

受（到）		shòu(dào)	v.	be subjected to
开始	開始	kāishǐ	v.	begin; start
变化	變化	biànhuà	n.	change; transformation
例子		lì.zi	n.	example; case; instance
改良		gǎiliáng	v./n.	improve; reform
最近		zuìjìn	adv.	recently
豆腐	豆腐	dòu.fu	n.	bean curd
超级市场	超級市場	chāojí shìchǎng	n.	supermarket
日常		rìcháng	adj.	daily; day-to-day
食品		shípǐn	n.	foodstuff; food
结果	結果	jiéguǒ	n.	result; outcome; consequence

词语例句

(1) 从来没 *v.* 过: have never v.-ed before

◆ 我在中国怎么从来没见过女人穿旗袍?

How come I've never seen women wearing *qipao* in China?

1. 你坐我的车可以放心。我开了十几年的车，从来没出过车祸。

   You can be worry-free when you're riding in my car. I have been driving for more than ten years and have never been in an accident.

2. 你出的主意怎么从来都没解决过一个问题?

   How come the ideas that you come up with have never resolved a single problem?

(2) 一般: usually

◆ 印度人一般都穿他们自己的服装。

The Indians usually wear their own (traditional) costumes.

1. 去饭馆吃饭很不方便，所以我们一般都在学校的食堂吃。

   It's inconvenient to go to a restaurant, so we usually eat at the school's dining hall.

2. 北京的老人一般喜欢在公园里锻炼身体。

   Old folks in Beijing usually like to exercise in the parks.

   一般 can also appear before a noun to modify it. In such cases it means "the common," "the usual," and is usually translated as "most" or "most of the." For example:

3. 一般的印度人都穿他们自己的服装。

   Most Indians wear their own (traditional) costumes.

   When something is said to be 一般，it means it is ordinary or common. For example:

4. 对印度人来说，他们的传统服装可能很一般；可是对我们来说，那种服装却很特别。

   To Indians their traditional costumes might seem very ordinary, but to us they are very unique.

(3) 好像: seem to be

◆ 中国人在穿着上好像不太坚持自己的传统。

In terms of clothing, the Chinese do not seem to be too insistent on keeping with their traditions.

1. 他今天不说话也不笑，好像不太高兴。

He isn't talking or smiling today. He seems to be unhappy.

2. 美国人天天谈的、想的都是美国的事，好像世界上只有美国一
个国家。

The things Americans talk and think about every day consist only of matters related to America, as if it were the only country on earth.

(4) 如果/要是…，（那）就…: if…, then …

◆ 如果为了坚持传统，每天穿着旗袍上课工作，那就太不方便了。

It would be too inconvenient if, for the sake of keeping with tradition, a woman wore a *qipao* to class or to work everyday.

The 那 here means "in this/that case," referring to that which is mentioned after "如果/要是." It is optional.

1. 如果你能跟我一块儿去西安，那就太好了。

It would be great if you could go to Xi'an with me.

2. 这件旗袍要是试穿以后觉得合身，我就买。

If, after trying it on, I think that this *qipao* fits me, I'll buy it.

(5) 值得 v. : deserve to be v.-ed ; worth v.-ing

◆ 这样的传统是不值得坚持的。

Such a tradition is not worth keeping.

1. 这是一本少有的好书，很值得看。

This is a good book that is rare to come by. It's really worth reading.

2. 像他那样的人，不值得你对他那么好。

A person like him does not deserve such good treatment from you.

(6) 接受: to accept; to receive

◆ 中国人在穿着上完全接受了西方的影响。

The Chinese completely follow the West's lead (accept the West's influence) in terms of clothing.

1. 你说的很有道理，我接受你的看法。

What you said makes good sense. I agree with you (accept your view).

2. 要是我们都能接受别人不同的看法，这个世界就好多了。

If we could all accept the different views of others, this world would be so much better.

(7) 一般来说: generally speaking

◆ 一般来说，中国人都用筷子吃饭。

Generally speaking, the Chinese use chopsticks to eat.

1. A: 中国人从小就用筷子吗?

   B: 一般来说是这样的。

   A: Do Chinese use chopsticks from an early age?

   B: That's usually the case.

2. 我觉得中国人一般来说比美国人保守些。

   I think Chinese are, generally speaking, more conservative than Americans.

3. 一般来说，文化交流的结果不会是一种文化取代另一种。

   Generally speaking, the interaction of cultures will not result in the replacement of one culture by another.

(8) V. 掉: v. away

◆ 没什么理由把筷子淘汰掉。

There's no reason to abolish (the use of) chopsticks.

1. 你别再说话了，快把汤喝掉!

   Don't talk anymore, finish the soup fast!

2. A: 糟了! 汤里有只苍蝇!

   B: 快舀掉! 别让人看到!

   A: Oh! My God! There's a fly in the soup!

   B: Scoop it out fast! Don't let anyone see it!

(9) …, 尤其是…: …, especially …

◆ 这个我同意，尤其是喝汤的时候，大家都用汤勺儿在汤碗里舀来舀去，看了让我恶心。

I agree with this point, especially when it comes to drinking soup — everyone takes from the (same) soup bowl with their own spoon, it really disgusts me.

1. 从美国飞一趟北京真累，尤其是转机的时候，更是受不了!

   Taking a plane from America to Beijing is really tiring, especially when you're changing flights — it's even more unbearable.

2. 她看起来很像中国人，尤其是穿上了旗袍，简直和中国人完全一样。

   She looks very much like a Chinese person, especially when she wears a *qipao* — she looks exactly like one.

47

(10) V. 来 V. 去: V. around; V. back and forth

◆ 大家都用汤勺儿在汤碗里舀来舀去。

Everybody uses the soup spoons to stir around in the soup bowl.

1. 你为什么一直在这儿走来走去？是不是在等人？

Why do you keep walking back and forth? Are you waiting for someone?

2. 他在书桌上找来找去，找了很久，还是没找到他的笔。

He searched all over the desk, but after searching for a long time, he still could not find his pen.

(11) 简直: simply; at all

◆ ⋯简直像在汤里洗筷子。

…This is just like washing one's chopsticks in the soup.

(简直 is used for exaggeration.)

1. 他怎么可以这样对他的父母？他简直不是人！

How could he treat his parents in this manner? He's simply inhuman!

2. 什么？你到现在还没把功课做完？简直太糟了！

What? You still haven't finished your homework? You're really terrible!

(12) 说明: to show; to illustrate; to explain

◆ 虽然这只是一件小事儿，但是却可以说明一个文化交流的现象。

Although it's only a trivial matter, it illustrates a phenomenon in (the process of) cultural exchanges.

1. 他不接受新的看法说明他这个人比较保守。

His refusal to accept new ideas shows that he's quite conservative.

2. 中国人到现在还在用筷子，这说明筷子很方便、很实用。

The Chinese continue to use chopsticks even today. This shows that chopsticks are convenient and useful.

(13) 取代: to replace; to supersede

◆ 中西文化交流的时候，并不一定是西方的取代中国的，或者中国的取代西方的。

When Eastern and Western cultures interact, the West doest not necessarily replace the East; nor does it have to be the other way around.

1. 新的取代旧的，好的取代坏的，这是很自然的。

The new replaces the old, and the good replaces the bad. It is only natural.

2. 清朝的改良做得不好，所以被民国取代了。

The Qing Dynasty did not do well in its reforms, therefore it was replaced by the Republic of China.

⒁ 结果: result; outcome; consequence

◆ 最近豆腐成了美国超级市场上一种日常食品，这就是中美文化交流的结果。

Bean curd has become a daily food in American supermarkets recently. This is exactly a result of Sino-American cultural exchanges.

1. 你吃得多，又不运动，发胖是很自然的结果。

You eat more than usual and do not exercise. Gaining weight is but a natural result.

2. A：你为什么要叫他骑自行车？他被车撞了，你知道吗？

　 B：我只是想让他省点儿钱，没想到会有这样的结果。

A：Why did you advise him to ride a bicycle? He was hit by a car, did you know that?

B：I was only thinking of helping him save a little money. I did not expect such an outcome.

练习

I. Choose the correct answer.

1. 我是去北京学习的，所以带几件普通的 _____ 就够了。
　　a. 穿着　b. 衣服　c. 服装

2. 昨天我请班上最漂亮的女生吃饭，她 _____ 了，我真高兴。
　　a. 受到　b. 收到　c. 接受

3. 他什么事都觉得无所谓，可是 _____ 工作 _____ 却特别认真。
　　a. 以…来说　b. 在…上　c. 对…来说

4. 那个人有点儿奇怪，总是 _____ 。
　　a. 一边站，一边写功课　b. 站着写功课　c. 写功课站着

5. 不上大学也可以成功，也可以赚很多钱。Bill Gates 就是最好
　 的 _____ 。
　　a. 例子　b. 结果　c. 理由

6. 你最好用公勺儿把汤 _____ 到你的碗里，再用自己的勺儿喝。要不
　 然别人会觉得恶心。
　　a. 伸　b. 夹　c. 舀

II. Choose the most appropriate word for each blank and fill in with its Chinese equivalent.

infect	conservative	fitting
to insist on	practical	replace

1. 母亲在孩子心中的地位，是任何人都不能 _____ 的。
2. 在医院里面不要走来走去，因为那样的地方比较容易 _____ 病。
3. 他的父母不放心他一个人去中国，可是他 _____ 要去。
4. 这些碗筷看起来很漂亮，可是一点儿也不 _____ 。
5. 你不能因为他年纪大就认为他一定很 _____ 。
6. 衣服的价钱贵不贵无所谓，最要紧的是一定得 _____ 。

III. Fill in the blank with the most appropriate word.

行动，印象，合身，定做，坚持，竟然，耽误
影响，当然，实用，淘汰，认为，如果，认为

我是一件很旧的旗袍。两百年前，是为皇帝的太太 _____ 的。我刚做好的时候，既 _____ ，又漂亮，皇帝的太太常常把我穿在身上，让所有见到她的人留下深刻的 _____ 。现在没有人愿意再看我一眼了。我知道女人穿上旗袍，工作、_____ 都不方便，容易 _____ 事情。所以大家 _____ 旗袍已经不 _____ 了，可能不久以后，旗袍就会被 _____ 掉。我想说的是：现代的中国人太容易受西方的 _____ 了，为了方便和实用可以不 _____ 传统。_____ 有一天中国的传统都没有了，那么，我们要到那里去找"中国"呢？

IV. Answer the following questions using the expressions provided.

1. 你看见过中国女人旗袍吗？（从来没 v. 过，说明）
2. 传统是很重要的，我们必须坚持所有的传统。（值得，例子）
3. 改革开放以后，中国的进步很大吧？（尤其是，在…上）
4. 有了汽车以后，应该把自行车淘汰掉。

（认为，又…又…，没什么理由 v.）
5. 中国的语言和文字都会很快地被英语取代。（简直，实用）

V. Composition

作者批评中国人忘了传统，因为他们不再穿旗袍了。你觉得不穿旗袍能不能说明中国人不坚持传统？在实用和坚持传统有冲突（chōngtū: conflict）的时候，你会选择哪一个？为什么？

繁体字课文

甲：這件衣服真漂亮，是在哪儿買的啊？

乙：不是買的，是定做的。現成的也有，可是沒這麼合身。

甲：這是什麼衣服啊？

乙：這是旗袍，據說是清朝女人穿的衣服，可是民國以後穿的人還是很多。

甲：可是我在中國怎麼從來沒見過(1)女人穿旗袍？

乙：因為穿了旗袍，行動工作都不方便，所以大家都不穿了。

甲：印度人一般(2)都穿他們自己的服裝。中國人在穿著上好像(3)不太堅持自己的傳統。

乙：穿衣服是天天都得做的事儿，最要緊的是方便和實用。如果(4)為了堅持傳統，每天穿著旗袍上課、工作，那就太不方便了。這樣的傳統是不值得(5)堅持的。

甲：中國人在穿著上完全接受(6)了西方的影響，但是在飲食上好像就比較保守了。一般來說(7)中國人都用筷子吃飯。在中國我還沒見過用刀叉吃飯的中國人。

乙：不用刀叉吃飯，倒不一定是為了維持傳統。用筷子又簡單又方便，沒什麼理由把筷子淘汰掉(8)。我認為兩種文化交流的時候，用什麼和不用什麼的標準只是實用，和維持傳統是沒有關係的。

甲：筷子方便是方便，但是我覺得不太衛生。大家一桌吃飯，都把筷子伸到盤子裏去夾菜。要是有人感冒，就很容易傳染。

乙：這個我同意。尤其是(9)喝湯的時候，大家都用湯勺儿在湯碗裏舀來舀去(10)，然後再放進嘴裏喝，還有人用筷子往湯碗裏夾東西吃，簡直(11)像在湯裏洗筷子，看了讓我覺得噁心。

甲：現在比較高檔的飯館儿都有公筷和公勺儿，大家已經不用自己的筷子和湯勺儿去夾菜舀湯了。

乙：你指出了一個很有趣的問題。雖然這只是一件小事儿，但是卻可以說明(12)一個文化交流的現象。中西文化交流的時候，並不一定是西方的取代(13)中國的，或者中國的取代西方的。有時中國受了西方的影響，開始有了變化，用公筷、公勺儿就是一個最好的例子，這叫"改良"。有時西方也受中國的影響，就像最近豆腐成了美國超級市場上一種日常食品，這就是中美文化交流的結果(14)。

第五课　一次性产品

甲：北京的饭店、旅馆用的都是一次性的东西，真是又方便又卫生。

乙：我最讨厌一次性的东西，不但质量差，而且也不见得(1)卫生。

　　上次去饭店，桌上的一双竹筷子黑黑的、黏黏的，看了真恶

　　心。后来服务员给(2)换了一双，但是一夹菜就断了。这种一次

　　性的筷子还不如(3)传统的筷子呢!

甲：我觉得大量使用一次性的产品还是一种进步。尽管(4)目前有些

　　产品的质量太差，但是使用一次性产品的这个方向是对的。

乙：我不同意你的话。用一次性的产品其实是一种浪费。像中国这

　　样人口多、资源少的国家应该尽量回收资源，重复使用，而不

　　是用一次就丢掉。这么做不但浪费资源而且污染环境。你想，

　　全中国十几亿人口，如果每个人吃一顿饭就扔一双筷子，一年

　　下来(5)得用掉多少竹子?

一次性		yícìxìng	*adj.*	one-time
——性		xìng	*suffix*	-ness; - ity 重要性/可能性/实用性
产品	産品	chǎnpǐn	*n.*	product
饭店	飯店	fàndiàn	*n.*	restaurant; hotel
讨厌	討厭	tǎoyàn	*v.*	dislike; loathe
质量	質量	zhìliàng	*n.*	quality
差		chà	*adj.*	poor; bad; not up to standard

不见得	不見得	bújiàn.dé	*adv.*	not necessarily; not likely
双	雙	shuāng	*AN*	measure word for things in pairs, e.g. chopsticks, socks, shoes, etc.
竹（子）		zhú(.zi)	*n.*	bamboo
黑		hēi	*adj.*	black; dark
黏		nián	*adj.*	sticky
服务员	服務員	fúwùyuán	*n.*	waiter
换	換	huàn	*v.*	change
断	斷	duàn	*v.*	break (used for something long and thin, e.g. thread, rope, or sticks)
不如		bùrú	*v.*	be unequal to; be inferior to
大量		dàliàng	*adv./adj.*	a large number; a great quantity 大量制造/大量的产品
使用		shǐyòng	*v.*	use; employ
进步	進步	jìnbù	*n./v.*	improvement; progress, improve; advance
尽管	儘管	jǐnguǎn	*conj.*	even though; despite
目前		mùqián	*n.*	at prcsent; at the moment
方向		fāngxiàng	*n.*	direction
人口		rénkǒu	*n.*	population
资源	資源	zīyuán	*n.*	natural resources
回收		huíshōu	*v.*	recycle; retrieve; reclaim
重复	重複	chóngfù	*v./adv.*	repeat, repeatedly; again and again
丢		diū	*v.*	discard
污染		wūrǎn	*v.*	pollute; contaminate
环境	環境	huánjìng	*n.*	environment
全		quán	*adj.*	whole; entire 全国/全校/全世界
亿	億	yì	*num.*	hundred million
扔		rēng	*v.*	throw away; throw; toss

甲：每一件事儿总是有好处也有坏处。难道(6)一次性产品就没有一点儿好处吗？

乙：好处当然有，就是方便。但是在我看来，以目前中国的经济条件来说(7)，大量使用一次性产品会造成许多资源的浪费和环境的污染。美国大概是世界上用一次性产品最多的国家。纸杯、纸盘、纸碗、纸巾，甚至于(8)纸内裤，都是用一次就丢。而做纸的原料是树木。现在已经有人为了保护森林、保护环境，提倡少用一次性产品，尤其是造成污染最严重的塑料产品。

甲：是啊！最近北京电视上已经有劝大家少用塑料袋的广告了。

乙：这真是一大进步！但是我觉得在中国垃圾回收的工作做得还不够，可回收和不可回收的垃圾常常混在一起。

甲：是的，在垃圾回收上(9)，我们分类的工作做得还不够。但是在中国有些人靠捡垃圾为生(10)，所以实际上(11)造成的浪费并没有你想像的那么大。

好处	好處	hǎo.chu	*n.*	advantage
坏处	壞處	huài.chu	*n.*	disadvantage
难道	難道	nándào	*adv.*	could it be that…? (used in a rhetorical question to make it more forceful)
经济	經濟	jīngjì	*n.*	economy

条件	條件	tiáojiàn	n.	condition; requirement; prerequisite; term
造成		zàochéng	v.	cause; bring about (problems or other undesirable consequences)
世界		shìjiè	n.	world
国家	國家	guójiā	n.	country; nation
纸杯	紙杯	zhǐbēi	n.	paper cup
纸巾	紙巾	zhǐjīn	n.	paper towel; tissue paper
甚至于	甚至於	shènzhìyú	conj.	even; even to the point that; so much so that
内裤	內褲	nèikù	n.	underpants; panties 内：inside 裤：裤子；pants
原料		yuánliào	n.	raw material; rough material
树木	樹木	shùmù	n.	trees; wood
保护	保護	bǎohù	v.	protect
森林		sēnlín	n.	forest
提倡		tíchàng	v.	advocate; promote
塑料		sùliào	n.	plastics
劝	勸	quàn	v.	urge; persuade; exhort
袋（子）		dài(.zi)	n.	bag; sack
广告	廣告	guǎnggào	n.	advertisement
垃圾		lājī	n.	garbage
混		hùn	v.	mix
分类	分類	fēnlèi	v.	sort; classify
靠		kào	v.	rely on; depend on
捡	撿	jiǎn	v.	pick up; collect; gather
靠…为生		kào…wéi shēng	n.	make a living by
实际上	實際上	shíjìshàng		in reality; in actual fact
想像		xiǎngxiàng	v.	imagine

乙：是的，我每次去风景区都看到有人在捡易拉罐儿或矿泉水的瓶子。我们应该感谢这些人为保护环境所做的工作。保护环境不只是为了我们自己，也是为了我们的下一代。

风景区	風景區	fēngjǐngqū	n.	scenic spot 风景：scenery 区：area; region
易拉罐儿	易拉罐儿	yìlāguànr	n.	pop-top; pull-top; flip-top
矿泉水	礦泉水	kuàngquánshuǐ	n.	mineral water
瓶子		píng.zi	n.	bottle
感谢	感謝	gǎnxiè	v.	thank; be grateful
下一代		xiàyídài	n.	next generation 上一代：previous generation 这一代：this generation

词语例句

(1) 不见得: not necessarily; not likely

◆ 我最讨厌一次性的东西，不但质量差，而且也不见得卫生。

I hate disposable things. They not only are of cheap quality, but aren't necessarily hygienic either.

(不见得 does not have a positive form; therefore, do not say 见得.)

1. A: 你不会念这个字，为什么不去问那个中国人呢？

   B: 他虽然是个中国人，可是不见得就会念这个字！

   A: Since you don't know how to pronounce this character, why don't you go and ask that Chinese person?

   B: Even though he is Chinese, he doesn't necessarily know how to read this character!

2. A: 旗袍穿起来那么不方便，谁会买呢？

   B: 那倒不见得。我就买了三件。

   A: Wearing *qipao* is so inconvenient. Who would buy anything like that?

   B: That's not necessarily the case! I, for one, bought three.

(2) 给 v.:

◆ 后来服务员给换了一双。

Then the waiter gave us another pair (of chopsticks.)

   (This 给 is the same as the one in 给他打电话，给我倒一杯茶. When the object of 给 is very obvious, it can be omitted.)

1. 你别担心。你有了困难，外事处的人一定会给想办法。

   Don't worry. If you have problems, the people in the foreign affairs office will definitely help you.

2. 我们一坐下来，他就给倒了两杯茶。

   As soon as we sat down, he offered us two cups of tea.

(3) A 不如 B: A cannot be compared to B; A is not as good as B

◆ 这种一次的筷子还不如传统的筷子呢！

Disposable chopsticks are even worse than traditional ones.

1. 这是一辆高档的自行车，可是骑起来还不如我那辆中档的快呢！

   This is a top-quality bike, yet (when you ride on it) it doesn't go as fast as my

59

mid-range bike.

2. 这家旅馆的服务不如那家好，我们走吧！

The service at this hotel is not as good as that at the other one. Let's leave!

(4) 尽管: even though; despite

◆ 尽管目前有些产品质量太差，但是使用一次性产品的这个方向是对的。

Despite the bad quality of some current disposable products, the increasing use of these products is a step in the right direction.

1. 尽管那家饭馆的桌子、椅子都是黑黑的、黏黏的，我还是喜欢到那儿去吃东西。

Even though the tables and chairs in that restaurant are all dark and sticky, I still enjoy eating there.

2. 他常去看中国电影，尽管他听不懂。

He frequently went to see Chinese movies, even though he couldn't understand Chinese.

(5) Time duration + 下来: after + time duration

◆ 一年下来，得用掉多少竹子？

How much bamboo will be used up in a year's time?

1. 你才来了一个星期就胖了三公斤，两个月下来还得了？

You have been here for only a week, yet you have gained three kilos. What's going to happen in two months?

2. 他说要体验中国人的生活，可是三天下来就受不了了。

He said he wanted to experience the Chinese way of life, but after just three days he couldn't take it anymore.

(6) 难道…吗？: Could it be possible that …?

◆ 难道一次性产品就没有一点儿好处吗？

Could it be possible that disposable products have no advantage at all?

1. 你每顿饭都用纸杯、纸盘，难道你不觉得很浪费吗？

You use paper cups and plates at every meal. Don't you find it wasteful?

2. 汽车和空调都不能开，纸巾和塑料袋也不能用，难道你要我们回到古代吗？

We shouldn't drive a car nor turn on the air-conditioning, and we shouldn't use paper towels or plastic bags too —— are you suggesting that we should go back to the ancient times?

(7) 以···来说: based on...; speaking from...; as far as ... is concerned

◆ 以目前中国的经济条件来说，大量使用一次性产品会造成许多资源的浪费和环境的污染。

With its present economic conditions, using disposable products on a large scale in China will cause a great waste of resources and create a lot of pollution.

1. 这种产品是贵了点儿，但是以质量来说，却比旧的好多了。

This new type of product is indeed a bit too expensive, but its quality is much better than the old one (but in terms of quality, it's much better than the old one.)

2. 以饮食来说，中国人好像很传统；但是以穿着来说，他们却完全接受了西方的影响。

Chinese seem very traditional in terms of food and drink, but when it comes to clothing, they completely follow the West's lead (they accept the Western influence completely.)

(8) 甚至（于）: even; even to the point that; so much so that

◆ 纸杯、纸盘、纸碗、纸巾，甚至于纸内裤，都是用一次就丢。

Paper cups, paper plates, paper bowls, paper towels, and even paper underpants are all disposed of after only one use.

1. 他什么东西都不扔，甚至空的矿泉水瓶子，他都收着。

He doesn't throw away anything. He keeps even empty mineral water bottles.

2. 在这儿开车很危险。要是出了车祸，不但伤得很重，甚至连命都可能没有了。

It's very dangerous to drive here. If you get into an accident, you might not only be seriously injured, but even lose your life!

(9) 在···上: in terms of

◆ 在垃圾回收上，我们分类的工作做得还不够。

In our collection of garbage (lit. "In terms of garbage collection"), we have not done enough work in making classification (of the garbage collected).

1. 我们在纸张的使用上，应该尽量做到不浪费。

When we use paper we should try not to waste any of it.

2. 在环境保护的工作上，我们还得更进一步。

We should go a step further in our work for protection of the environment.

(10) 靠···为生: rely on ... for living; do ... for living

◆ 在中国有些人靠捡垃圾为生。

In China there are some people who make a living by collecting garbage.

1. 他是靠开出租车为生的，所以对这儿的交通规则特别熟。

He drives a cab for living, so he knows the traffic regulations here very well.

2. 你天天都在写小说，你想以后靠写小说为生吗？

You are writing your novel every day. Are you thinking of writing novels to make a living in the future?

(11) 实际上: actually; in reality; in actual fact

◆ ···所以实际上造成的浪费并没有你想像的那么大。

... so the amount of waste that is actually created is not as much as you have imagined.

1. 这些房子看起来很古老，实际上是去年才盖的。

These houses look old, but actually they were only built last year.

2. 你以为大家都在担心环境问题，实际上很多人都不知道这个问题有多严重。

You assume that everyone is worried about environmental problems, but in fact, many people do not know how serious they are.

练习

I. Choose the correct answer.

1. 我的中国朋友都 ＿＿＿＿＿＿ 我不要骑自行车上街。

    a. 提倡　b. 劝　c. 同意

2. 对不起，今天我 ＿＿＿＿＿＿ ，所以不能去上课了。

    a. 感冒得很厉害　b. 有一个厉害的感冒　c. 有一个坏的感冒

3. 塑料产品大多是不可回收的产品，所以污染环境最 ＿＿＿＿＿＿ 。

    a. 严重　b. 重要　c. 严

4. 我想，＿＿＿＿＿＿ 他现在的电脑水平 ＿＿＿＿＿＿ ，找到一个工作应该很容易。

    a. 以…来说　b. 在…上　c. 据…说

II. Choose the most appropriate word for each blank and fill in with its Chinese equivalent.

repeat	classify	pollution	advocate
next generation	protect	persist in	mix

1. 很多外国人到了美国后努力地学英文，可是却要他们的 ＿＿＿＿＿ 尽量 ＿＿＿＿＿ 他们自己国家的传统。

2. 你丢垃圾以前，要记得把垃圾先 ＿＿＿＿＿ ，别把纸和易拉罐 ＿＿＿＿＿ 在一起。

3. 学一个外语的时候，学生必须大量练习，大量 ＿＿＿＿＿ ，这样才能学好外语。

4. 为了 ＿＿＿＿＿ 环境，许多人 ＿＿＿＿＿ 少用造成严重 ＿＿＿＿＿ 的塑料产品。

III. Choose the phrase that is closest in meaning to the underlined phrase in the sentence.

1. 一次性产品就是用一次就<u>丢</u>的东西。

    a. 捡　b. 换　c. 扔

2. 不改变并<u>不见得</u>就是坚持传统最好的法子。

    a. 不一定　b. 不必　c. 不得

3. 朋友告诉我，纽约的地铁<u>实际上</u>并不像别人说的那么危险。

a. 实在   b. 真的   c. 其实

4.<u>在垃圾回收上</u>，我们的工作还做得很不够。

a. 在垃圾回收方面   b. 在垃圾回收方向   c. 在垃圾回收的上面

IV. Complete the following dialogues using the expressions given.

1. A: 既然是他撞了你，为什么他不负责你的医疗费？

B: _____ 。（尽管···，但是···）

2. A: _____ 。（难道···吗？）

B: 我不是不知道他住院了，只是没有时间去看他。

3. A: 听说他在外国生活的不太好，是不是真的？

B: _____ 。（靠···为生，甚至于）

V. Write a passage in response to the question.

对中国来说，使用一次性产品为什么是一种进步也是一种浪费？大量使用一次性产品会造成什么结果？

繁体字课文

甲：北京的飯店、旅館用的都是一次性的東西，真是又方便又衛生。

乙：我最討厭一次性的東西，不但質量差，而且也不見得(1)衛生。上次去飯店，桌上的一雙竹筷子黑黑的、粘粘的，看了真噁心。後來服務員給(2)換了一雙，但是一夾菜就斷了。這種一次性的筷子還不如(3)傳統的筷子呢！

甲：我覺得大量使用一次性的產品還是一種進步。儘管(4)目前有些產品的質量太差，但是使用一次性產品的這個方向是對的。

乙：我不同意你的話。用一次性的産品其實是一種浪費。像中國這樣人口多、資源少的國家應該儘量回收資源，重複使用，而不是用一次就丟掉。這麼做不但浪費資源而且污染環境。你想，全中國十幾億人口，如果每個人吃一頓飯就扔一雙筷子，一年下來(5)得用掉多少竹子？

甲：每一件事儿總是有好處也有壞處。難道(6)一次性産品就沒有一點儿好處嗎？

乙：好處當然有，就是方便。但是在我看來，以目前中國的經濟條件來說(7)，大量使用一次性産品會造成許多資源的浪費和環境的污染。美國大概是世界上用一次性産品最多的國家。紙杯、紙盤、紙碗、紙巾，甚至於(8)於紙內褲，都是用一次就丟。而做紙的原料是樹木。現在已經有人爲了保護森林、保護環境，提倡少用一次性産品，尤其是造成污染最嚴重的塑料産品。

甲：是啊！最近北京電視上已經有勸大家少用塑料袋的廣告了。

乙：這真是一大進步！但是我覺得在中國垃圾回收的工作做得還不夠，可回收和不可回收的垃圾常常混在一起。

甲：是的，在垃圾回收上(9)，我們分類的工作做得還不夠。但是在中國有些人靠撿垃圾爲生(10)，所以實際上(11)造成的浪費並沒有你想像的那麼大。

乙：是的，我每次去風景區都看到有人在撿易拉罐儿或礦泉水的瓶子。我們應該感謝這些人爲保護環境所做的工作。保護環境不只是爲了我們自己，也是爲了我們的下一代。

第六课　　防盗和防火

甲：师傅，我早晨起来想去校园里跑跑步，锻炼锻炼，可是大门锁

着，出不去。能不能换个锁，让宿舍里面的人出得去，但是外

面的人进不来？

乙：里面的人出去了，万一没把门锁上，外头的人不是就进得来了

吗？我们是为了学生的安全才(1)锁门的。

甲：我觉得这样锁门，不但不方便而且也不安全。

乙：锁上门，外头的人进不来了，怎么会不安全呢？

甲：你们总以为(2)只要外面的人进不来就安全了，可是你们没想到

里面的人出不去才更危险。

乙：我们是晚上十二点以后才锁门的，大家都睡觉了，为什么还要

出去呢？

甲：万一失火了，门锁着出不去，大家不是都烧死了吗？

乙：失火？我在这个单位工作二十几年了，从来没失过火，可是偷

东西的事儿却常听说(3)。你觉得防火比防盗更重要吗？

甲：小偷儿固然(4)应该防范，但是火灾造成的伤害比偷窃严重得多。

小偷儿顶多(5)不过(6)偷个照相机或偷点儿现金，但是一旦(7)失

| 防盗 | | fángdào | v.-o. | guard against theft |
| | | | | 防：防止 (fángzhǐ) prevent |

				盗：盗窃（dàoqiè）theft; burglary
防火		fánghuǒ	v.-o.	prevent fires 火：fire
校园	校園	xiàoyuán	n.	campus
跑步		pǎo//bù	v.-o.	jog 跑：run 步：step
大门	大門	dàmén	n.	main entrance
锁	鎖	suǒ	v./n.	lock (up), lock
以为	以爲	yǐwéi	v.	think, believe or consider erroneously; assume incorrectly
失火		shī//huǒ	v.-o.	catch fire; be on fire 那幢房子失火了！
烧	燒	shāo	v.	burn
死		sǐ	v.	die
单位	單位	dānwèi	n.	work unit
偷		tou	v.	steal
听说	聽說	tīngshuō	v.	hear of; be told
重要		zhòngyào	adj.	important
小偷儿	小偷儿	xiǎotōur	n.	thief
固然		gùrán	conj.	it is true; no doubt
防范	防範	fángfàn	v.	be on guard; keep a lookout
火灾	火災	huǒzāi	n.	fire disaster
伤害	傷害	shānghài	n./v.	harm, injure; harm
偷窃	偷竊	tōuqiè	n./v.	theft; stealing, steal
顶多	頂多	dǐngduō	adv.	at (the) most
不过	不過	búguò	adv.	merely; only
照相机	照相機	zhàoxiàngjī	n.	camera
或		huò	conj.	或者；or 今天或明天/中文或英文
现金	現金	xiànjīn	n.	cash
一旦		yídàn	conj.	once; some time or other

火，却可能烧死几十个甚至(8)几百个人，财产的损失更是远远超过偷窃了。

乙：失火你可能一辈子碰不到一次，可是小偷儿却可能就在你身边儿。我们锁大门主要还是从防盗这一点着想(9)。我们从来没想过锁门跟火灾有什么关系。不过，听你这么一说，好像也很有道理。我明天和领导汇报一下吧！

可能		kěnéng	*adv./ adj.*	probably; maybe, possible; probable; may 他可能不来了。 这是不可能的事。
甚至		shènzhì	*adv.*	even (to the point of); so much so that
财产	財産	cáichǎn	*n.*	property
损失	損失	sǔnshī	*n./v.*	loss, lose
远远	遠遠	yuǎnyuǎn	*adv.*	to a great degree; extremely; greatly A 远远不如 B。/远远不够
超过	超過	chāoguò	*v.*	exceed; surpass
一辈子	一輩子	yíbèi.zi	*n.*	all one's life; a lifetime
碰		pèng	*v.*	encounter; run into
主要		zhǔyào	*adv.*	mainly
着想	著想	zhuóxiǎng	*v.*	give consideration to (the interests of somebody or something)
领导	領導	lǐngdǎo	*n.*	leader; leadership
汇报	匯報	huìbào	*v.*	report; give an account of

词语例句

(1) 为了··· 才···: It's only for the sake of sb./sth. that one …

◆ 我们是为了学生的安全才锁门的。

  It was only for the sake of the students' safety that we locked the door.

1. 他是为了到中国去做生意才开始学中文的。

   He began learning Chinese in order to do business in China.

2. 我刚到的时候常常坐出租车，后来为了省钱才租了辆自行车。

   I took cabs frequently when I first got here. Later, in order to save some money, I rented a bike.

(2) 以为: to think, believe or consider erroneously; to assume incorrectly

◆ 你们总以为只要外面的人进不来就安全了，可是你们没想到里面的人出不去才更危险。

  You always assume that it will be safe as long as outsiders can't get in, but you overlook the fact that it's even more dangerous when people can't get out.

1. 他看我的门锁着，以为我出去了，其实我还在睡大觉呢!

   When he saw that my door was locked, he thought that I had gone out, but in fact I was still sleeping like a log!

2. 你不要以为一定不会有问题，等真的出了事就太晚了。

   Don't assume that nothing will go wrong. If something really does happen, it will be too late to do anything.

(3) 听说: to hear that; be told

◆ 我在这个单位工作二十几年了，从来没失过火，可是偷东西的事儿却常听说。

  I have worked in this unit for more than twenty years. There was never a fire, but we often heard that things were stolen.

A: 我听说老李被车撞了，是真的吗?

B: 没这样的事儿。你是听谁说的?

A: 我是听老张说的。

A: I heard that Old Li was hit by a car, is it true?

B: No! Who told you this? (lit: who did you hear it from?)

A: I heard it from Old Zhang.

(4) 固然···，但是···: It's true that …, but …

◆ 小偷固然应该防范，但是火灾造成的伤害比偷窃严重得多。

There's no doubt that we should guard against thieves, but the damage caused by a fire is much more serious than that caused by stealing.

1. 传统固然重要，可是我们不应该为了坚持传统而不要进步。

It's true that tradition is very important but we shouldn't give up progress merely for the sake of keeping with tradition.

2. 你说的固然比他说的有道理，但他是领导，我得听他的。

Undoubtedly what you said makes more sense (than what he said), but he's the supervisor, so I have to listen to him.

(5) 顶多：at (the) most

◆ 小偷顶多不过偷个照相机或偷点儿现金，但是一旦失火却可能烧死几十个甚至几百个人。

At most a thief will steal a camera or a little cash, but once a fire breaks out, it might cost tens or even hundreds of lives.

1. 这辆自行车这么旧了，顶多能骑几个月，你还是买辆高档的新车吧！

This bike is so worn out that it will last only a few more months at the most. I suggest you buy a new one of high quality.

2. 去趟西安顶多耽误一点儿功课，有什么好担心的呢？

Going to Xi'an will only hold up your studies a little bit. So what is there to worry about?

(6) 不过：merely; only

◆ 小偷顶多不过偷个照相机或偷点儿现金。

1. 我不过是指出了他的一个问题，他就受不了了。

I merely pointed out one of his problems, but he couldn't take it.

2. 不过一两块钱的东西，丢了就丢了吧！

It's only worth a dollar or two. If it gets lost, let it be!

(7) 一旦：once

◆ …一旦失火却可能烧死几十个甚至几百个人。

1. 你还是把这些东西分好吧！一旦混起来了，想再分类就难了。

It's better that you organize these things properly now. Once they're mixed up, it's hard to sort them again.

2. 人们总是喜欢新的东西而讨厌旧的。他们一旦看到新产品，就想把旧的换掉。

People always like new things and dislike old ones. Once they see a new product, they will want to replace the old one.

(8) 甚至: even (to the point of); so much so that

◆ 小偷顶多不过偷个照相机或偷点儿现金，但是一旦失火，却可能烧死几十个甚至几百个人。

1. 这个宿舍的大门从来不锁，甚至晚上也不锁。

The door of this dormitory is never locked, even at night.

2. 那些筷子的质量太差了，甚至一夹菜就断了。

The quality of those chopsticks was so poor that they even broke when they were used to pick up food.

(9) 着想: consider; take into consideration

◆ 我们锁大门主要还是从防盗这一点着想。

The reason that we lock the door is for guarding against theft.

1. 她是为你着想才那样做的。

She did that for your own good.

2. 我们提倡用纸袋，是从保护环境着想。

We promote the use of paper bags for the protection of the environment.

练习

I. Choose the correct answer.

1. 这件事情我不能自己决定，我得跟领导 _____ ，再告诉你结果。

    a. 汇报汇报　　b. 汇一下报　　c. 汇汇报报

2. 请最后一个离开实验室的人关灯，把门 _____ 。

    a. 锁着　　b. 锁　　c. 锁上

3. 他很聪明，也很努力，他 _____ 有机会，就会成为一个有名的人。

    a. 万一　　b. 一旦　　c. 尽管

4. 他真像个小孩子，我 _____ 跟他开了个玩笑，他就生气了。

    a. 顶多　　b. 最多　　c. 不过

5. 父母离婚的时候，常常是孩子受到最大的 _____ 。

a. 伤害　　　b. 伤　　　c. 损失

II. Choose the most appropriate word for each blank and fill in with its Chinese equivalent.

| assume incorrectly | be on guard | loss |
| even (to the extent of) | run into | catch fire |

1. 我 _____ 他的英文很好，后来才知道他一点儿也不会说。

2. 他什么坏事都会做， _____ 会伤害自己的朋友。

3. 昨天我在街上 _____ 一个十年没见的朋友，我们谈得很高兴。

4. 你不应该把孩子锁在家里，万一 _____ ，孩子会被烧死的。

5. _____ 森林火灾是这个单位主要的工作。

6. 一旦失火，生命、财产的 _____ 都会很严重。

III. Answer the question using the expressions given.

1. 你觉得防盗跟防火哪一个重要？

　　　（远远，固然，顶多，甚至，碰到，一旦）

2. 为什么中国学生宿舍的师傅晚上十二点以后要锁大门？

　　　（为了…才…，以为，只要，从…着想，跟…有关系）

IV. Composition

　　　你感冒了。要是你坚持上课，就不会耽误功课；要是你请两三天假，就可以防范把感冒传染给同学。你要怎么做？也请说明你这么做的理由。

繁体字课文

甲：師傅，我早晨起來想去校園裏跑跑步，鍛鍊鍛鍊，可是大門鎖著，出不去。能不能換個鎖，讓宿舍裏面的人出得去，但是外面的人進不來？

乙：裏面的人出去了，萬一沒把門鎖上，外頭的人不是就進得來了嗎？我們是爲了學生的安全才(1)鎖門的。

甲：我覺得這樣鎖門，不但不方便而且也不安全。

乙：鎖上門，外頭的人進不來了，怎麼會不安全呢？

甲：你們總以爲(2)只要外面的人進不來就安全了，可是你們沒想到裏面的人出不去才更危險。

乙：我們是晚上十二點以後才鎖門的，大家都睡覺了，爲什麼還要出去呢？

甲：萬一失火了，門鎖著出不去，大家不是都燒死了嗎？

乙：失火？我在這個單位工作二十幾年了，從來沒失過火，可是偷東西的事兒却常聽說(3)。你覺得防火比防盜更重要嗎？

甲：小偷固然(4)應該防範，但是火災造成的傷害比偷竊嚴重得多。小偷頂多(5)不過(6)偷個照相機或偷點兒現金，但是一旦(7)失火，却可能燒死幾十個甚至(8)幾百個人，財產的損失更是遠遠超過偷竊了。

乙：失火你可能一輩子碰不到一次，可是小偷却可能就在你身邊兒。我們鎖大門主要還是從防盜這一點著想(9)。我們從來沒想過鎖門跟火災有什麼關係。不過，聽你這麼一說，好像也很有道理。我明天和領導匯報一下吧！

第七课　　我不给乞丐钱

甲：今天下午我从西单购物中心出来的时候，被一群小乞丐给(1)围住
　　了，其中(2)一个扯住了我的裙子。你瞧，好好儿的一条裙子给弄(3)
　　成这样！我很生气，一毛钱都没给他们。

乙：你怎么一点儿同情心都没有呢？他们也是别人的孩子啊！他们出
　　来做乞丐也是不得已(4)啊！

甲：我觉得给乞丐钱就是鼓励他们不劳而获。不工作的人没饭吃是
　　公平的，也是应该的。你所谓的(5)"同情心"不但解决不了他
　　们的生活问题，而且还会养成他们懒惰和依靠别人的习惯。所
　　以，在我看来(6)，给乞丐钱不但不是帮他们的忙，反而(7)是害
　　了他们。

乙：找不到工作并不一定是他们懒，而是(8)社会制度不合理，贫富

乞丐		qǐgài	*n.*	beggar
西单购物中心	西單購物中心	Xīdān Gòuwù Zhōngxīn	*n.*	Xidan Shopping Center
群		qún	*AN*	measure word for groups or flocks
围住	圍住	wéi//zhù	*v.-c.*	surround; encircle
其中		qízhōng	*n.*	among (which, them, etc.)
扯住		chě//zhù	*v.-c.*	pull and hold tight
裙子		qún.zi	*n.*	skirt

瞧		qiáo	*v.*	look at; see
好好儿		hǎohāor	*adj./ adv.*	in perfectly good condition, nicely; well; to one's heart's content 好好儿的一支笔，却丢了。 你得好好儿想一想。
条	條	tiáo	*AN*	measure word for long, narrow things 一条裙子/两条腿/一条命
弄		nòng	*v.*	make
毛		máo	*AN*	ten cents; 1/10 yuan
同情心		tóngqíng xīn	*n.*	sympathy; compassion
不得已		bùdéyǐ	*v.*	have no alternative but to; have to
鼓励	鼓勵	gǔlì	*v.*	encourage
不劳而获	不勞而獲	bù láo ér huò	*idm.*	reap without sowing; get without any labor
公平		gōngpíng	*adj.*	fair
所谓	所謂	suǒwèi	*adj.*	so-called
解决		jiějué	*v.*	solve; resolve
v.不了		...bù liǎo	*v.-c.*	not able to ; cannot bc v.-ed
养成	養成	yǎngchéng	*v.*	develop; cultivate; form (habit)
懒惰	懶惰	lǎnduò	*adj.*	lazy; indolent
依靠		yīkào	*v.*	rely on
习惯	習慣	xíguàn	*n.*	habit
反而		fǎn'ér	*adv.*	on the contrary; instead
害		hài	*v.*	harm; impair; cause trouble to
懒	懶	lǎn	*adj.*	lazy
社会制度	社會制度	shèhuì zhìdù	*n.*	social system
合理		hélǐ	*adj.*	reasonable; equitable
贫富不均	貧富不均	pínfù bùjūn	*phr.*	large gap between the rich and the poor; there is a large gap between the rich and the poor

不均。有钱的人越来越有钱，穷的人越来越穷。所以，有些人成了乞丐，并不是不努力，而是社会的过错。

甲：把个人失败的责任推给社会，这是最不负责任的态度。任何一个社会都免不了(9)有竞争，只要有竞争就免不了有人失败。我们不能把失败者的生活变成成功者的负担。这种表面上看来充满同情心的做法其实(10)是阻碍社会发展的。

乙：你说的也不是完全没有道理。

甲：从前在办公室里努力工作的人和天天喝茶看报的人都拿一样的工资，那样的制度合理吗？凡是觉得竞争不合理的人都(11)是失败的人。一个有能力又努力的人是不会害怕竞争的。

乙：如果人人都像你这样对穷人一点儿都不同情，这个社会一定会变得非常残酷。

甲：进步是有代价的。如果因为有了乞丐、有了无家可归的人就怀

穷	窮	qióng	*adj.*	poor; poverty-stricken
过错	過錯	guòcuò	*n.*	fault; mistake
个人	個人	gèrén	*n.*	individual (person)
失败	失敗	shībài	*v.*	fail; lose
责任	責任	zérèn	*n.*	responsibility; duty
推		tuī	*v.*	shift; push away
负责任	負責任	fù zérèn	*adj.*	responsible
态度	態度	tài.du	*n.*	attitude
任何		rènhé	*adj.*	any; whatever
免不了		miǎnbùliǎo	*v.*	be unavoidable; be bound to be

竞争	競爭	jìngzhēng	n./v.	competition, compete
——者		zhě	suffix	one who … 社会工作者/研究者
变成	變成	biànchéng	v.	turn into; become
成功		chénggōng	v./n.	succeed, success
负担	負擔	fùdān	n.	burden
表面上		biǎomiàn shàng	adv.	on the surface; in name only
看来		kànlái	adv.	it looks; it appears; 看起来
充满	充滿	chōngmǎn	v.	be full of
做法		zuòfǎ	n.	way of doing or making a thing; a method of work
阻碍	阻礙	zǔài	v.	hinder; impede
有道理		yǒu dàolǐ	v.	make sense
从前	從前	cóngqián	n	past
办公室	辦公室	bàngōngshì	n.	office
喝茶		hē//chá	v.-o.	drink tea
看报	看報	kàn//bào	v.-o.	read newspaper
拿		ná	v.	receive
工资	工資	gōngzī	n.	wages; pay
凡是		fánshì	conj.	all; any
能力		nénglì	n.	ability
害怕		hàipà	v.	fear
同情		tóngqíng	v.	sympathize; show sympathy for 我很同情她。
残酷	殘酷	cánkù	adj.	cruel
代价	代價	dàijià	n.	price; cost
无家可归	無家可歸	wú jiā kě guī	idm.	be homeless; wander about without a home to go back to
怀疑	懷疑	huáiyí	v.	suspect; doubt

疑改革开放的方向，那么我们就只好永远在大锅饭的制度下(12)

过着喝稀饭、吃馒头的日子了。

改革开放	改革開放	gǎigé kāifàng	n.	the economic reform and open up policy that began in 1979
永远	永遠	yǒngyuǎn	adv.	forever
大锅饭	大鍋飯	dàguōfàn	n.	"big pot rice"——a metaphor for life in China before the reform; everybody eating from the same big pot —— equalitarian treatment of enterprises and individuals regardless of their performance
稀饭	稀飯	xīfàn	n.	rice gruel; congee
馒头	饅頭	mán.tou	n.	steamed bun

词语例句

(1) 给: (used in a passive sentence to introduce either the doer of the action or the action itself.)

◆ 今天下午我从西单购物中心出来的时候，被一群小乞丐给围住了。
This afternoon when I came out from the Xidan Shopping Center, I was surrounded by a group of young beggars.

1. 后来我才发现我给小贩骗了。
   It was only later I found out that I was cheated by the vender.
2. 那个小偷刚要偷东西的时候就给抓住了。
   The thief was caught just as he was about to steal something.

(2) 其中: among (which, them, etc.)

◆ 今天下午我从西单购物中心出来的时候，被一群小乞丐给围住了，其中一个扯住了我的裙子。
This afternoon when I came out from the Xidan Shopping Center, I was surrounded by a group of young beggars; one of them pulled my skirt and wouldn't let go.

1. 这个学期我选了四门课，其中功课最重的就是中文课。
   I am taking four courses this semester; of them, Chinese is the one with the heaviest work load.
2. 中国的社会问题很多，其中贫富不均是最严重的一个。
   There are many social issues in China; among them the difference between the rich and the poor is the most serious one.

(3) 弄: to make

◆ 你瞧，好好的一条裙子给弄成这样！
See, a fine skirt ended up like this (lit. "made to become like this")!

1. 小心别把衣服弄脏了。
   Be careful; don't get your clothes dirty.
2. 他的话真把我弄糊涂了。
   What he said really confuses me (lit. "makes me confused").

(4) 不得已: to have no alternative

◆ 他们出来做乞丐也是不得已啊！
They became beggars only because they had no choice.

1. 我不得已才请了几天假。

I had no choice but to ask for a few days' leave.

2. 请你原谅她吧，她这么做是不得已的。

Please forgive her. She did it because she had no choice.

(5) 所谓的 n.：the so-called n.

◆ 你所谓的"同情心"不但解决不了他们的生活问题，而且还会养成他们懒惰和依靠别人的习惯。

Your so-called "sympathy" not only couldn't solve their problems in life, but will also form their bad habits of being lazy and depending on others.

1. 他们所谓的"垃圾分类"只把垃圾分成两类，做得很不够。

What they call "garbage classification" divides garbage into two categories only; it is far from enough.

2. 那个所谓的"风景区"，只是几个破旧的建筑，没什么好看的。

That so-called "scenic spot" is nothing but a few run-down buildings. There is not much to see.

(6) 在 sb. 看来：in sb.'s view

◆在我看来，给乞丐钱不但不是帮他们的忙，反而(7)是害了他们。

In my view, giving the beggars money is not helping them; on the contrary, it hurts them.

1. 在你看来，这件事很简单，可是在他看来却困难得很。

To you this is a very simple matter, but to him it couldn't be more difficult.

2. 在美国人看来，言论自由是最基本的人权。

The way Americans see it, freedom of speech is the most basic human right.

(7)不但不···，反而···: not only..., on the contrary...

◆ 给乞丐钱不但不是帮他们的忙，反而是害了他们。

Giving the beggars money is not helping them; on the contrary, it hurts them.

1. 在我看来，用塑料产品不但不是一种进步，反而会严重地污染环境。

In my opinion, using plastic products is not progress; on the contrary, it pollutes the environment seriously.

2. 中国人在服装方面不但不保守，反而开放得很。

When it comes to clothing, the Chinese are not conservative at all; on the contrary, they are very liberal.

(8) 不是 A，而是 B: it's not A, but B

◆ 找不到工作并不一定是他们懒，而是社会制度不合理。

It may not be because they are lazy that they can't find a job, but because the social system is unjust.

1. 有些人很成功并不是因为他们很努力，而是因为他们依靠父母。

Some people were very successful not because they worked hard, but because they depended on their parents.

2. 对他来说，最大的痛苦不是没有钱、没有朋友，而是没有书看。

To him, the greatest suffering is not to have no money or no friends, but having no books to read.

(9) 免不了: inevitable; unavoidable

◆ 任何一个社会都免不了有竞争。

Competition is inevitable in every society.

1. 考试考得不太好免不了让他很难过。

It is inevitable that he feels sad when he did not do well on the examination.

2. 刚到外国，免不了有点儿不习惯。

One will inevitably find it a little difficult to adapt when one first goes abroad.

(10) 表面上···，其实···: on the surface…, in fact …

◆ 这种表面上看来充满同情心的做法其实是阻碍社会发展的。

This kind of practice looks very sympathetic, but in fact it will hinder the development of society.

1. 在中国，汽车快速增加，表面上为人们提供了许多方便，其实造成了严重的交通堵塞。

On the surface the rapid increase of cars in China affords people a lot of convenience; actually it causes serious traffic jams.

(11) 凡是··· 都···: all; any

◆ 凡是觉得竞争不合理的人都是失败的人。

Anyone who finds competition unreasonable is a loser.

1. 凡是到了十八岁的人，都有选举权。

Everyone who has reached the age of 18 has the right to vote.

2. 你搬家的时候，凡是你不要的东西，都可以留给我。

Leave anything that you don't want to me when you move.

(12) 在···下: under

◆ 如果因为有了乞丐就怀疑改革开放的方向，那么我们就只有永远在大锅饭的制度下过着喝稀饭、吃馒头的日子了。

If we doubt the direction of reform and open-up just because there are beggars, then we would forever live a (poor) life of eating rice gruel and steamed buns under the "big pot rice" system.

1. 在目前人口多而资源少的情况下，中国提倡使用一次性产品是很不实际的。

   Under the present situation of a large population and few natural resources, it is very unpractical to promote the use of disposable products in China.

2. 在市场经济的条件下，贫富不均是避免不了的。

   Under the conditions of a market economy, the big gap between the rich and the poor is inevitable.

练习

I. Make a sentence using the underlined expression.

1. 我觉得给乞丐钱<u>就是</u>鼓励他们不劳而获。

2. <u>在</u>我<u>看来</u>，给乞丐钱<u>不但不</u>是帮他们的忙，<u>反而</u>是害了他们。

3. 有些人成了乞丐，<u>并不是</u>不努力，<u>而是</u>社会的过错。

4. 把个人失败的责任推给社会，<u>这是最不负责任的态度</u>。

5. 任何一个社会都<u>免不了</u>有竞争。

6. 这种<u>表面上</u>看来充满同情心的做法<u>其实</u>是阻碍社会发展的。

7. <u>如果人人都像</u>你<u>这样</u>对穷人一点儿都不同情，这个社会<u>一定会</u>变得非常残酷。

II. Choose the most appropriate word for each blank and fill in with its Chinese equivalent.

have no alternative	not able to solve	rely on
reasonable	be full of	inevitable
hinder	be responsible for	suspect; doubt

1. 你应该去找工作，不能总是 _____ 父母的钱过日子。

2. 每一种社会制度都 _____ 有不合理的地方。

3. 我们不能为了坚持传统而 _____ 社会的进步。

4. 他是 _____ 才偷东西的，请你再给他一次机会吧！

5. 大家都知道这件事是 _____ 的，所以没有人愿意 _____ 。

6. 我 _____ 这种新产品质量有问题，因为只用了一次就坏了。

III. Complete the following dialogues with the expressions provided.

1. A: 大锅饭的制度让每个人都有饭吃，这不是很合理吗？

   B: _____。（表面上…，其实…）

2. A: 你不愿意上最好的大学，是不是害怕竞争啊？

   B: _____。（不是 A，而是 B）

3. A: _____。（凡是…都…）

   B: 我不同意。一次性的产品也有质量很好的。

IV. Answer the following questions using the words given.

1. 你在街上看到乞丐，会不会给他们钱？为什么？你同意不同意给
乞丐钱是鼓励他们不劳而获？

     （养成，习惯，公平，依靠，懒惰，过错，同情心，残酷）

2. 美国有没有贫富不均的问题？你认为造成这个问题的原因是什
么？政府可以用什么方法来解决这个问题？

     （竞争，失败，责任，合理，制度，鼓励，工资，发展，改革）

3. 竞争是不是一定是残酷的？你对竞争的态度是什么？在竞争中的成功
者有没有责任帮助失败者？有钱的人对穷人有没有责任？

     （怀疑，永远，有能力，阻碍，方向，变成，负担，代价，

     推给）

V. Composition

    美国的无家可归者

繁体字课文

甲：今天下午我從西單購物中心出來的時候，被一群小乞丐給(1)圍住
了。其中(2)一個扯住了我的裙子。你瞧，好好儿的一條裙子給弄(3)
成這樣！我很生氣，一毛錢都沒給他們。

乙：你怎麼一點儿同情心都沒有呢？他們也是別人的孩子啊！他們出
來做乞丐也是不得已(4)啊！

甲：我覺得給乞丐錢就是鼓勵他們不勞而獲。不工作的人沒飯吃是
公平的，也是應該的。你所謂的(5)"同情心"不但解決不了他
們的生活問題，而且還會養成他們懶惰和依靠別人的習慣。所
以，在我看來(6)，給乞丐錢不但不是幫他們的忙，反而(7)是害
了他們。

乙：找不到工作並不一定是他們懶，而是(8)社會制度不合理，貧富
不均。有錢的人越來越有錢，窮的人越來越窮。所以，有些人
成了乞丐，並不是不努力，而是社會的過錯。

甲：把個人失敗的責任推給社會，這是最不負責任的態度。任何一
個社會都免不了(9)有競爭，只要有競爭就免不了有人失敗。我
們不能把失敗者的生活變成成功者的負擔。這種表面上看來充
滿同情心的做法其實(10)是阻礙社會發展的。

乙：你說的也不是完全沒有道理。

甲：從前在辦公室裏努力工作的人和天天喝茶看報的人都拿一樣的
工資，那樣的制度合理嗎？凡是覺得競爭不合理的人都(11)是失
敗的人。一個有能力又努力的人是不會害怕競爭的。

乙：如果人人都像你這樣對窮人一點儿都不同情，這個社會一定
　　會變得非常殘酷。

甲：進步是有代價的。如果因爲有了乞丐、有了無家可歸的人就懷
　　疑改革開放的方向，那麼我們就只好永遠在大鍋飯的制度下⑿
　　過著喝稀飯、吃饅頭的日子了。

第八课　打官司

甲：美国人真是世界上最喜欢打官司⑴的人！

乙：这话怎么说呢？

甲：我昨天在报上看到有个人在麦当劳买了一杯咖啡，因为咖啡太烫，烫伤了手，于是⑵她就告⑶麦当劳，麦当劳还赔了她好几十万元呢！这在中国是不可思议的。

乙：是啊！在美国什么事儿都可以告到法院去。从一杯咖啡到人权，从交通事故到国家大事都可以告。政府可以告老百姓，老百姓也可以告政府；单位可以告个人，个人也可以告单位。像那个人告麦当劳，这种事儿是常有的，一点儿也不稀奇。

甲：美国这么多人打官司，律师的生意一定很好咯？

乙：你说得一点儿也不错。律师是美国最赚钱的职业之一。出了车祸得找⑷律师，买卖房子得找律师，离婚得找律师，甚至于立遗嘱还得找律师。美国人一生之中，从生到死都得跟律师打交道。

甲：律师在中国还是个比较新的行业。过去两个人有了争执，常常是找单位领导来解决问题，除非⑸不得已是不打官司的。中国人自古就不提倡打官司。

打官司		dǎ guān.si	v.-o.	go to court; engage in a lawsuit
				他跟麦当劳打官司。

麦当劳	麥當勞	Màidāngláo	*n.*	McDonald's
咖啡		kāfēi	*n.*	coffee
烫	燙	tàng	*adj./v.*	very hot; scalding, burn; scald
于是	於是	yúshì	*conj.*	consequently; hence; thereupon
告		gào	*v.*	sue; accuse
赔	賠	péi	*v.*	compensate; pay for
好几	好幾	hǎojǐ	*adj.*	quite a few
不可思议	不可思議	bùkě sīyì	*idm.*	unimaginable; inconceivable
法院		fǎyuàn	*n.*	court
人权	人權	rénquán	*n.*	human rights
交通		jiāotōng	*n.*	traffic
事故		shìgù	*n.*	accident
大事		dàshì	*n.*	a great event; a major important matter
老百姓		lǎobǎixìng	*n.*	common people; civilians
单位	單位	dānwèi	*n.*	work unit
个人	個人	gèrén	*n.*	individual (person)
稀奇		xīqí	*adj.*	rare; unusual and seldom seen
律师	律師	lǜshī	*n.*	lawyer
咯		.lo	*part.*	(used at the end of a sentence or question to show obviousness)
职业	職業	zhíyè	*n.*	occupation
…之一		…zhīyī		one of …
离婚	離婚	lí//hūn	*v.-o.*	get a divorce
甚至于	甚至於	shènzhìyú	*adv.*	even; so much so that
立		lì	*v.*	set up; (here) write up
遗嘱	遺囑	yízhǔ	*n.*	will; dying words
一生		yìshēng	*n.*	all one's life
行业	行業	hángyè	*n.*	profession
争执	爭執	zhēngzhí	*n./v.*	dispute; be at odds with, dispute
除非		chúfēi	*conj.*	unless; only if
自古		zìgǔ		since ancient time

乙：美国人喜欢打官司，表示美国是个法治的社会，大家对司法制
度有信心，相信打官司可以得到(6)公平合理的解决。最近几年
因为侵害知识产权的案子大量增加，律师的生意就更好了。

甲：拿现在跟改革开放以前比较(7)，中国人打官司也在增加，老百
姓渐渐学着(8)用法律来解决相互的争执。有些人担心这种打官
司的风气会影响到社会的和谐，我倒不担心。

乙：我觉得老百姓开始打官司是件好事儿。中国几千年来都是人治，
现在也渐渐走上了法治的道路(9)，所以打官司就成了不可避免
的事儿，而(10)律师也成了一个重要的行业了。

表示		biǎoshì	*v.*	show; indicate
法治		fǎzhì	*n.*	rule by law; governed by law
司法		sīfǎ	*adj.*	judicial
信心		xìnxīn	*n.*	confidence
有信心		yǒu xìnxīn	*adj.*	be confident of 他对自己很有信心。
得到		dédào	*v.*	gain; get
侵害		qīnhài	*v.*	infringe upon
知识产权	知識産權	zhī.shi chǎnquán	*n.*	intellectual property right
案子		àn.zi	*n.*	(law) case
大量		dàliàng	*adj. /adv.*	a large number; a great quantity, in great quantity
比较	比較	bǐjiào	*v.*	compare
渐渐	漸漸	jiànjiàn	*adv.*	gradually

学着	學著	xué.zhe	*v.*	imitate; copy; mimic; learn to
				学着用筷子/学着喝热茶
法律		fǎlù	*n.*	law
相互		xiānghù	*adj.*	mutual
			/adv.	相互的关系/相互的影响
				相互关心/相互了解
风气	風氣	fēngqì	*n.*	common practice
影响	影響	yǐngxiǎng	*v.*	affect; impair
				影响健康/影响质量/影响学习
和谐	和諧	héxié	*n./adj.*	harmony, harmonious
人治		rénzhì	*n.*	rule by man; rule of man
道路		dàolù	*n.*	road; way; path
不可避免		bùkě bìmiǎn	*phr.*	inevitable; unavoidable

词语例句

(1) 打官司: go to court

◆ 美国人真是世界上最喜欢打官司的人。

Americans like to take matters to court more than anyone else in the world.

1. 这位律师去年帮人打赢了六场官司。

This lawyer won six lawsuits for his clients last year.

2. 他最近正在跟一家出版社打官司，因为他们没得到他的同意就出版了他的一本书。

He has been suing a publishing house recently because they published one of his books without his permission.

(2) 于是: consequently; hence; thereupon

◆ …于是她就告麦当劳。

…therefore she sued McDonald's.

1. 他总是劝我早起，于是我试着每天 6 点钟起床。

He always urged me to get up early, so I tried to get up at six every day.

2. 他的自行车丢了，于是我把我的旧车给了他。

His bike was stolen. Therefore I gave my old one to him.

(3) 告: to sue; to take (sb.) to court

◆ …于是她就告麦当劳。

…therefore she sued McDonald's.

1. 我的邻居威胁我说，要是我不把狗拴起来，他就去告我。

My neighbor threatened to sue me if I didn't keep my dog tied up.

2. 这个老人因为儿子不养他而把儿子告到了法院。

Because his son didn't support him, the old man took his son to court.

(4) 找: to call on (sb.); to seek (the help of sb.)

◆ 出了车祸找律师，买卖房子找律师，离婚找律师，甚至于立遗嘱还得找律师。

You have to find a lawyer if you get into a car accident, if you want to buy or sell a house, or to get a divorce; you'll need a lawyer even to write up a will.

1. 你最好找朋友帮忙。

You'd better call on your friends to help you.

2. 过去中国人有了争执，常常找领导来解决问题。

In the past, Chinese people usually sought out their supervisors for a resolution when they had conflicts with each other.

(5) 除非: only if; unless

◆ 中国人除非不得已，是不打官司的。

Chinese people would not go to court unless they had no choice.

1. 除非她先道歉，要不然我不道歉。

I won't apologize unless she apologizes first.

2. 他一般不会迟到，除非他没赶上车。

Unless he misses the bus, he's usually not late.

(6) 得到 v. : get; gain; be v.-ed

◆ 大家相信打官司可以得到公平合理的解决。

Every one believes that (one's dispute) will be settled fairly and reasonably by going to court.

1. 生活水平提高了，饮食当然也得到了改善。

The living standard has been raised, so of course people's diet has improved too.

2. 必须有完备的法律，人民的权利才能得到保证。

Only when the law is perfect can people's rights be guaranteed.

(7) 拿 A 跟 B 比较, …: Compare A with B, …

◆ 拿现在跟改革开放以前比较，中国人打官司也在增加。

Comparing the present with the time before the "reform and opening-up," Chinese people who go to court are increasing.

1. 拿这个跟那个比较，你就知道哪个好了。

Comparing this with that, you will see which one is better.

2. 要是你总拿自己的长处跟别人的短处比较，你是永远不会进步的。

You won't make any progress if you are always comparing your strengths with others' weak points.

(8) 学着 v. : imitate; copy; mimic

◆ 老百姓渐渐学着用法律来解决相互的争执。

Chinese people are gradually learning to solve their disputes between one another by law.

1. 你既然住在中国，就应该学着喝热水，像中国人一样。

Since you're in China, you should get used to drinking hot water like the Chinese do.

2. 本来我只喝茶，到了美国以后，我就开始学着喝咖啡。

I used to drink tea. I started to drink coffee after I arrived in America.

(9) 走上…的道路: follow the path of; take the route of

◆中国几千年来都是人治，现在也渐渐走上了法治的道路。

China has long been a country ruled by man. Now it has gradually moved along the path of rule by law.

1. 八十年代以后，中国渐渐走上了改革开放的道路。

Since the eighties, China has gradually taken the route of reform and open-up.

2. 自从二十世纪初期，中国快速地走上了西化的道路。

Since the beginning of the 20th century, China has adopted Westernization.

(10) 而: (used to connect clauses or sentences to indicate coordination.)

◆打官司成了不可避免的事儿，而律师也成了一个重要的行业了。

Solving disputes by going to court has become inevitable, and the profession of lawyer has also become an important profession.

1. 工厂增加了，而环境保护也因此更重要了。

The number of factories has increased, and the protection of the environment has also become more important.

2. 中国社会比从前开放了，而妇女的地位也提高了。

Chinese society has become more open, and the position of women has also improved.

练习

I. Choose the correct answer.

1. 由于知识产权的问题，这两家公司一直在（打官司，告）。

2. 我对这个律师没有什么（相信，信心），因为我听说他输(shū, lose)了很多次。

3. 为了停车，他们两个人（发生了争执，有了一个争执）。

II. Choose the most appropriate word for each blank and fill in with its Chinese equivalent.

sue	write up	compensate	rare
a will	unimaginable	learn to	all one's life

1. 你把我的车撞坏了，要是你不 _____ ，我就去法院 _____ 你。

2. 他过去不喝咖啡，到了美国以后也开始 _____ 喝咖啡了。

3. 这位老人在死以前， _____ 了一份 _____ ，把所有的钱都给了一所大学。

4. A：你听说了吗？那个女人已经三十岁了，还没结婚，真 _____ 。

   B：这没什么嘛！在美国 _____ 没结婚的人并不少。

5. 真 _____ ，他跟女朋友认识了才两个星期就结婚了。

III. Make a sentence using the underlined expression.

1. 麦当劳因为咖啡烫伤了顾客的手而赔顾客钱，<u>这在中国是不可思议的</u>。

2. 像那个人告麦当劳，<u>这种事是常有的，一点儿也不稀奇</u>。

3. 律师是美国最赚钱的职业<u>之一</u>。

4. 中国几千年来都是人治，现在也渐渐<u>走上</u>了法治<u>的道路</u>。

5. 中国自古就不提倡打官司，所以人们<u>除非</u>不得已是不打官司的。

IV. Write a paragraph to answer each of the following questions:

1. 律师为什么是最赚钱的职业之一？美国人一般对律师的印象怎么样？

2. 打官司增加的现象，是不是说明社会不和谐？

3. "法治"和"人治"各有什么好处和坏处？

V. Read the following paragraph, then use Chinese to summarize it and write your impression of it.

On February 27, 1992, Stella Liebeck, a 79-year-old woman from Albuquerque, New Mexico, ordered a 49¢ cup of coffee from the drive-through window of a local McDonald's restaurant. Liebeck was in the passenger's seat of her Ford Probe, and her grandson Chris parked the car so that Liebeck could add cream and sugar to her coffee. She placed the coffee cup between her knees and pulled the far side of the lid toward her to remove it. In the process, she spilled the entire cup of coffee on her lap.[9] Liebeck was wearing cotton sweatpants; they absorbed the coffee and held it against her skin as she sat in the puddle of hot liquid for over 90 seconds, scalding her thighs, buttocks, and groin.[10] Liebeck was taken to the hospital, where it was determined that she had suffered third-degree burns on six percent of her skin and lesser burns over sixteen percent.[11] She remained in the hospital for eight days while she underwent skin grafting. During this period, Liebeck lost 20 pounds (nearly 20% of her body weight), reducing her down to 83 pounds.[12] Two years of medical treatment followed.

VI. Composition

"美国人真是世界上最喜欢打官司的人！"这句话说得对不对？

繁体字课文

甲：美國人真是世界上最喜歡打官司⑴的人！

乙：這話怎麼說呢？

甲：我昨天在報上看到有個人在麥當勞買了一杯咖啡，因爲咖啡太
　　燙，燙傷了手，於是⑵她就告⑶麥當勞，麥當勞還賠了她好幾
　　十萬元呢！這在中國是不可思議的。

乙：是啊！在美國什麼事兒都可以告到法院去。從一杯咖啡到人權，
　　從交通事故到國家大事都可以告。政府可以告老百姓，老百姓
　　也可以告政府；單位可以告個人，個人也可以告單位。像那個
　　人告麥當勞，這種事兒是常有的，一點兒也不稀奇。

甲：美國這麼多人打官司，律師的生意一定很好咯？

乙：你說得一點兒也不錯。律師是美國最賺錢的職業之一。出了車禍
　　得找⑷律師，買賣房子得找律師，離婚得找律師，甚至於立遺
　　囑還得找律師。美國人一生之中，從生到死都得跟律師打交
　　道。

甲：律師在中國還是個比較新的行業。過去兩個人有了爭執，常常
　　是找單位領導來解決問題，除非⑸不得已是不打官司的。中國
　　人自古就不提倡打官司。

乙：美國人喜歡打官司，表示美國是個法治的社會，大家對司法制
　　度有信心，相信打官司可以得到⑹公平合理的解決。最近幾年
　　因爲侵害知識産權的案子大量增加，律師的生意就更好了。

甲：拿現在跟改革開放以前比較(7)，中國人打官司也在增加，老百姓漸漸學著(8)用法律來解決相互的爭執。有些人擔心這種打官司的風氣會影響到社會的和諧，我倒不擔心。

乙：我覺得老百姓開始打官司是件好事儿。中國幾千年來都是人治，現在也漸漸走上了法治的道路(9)，所以打官司就成了不可避免的事儿，而(10)律師也成了一個重要的行業了。

第九课　　电子邮件

甲：自从电子邮件广泛使用以后(1)，人们的交流和信息的传递有了
　　很大的改变，现在差不多没有人写信了。

乙：是啊！以前我一个星期至少(2)给家里写一封信，现在发个电子
　　邮件比写封信容易多了。写信得买信纸、信封儿、邮票，不但
　　贵而且慢。电子邮件又便宜又快，在学校里用电脑还是免费的
　　呢！

甲：可是，我觉得电子邮件和信还是有些不同。收到信可以拿在手
　　上慢慢儿地看，一次一次地看，看完了还可以留起来。收到电
　　子邮件就没有这么真实的感觉了。

乙：你真是太落伍了！收到电子邮件一样可以用打印机把它印出
　　来，这跟信有什么不同呢？

甲：这个道理我知道，但是那种感觉还是有点儿不同。

乙：这只是一个习惯问题。二十一世纪的孩子除了电子邮件，根本(3)
　　不知道还有别的写信的法子。他们收到电子邮件的时候肯定(4)
　　跟你收到信是一样的感觉。

电子邮件	電子郵件	diànzǐ yóujiàn	n.	electronic mail 电子: electronic 邮件: mail; postal items

自从	自從	zìcóng	*prep.*	since; ever since
广泛	廣泛	guǎngfàn	*adj./* *adv.*	extensive; wide-ranging, extensively; widely
信息		xìnxī	*n.*	information; news
传递	傳遞	chuándì	*v./n.*	transmit; deliver; transfer, transmission
改变	改變	gǎibiàn	*n./v.*	change; transformation, change; transform
差不多		chà.buduō	*adv.*	almost
信		xìn	*n.*	letter
至少		zhìshǎo	*adv.*	at least
封		fēng	*AN*	measure word for letters
发	發	fā	*v.*	send out
信纸	信紙	xìnzhǐ	*n.*	letter paper
信封儿		xìnfēngr	*n.*	envelope
邮票	郵票	yóupiào	*n.*	stamp
电脑	電腦	diànnǎo	*n.*	computer
免费	免費	miǎnfèi	*v.*	free of charge
有些		yǒuxiē	*adv.*	somewhat; rather 有些不好意思/有些怀疑
收		shōu	*v.*	receive
留		liú	*v.*	keep; reserve
真实	真實	zhēnshí	*adj.*	true; real; authentic
感觉	感覺	gǎnjué	*n.*	feeling
落伍		luòwǔ	*adj.*	out of date; behind the times
打印机	打印機	dǎyìnjī	*n.*	printer
它		tā	*pron.*	it
印		yìn	*v.*	print
世纪	世紀	shìjì	*n.*	century
孩子		hái.zi	*n.*	child; children; kids
根本		gēnběn	*adv.*	at all; simply
肯定		kěndìng	*adv.*	definitely; surely

甲：你说的有道理。

乙：过去几年，对我们日常生活影响最大的，除了电子邮件以外，就是(5)互联网。有了互联网，你不必出门就能知道天下事了。

甲：从前中国人常拿"不出门，知天下事"来形容(6)一个特别聪明的人。其实现在只要有个电脑，上网一看，任何人都能做到"不出门，知天下事"。

乙：科技的进步使许多以前认为不可能的事都变得(7)可能了。科技缩短了距离，增加了速度，因此(8)也改善了我们的生活。

甲：电子邮件已经成了我们生活中不可少的一个东西。我爱电子邮件！

互联网	互聯網	hùliánwǎng	n.	Internet
出门	出門	chū//mén	v.-o.	go out; leave home
天下事		tiānxiàshì	n.	things in the world 天下: under the heaven "不出门知天下事" is abbreviated from the common saying "秀才不出门，能知天下事。" 秀才 xiùcái, one who passed the imperial examination at the county level in the Ming and Qing dynasties
形容		xíngróng	v.	describe
上网	上網	shàng//wǎng	v.-o.	get on or log on to the internet
任何		rènhé	adj.	any
科技		kējì	n.	science and technology
使		shǐ	v.	make; enable; cause

缩短	縮短	suōduǎn	v.	shorten
增加		zēngjiā	v.	increase
速度		sùdù	n.	speed; pace
因此		yīncǐ	conj.	therefore; hence; consequently
改善		gǎishàn	v.	improve
成		chéng	v.	become
爱	愛	ài	v.	love

词语例句

(1) 自从…以后: since …; ever since …

◆自从电子邮件广泛使用以后，人们的交流和信息的传递有了很大的改变。

Ever since electronic mail was first extensively used, there has been a great change in the way people communicate and the exchange of information.

1. 他自从在车祸中把腿撞断了以后，就很少出门了。

Ever since he broke his leg in an accident, he has seldom gone out.

2. 自从有了一次性的筷子以后，一般的饭馆儿都不用传统的筷子了。

Ever since disposable chopsticks came into use, most restaurants have stopped using traditional chopsticks.

(2) 至少: at least

◆ 以前我一星期至少给家里写一封信。

In the past I would write at least one letter to my family every week.

1. 定做一件旗袍，至少得三四百块钱。

It should cost you at least three or four hundred dollars to get a tailor-made *qipao*.

2. 他住院了，你不去看他，至少也应该给他打个电话啊！

He has been hospitalized, so even if you're not going to visit him, you should at least give him a call.

(3) 根本: at all; simply

◆ 二十一世纪的孩子除了电子邮件，根本不知道还有别的写信的法子。

Children of the 21st century simply do not know that there are other ways to write letters besides e-mail.

1. 他说他是学中国古代建筑的，但他其实根本不懂建筑。

He claimed that he majored in ancient Chinese architecture, but in fact he knows nothing at all about architecture.

2. A: 你为什么没问过我就拿了我的信？

B: 我根本没去过你的房间，怎么可能拿了你的信呢?!

A: Why did you take away my letter without asking me?

B: I didn't even go in your room; how could I have possibly taken your letter?

(4) 肯定: definitely; surely

◆ 他们收到电子邮件的时候，肯定跟你收到信是一样的感觉。

When they receive e-mails, they definitely feel the same way as you do when you receive letters.

1. 只有他来过我的房间，所以我的信肯定是他拿走的。

He's the only one who has been into my room, so he must be the one who took away my letter.

2. 现在什么都电脑化了，不会用电脑的人肯定会被社会淘汰。

Nowadays everything is computerized. Those who do not know how to use a computer will surely lag behind the others (lit. be kicked out by society).

(5) 除了…以外，就是… : other than/besides…, there's …

◆ 对我们日常生活影响最大的，除了电子邮件以外，就是互联网。

Other than e-mail, the Internet has had the greatest influence on our daily lives.

1. 现在的孩子除了看电视以外，就是对着电脑，什么运动都不做。

Besides watching television, what kids nowadays do is sit in front of the computer. They don't do any exercise.

2. 一次性产品的好处除了卫生一点儿以外，就是方便。

The advantage of disposable products is that, besides being a little more hygienic, they are so convenient.

(6) 拿 A 来形容 B: use A to describe B

◆ 从前中国人常拿"不出门，知天下事"来形容一个特别聪明的人。

In the past, Chinese often used the phrase "he who knows the world under heavens without stepping out of the house" to describe a very smart person.

（The 拿 here can be replaced by 用．）

1. 你怎么可以用电脑来形容人脑呢？一个会想，另一个可不会啊!

How can you use a computer to describe a human brain? One can think, but the other can't.

2. 我不知道应该拿什么来形容我现在的感觉。

I don't know how to describe my feeling right now.

(7) A 使 B 变得… : A makes B (change to be) …

◆ 科技的进步使许多以前认为不可能的事变得可能了。

Improvements in science and technology have made possible things that were thought to be impossible in the past.

1. 使用电脑可以使一些很困难的事变得很简单。

Using a computer can make some difficult tasks very easy.

2. 穿旗袍不见得会使一个女人变得更好看。

Wearing a *qipao* doesn't necessarily make a woman look better.

(8) 因此: therefore; hence; consequently

◆ 科技缩短了距离，增加了速度，因此也改善了我们的生活。

Science and technology has shortened the distance and increased the speed; therefore it also has improved our lives.

1. 他没有电脑，因此不能发电子邮件。

He has no computer, so he couldn't send e-mail.

2. 他的手被烫伤了，因此请了三天病假。

His hand was scalded; therefore he asked for sick leave for three days.

练习

I. Choose the correct answer.

1. _____ 朋友的信的时候，我常常马上回信，可是如果是父母的
   信，就等几天再给他们回信。

   　　a. 接受　　b. 收到　　c. 受到

2. 政府提倡我们不要把用过的塑料袋扔掉，要留_____，以后重复使
   用。

   　　a. 起来　　b. 出来　　c. 进来

3. 他以前很努力，上了大学以后却_____很懒，做什么事都只想不劳
   而获。

   　　a. 变成　　b. 变了　　c. 变得

II. Choose the most appropriate word for each blank and fill in with its Chinese equivalent.

extensive/wide-ranging　　free　　　　describe　　　　change
get on to the Internet　　　mainly　　　behind the times　　transmit

1. 据说美国的高中学生每天花大量时间 _____ ，_____ 是跟朋友聊
   天或者做一些没有意义的事情。

2. 为了让更多的人用自己的产品，电脑公司常常为顾客提供 _____的
   服务。

3. 中国人用"脱了裤子放屁"来 _____ 做了多余的事情。

4. 最近二十年来，尤其是改革开放以后，美国和中国在政治上、经
   济上、文化上都有了 _____ 的交流。

5. 认为孩子越多父母越有福气的想法早就 _____ 了。

III. Answer the following questions using the expressions given.

1. 你还常常写信给朋友吗？（自从…以后，上网，发）

2. 要看懂中文报纸，得会多少中国字？（至少）

3. 我觉得收到电子邮件和收到信感觉完全不同。（根本）

4. 你上网的时候都做些什么事？（除了…，就是…）

5. 在中国，律师的生意越来越好，是因为什么呢？（因此）

IV. Answer the question using the expressions given.

1. 科技进步真的缩短了人们之间的距离了吗？请用飞机、电视、电子邮件等例子来说明。

（改善，改变，增加，速度，影响，落伍，日常生活，广泛，交流，信息）

2. 要是你想告诉一个人你很喜欢她，你会写信给她，还是发电子邮件给她？为什么？

（封，信纸，信封儿，邮票，感觉，真实，留起来，打印，不必）

V. Composition

1. 我和电子邮件
2. 我们还需要更多新的科技产品吗？

繁体字课文

甲：自從電子郵件廣泛使用以後(1)，人們的交流和信息的傳遞有了
很大的改變，現在差不多沒有人寫信了。

乙：是啊！以前我一個星期至少(2)給家裏寫一封信，現在發個電子
郵件比寫封信容易多了。寫信得買信紙、信封儿、郵票，不但
貴而且慢。電子郵件又便宜又快，在學校裏用電腦還是免費的
呢！

甲：可是，我覺得電子郵件和信還是有些不同。收到信可以拿在手
上慢慢儿地看，一次一次地看，看完了還可以留起來。收到電
子郵件就沒有這麼真實的感覺了。

乙：你真是太落伍了！收到電子郵件一樣可以用打印機把它印出
來，這跟信有什麼不同呢？

甲：這個道理我知道，但是那種感覺還是有點儿不同。

乙：這只是一個習慣問題。二十一世紀的孩子，除了電子郵件根本(3)
不知道還有別的寫信的法子。他們收到電子郵件的時候肯定(4)
跟你收到信是一樣的感覺。

甲：你說的有道理。

乙：過去幾年，對我們日常生活影響最大的，除了電子郵件以外，
就是(5)互聯網。有了互聯網，你不必出門就能知道天下事了。

甲：從前中國人常拿"不出門，知天下事"來形容(6)一個特別聰明
的人。其實現在只要有個電腦，上網一看，任何人都能做到
"不出門，知天下事"。

乙：科技的進步使許多以前認爲不可能的事都變得(7)可能了。科技
　　縮短了距離，增加了速度，因此(8)也改善了我們的生活。

甲：電子郵件已經成了我們生活中不可少的一個東西。我愛電子郵
　　件！

第十课　鲜花插在牛粪上

甲：最近在中国老夫少妻的婚姻越来越普遍了。我家隔壁的那对夫妇，男的比女的大二十几岁！

乙：大二十几岁？这哪儿(1)像夫妇啊！简直是父女嘛！我真不懂这么年轻漂亮的小姐为什么要嫁给一个又老又丑的老头儿。真是鲜花插在牛粪上！

甲：我看他们生活得很幸福，一点儿问题也没有。那个男的虽然年纪大一点儿，但是学问好，收入高，对妻子又体贴。在我看来，是很理想的一对儿。

乙：刚结婚的时候，老夫少妻的问题往往(2)看不出来(3)，但是十年、二十年以后，他们的问题就会变得很严重了。

甲：怎么说呢？

乙：十年、二十年以后，男的在体力上会明显地不如女的。而且就

鲜花	鲜花	xiānhuā	*n.*	fresh flower
插		chā	*v.*	stick in; insert
牛粪	牛粪	niúfèn	*n.*	cow dung
鲜花插在牛粪上	鲜花插在牛粪上	xiānhuā chā zài niúfèn shàng	*idm.*	fresh flower sticking in cow dung——what a waste!

老夫少妻		lǎofū shàoqī	*n.*	old husband and young wife
婚姻		hūnyīn	*n.*	marriage
普遍		pǔbiàn	*adj.*	common; prevalent
隔壁		gébì	*n.*	next door
夫妇	夫婦	fūfù	*n.*	husband and wife; 夫妻
父女		fùnǚ	*n.*	father and daughter 父：父亲；father 女：女儿；daughter
嘛		.ma	*part.*	(used at the end of a sentence to indicate that sth. is obvious) 这个问题很简单嘛！
年轻	年輕	niánqīng	*adj.*	young
小姐		xiǎo.jiě	*n.*	young (unmarried) lady
嫁		jià	*v.*	(of a woman) marry
丑	醜	chǒu	*adj.*	ugly
老头儿	老頭儿	lǎotóur	*n.*	old man; old chap
生活		shēnghuó	*v.*	live
幸福		xìngfú	*adj.*	happy; fortunate
年纪	年紀	niánjì	*n.*	age
学问	學問	xuéwèn	*n.*	knowledge
收入		shōurù	*n.*	income; earning
妻子		qī.zi	*n.*	wife
体贴	體貼	tǐtiē	*v.*	show consideration for; give every care to
理想		lǐxiǎng	*adj.*	ideal
一对儿	一對儿	yíduìr	*n.*	a couple; a pair
结婚	結婚	jié//hūn	*v.-o.*	get married
往往		wǎngwǎng	*adv.*	more often than not; often; frequently
体力	體力	tǐlì	*n.*	physical strength
明显	明顯	míngxiǎn	*adj./adv.*	obvious; clear; apparent, obviously; clearly

常识来说(4)，男人的平均寿命比女人的短，所以年轻的妻子守

寡的可能就很高。

甲：现在是二十一世纪的新中国，妻子死了，丈夫可以再娶；丈夫

死了，妻子也可以再嫁。在我父母那个时代，再嫁的女人是让

人看不起的，现在可没这个问题了。

乙：对老夫少妻的婚姻，我常常怀疑夫妻之间(5)是不是真的有爱

情。我觉得一个年轻女人嫁给一个老头儿，往往是为了他的地

位和财富，女的并不是真的爱男的。

甲：这个我不同意。婚姻完全是一件个人的事儿。要嫁给谁，要娶

谁，都只是他们两个人的事儿。两人之间有没有爱情，只有他

们自己知道。

乙：你见过一个漂亮的女人嫁给一个又老又丑又穷又没有地位的男

人吗？

甲：这个……这个……我一时(6)想不出一个例子来。

乙：所以我说一个男人年龄大不大不要紧，只要他有钱有地位，就

能娶到年轻漂亮的女人。

甲：你这样说，对女人是不公平的。即使一个女人为了钱为了地位

而嫁给一个比她大十几二十几岁的男人，那也(7)是她自己的选

择。再说(8)，男人也有为了金钱和地位而(9)跟一个比自己年长

的女人结婚的。我希望不但有"老夫少妻"，也有"老妻少

常识	常識	chángshí	n.	common knowledge
平均		píngjūn	adj.	average
寿命	壽命	shòumìng	n.	life span
短		duǎn	adj.	short (in length, duration, height)
守寡		shǒu//guǎ	v.-o.	remain a widow; live in widowhood
可能		kěnéng	n.	possibility
丈夫		zhàng.fu	n.	husband
娶		qǔ	v.	(of men) marry; take (a wife)
父母		fùmǔ	n.	parents
时代	時代	shídài	n.	times; age; era
看不起		kàn.buqǐ	v.-c.	look down upon
怀疑	懷疑	huáiyí	v.	suspect; doubt
爱情	愛情	àiqíng	n.	romantic love
地位		dìwèi	n.	(social) status
财富	財富	cáifù	n.	wealth
件		jiàn	AN	measure word for matters in general
个人	個人	gèrén	n.	individual
穷	窮	qióng	adj.	(financially) poor
一时	一時	yìshí	adv.	for the moment
例子		lì.zi	n.	example; case; instance
年龄	年齡	niánlíng	n.	年纪; age
不要紧	不要緊	búyàojǐn	adj.	it doesn't matter; never mind
公平		gōngpíng	adj.	fair; just
即使		jíshǐ	conj.	even; even if; even though
选择	選擇	xuǎnzé	n./v.	choice, select; choose
再说	再説	zàishuō	conj.	what's more; besides
金钱	金錢	jīnqián	n.	money
年长	年長	niánzhǎng	adj.	older
希望		xīwàng	v.	hope; wish

夫", 这样才能显出⑽这个社会确实开放了, 选择增加了。"老
夫少妻"也好, "老妻少夫"也好, 这都⑾是他们自己的事儿,
别人是没有权利干涉的。

显出	顯出	xiǎnchū	*v.*	show; reveal
确实	確實	quèshí	*adv.*	indeed; really
开放	開放	kāifàng	*adj.*	open-minded; liberal
权利	權利	quánlì	*n.*	right
干涉		gānshè	*v.*	interfere; intervene; meddle

词语例句

(1) S. 哪儿 v. !: (rhetorical question)

◆ 这哪儿像夫妇啊!

This couple doesn't really look like a couple!

1. 这是他的私事，我哪儿知道啊?

This is his private matter. How would I know it?

2. 他是个穷学生，哪儿有钱租这么贵的房子!

He is a poor student. How could he be able to rent such an expensive house?

(2) 往往: tend to be

◆ 刚结婚的时候，老夫少妻的问题往往看不出来。

It's always hard to see the problem of an "old husband and young wife" marriage at the beginning.

(往往 expresses a tendency or likelihood.)

1. 对一门课没有兴趣，往往就学不好。

If you're not interested in a subject, you tend not to learn it well.

2. 现代化的东西方便是方便，可是往往造成很大的浪费。

Modern things are convenient, but they usually cause a lot of waste.

(3) v. 不出 o. 来: unable to v. – o.

◆ 刚结婚的时候，老夫少妻的问题往往看不出来。

1. 我太紧张了，所以想不出答案来。

I was too nervous, so I couldn't think of an answer.

2. 他难过得说不出话来。

He feels so bad that he can't even speak.

(4) 就···来说: based solely on...; speaking solely of...

◆ 就常识来说，男人的平均寿命比女人的短。

We know by common knowledge that a man's average life span is shorter than a woman's.

1. 就交通来说，住在纽约是很方便的。

If you're speaking solely in terms of transportation, living in New York is very convenient.

2. 就收入来说，老李的比老张的高，可是就学问来说，老李却不如老张。

Based solely on their incomes, you could say that Old Li is much wealthier than Old Zhang, but in terms of knowledge, Old Li cannot be compared with Old Zhang.

(5) A 和 B 之间: between A and B

◆ 对老夫少妻的婚姻，我常常怀疑夫妻之间是不是真的有爱情。
When I see an "old husband and young wife" marriage, I often wonder if there is really love between the couple.
　　1. 父母和孩子之间有不能说的话吗？
　　Are there things that cannot be said between parents and their children?
　　2. 中国人和美国人之间的不同不是一个对和错的问题。
　　The difference between a Chinese person and an American is not a matter of right or wrong.

(6) 一时: at the moment; for the moment

◆ 我一时想不出一个例子来。
I can't think of an example at the moment.
　　1. 我脑子很乱，一时不知道该怎么办。
　　My mind is in a mess, so for now I don't know what to do.
　　2. 他听到坏消息，一时很难过，竟然哭了起来。
　　Upon hearing the bad news, he was momentarily overcome by grief and actually began to cry.

(7) 即使…，也…: even if …

◆即使一个女人为了钱为了地位而嫁给一个比她大十几二十几岁的男人，那也是她自己的选择。
Even if a woman marries a man ten or twenty years older than her for the sake of money and status, it's still her own choice.
　　1. 他即使变得又老又丑又穷，我也会爱他！
　　Even if he becomes old, ugly and poor, I'll still love him!
　　2. 即使你跟他结了婚，也不一定会幸福。
　　Even if you marry him, you (still) might not be happy.

(8) 再说: moreover; furthermore

◆再说，男人也有为了金钱和地位而跟一个比自己年长的女人结婚的。
Moreover there are also men who marry older women for their money and status.

1. 你应该结婚了。你有了工作，女朋友又那么好。再说，你年纪
   也不小了。

   It's time you got married. You have a job, and your girlfriend is great, and what's more, you are no longer young.

2. 我工作太忙，钱又不多。再说，对出国也没兴趣，所以不跟你
   们去中国了。

   I am too busy with my work and do not have much money; furthermore, I'm not interested in going abroad, so I won't go with you to China.

(9) 为了···而···: do sth. for the sake of ...

◆ 男人也有为了金钱和地位而跟一个比自己年长的女人结婚的。

1. 你会为了爱情而死吗？

   Would you die for love?

2. 有的父母为了让孩子上好的学校而搬家。

   Some parents move (to another place) so that their children can go to a good school.

(10) 显出: show

◆ 这样才能显出这个社会确实开放了，选择增加了。

   Only then can we show that our society has really opened up and that we have more choices.

1. 你得多体贴你的女朋友，才能显出你爱他。

   You have to take better care of your girlfriend in order to show that you love her.

2. 她听了我说的话，显出怀疑的样子。

   She had suspicion written on her face after hearing what I said.

(11) A 也好，B 也好，都···: no matter whether; whether ... or ...

◆ "老夫少妻"也好，"老妻少夫"也好，这都(11)是他们自己的事儿。

   Either "old husband marries a young wife" or "old wife marries a young husband," these are both their own business.

1. 再嫁也好，再娶也好，谁都不能看不起他们。

   No one should look down upon women and men who remarry.

2. 你喜欢也好，不喜欢也好，电子邮件已经成了生活中不可少的
   东西了。

   No matter if you like it or not, e-mail has become something indispensable in our lives.

练习

I. Make a sentence using the underlined expression(s).

1. 这哪儿像夫妇啊！简直是父女嘛！

2. 在我父母的时代，再嫁的女人是让人看不起的。

3. 即使一个女人为了钱为了地位而嫁给一个比她大二十几岁的男人，也是她自己的选择。

4. 李小姐为了地位而嫁给一个比她大二十几岁的男人。

5. 就常识来说，男人的平均寿命比女人的短，所以年轻妻子守寡的可能就很高。

6. 我希望不但有"老夫少妻"，也有"老妻少夫"，这样才能显出这个社会确实开放了。

7. 这是他们自己的事儿，别人是没有权利干涉的。

II. Choose the most appropriate word for each blank and fill in with its Chinese equivalent.

show/reveal	look down upon	obvious/clear
interfere	for the moment	give every care to

1. 因为怕被别人 ＿＿＿＿＿ ，他不敢告诉别人他很穷。

2. 这次的考试，他有很 ＿＿＿＿＿ 的进步。

3. 她希望她的丈夫能对她 ＿＿＿＿＿ 一点儿。

4. 我当然认识他，不过 ＿＿＿＿＿ 想不起来他叫什么名字。

5. 那是他的事，你最好不要 ＿＿＿＿＿ 。

III. Answer the question using the expressions given.

1. 一般人对老夫少妻的态度是什么？
（怀疑，地位，往往，公平，财富，年轻，丑，看不起，爱情）

2. 你最好的朋友跟一个又老又丑又没有钱的人认识了一个月，就决定嫁给他。你想劝她再考虑考虑。你会怎么说呢？
（幸福，鲜花插在牛粪上，年纪，学问，体贴，理想，严重，体力，寿命，守寡，再嫁，选择）

IV. Answer the following questions using the expressions provided.

1. 你为什么不去参观北京有名的景点呢？（哪儿，简直）

2. 你习惯这儿的生活了没有？（刚，但是）

3. 你想租个什么样的房子呢？一定得有空调吗？

    （…不要紧，只要…就…）

4. 听说这门课功课很重，又特别困难，你为什么要选这样的一门课

    呢？（再说）

5. 你觉得我应该学中文还是学日文呢？（A也好，B也好，都…）

6. 上课的时候老师问了你一个问题，你为什么不回答呢？（一时）

V. Composition

1. 老夫少妻的婚姻可能有哪些问题？你对这种婚姻的态度是什么？
    你会不会跟一个比自己年纪大很多或者小很多的人结婚呢？为什
    么？

2. 为什么"老妻少夫"的婚姻比"老夫少妻"的婚姻少呢？请谈谈
    你的看法。

繁体字课文

甲：最近在中國老夫少妻的婚姻越來越普遍了。我家隔壁的那對夫
　　婦，男的比女的大二十幾歲！

乙：大二十幾歲？這哪儿⑴像夫婦啊！簡直是父女嘛！我真不懂這麼
　　年輕漂亮的小姐爲什麼要嫁給一個又老又醜的老頭儿。真是鮮
　　花插在牛糞上！

甲：我看他們生活得很幸福，一點儿問題也沒有。那個男的雖然年紀大
　　一點儿，但是學問好，收入高，對妻子又體貼。在我看來，是很
　　理想的一對儿。

乙：剛結婚的時候，老夫少妻的問題往往⑵看不出來⑶，但是十年、
　　二十年以後，他們的問題就會變得很嚴重了。

甲：怎麼說呢？

乙：十年、二十年以後，男的在體力上會明顯地不如女的。而且就
　　常識來說⑷，男人的平均壽命比女人的短，所以年輕的妻子守
　　寡的可能就很高。

甲：現在是二十一世紀的新中國，妻子死了，丈夫可以再娶；丈夫
　　死了，妻子也可以再嫁。在我父母那個時代，再嫁的女人是讓
　　人看不起的，現在可沒這個問題了。

乙：對老夫少妻的婚姻，我常常懷疑夫妻之間⑸是不是真的有愛
　　情。我覺得一個年輕女人嫁給一個老頭儿，往往是爲了他的地
　　位和財富，女的並不是真的愛男的。

甲：這個我不同意。婚姻完全是一件個人的事ㄦ。要嫁給誰，要娶誰，都只是他們兩個人的事ㄦ。兩人之間有沒有愛情，只有他們自己知道。

乙：你見過一個漂亮的女人嫁給一個又老又醜又窮又沒有地位的男人嗎？

甲：這個……這個……我一時(6)想不出一個例子來。

乙：所以我說一個男人年齡大不大不要緊，只要他有錢有地位，就能娶到年輕漂亮的女人。

甲：你這樣說，對女人是不公平的。即使一個女人爲了錢爲了地位而嫁給一個比她大十幾二十幾歲的男人，那也(7)是她自己的選擇。再說(8)，男人也有爲了金錢和地位而(9)跟一個比自己年長的女人結婚的。我希望不但有"老夫少妻"，也有"老妻少夫"，這樣才能顯出(10)這個社會確實開放了，選擇增加了。"老夫少妻"也好，"老妻少夫"也好，這都(11)是他們自己的事ㄦ，別人是沒有權利干涉的。

第十一课 总统有了女朋友

甲：最近电视上、报纸上，天天都报导美国总统有女朋友的事儿。有人觉得美国人真丢脸，怎么选了一个人品这么差的总统。

乙：我一点儿也不觉得丢脸，我觉得这是美国人最值得骄傲的地方。这说明美国有非常完备的法律制度，任何人都受到法律的保护，也受到法律的制裁，即使总统也不例外。我想全世界也许只有美国能把这样的丑闻宣布出来。我们觉得任何贪污腐化都得公布出来，公布出来是制裁贪污腐化最有效的办法。有些国家的报纸和电视上看不到任何贪污腐化的新闻，那才是最黑暗的。

甲：这个我同意。但是我觉得美国人有点儿小题大做。有没有女朋友是总统个人的事儿，这跟他是不是一个好总统没有关系。要是总统夫人不管这件事儿，没有任何人可以管这件事儿。可是在美国，好像什么人都可以过问总统个人的事情。有一回我在电视

总统	總統	zǒngtǒng	n.	president
女朋友		nǚ péng.you	n.	girlfriend
报纸	報紙	bàozhǐ	n.	newspaper
报导	報導	bàodǎo	v.	report
丢脸	丟臉	diū//liǎn	v.-o.	lose face; be disgraced

				丢：lose
				脸：face
选	選	xuǎn	v.	elect; select; choose
人品		rénpǐn	n.	moral standing; moral quality; character
骄傲	驕傲	jiāoào	v.	take pride in; be proud
完备	完備	wánbèi	adj.	complete; perfect (not to be used for people)
制裁		zhìcái	v.	sanction; punish
例外		lìwài	v./n.	be an exception, exception
丑闻	醜聞	chǒuwén	n.	scandal
				闻：news; story
宣布		xuānbù	v.	announce; declare
贪污	貪污	tānwū	v./n.	embezzle; practice graft, embezzlement
腐化		fǔhuà	v./n.	become corrupt, corruption
公布		gōngbù	v.	make public; announce; promulgate
有效		yǒuxiào	adj.	effective
办法	辦法	bànfǎ	n.	way; means
新闻	新聞	xīnwén	n.	news
黑暗	黑暗	hēiàn	adj.	dark
小题大做	小題大做	xiǎotí dàzuò	idm.	make a big fuss over a trifle; make a mountain out of a molehill
夫人		fū.rén	n.	Lady; Madam; Mrs.
				总统夫人：the first lady
过问	過問	guòwèn	v.	make inquiry about; concern oneself with; take an interest in
				你没有权利过问我的私事。
事情		shì.qing	n.	matter; affair; business
回		huí	AN	measure word for occurrences; 次

上看到一个记者，当着许多外国元首的面(1)问总统："你到底跟那个女人发生过关系没有？"我觉得这未免太让总统下不了台了。美国人在这件事情上，好像最关心的是总统跟这个女人睡过觉没有，至于(2)他是不是一个能干的总统反而(3)不是一个话题。美国人不是最重视个人的隐私权吗？这件事儿，在我看来，总统的隐私权受到了很大的侵害。

乙：我们一方面强调(4)个人的隐私权，但另一方面更强调政治领袖得诚实。其实大部分美国人也并不在乎(5)总统有没有女朋友，这是他个人的事儿，但是他说谎就不对了。我们不能要一个不诚实的总统。

甲：其实，哪个人不说谎啊？我也不觉得美国人对诚实的要求(6)特别高。我看，总统有女朋友的事儿还是政治斗争。

乙：政治斗争肯定是有的，但是新闻单位也起了大作用(7)。美国的新闻单位是监督政府最严密的组织，他们恨不得(8)每天都找到

记者	記者	jìzhě	n.	reporter; journalist
当着…的面	當着…的面	dāng.zhe … .de miàn	adv.	in one's presence; face to face
元首		yuánshǒu	n.	head of state
发生	發生	fāshēng	v.	occur; happen; take place
关系	關係	guān.xi	n.	relation
发生关系	發生關係	fāshēng guān.xi		have sexual relations (with sb.)

下不了台	下不了臺	xià .bu liǎo tái	v.	be unable to get out of a predicament or an embarrassing situation 下台：step down from the platform or stage
睡觉	睡覺	shuì//jiào	v.-o.	sleep; (here) have sexual relations (with sb.)
至于	至於	zhìyú	prep.	as for
能干	能幹	nénggàn	adj.	capable; able; competent
反而		fǎn'ér	adv.	on the contrary
话题	話題	huàtí	n.	topic of conversation
重视	重視	zhòngshì	v.	take something seriously; value
隐私	隱私	yǐnsī	n.	privacy
——权	——權	quán	suffix	right
隐私权	隱私權	yǐnsīquán	n.	the right to keep one's privacy
侵害		qīnhài	v.	encroach upon; infringe upon
强调	強調	qiángdiào	v.	emphasize; stress
政治		zhèngzhì	n.	politics
领袖	領袖	lǐngxiù	n.	leader
诚实	誠實	chéngshí	adj.	honest
大部分		dàbù.fen	adj.	most of; a great part of; majority
在乎		zài.hu	v.	care about; mind
说谎	說謊	shuō//huǎng	v.-o.	tell a lie
要求		yāoqiú	n.	request; demand; requirement
斗争	鬥爭	dòuzhēng	n.	struggle
作用		zuòyòng	n.	effect; function
起作用		qǐ zuòyòng	v.-o.	take effect
监督	監督	jiāndū	v.	keep watch on and to supervise
严密	嚴密	yánmì	adj.	closely-knit; tight
组织	組織	zǔzhī	n.	organization
恨不得		hèn.bu.de	v.	very anxious to; itch to; how one wishes one could (do something that is impossible)

政府贪污腐化的地方，这样报纸的销路才会更好，电视收视率才会提高。但是也正因为他们监督得那么严，政府才不至于(9)太腐化。

甲：要是克林顿这一次还能竞选总统，你会不会投他的票？

乙：我肯定会再投他的票！与其选一个喜欢打仗的总统，不如(10)选一个喜欢谈恋爱的总统。

销路	銷路	xiāolù	n.	sales
收视率	收視率	shōushìlǜ	n.	(of television programs) the rate of being viewed
——率		lǜ	suffix	rate; ratio; proposition
提高		tígāo	v.	raise; increase; heighten
严	嚴	yán	adj.	strict
不至于	不至於	búzhìyú	adv.	cannot or be unlikely to go so far as to
克林顿	克林頓	Kèlíndùn	n.	Bill Clinton
竞选	競選	jìngxuǎn	v.	run for (office)
投票	投票	tóu//piào	v.-o.	cast a vote; vote 我还没有投票的权利。 你要投谁的票？
与其A不如B	與其A不如B	yǔqí A bùrú B	conj.	rather then A, it would be better B
打仗		dǎ//zhàng	v.-o.	fight a battle; go to war A 跟 B 打仗。
谈恋爱	談戀愛	tán liàn'ài	v.-o.	be in love 谈: talk about 恋爱: romantic love 他跟谁谈恋爱？是他的同学吗？

词语例句

(1) 当着 sb. 的面: in the presence of sb.

◆有一回我在电视上看到一个记者，当着许多外国元首的面问总
　统…

Once I saw a journalist on television.　He asked the President in front of many
foreign political leaders...

1. 他当着我的面什么都不说，却在别人面前批评我。

   He didn't say anything in front of me, but he criticized me in front of someone
   else.

2. 当着那么多老师的面，我怎么好意思说我不知道呢。

   How can I say that I don't know in the presence of so many teachers?

(2) 至于: as for

◆美国人在这件事情上，好像最关心的是总统跟这个女人睡过觉没
　有，至于他是不是一个能干的总统反而不是一个话题。

It seems that what Americans care about most in this matter is whether the
President has slept with this woman; as for whether he's a capable president, that
is, on the contrary, not an issue.

1. 我觉得北京的吃和住都很不错，至于交通，却实在让人受不
   了。

   I think the food and accommodations in Beijing are both quite good.　As for the
   traffic there, I find it unbearable.

2. 只要她很能干、负责就行了，至于人品怎么样，我们不必管。

   It's fine as long as she is capable and responsible.　As for her personality, we
   don't need to be concerned about that.

(3) 反而: on the contrary

◆美国人在这件事情上，好像最关心的是总统跟这个女人睡过觉没
　有，至于他是不是一个能干的总统反而不是一个话题。。

1. 我给他出了个好主意，可是他不但不感谢我，反而说我侵害了
   他的隐私。

   I came up with a good idea for him, but he was not only ungrateful (to me,) he
   even went on to say that, on the contrary, I have infringed upon his privacy.

2. 她又年轻又漂亮，我以为她会嫁给一个年轻人，她反而嫁给了
   一个老头。

She is young and pretty. I thought that she was going to marry a young man, but on the contrary, she married an old guy.

(4) 一方面…, 另一方面…: on one hand…, on the other hand…

◆我们一方面强调个人的隐私权，但另一方面更强调政治领袖得诚实。

On one hand we emphasize the rights of an individual to his privacy, but on the other hand, we stress even more the honesty of a political leader.

1. 我一方面同情乞丐，另一方面也不想养成他们不劳而获的习惯。

On one hand I sympathize with beggars very much, but on the other hand, I don't want to form their bad habits of being lazy and depending on others.

2. 一方面旗袍很好看，但另一方面穿着旗袍工作行动的确很不方便。

On one hand, *qipao* are really pretty, but on the other hand, it is indeed very inconvenient to wear them to work or move about.

(5) 在乎: care about; mind

◆其实大部分美国人也并不在乎总统有没有女朋友。

In fact, most Americans don't care if the President has a girlfriend or not.

1. 你不必太在乎他说的话，他还是个小孩儿。

Don't take what he said too hard; he's just a kid.

2. 她很在乎别人对她的看法，所以活得特别累。

She cares a lot about what people think of her, so she makes life hard for herself (lit. "so living is especially tiring for her").

(6) 对… 的要求: what one asks of …

◆我也不觉得美国人对诚实的要求特别高。

I don't think Americans set a very high standard for honesty.

1. 我对生活的要求很简单，只要有饭吃、有地方住就可以了。

What I ask of life is very simple. As long as I have food and lodging, that's enough.

2. 对别人不要有太高的要求，对自己却要严些。

Don't ask too much of others, but be more strict with yourself.

(7) 起作用/不起作用: have effect

◆政治斗争肯定是有的，但是新闻单位也起了大作用。

Political struggles definitely do exist, but the media has also played a large part (lit. "created great effect").

1. 据说这种药很有效，但我吃了两个星期，怎么还不起作用呢？

   This medicine is said to be very effective, but I've taken it for two weeks — why hasn't it taken effect?

2. 无论我跟他说什么都起不了作用，他还是坚持自己的看法。

   No matter what I say (to him), I cannot influence him (lit. "have no effect on him); he still insists on his own views.

(8) 恨不得: one wishes one could; be dying to

◆ 他们每天都恨不得找到政府贪污腐化的地方。

   Each day, they hope to find evidence of embezzlement and corruption by the government.

1. 我真受不了这么冷的天气！我恨不得夏天明天就到！

   I can't stand this cold weather! Man, I wish it could be summer tomorrow!

2. 天天上班的生活太忙碌了，我真恨不得还是个学生！

   It is so busy to work everyday. I really wish that I were still a student.

(9) 不至于: cannot or be unlikely to go so far as to

◆ 正因为他们监督得那么严，政府才不至于太腐化。

   It's precisely because they have kept such a close watch that the government does not become too corrupt.

1. 这么简单的中文课文，他不至于看不懂吧？

   This Chinese lesson is very simple. Can't he understand it? (His Chinese cannot be so bad that he can't understand it, can it?)

2. 虽然他不太诚实，但是不至于当着那么多人的面说谎吧？

   Even though he's not very honest, he wouldn't go so far as to lie in front of so many people, would he?

(10) 与其 A，不如 B: rather then A, it would be better B

◆ 与其选一个喜欢打仗的总统，不如选一个喜欢谈恋爱的总统。

   Instead of electing a president who likes to go to war, it would be better to choose one who likes to fall in love.

1. 与其跟一个自己不爱的人结婚，不如一个人生活更好。

   It would be better to live alone rather than marrying someone you don't love.

2. 付钱坐出租车划得来吗？你与其浪费钱，不如走走路、锻炼锻炼身体呢！。

   Is it worth it to pay for the taxi fare? Instead of wasting your money, you would be better off walking and getting some exercise!

练习

I. Choose the correct answer.

1. 总统不是一个 _____ 的人，所以他的人品怎么样当然是一件很重要的事。

    a. 普通   b. 普遍   c. 普及

2. _____ 美国人都认为总统有没有女朋友跟他是不是好总统没有关系。

    a. 最多   b. 大都   c. 大部分

3. 我很喜欢这个地方的环境和建筑，_____ 天气，我有点儿不习惯。

    a. 至于   b. 关于   c. 对于

4. 我觉得他的人品太差，不但有婚外关系，_____ 还说谎。

    a. 即使   b. 甚至   c. 连

5. 中国人主张"多子多福"是有一定道理的。因为中国没有_____ 的保险制度，人到了老年就得靠孩子生活。

    a. 完备   b. 完全   c. 全

6. 经济情况这么好，说明总统很 _____ 。

    a. 能力   b. 能干   c. 有能干

7. 我要租一辆车，只要能骑就行，我 _____ 好看不好看。

    a. 不在乎   b. 无所谓   c. 不要紧

II. Choose the most appropriate word for each blank and fill in with its Chinese equivalent.

make a big fuss over a trivial matter		
look down upon	be effective	be in love
value	announce	for the moment
be dying to	face to face	

1. 一方面我们 _____ 个人的隐私权，另一方面也要把政治领袖的

    丑闻 _____ 出来。

2. 听说儿子出了车祸，妈妈心里很着急，_____ 马上飞到北京去看

    他。

3. 难怪最近他那么高兴，脸上总是带着笑容，原来他在 _____ 。

4. 你只是得了一点儿感冒，就要你父母来看你，未免太 _____ 了。

5. 我真没想到你竟然 _____ 着大家的 _____ 说谎。

6. 中国的人口没有从前增长得那么快了，说明一家一个孩子的政策很 _____ 。

III. Answer the question using the words given:

1. 作者为什么说美国的报纸天天报导总统有了女朋友不但不让美国丢脸，反而值得骄傲？

        （说明，制裁，例外，即使，只有，公布，黑暗，腐化）

2. 新闻单位的作用是什么？你觉得美国的新闻单位在总统有了女朋友这件事情上做得对不对？

        （监督，腐化，不至于，侵害，管，关心，收视率，下不了台）

IV. Composition

1. 要是克林顿还竞选总统，你会不会投他的票？为什么？你对一个政治领导的要求是什么？

2. 你是一个新闻记者，最近报导了许多关于总统和他女朋友的丑闻，让总统下不了台，而受伤最深的可能是总统的家人。就新闻工作来说，你所做的完全是对的，可是你觉得对不起总统夫人，所以你打算写一封信给总统夫人。

    请尽量多用下面的新词：

报导	丢脸	骄傲	制裁
宣布	小题大做	过问	发生
至于	反而	重视	隐私
侵害	强调	在乎	监督
说谎	提高	不至于	强调
恨不得	与其 A 不如 B		

繁体字课文

甲：最近電視上、報紙上，天天都報導美國總統有女朋友的事儿。有
人覺得美國人真丟臉，怎麼選了一個人品這麼差的總統。

乙：我一點儿也不覺得丟臉，我覺得這是美國人最值得驕傲的地方。
這說明美國有非常完備的法律制度，任何人都受到法律的保
護，也受到法律的制裁，即使總統也不例外。我想全世界也許
只有美國能把這樣的醜聞宣布出來。我們覺得任何貪污腐化都
得公布出來，公布出來是制裁貪污腐化最有效的辦法。有些國
家的報紙和電視上看不到任何貪污腐化的新聞，那才是最黑暗
的。

甲：這個我同意。但是我覺得美國人有點儿小題大做。有沒有女朋友
是總統個人的事儿，這跟他是不是一個好總統沒有關係。要是
總統夫人不管這件事儿，沒有任何人可以管這件事儿。可是在美
國，好像什麼人都可以過問總統個人的事情。有一回我在電視
上看到一個記者，當著許多外國元首的面(1)問總統："你到底
跟那個女人發生過關係沒有？"我覺得這未免太讓總統下不了
臺了。美國人在這件事情上，好像最關心的是總統跟這個女人
睡過覺沒有，至於(2)他是不是一個能幹的總統反而(3)不是一個
話題。美國人不是最重視個人的隱私權嗎？這件事儿，在我看
來，總統的隱私權受到了很大的侵害。

乙：我們一方面強調(4)個人的隱私權，但另一方面更強調政治領袖
得誠實。其實大部分美國人也並不在乎(5)總統有沒有女朋友，

這是他個人的事儿，但是他說謊就不對了。我們不能要一個不誠實的總統。

甲：其實，哪個人不說謊啊？我也不覺得美國人對誠實的要求(6)特別高。我看，總統有女朋友的事儿還是政治鬥爭。

乙：政治鬥爭肯定是有的，但是新聞單位也起了大作用(7)。美國的新聞單位是監督政府最嚴密的組織，他們恨不得(8)每天都找到政府貪污腐化的地方，這樣報紙的銷路才會更好，電視收視率才會提高。但是也正因爲他們監督得那麼嚴，政府才不至於(9)太腐化。

甲：要是克林頓這一次還能競選總統，你會不會投他的票？

乙：我肯定會再投他的票！與其選一個喜歡打仗的總統，不如(10)選一個喜歡談戀愛的總統。

第十二课 保险套与社会道德

甲：真是太不像话了！这样的东西竟然放在街上卖！给小孩儿看见了

多不好啊！

乙：什么东西啊？

甲：就是你晚上用的那个玩意儿。

乙：晚上用的？你是说安眠药啊？

甲：不是！是你最讨厌的那个东西。

乙：你在说什么啊？

甲：就是…就是…，（一边儿说，一边儿用手比划）就是那个嘛！

乙：噢，你是说"套子"啊！在哪儿卖啊？

甲：就在隔壁杂货店门口儿。他们放了一个自动售货机，只要放一块

钱就自动出一个，比买香烟还方便！

乙：中国真是现代化了！连保险套都能在自动售货机上买到了。这

真是改革开放最好的证明(1)啊！

甲：用自动售货机卖保险套跟改革开放有什么关系啊？该开放的不

开放，不该开放的倒开放了(2)。

乙：用自动售货机卖保险套，表示大家在思想上已经开通了。在先

进国家早就这么做了(3)，这有什么好大惊小怪的呢(4)！

甲：这样随便卖保险套不是鼓励婚前和婚外的性关系吗？现在社会

保险套	保險套	bǎoxiǎntào	n.	condom
与	與	yǔ	conj.	and; 跟
道德		dàodé	n.	morality
不像话	不像話	búxiànghuà	adj.	outrageous; shocking; bad beyond description (there is no positive form except in rhetorical questions)
小孩儿		xiǎoháir	n.	kid
玩意儿		wányìr	n.	thing (used in a derogatory sense)
安眠药	安眠藥	ānmiányào	n.	sleeping pill
比划	比劃	bǐ.hua	v.	make hand gestures
套子		tào.zi	n.	cover; case; (here) condom
杂货店	雜貨店	záhuòdiàn	n.	grocery
自动	自動	zìdòng	adj.	automatic
售货机	售貨機	shòuhuòjī	n.	vending machine
香烟		xiāngyān	n.	cigarette
现代化	現代化	xiàndàihuà	v.	modernize
改革开放	改革開放	gǎigé kāifàng	n.	the economic reform and opening-up of China that began in 1979
证明	證明	zhèngmíng	n./v.	proof, prove
该	該	gāi	aux.	should; ought to; 应该
思想		sīxiǎng	n.	thought; thinking
开通	開通	kāitōng	adj.	open-minded; liberal
先进	先進	xiānjìn	adj.	advanced
大惊小怪	大驚小怪	dàjīng xiǎo guài	idm.	be surprised or alarmed at something perfectly normal or trivial; make a fuss about nothing
随便	隨便	suíbiàn	adv.	carelessly; willfully
鼓励	鼓勵	gǔlì	v.	encourage
婚前		hūnqián	n.	before getting married
婚外		hūnwài	adj.	out of marriage
性		xìng	n.	sex

已经够乱了，随时随地(5)都能买到保险套，男女关系不知道要乱到什么地步(6)呢！

乙：让大家比较容易买到保险套，不但可以方便避孕，还可以防止性病的传染，这当然是一大进步咯！你以为买不到保险套就能减少婚前和婚外的性关系了吗？我告诉你，在孔子那个时代，连保险套是什么都不知道，可是一样有婚前和婚外的男女关系。

甲：你在胡说什么啊！保险套跟孔子有什么关系？今天在自动售货机上可以买到保险套，明天说不定(7)就能买到春药，这样下去(8)，社会道德就越来越糟了。

乙：我觉得用不用保险套跟社会道德是没有关系的。一个买不到保险套的社会是比较不文明不进步的，而不是社会道德水平比较高；同样的，一个能方便地买到保险套的社会是比较开放比较进步的，并不是社会道德比较低。方便避孕、防止性病传染就是改善生活，给大家带来(9)幸福。我觉得不应该放在自动售货机上卖的东西不是保险套，而是香烟。

乱	亂	luàn	adj.	in a mess; disordered
随时随地	隨時隨地	suíshí suídì	adv.	at any time and any place
地步		dìbù	n.	extent; stage
方便		fāngbiàn	v.	make things convenient

避孕		bì//yùn	v.-o.	practice contraception 避：avoid 孕：pregnancy
防止		fángzhǐ	v.	prevent
性病		xìngbìng	n.	venereal disease
减少		jiǎnshǎo	v.	reduce; cut down
孔子		Kǒngzǐ	n.	Confucius
胡说	胡說	húshuō	v.	talk nonsense
说不定	說不定	shuō.budìng	adv.	perhaps; maybe
春药	春藥	chūnyào	n.	aphrodisiacs; drugs that induce sexual desire
文明		wénmíng	adj./n.	civilized, civilization
水平		shuǐpíng	n.	level; standard

词语例句

(1) 证明: proof; prove

◆ 这真是改革开放最好的证明啊！
This is the best evidence of China's reform and open-up policy!

1. 你得证明这件事不是你做的，我们才会相信你。
   You'll have to prove you didn't do it before we will believe you.

2. 他从来不说谎，证明他人品不差。
   He never lies. This proves that he has good character.

(2) 该 v. 的不 v., 不该 v. 倒 v.: those that are supposed to v. do not v., but those that are not supposed to v. do v.

◆ 该开放的不开放，不该开放的倒开放了。
What should be opened up is not opened up; instead it's what shouldn't be opened up that in fact is.

1. "吃饭"、"睡觉"这些简单的中文你说不好，骂人的话却说得那么熟。真是该学的不学，不该学的倒学得特别快！

You can't even say simple Chinese words like "*chifan*" and "*shuijiao*" well, but you're so fluent in curse words. You didn't learn what you should have learned, but what you shouldn't have learned, you sure learned fast!

2. 该学习的时候你在睡觉，不该学习的时候你却拿着书，你这个
人真怪！

You slept when it was time to study. When it wasn't time for studying, you would hold a book instead. You're such a weirdo!

(3) 早就 v. 了: has v.-ed a long time ago

◆ 在先进国家早就这么做了。

 It has been done a long time ago in developed countries.

1. 我早就知道了，你不必再说了。

 I knew this a long time ago. You don't need to say any more.

2. 这个问题早就解决了。

 This problem has been solved quite a while ago.

(4) 有什么好 v. 的呢？ : What is there to v. ?

◆ 这有什么好大惊小怪的呢?

What is all the fuss about? (There is nothing to fuss about.)

1. 这儿的风景这么普通，有什么好看的呢?

 The scenery here is really ordinary, what is there to see? (There is nothing worth seeing.)

2. 你已经决定了，我还有什么好说的呢?

 Since you have already decided, what else can I say? (There is nothing else that I can say.)

(5) 随时随地都……: at any time and at any place

◆ 随时随地都能买到保险套。

One can buy condoms at any time and at any place.

1. 互联网的好处就是让你随时随地都可以收到国外的信息。

 The advantage of the Internet is that it allows you to get news from other countries anytime and anywhere.

2. 人类随时随地都在污染环境。

 Man pollutes the environment all the time and everywhere.

(6) v./adj. 到···地步: v./adj. to the extent of ...

◆ 男女关系不知道要乱到什么地步呢!

I don't know how much more promiscuous (man-woman) relationships will get.

1. 这儿的垃圾已经多到没办法回收的地步。

   There is so much garbage here that we have no way to collect it.

2. 他抽烟抽到不抽就活不下去的地步。

   He smokes so heavily that if he didn't smoke, he couldn't go on living.

(7) 说不定: perhaps; maybe

◆ 今天在自动售货机上可以买到保险套，明天说不定就能买到春药。

If one can buy condoms in a vending machine today, it's possible that one could also find aphrodisiacs in it tomorrow!

1. A：已经九点了，美生还没回来，我真担心！

   B：有什么好担心的？说不定她去同学家玩儿了！

   A：It's already nine and Meisheng is still not back yet. I'm really worried.

   B：What's there to worry about? She's probably at her classmate's house having fun.

2. 你的话比总统的还有道理！你去竞选说不定有很多人投你的票呢！

   What you've said makes more sense than what the President said. If you ran (for the presidency), a lot of people might vote for you!

(8) 这样下去: go on like this

◆ 这样下去，社会道德就越来越糟了。

   If things go on like this, the social morals will be getting worse.

1. 你这么不用功，这样下去，怎么会进步呢？

   You are so lazy. If you go on like this, how will you make any progress?

2. 要是新闻单位没有权利监督政府，这样下去，政治肯定会越来越糟。

   If the media has no right to supervise the government and things go on like this, politics will certainly be getting worse.

(9) A 给 B 带来…: A brings …to B

◆ 方便避孕、防止性病传染就是改善生活，给大家带来幸福。

Making contraception convenient and preventing the spread of venereal diseases makes our lives better, and brings happiness to all.

1. 你戒烟吧！抽烟是不会给你带来任何好处的。

   Why don't you quit smoking? It's not going to do you any good.

2. 虽然一次性产品给我们带来了方便，但是也造成了更大的浪费。

Although disposable products bring convenience (to our lives), they also cause more waste.

练习

I. Read the model sentence; and complete the sentences or dialogues that follow based on the same patterns.

A: 他们<u>竟然</u>把保险套放在街上卖，<u>真是</u>太不像话<u>了</u>。

  1. 总统竟然……

  2. 这些记者为了提高收视率，竟然……

  3. 买一辆自行车竟然要……

  4. 一个记者竟然当着那么多人的面……

B: A: 现在的社会实在很乱。

  B: 现在的社会<u>乱到什么地步了呢？</u>

  A: 现在的社会已经<u>乱到没有枪不敢出门的地步了。</u>

  1. A: 这个人很坏。

    B: ……

    A: ……

  2. A: 那个城市的小偷很多。

    B: ……

    A: ……

  3. A: 他可真懒。

    B: ……

    A: ……

  4. A: 北京的空气污染太严重了。

    B: ……

    A: ……

C: <u>要是</u>用自动售货机来卖保险套，<u>就</u>随时随地都能买到保险套。

　　1. 要是我有手机，……

　　2. 要是没有电子邮件，……

　　3. 要是那些报纸的记者……，……

D: <u>今天</u>在自动售货机上买得到保险套，<u>明天也许就能买到春药。这样下去</u>，社会道德就越来越糟了。

　　1. 要是你的孩子今天打人而你不批评他，……

　　2. 今天总统有了女朋友而我们不把这件事公布出来，……

　　3. 要是今天一个人偷了小东西而不受到制裁，……

　　4. 要是今天你给一个乞丐五毛钱，这个乞丐明天也许就……

II. Choose the most appropriate word for each blank and fill in with its Chinese equivalent.

improvement　　outrageous　　open-minded; liberal
encourage　　automatic　　make hand gestures
be surprised or alarmed at something perfectly normal

1. 你实在不必 _____ ，这是一件很平常的事儿，一点儿也不稀奇。

2. 她的父母相当 _____ ，她无论嫁给外国人或老头儿他们都觉得无所谓。

3. 我说了好几遍他都没听懂，我只好用手 _____ ，他这才懂了。

4. 真 _____ ，他这一个星期都没来上课。

5. 自从改革开放以后，人们的生活条件有了很大的 _____ 。

III. Composition

1. 你认为用自动售货机卖保险套是不是鼓励婚前和婚外性关系？你对堕胎(duòtāi: abortion) 有什么看法？这两种做法是一个健康问题还是道德问题？

2. 你认为美国的社会道德是不是越来越糟了？你担心不担心这个问题？一个社会的道德受什么影响？谁又应该为社会道德的发展负责呢？

繁体字课文

甲：真是太不像話了！這樣的東西竟然放在街上賣！給小孩兒看見了
多不好啊！

乙：什麼東西啊？

甲：就是你晚上用的那個玩意兒。

乙：晚上用的？你是說安眠藥啊？

甲：不是！是你最討厭的那個東西。

乙：你在說什麼啊？

甲：就是…就是…，（一邊兒說，一邊兒用手比劃）就是那個嘛！

乙：噢，你是說"套子"啊！在哪兒賣啊？

甲：就在隔壁雜貨店門口兒。他們放了一個自動售貨機，只要放一塊
錢就自動出一個，比買香烟還方便！

乙：中國真是現代化了！連保險套都能在自動售貨機上買到了。這
真是改革開放最好的證明(1)啊！

甲：用自動售貨機賣保險套跟改革開放有什麼關係啊？該開放的不
開放，不該開放的倒開放了(2)。

乙：用自動售貨機賣保險套，表示大家在思想上已經開通了。在先
進國家早就這麼做了(3)，這有什麼好大驚小怪的呢(4)！

甲：這樣隨便賣保險套不是鼓勵婚前和婚外的性關係嗎？現在社會
已經夠亂了，隨時隨地(5)都能買到保險套，男女關係不知道要
亂到什麼地步(6)呢！

乙：讓大家比較容易買到保險套，不但可以方便避孕，還可以防止
性病的傳染，這當然是一大進步咯！你以爲買不到保險套就能

減少婚前和婚外的性關係了嗎？我告訴你，在孔子那個時代，連保險套是什麼都不知道，可是一樣有婚前和婚外的男女關係。

甲：你在胡說什麼啊！保險套跟孔子有什麼關係？今天在自動售貨機上可以買到保險套，明天說不定(7)就能買到春藥，這樣下去(8)，社會道德就越來越糟了。

乙：我覺得用不用保險套跟社會道德是沒有關係的。一個買不到保險套的社會是比較不文明不進步的，而不是社會道德水平比較高；同樣的，一個能方便地買到保險套的社會是比較開放比較進步的，並不是社會道德比較低。方便避孕、防止性病傳染就是改善生活，給大家帶來(9)幸福。我覺得不應該放在自動售貨機上賣的東西不是保險套，而是香烟。

第十三课 小学生做生意

下面是贵州一位市民写给《人民日报》的一封信，反映了目前中国中小学生的部分生活。

前些日子，家中的随身听不见了，问到读小学六年级的女儿，才知道她以(1)每天 0.5 元出租费租给了班上的同学。我很生气地问她为什么不借给同学听而(2)去收租金，她却振振有词地回答说："爸，班上同学都这样做。"

通过(3)女儿出租随身听的线索，我还惊奇地发现，不仅女儿在班上做生意，就连我妹妹的女儿（正读初一）也(4)是这样。两姐妹经常暗地发生生意往来。我还从女儿那里了解到，她们班上有的同

做生意		zuò shēng.yi	v.-o.	do business
贵州	貴州	Guìzhōu	n.	Guizhou Province
市民		shìmín	n.	city resident; townspeople
人民日报	人民日報	Rénmín Rìbào	n.	the People's Daily
反映		fǎnyìng	v.	reflect
中小学生	中小學生	zhōng xiǎo xuéshēng	n.	middle school and primary school students; short for 中学生 and 小学生
部分		bù.fen	adj.	part 部分原因/部分学生
前些日子		qián xiē rì.zi	n.	few days ago
随身听	隨身聽	suíshēntīng	n.	walkman

不见	不見	bújiàn	*v.*	disappear
读	讀	dú	*v.*	attend (school, class, etc.)
年级	年級	niánjí	*n.*	grade; year (in school, etc.)
女儿	女兒	nǚ.er	*n.*	daughter
以		yǐ	*prep.*	for; by
出租费	出租費	chūzūfèi	*n.*	rental fee
出租		chūzū	*v.*	rent out; let out
租给	租給	zūgěi	*v.*	rent sth. to sb.
生气	生氣	shēng//qì	*v.-o.*	get angry; be angry at 你生谁的气?
借给	借給	jiègěi	*v.*	lend to 他借给我两本书。
而		ér	*conj.*	but; however
收		shōu	*v.*	collect; gather
振振有词	振振有詞	zhènzhèn yǒucí	*idm.*	speak plausibly and volubly (in self-justification)
回答		huídá	*v.*	answer; reply
通过	通過	tōngguò	*prep.*	by means of; through
线索	線索	xiànsuǒ	*n.*	clue; hint
惊奇地	驚奇地	jīngqí.de	*adv.*	with surprise; surprisingly
发现	發現	fāxiàn	*v.*	find out; discover
不仅	不僅	bùjǐn	*conj.*	not only
妹妹		mèi.mei	*n.*	younger sister
初一		chūyī	*n.*	first year in junior high school
姐妹		jiěmèi	*n.*	older sister and younger sister; sisters
经常	經常	jīngcháng	*adv.*	frequently; often
暗地		àndì	*adv.*	secretly
发生	發生	fāshēng	*v.*	take place; occur
往来		wǎnglái	*n.*	intercourse; contact
了解		liǎojiě	*v.*	learn about; find out

学出租杂志、书籍、磁带，春节前夕还有人转卖明信片。

青少年上学期间(5)，是培养人生美德的关键时期。即使在现在的社会主义市场经济条件下，小学生做生意，我认为也还是太早了。这种"生意经"不仅会影响孩子的思想品德的培养，也会影响孩子的学习成绩。

《人民日报》1999 年 7 月 24 日

杂志	雜誌	zázhì	*n.*	magazine
书籍	書籍	shūjí	*n.*	books
磁带	磁帶	cídài	*n.*	cassette
春节	春節	Chūnjié	*n.*	Chinese New Year; Spring Festival
前夕		qiánxī	*n.*	eve
转卖	轉賣	zhuǎnmài	*v.*	resell
明信片		míngxìnpiàn	*n.*	postcard
青少年		qīngshàonián	*n.*	teenager
期间	期間	qījiān	*n.*	time; period
培养	培養	péiyǎng	*v.*	foster; develop; educate; cultivate
人生		rénshēng	*n.*	life
美德		měidé	*n.*	virtue; moral excellence
关键	關鍵	guānjiàn	*adj.*	crucial; key; very important
	時期	shíqī	*n.*	period (of time)
	社會主義	shèhuì zhǔyì	*n.*	socialism
	市場經濟	shìchǎng jīngjì	*n.*	market economy; market-oriented economy
	條件	tiáojiàn	*n.*	condition

生意经	生意經	shēngyijīng	*n.*	knack of doing business; shrewd business sense
品德		pǐndé	*n.*	moral character
成绩	成績	chéngjì	*n.*	results (of work or study); achievement; grade

词语例句

(1) 以: by; for

◆ 她以每天 0.5 元出租费租给了班上的同学。

She rented it to her classmates for 0.5 *yuan* a day.

   1. 这个城市的人口以每年一百万的速度快速增长。

     The population of this city is increasing rapidly by about a million people a year.

   2. 这幅画我可以以 2000 块钱卖给你。

     I can sell this painting to you for 2000 dollars.

(2) 而: but; however

◆ 我很生气地问她为什么不借给同学听而去收租金。

   I angrily asked her why she charged her classmates for the use of her walkman instead of lending it to them.

   1. 我和妹妹的性格完全不同，她喜欢和人交往，而我最怕跟别人说话。

     My sister and I have completely different characters; she likes to socialize with people, but what I fear most is talking to people.

   2. 为什么你自己不来见我，而让你妹妹来呢?

     Why did you let your sister meet me rather than meeting me yourself?

(3) 通过: through; by means of

◆通过女儿出租随身听的线索，我还惊奇地发现…

Through the clue that my daughter rented her walkman to her classmates, I discovered to my surprise that …

1. 通过我妹妹的介绍，我认识了她的老师。

  I got to know her teacher through my younger sister.

2. 由于不懂中文，他只能通过翻译跟中国人交谈。

  As he didn't know any Chinese, he had to speak through an interpreter.

(4) 不仅…，就连…也…: not only …, even…

◆ 不仅女儿在班上做生意，就连我妹妹的女儿也是这样。

My daughter was not the only one who collected rent money in class; even my niece did so as well.

1. 不仅学生不认识这个字，就连中文老师也不认识这个字。

  Not only do the students not know this character; even the Chinese teachers don't know it either.

2. 不仅中国人用筷子，就连外国人吃中国饭的时候也用筷子。

  Not only do Chinese use chopsticks; even foreigners use chopsticks too when eating Chinese food.

(5) （在）…期间: during the course of …; for the duration of …

◆青少年上学期间，是培养人生美德的关键时期。

The time adolescents spend in school is crucial to cultivating their virtue.

1. 上大学期间，是交朋友最好的时候。

  It is the best time to make friends when one is in college.

2. 在北京旅游期间，我印象最深刻的就是去参观故宫。

  When I was touring Beijing, what impressed me most was the visit to the Imperial Palace.

练习

I. Choose the correct answer.

1. 老师 _____ 了解到最近两个星期他都病得很严重。

    a. 从他的同屋   b. 向他的同屋那里   ⓒ 从他的同屋那里

2. 他发现钱包 _____ ，怀疑是被旁边的人偷了。

    a. 没见了   b. 不看见了   ⓒ 不见了

3. 只有 _____ ，他才会让我用他的电脑。

    a. 在他不用下   ⓑ 在他不用的情况下   c. 在他不用的情况上

4. 女儿问我："爸爸，今天晚上我能不能_____ 你的车？"

    a. 借给   ⓑ 借   c. 从你借

5. 即使这两个国家关系紧张，他们也还经常 _____ 生意往来。

    ⓐ 发生   b. 发现   c. 做出

II. Fill in the blank with the most appropriate word. Each word should be use only once.

    却，地，被，给，到，才，再

    今天早晨我发现家里的车撞坏了，问 __①到__ 女儿 __②才__ 知道她昨天晚上开车出去，不小心 __③被__ 后面的车 __④给__ 撞了。我生气 __⑤地__ 问她为什么不先问问我 __⑥再__ 把车开出去，她 __⑦却__ 回答说："那个时候你已经睡着了。"

III. Choose the most appropriate word for each blank and fill in with its Chinese equivalent.

    cultivate; foster   reflect   secretly
    moral excellence   affect   learn about; find out

1. 好的学习习惯是可以 __培养__ 的。

2. 真没想到他竟然 __暗地__ 把图书馆的书拿到自己的屋子去。

3. 我从报纸上 __了解__ 到中国农村的生活条件还很差。

4. 政治领导贪污腐化肯定会 __影响__ 到政府的成绩。

5. 诚实是一种 __美德__ ，诚实的人应该受到鼓励。

6. 他的话 __反映__ 了大部分学生对这件事的看法。

IV. Make sentences using the underlined expressions.

1. <u>我问</u>她为什么不借给同学听而去收租金，<u>她却振振有词地回答</u>说："爸，班上同学都这样。"

2. 昨天我<u>跟</u>朋友<u>借</u>了一本非常好看的书。

3. 读大学<u>期间</u>，<u>是</u>交朋友的关键时期。

4. <u>即使</u>在现在的社会主义市场经济条件下，小学生做生意<u>也</u>还是太早了。

5. <u>不仅</u>女儿在班上做生意，<u>就连</u>我妹妹的女儿<u>也</u>是这样。

6. 她<u>以</u>每天 0.5 元出租费把随身听租给了班上的同学。

7. 这种生意经<u>不仅</u>会影响孩子的思想品德，<u>也</u>会影响孩子的学习成绩。

8. 跟女儿谈过话<u>以后</u>，<u>我很惊奇地发现</u>，许多中小学生在班上做生意。

V. Answer the following questions.

1. 在你看来，小学生做生意的坏处是什么？

2. 做生意会不会影响人生美德的培养？

3. 美国小学生做不做生意？他们的父母担心不担心他们的思想品德受到不好的影响？

繁体字课文

　　下面是貴州一位市民寫給《人民日報》的一封信，反映了目前中國中小學生的部分生活。

　　前些日子，家中的隨身聽不見了，問到讀小學六年級的女兒，才知道她以(1)每天 0.5 元出租費租給了班上的同學。我很生氣地問她爲什麼不借給同學聽而(2)去收租金，她却振振有詞地回答說："爸，班上同學都這樣做。"

　　通過(3)女兒出租隨身聽的線索，我還驚奇地發現，不僅女兒在班上做生意，就連我妹妹的女兒（正讀初一）也(4)是這樣。兩姐妹經常暗地發生生意往來。我還從女兒那裏了解到，她們班上有的同學出租雜誌、書籍、磁帶，春節前夕還有人轉賣明信片。

　　青少年上學期間(5)，是培養人生美德的關鍵時期。即使在現在的社會主義市場經濟條件下(6)，小學生做生意，我認爲也還是太早了。這種"生意經"不僅會影響孩子的思想品德的培養，也會影響孩子的學習成績。

第十四课 寂寞的孩子

jì mò

东北 76 所学校对一万多名学生所做的一项心理测试显示，32%
的中小学生不同程度地(1)存在心理异常：讨厌上学、想离家出走等
等。分析表明，家庭环境是造成孩子心理障碍的主要原因。许多父
母以为，只要为孩子投入大量金钱和精力，孩子身体健康，学习成
绩好就行了，而忽视了不容易察觉的心理健康问题。家长需要提高
自身素质，学习一些关于(2)心理健康教育方面的知识。

孩子的身体状况也令人(3)忧虑。经济发达了，人民生活水平提

寂寞		jìmò	*adj.*	lonely; lonesome
东北	東北	Dōngběi	*n.*	Northeastern China
所		suǒ	*AN*	measure word for houses, institutions, etc.
万	萬	wàn	*n.*	ten thousand
名		míng	*AN*	measure word for people 两名学生/一名警察
项	項	xiàng	*AN*	measure word for items, clauses, etc.
心理		xīnlǐ	*n.*	psychology
测试	測試	cèshì	*n.*	test; testing; measurement
显示	顯示	xiǎnshì	*v.*	reveal; display; show
程度		chéngdù	*n.*	degree; extent
存在		cúnzài	*v.*	exist; be

异常	異常	yìcháng	*adj.*	abnormal; unusual
离家出走	離家出走	líjiā chūzǒu	*v.*	run away from home
等等		děngděng		and so on; etc
分析		fēnxī	*n./v.*	analysis, analyze
表明		biǎomíng	*v.*	demonstrate; make clear
家庭		jiātíng	*n.*	family; household
障碍	障礙	zhàng'ài	*n.*	obstacle; barrier; impediment
心理障碍	心理障礙	xīnlǐ zhàng'ài	*n.*	psychological disorder
原因		yuányīn	*n.*	reason; cause
投入		tóurù	*v.*	put into; invest in
金钱	金錢	jīnqián	*n.*	money
精力		jīnglì	*n.*	energy; vigor
健康		jiànkāng	*adj.*	healthy
忽视	忽視	hūshì	*v.*	overlook; neglect; ignorc
察觉	察覺	chájué	*v.*	be conscious of; bccomc awarc of; perceive
家长	家長	jiāzhǎng	*n.*	parents or guardian of a child
需要		xūyào	*n.*	need to
自身		zìshēn	*n.*	self; oneself
素质	素質	sùzhì	*n.*	quality
关于	關於	guānyú	*prep.*	about; concerning; regarding
教育		jiàoyù	*n.*	education
知识	知識	zhī.shi	*n.*	knowledge
状况	狀況	zhuàngkuàng	*n.*	condition; situation
令人…		lìngrén	*v.*	make people feel…
忧虑	憂慮	yōulǜ	*v.*	worry; be anxious; be concerned
经济	經濟	jīngjì	*n.*	economy
发达	發達	fādá	*adj.*	developed; advanced; prosperous
人民		rénmín	*n.*	people
水平		shuǐpíng	*n.*	level; standard

高了，青少年的营养状态反而下降了，肥胖型(4)儿童越来越多。这是因为学生学习负担过重，活动量小。另外(5)也与孩子偏食等不良习惯有关。

　　另一个不容(6)忽视的问题是孩子们对劳动的认识和态度。近年来，由于(7)升学压力，家长、教师似乎对孩子只有一个要求：学习好就行了，而忽视了对孩子劳动能力的培养。1997 年的一项调查显示，我国城市孩子平均每日劳动时间只有 0.2 小时，而美国是 1.2 小时，韩国是 0.7 小时，法国是 0.6 小时，英国是 0.6 小时。

　　近年来，进入结婚年龄的独生子女，结婚后双方不会料理家

营养	營養	yíngyǎng	*n.*	nutrition; sustenance
状态	狀態	zhuàngtài	*n.*	state; condition
下降		xiàjiàng	*v.*	descend; drop off; decrease
肥胖		féipàng	*adj.*	fat; corpulent; obese
——型		xíng	*suffix*	type; shape
				大型/小型/新型
儿童	兒童	értóng	*n.*	children
负担	負擔	fùdān	*n.*	burden; load
过——	過——	guò	*adv.*	excessively; over-
重		zhòng	*adj.*	heavy
活动量	活動量	huódòng liàng	*n.*	amount of physical activity
另外		lìngwài	*conj.*	in addition; moreover; besides

与	與	yǔ	*prep.*	with; to (used to introduce the target of the action) 与（人）打交道/与 sth. 比较/A 与 B 有关
偏食		piānshí	*v.*	be partial to a limited variety of food
不良		bùliáng	*adj.*	bad; harmful
不容——		bùróng	*v.*	not tolerate; not allow 这个做法不容怀疑。 知识产权不容侵害。
劳动	勞動	láodòng	*n.*	physical labor
认识	認識	rèn.shi	*n.*	understanding
态度	態度	tài.du	*n.*	attitude
近年来	近年來	jìnniánlái	*phr.*	in recent years
由于	由於	yóuyú	*prep.*	owing to; due to
升学	升學	shēng//xué	*v.-o.*	enter a higher school; advance to a higher school
压力	壓力	yālì	*n.*	pressure
教师	教師	jiàoshī	*n.*	teacher
似乎		sìhū	*adv.*	it seems that; it appears that; it appears as if
调查	調查	diàochá	*n./v.*	investigation; survey, investigate
城市		chéngshì	*n.*	city
韩国	韓國	Hán'guó	*n.*	Korea
法国	法國	Fǎguó	*n.*	France
英国	英國	Yīngguó	*n.*	England
进入	進入	jìnrù	*v.*	enter into; get into
年龄	年齡	niánlíng	*n.*	age
独生子女	獨生子女	dúshēng zǐnǚ	*n.*	the only child
双方	雙方	shuāngfāng	*n.*	both sides; the two parties
料理		liàolǐ	*v.*	attend to; take care of; manage
家务	家務	jiāwù	*n.*	household chores; housework

务，不愿干家务而引起(8)家庭生活不和睦，甚至离婚的事很多。事实说明，热爱劳动与儿童道德的发展有直接密切的关系。热爱劳动的孩子独立性强、责任心强，劳动还有助于(9)培养孩子勤劳俭朴的美德。劳动让他们懂得(10)珍惜劳动成果，知道父母的血汗钱来得不容易，而更加(11)孝敬父母。同时，劳动会给孩子一个健康的身体。

现在有些父母只想挤进中产阶级，只顾(12)努力地工作，努力地赚钱，而忽视了孩子的教育问题。在今天竞争日益(13)激烈的社会里，拼命挣钱没什么可指责的(14)，但别忘了，要尽可能(15)多挤出一点儿时间给孩子。今天花费几分钟时间，也许会有益于(16)孩子的一生。

《人民日报》1999 年 7 月 10 日

愿	願	yuàn	*aux.*	be willing to; 愿意
干	幹	gàn	*v.*	do
引起		yǐnqǐ	*v.*	give rise to; bring about
和睦		hémù	*adj.*	harmonious
事实	事實	shìshí	*n.*	fact
热爱	熱愛	rè'ài	*v.*	love fervently
直接		zhíjiē	*adj.*	direct; immediate
密切		mìqiè	*adj.*	close; intimate
独立性	獨立性	dúlìxìng	*n.*	ability to be independent
强		qiáng	*adj.*	strong
责任心	責任心	zérènxīn	*n.*	sense of responsibility
有助于	有助於	yǒuzhùyú	*v.*	contribute to; be conducive to
勤劳		qínláo	*adj.*	diligent; hardworking
俭朴	儉樸	jiǎnpǔ	*adj.*	thrifty and simple; economical 生活俭朴/穿着俭朴

品德		pǐndé	*n.*	(moral) character; morals
懂得		dǒng.de	*v.*	understand; know
珍惜		zhēnxī	*v.*	cherish; treasure; value
成果		chéngguǒ	*n.*	achievement; fruit; gain; positive result
血汗钱	血汗錢	xuèhànqián	*n.*	money earned by hard toil (lit. "blood and sweat money")
更加		gèngjiā	*adv.*	even more
孝敬		xiàojìng	*v.*	show filial piety and respect for one's parents
同时	同時	tóngshí	*conj.*	at the same time; in the mean time
挤进	擠進	jǐ//jìn	*v.-c.*	squeeze in; push one's way in; join eagerly
中产阶级	中産階級	zhōngchǎn jiējí	*n.*	middle class
只顾	只顧	zhǐgù	*adv.*	be preoccupied solely with
努力		nǔlì	*adv.*	make great efforts; try hard; exert oneself
赚钱	賺錢	zhuàn//qián	*v.-o.*	make money; gain money
日益——		rìyì	*adv.*	increasingly; day by day
激烈		jīliè	*adj.*	intense; fierce
拼命		pīnmìng	*adv.*	do something desperately; with all one's might 拼命工作/拼命努力
挣钱	掙錢	zhèng//qián	*v.-o.*	赚钱；make money
指责	指責	zhǐzé	*v.*	censure; criticize; find fault with
尽可能	盡可能	jǐn kěnéng	*adv.*	as far as possible; to the best of one's ability
挤出	擠出	jǐ//chū	*v.-c.*	squeeze
花费	花費	huāfèi	*v.*	spend
有益于	有益於	yǒuyìyú	*v.*	be good for; do good to; benefit
一生		yìshēng	*n.*	all one's life; throughout one's life

词语例句

(1) 不同程度地: to varying degrees

◆ 32%的中小学生不同程度地存在心理异常。

Thirty-two percent of elementary and middle school students have abnormal psychological problems of varying degrees.

1. 在北京住了一个夏天，所有学生的中文水平都不同程度地提高了。

All the students improved their Chinese to varying degrees after living in Beijing for a summer.

2. 环境、毒品等问题是全球性的，每个国家都不同程度地存在这类问题。

Environmental pollution and drugs are global issues that more or less exist in every country.

(2) 关于: about; on

◆ 家长需要提高自身素质，学习一些关于心理健康教育方面的知识。

Parents need to improve themselves by studying psychological health.

1. 每天《中国日报》都有关于新电影、新书、新饭馆儿的报导。

There are reports on new movies, books, and new restaurants in the *China Daily* every day.

2. 《中国日报》也有比较长的文章，多半是关于商业或者中国各地情况的报导。

There are also longer articles in the *China Daily,* and most of them are reports about business or about different regions of China.

(3) 令人 v./adj. : make somebody (feel) ...

◆ 孩子的身体状况也令人忧虑。

Children's health is also worrisome.

1. 那对夫妻之间有没有爱情真令人怀疑。

People are very skeptical whether there is love between that couple.

2. 这家饭馆的服务令人很不满意。

The service of this restaurant is really not satisfactory.

(4) —型: —type; —shaped

◆ 肥胖型儿童越来越多。

Obese children ("fat-shaped children") are becoming more and more numerous.

1. 他过生日的时候，朋友们送给他一个心型蛋糕。
   His friends gave him a heart-shaped cake for his birthday.
2. 在传统的社会里，"事业型"的妇女并不受欢迎。
   In traditional society, working women ("career-type") are not welcome.

(5) 另外: in addition; moreover; besides

◆ 肥胖型儿童越来越多。这是因为学生学习负担过重，活动量小。
   另外也与孩子偏食等不良习惯有关。
   Obese children are becoming more and more numerous. The reason is that
   students' work load is too heavy and their physical activities are too little.
   Besides, it also has something to do with bad habits of dietary preference.

1. 我想租一辆自行车。另外，我也得买几把椅子。
   I would like to rent a bicycle. In addition, I have to buy a few chairs.
2. 报纸、电视的主要责任是传递信息，另外也能起监督政府的作
   用。
   The major responsibility of newspaper and television is to transmit information;
   they also have the function of supervising the government.

(6) 不容 v. : not allow; admit of no …

◆ 另一个不容忽视的问题是孩子们对劳动的认识和态度。
   Another issue that shouldn't be ignored is the children's attitude toward and
   understanding of physical labor.

1. 这是中国的问题，不容外国干涉。
   This is a Chinese issue which tolerates no foreign interference.
2. 心理健康的重要性是不容怀疑的。
   The importance of mental health allows no doubt.

(7) 由于: due to; owing to

◆ 由于升学压力，家长、教师似乎对孩子只有一个要求：学习好就
   行了。
   Due to the pressure of entering a higher school, it seems that parents and teachers
   ask nothing from children but that they study well.

1. 由于他们两人之间没有爱情了，他们就离婚了。
   Because there is no love between them anymore, they got a divorce.
2. 由于偏食，这几个孩子的营养状态很差。
   Due to dietary preferences, these kids' nutrition is very poor.

155

(8) 引起: lead up to; give rise to

◆ 进入结婚年龄的独生子女，结婚后不愿干家务而引起家庭生活不和睦，甚至离婚的事很多。

It is common that "only-children," upon reaching the age of marriage, are not willing to do domestic work once they are married, making family life unharmonious and even leading to divorce.

1. 这个问题引起了学生热烈的讨论。

This issue evoked a heated discussion in class.

2. 他的样子非常紧张，引起了警察的怀疑。

His overly nervous look aroused the suspicion of the police.

(9) 有助于: help to; contribute to

◆ 劳动有助于培养孩子勤劳俭朴的美德。

Doing housework is good for nurturing moral character that values hard work, thrift, and simplicity.

1. 两国总统的互相访问有助于两国的互相了解。

The mutual visits of the two countries' presidents have contributed to a better understanding between the two countries.

2. 《中国日报》上有大量的广告，这有助于降低报纸的成本。

China Daily has plenty of advertisements, which helps to cut the costs of making the newspaper.

(10) 懂得: understand; know

◆ 劳动让他们懂得珍惜劳动成果。

Taking a laborious job will make them know how to cherish the product of their labor.

1. 被惯坏的独生子女根本不懂得怎么孝敬父母.

The only-child who is spoiled doesn't know how to respect his parents.

2. 他虽然年纪很小，可是却懂得照顾别人

He may be young, but he knows how to take care of others.

(11) 更加 adj. : even more adj.; more adj.

◆ 劳动让孩子知道父母的血汗钱来得不容易，而更加孝敬父母。

Taking a laborious job will make children know it is not easy for their parents to earn money, and they will therefore show more respect to their parents.

1. 听说不仅女儿出租随身听，连我妹妹的女儿也做生意，我更加

生气了。

When I heard that not only did my daughter rent her walkman, but my sister's daughter also did business, I got even angrier.

2. 上大学以后，他更加努力了。

 He worked even harder after he went to university.

(12) 只顾···，而···: be preoccupied solely with...

◆ 现在有些父母只想挤进中产阶级，只顾努力地工作，努力地赚钱，而忽视了孩子的教育问题。

There are some parents nowadays who try hard to squeeze into the middle class; they are so completely absorbed in working and making money that they neglect their children's education.

1. 这家工厂只顾赚钱，而忽视了工人的心理健康。

This factory cares only about making money and neglects their workers' mental health.

2. 你还是个学生，不能只顾谈恋爱而老不上课。

You are a student. You can't simply date someone and not go to class.

(13) 日益 v. /adj. : v./adj. day by day

◆在今天竞争日益激烈的社会里，拼命挣钱没什么可指责的。

In an increasingly competitive society, there is no reason to criticize earning money desperately.

1. 随着经济的发展，人民的生活日益改善。

With the development of the economy, people's living condition are improving increasingly.

2. 现代社会有心理问题的人数日益增加。

The number of people who have psychological problems is increasing with each passing day in modern society.

(14)没什么可 v. 的: there is nothing worth v.

◆在今天竞争日益激烈的社会里，拼命挣钱没什么可指责的。

1. 这个电影很无聊，没什么可看的。

This movie is too boring to watch.

2. 这是常见的事，有什么可大惊小怪的?

This is nothing special. What's there to be so surprised about?

(15) 尽可能: as far as possible

◆ 父母要尽可能多挤出一点儿时间给孩子。

Parents should try to squeeze in as much time with their children as possible.

1. 你做功课的时候，应该尽可能自己做。

You should do your homework by yourself as much as possible.

2. 我尽可能每天都运动。

I try as much as possible to work out every day.

(16) 有益于: to do good to; to benefit

◆ 父母多花一点儿时间跟孩子在一起，也许会有益于孩子的一生。

If the parents spent a little more time with their children, it might be beneficial throughout the children's life.

1. 社会的稳定有益于经济的发展。

The stability of society is good for the development of the economy.

2. 天天运动有益于健康。

Exercising daily is good for one's health.

练习

I. Choose the phrase that is closest in meaning to the underlined phrase in the sentence.

1. 孩子的身体状况也令人忧虑。

    a. 担心   b. 放心   c. 小心

2. 由于升学压力，老师和家长似乎对孩子只有一个要求：学习好就行了。

    a. 可能   b. 也许   c. 好像

3. 为了保护环境，人人都应该尽可能少用塑料产品。

    a. 绝对   b. 尽量   c. 肯定

4. 另一个不容忽视的问题是中国孩子对劳动的态度。

    a. 不容易   b. 不可能   c. 不应该

5. 每天报纸、电视上都有很多关于总统婚姻的新闻。

    a. 有关的   b. 有关   c. 有关系

6. 八十年代以来，高考的竞争日益激烈。

    a. 每天   b. 一天比一天   c. 天天

II. Complete the following sentences using the underlined expressions.

1. 家庭环境是<u>造成</u>孩子心理障碍<u>的主要原因</u>。

      这个司机喝酒以后开车是……。

      父母关系不和睦，常常吵架是……。

2. 一些父母只顾赚钱，<u>而忽视了</u>孩子的心理问题。

      小学生做生意的坏处是……。

      他们离婚的主要原因是……。

3. 劳动<u>有助于</u>培养孩子勤劳俭朴的美德。

      用自动售货机卖保险套……。

      多读中文报纸，多看中文电影，……。

4. 父母应该<u>尽可能</u>多挤出一些时间给孩子。

      资源少、人口多的国家得……。

      在中国住的时候最好……。

5. 肥胖型儿童越来越多，是因为孩子学习负担重，活动量小；<u>另外</u>也与孩子偏食有关。

      这次我来中国，学了中文，……。

      我反对你跟那个人结婚是因为……。

III. Make a sentence using the underlined expression.

1. 32%的学生<u>不同程度地</u>存在心理异常的情况。

2. 事实说明，热爱劳动<u>跟</u>儿童道德的发展<u>有直接密切的关系</u>。

3. 在今天竞争日益激烈的社会里，拼命赚钱<u>没有什么可指责的</u>。

4. 经济发达了，人民生活水平提高了，可是青少年的营养状态<u>反而</u>下降了。

IV. Answer the following questions.

1. 读了这篇报导以后，你同意不同意中国的孩子是"寂寞的孩子"？为什么？

2. 谈到父母和孩子在一起的时间，美国人常提到"quality"和"quantity"，请你说明这两个词儿的意思。

3. 美国父母怎么培养孩子的勤劳俭朴的美德？

繁体字课文

　　東北 76 所學校對一萬多名學生所做的一項心理測試顯示，32%的中小學生不同程度地(1)存在心理異常：討厭上學、想出走等等。分析表明，家庭環境是造成孩子心理障礙的主要原因。許多父母以爲，只要爲孩子投入大量金錢和精力，孩子身體健康，學習成績好就行了，而忽視了不容易察覺的心理健康問題。家長需要提高自身素質，學習一些關於(2)心理健康教育方面的知識。

　　孩子的身體狀況也令人(3)憂慮。經濟發達了，人民生活水平提高了，青少年的營養狀態反而下降了，肥胖型(4)兒童越來越多。這是因爲學生學習負擔過重，活動量小。另外(5)也與孩子偏食等不良習慣有關。

　　另一個不容(6)忽視的問題是孩子們對勞動的認識和態度。近年來，由於(7)升學壓力，家長、教師似乎對孩子只有一個要求：學習好就行了，而忽視了對孩子勞動能力的培養。1997 年的一項調查顯示，我國城市孩子平均每日勞動時間只有 0.2 小時，而美國是 1.2 小時，韓國是 0.7 小時，法國是 0.6 小時，英國是 0.6 小時。

　　近年來，進入結婚年齡的獨生子女，結婚後雙方不會料理家務，不願幹家務而引起(8)家庭生活不和睦，甚至離婚的事很多。事實說明，熱愛勞動與兒童道德的發展有直接密切的關係。熱愛勞動的孩子獨立性强、責任心强，勞動還有助於(9)培養孩子勤勞儉樸的美德。勞動讓他們懂得(10)珍惜勞動成果，知道父母的血汗錢來得不容易，而更加(11)孝敬父母。同時，勞動會給孩子一個健康的身體。

　　現在有些父母只想擠進中產階級，只顧⑿努力地工作，努力地賺錢，而忽視了孩子的教育問題。在今天競爭日益⒀激烈的社會裏，拼命掙錢沒什麼可指責的⒁，但別忘了，要盡可能⒂多擠出一點儿時間給孩子。今天花費幾分鐘時間，也許會有益於⒃孩子的一生。

第十五课 金钱是交往的通行证吗?

(一) 给钱才帮忙

学期刚结束, 杭州胜利小学校长见到记者, 谈到学生的道德教育工作时, 讲起学期结束前发生的一场大讨论。

事情非常简单。有个男学生有三道数学题不会做, 想请同学帮忙, 可是从第一排问到最后一排, 竟没有一个同学愿意教他。马上就要交作业了, 情急之下(1), 这位失望的男学生掏出五毛钱, 说: "谁教我, 我就给谁五毛钱(2)!" 金钱马上起了作用。一个女学生走过来, 难题很快解开了。那个女生理所当然(3)得到了五毛钱。拿到了报酬, 这位女学生得意地对同学说: "今后教同学都该这样收

交往		jiāowǎng	n./v.	association; relationship, have an association with
通行证	通行證	tōngxíng zhèng	n.	pass; permit
帮忙	幫忙	bāng//máng	v.-o.	help; do a favor 你能不能帮帮我的忙?
学期	學期	xuéqī	n.	semester
结束	結束	jiéshù	v.	end; conclude
杭州		Hángzhōu	n.	Hangzhou; capital city of Zhejiang Province
胜利	勝利	shènglì	n.	victory; success; (here) name of a school
校长	校長	xiàozhǎng	n.	(of a primary or secondary school) principal; head master,

				(of a college or university) president
谈到	談到	tándào	*v.-c.*	speak about or of; mention
讲起	講起	jiǎngqǐ	*v.-c.*	talk about
场	場	chǎng	*AN*	measure word for games, performance, etc.
讨论	討論	tǎolùn	*n./v.*	discussion, discuss
道		dào	*AN*	measure word for a question in a test or assignment
数学	數學	shùxué	*n.*	mathematics
题	題	tí	*n.*	question in a test or assignment
排		pái	*n.*	row
竟		jìng	*adv.*	unexpectedly; 竟然
愿意	願意	yuàn.yì	*aux.*	be willing to; be ready to
马上	馬上	mǎshàng	*adv.*	at once; right away
交		jiāo	*v.*	hand over; hand in
作业	作業	zuòyè	*n.*	school assignment; homework
情急之下		qíngjí zhī xià	*phr.*	in a moment of desperation
失望		shīwàng	*adj.*	disappointed
掏出		tāo//chū	*v.-c.*	take out; fish out; draw out
毛		máo		*mao*, ten cents
女生		nǚshēng	*n.*	girl student; school girl
难题	難題	nántí	*n.*	difficult question
解开	解開	jiě//kāi	*v.-c.*	solve (a mathematical problem, etc.)
理所当然	理所當然	lǐ suǒ dāng rán	*idm.*	deservedly; as a matter of fact; be natural and right
报酬	報酬	bàochóu	*n.*	reward; pay
得意		déyì	*adj.*	proud of oneself; pleased with oneself
今后	今後	jīnhòu	*n.*	from now on
收钱	收錢	shōu//qián	*v.-o.*	charge; collect fees

钱。"这件事很快就传到了班主任的耳朵里(4)。"起先(5)我很生气,"她说:"没想到这个表现不错的学生竟这么自私。但事后一想,这件事不能简单地以对或错来(6)判断。"她找这两位学生谈话。第二天,那位女学生勉强(7)把钱还给了那个男学生。

事情到此似乎也就结束了,然而(8)……

(二) 该不该收钱?

几天以后,班主任在家长会上讲了这件事,希望家长配合学校,注意学生道德上的培养。出人意料(9)的是家长的反应竟截然不同:有对孩子行为表示赞成,称赞孩子聪明,长大了不会吃亏的(10);有担心孩子小小年纪就学会金钱交易,长大了会唯利是图的。有家长说:孩子的心灵洁白如纸,过早的金钱意识会污染他们的天真;也有家长认为钱该收,社会美德也该发扬,不必对这件事大惊小怪。

传到	傳到	chuándào	v.-c.	spread to
班主任		bān zhǔrèn	n.	head teacher of a class
耳朵		ěr.duo	n.	ear
起先		qǐxiān	adv.	at first; in the beginning
表现	表現	biǎoxiàn	n.	performance
自私		zìsī	adj.	selfish
事后	事後	shìhòu	phr.	after the event; afterwards
判断	判斷	pànduàn	v.	judge
勉强		miǎnqiǎng	adv.	reluctantly; unwillingly

还	還	huán	v.	return; give back
此		cǐ	n.	this; this moment
然而		rán'ér	conj.	however
家长会	家長會	jiāzhǎnghuì	n.	parents' meeting
配合		pèihé	v.	work with; cooperate
注意		zhùyì	v.	pay attention to; keep an eye on; take notice of
出人意料		chū rén yìliào	phr.	come as a surprise; contrary to one's expectation; beyond all expectations
反应	反應	fǎnyìng	n.	response
截然不同		jiérán bùtóng	adj.	completely different
行为	行爲	xíngwéi	n.	behavior
赞成	贊成	zànchéng	v.	approve of; be in favor of
称赞	稱贊	chēngzàn	v.	praise; acclaim
聪明	聰明	cōng.míng	adj.	smart
长大	長大	zhǎngdà	v.-c.	grow up
吃亏	吃虧	chī//kuī	v.-o.	suffer losses; be in an unfavorable situation
小小年纪	小小年紀	xiǎoxiǎo niánjì	phr.	at a very young age
交易		jiāoyì	n.	trade; deals; business
唯利是图	唯利是圖	wéi lì shì tú	idm.	be intent on nothing but money; seek only profit
心灵	心靈	xīnlíng	n.	heart; soul; spirit
洁白	潔白	jiébái	adj.	spotlessly white
如		rú	v.	like; as; as if
意识	意識	yì.shí	n.	sense; awareness
天真		tiānzhēn	adj.	innocent
发扬	發揚	fāyáng	v.	develop; promote; carry forward; carry on (the object is always an abstract noun)

一位家长说:"老师搞家教可以收钱,学生为什么就不可以? 让学生从小学会通过劳动获得报酬,这对他们今后走入社会很有好处。"也有家长认为:五毛钱风波实际上是社会现象的反映。某些单位或机关给钱就办事,不给钱就不办事。这种现象很容易使孩子接受金钱万能的观念。总之(11),孩子的行为是社会思想的反映(12),不能怪孩子。

会议结束了以后,班主任组织同学展开讨论。谁知道(13)讨论变成了辩论,同学们有两种截然相反的意见。一方认为: 这个世界有比金钱更宝贵的东西。英雄救人的时候,如果想到钱,还肯去救吗? 要是同学之间互相帮助都要付钱,那么这个世界除了金钱还有什么? 互相帮助是一种美德,不能让金钱取代! 另一方则(14)认为:帮助别人就应该得到报酬。街上、电视上的寻物启事不都说"当面重谢"吗? 没有重谢,又有多少失物能找回呢? 这五毛钱该收! 钱是生活中的通行证!

搞		gǎo	v.	do; be engaged in 他这几年一直在搞科学研究工作。/这个词儿的意思我还没搞清楚。
家教		jiājiào	n.	private tutoring
获得	獲得	huòdé	v.	obtain; gain
有好处	有好處	yǒu hǎochù	v.	be good for; be of benefit

风波	風波	fēngbō	*n.*	disturbance (lit. "wind and wave")
实际上	實際上	shíjìshàng	*adv.*	in fact; in reality
某		mǒu	*pron.*	certain; some
机关	機關	jīguān	*n.*	government work unit
金钱万能	金錢萬能	jīnqián wànnéng	*phr.*	money is omnipotent
观念	觀念	guānniàn	*n.*	sense; idea; concept
总之	總之	zǒngzhī	*conj.*	in a word; in short
怪		guài	*v.*	blame
会议	會議	huìyì	*n.*	meeting; conference
组织	組織	zǔzhī	*v.*	organize; arrange
展开	展開	zhǎnkāi	*v.*	launch; carry out
变成	變成	biànchéng	*v.*	become; turn into
辩论	辯論	biànlùn	*n./v.*	debate; argument, debate
相反		xiāngfǎn	*adj.*	opposite; contrary 他的意见跟我的相反。
意见		yìjiàn	*n.*	idca; vicw; opinion
一方		yìfāng	*n.*	one side; one party 另一方: the other side
宝贵	寶貴	bǎoguì	*adj.*	valuable; precious
英雄		yīngxióng	*n.*	hero
救人		jiù//rén	*v.-o.*	save life
肯		kěn	*aux.*	be willing to
互相		hùxiāng	*adv.*	mutually; each other; one another
取代		qǔdài	*v.*	replace; substitute
则	則	zé	*conj.*	(written language) however
寻物启事	尋物啓事	xúnwù qǐshì	*n.*	lost and found notice
当面	當面	dāng//miàn	*adv.*	to somebody's face; in somebody's presence
重谢	重謝	zhòngxiè	*v.*	present a grand reward
失物		shīwù	*n.*	lost items

　　这场风波的主角怎么看这件事呢?那位男生说:"我没出钱时,同学都爱理不理;我一出钱,就有同学来帮助了,这不是说明钱很有用吗?今后我还是会这样做的。"而那位女学生却不明白自己错在哪里。她说:"老师教学生是老师的义务,学生却没有义务教同学。现在办什么事都要钱,我既然付出劳动,就⒂应该得到钱。我没有错!"

《光明日报》1998 年 7 月 16 日

主角		zhǔjué	n.	main character; leading role
出钱	出錢	chū//qián	v.-o.	put forth money; offer money
爱理不理	愛理不理	àilǐ bùlǐ	phr.	look cold and indifferent
明白		míng.bai	v.	understand; catch on
义务	義務	yìwù	n.	duty; obligation
付出		fù//chū	v.-c.	pay 付出劳动/付出代价

词语例句

(1) 情急之下: in a moment of desperation

◆ 情急之下，这位失望的男学生掏出五毛钱，说："谁教我，我就给谁五毛钱！"。

In a moment of desperation, the disappointed boy pulled out five *mao,* and said, "Whoever will teach me, I'll pay him five *mao.*"

　1. 他在饭馆儿吃完饭以后，却找不到钱包。情急之下，他只好给朋友打电话借钱。

　　He couldn't find his wallet after having eaten in a restaurant; therefore, in a moment of desperation, he called his friend to borrow some money.

　2. 他要吃鸡肉，可是服务员听不懂他的话。情急之下，他在纸上画了一只鸡。

　　He wanted to eat chicken, but the waiter couldn't understand what he said; therefore, in a moment of desperation, he drew a chicken on a piece of paper.

(2) …question word…, … question word …: whoever; whatever; whenever

◆ 谁教我，我就给谁五毛钱。

　Whoever will teach me, I will pay him five *mao.*

　1. 谁对我好，我就对谁好。

　　I will be nice to whoever is nice to me.

　2. 你什么时候方便，就什么时候来。

　　Come whenever is convenient for you.

(3) 理所当然: as a matter of fact; be natural and right

◆那个女生理所当然得到了五毛钱。

　Of course that girl student got the five *mao.*

　1. 帮助自己的朋友是理所当然的。

　　It is only right and natural to help one's friend.

　2. 父母都希望孩子成功，理所当然非常关心他们的学习成绩。

　　All parents hope for the success of their children; it's only natural that they are concerned about their children's study achievements.

(4) 传到…的耳朵里: to be heard by …

◆这件事很快就传到了班主任的耳朵里。

　This matter was heard by the class teacher immediately.

1. 他竟然交了一个女朋友，这件事要是传到他太太的耳朵里，她非跟他离婚不可。

   He has gone so far as to have a girlfriend. If his wife were to hear of this, she would definitely divorce him.

2. 他把随身听租给同学，这件事传到他父母的耳朵里，他们非常生气。

   He rented his walkman to his classmates. His parent got very angry after they heard of this.

(5) 起先…，但事后一想…: At first …, but when thinking back afterwards…

◆ 起先我很生气，但事后一想，这件事不能简单地以对或错来判断。

At first I was very angry, but when I thought back after the event, I found that this matter could not simply be judged by right and wrong.

1. 起先我觉得她太没有同情心，但事后一想，她的做法也不是没有道理。

   At first I felt that she was indifferent, but when I thought back afterwards, her way of doing it was not altogether without reason.

2. 起先我反对让孩子做家务，但事后一想，培养孩子的劳动习惯的确对他们有好处。

   At first I was opposed to asking the children to do household jobs, but later on I found that it was indeed beneficial to them to cultivate their habit of doing manual labor.

(6) 以…来 v. : use … to …

◆ 这件事不能简单地以对或错来判断。

1. 你一般以什么标准来判断一个电影好不好？

   What standard do you normally use to judge whether a movie is good or not?

2. 不能以一次考试来决定学生的成绩。

   You can't decide students' grade just by one quiz.

(7) 勉强: reluctantly

◆ 那位女学生勉强把钱还给了那个男学生。

The girl student reluctantly returned the money to the boy student.

1. 他勉强同意了。

   He agreed reluctantly.

2. 他接受了我们的建议，但是很勉强。

   He accepted our suggestion, but rather grudgingly.

(8) 然而: however; nevertheless; but

◆ 事情到此似乎也就结束了，然而……

It seemed that this matter had come to an end at this point; however …

1. 他请同学帮忙，然而没有一个人愿意教他。

He asked for help from his classmates; however, no one was willing to teach him.

2. 孩子的心理健康非常重要，然而许多父母却忽视了这个比较不容易察觉的问题。

Children's mental health is very important. However, many parents neglect this issue because it is not so easy to discover.

(9) 出人意料: to one's surprise

◆ 出人意料的是家长的反应竟截然不同。

To his surprise, the parents are completely split (on this issue.) (lit. "the reaction of the parents are completely split.")

1. 他的回答出人意料。

His answer surprised people.

2. 很多人觉得他们会很快离婚。出人意料的是：三年以后，他们还很幸福地生活在一起。

Many people thought their marriage wouldn't last long. However, to much surprise, they are still living happily together three years later.

(10) 有…的，有…的: some …, some …

◆ 有对孩子行为表示赞成的；有担心孩子小小年纪就学会金钱交易，长大了会唯利是图的；有认为不必大惊小怪的。

Some parents expressed approval of the children's behaviors; some worried that if children from a very young age learn about money, they will care about nothing but making money when they grow up; some say there is no need to fuss about little things.

1. 毕业以前，学生们都很忙。有忙着找工作的，有忙着写论文的，有忙着申请研究所的。

Before graduation, all students are very busy. Some are busy with finding work; some are busy with writing their theses; some are busy with applying for graduate school.

2. 在夜市里有各种各样的小摊儿。有卖小吃的，有卖服装的，有卖日用品的。

At the night market there are all kinds of vendor's stands. Some sell snacks;

some sell clothes; some sell everyday items.

(11) 总之: in a word; in short

◆ ……。总之,孩子的行为是社会思想的反映,不能怪孩子。

In a word, it is not the children's fault since their behaviors reflect the values of society.

1. 那个地方没有自来水,也没有电。总之,非常落后。

That place has neither tap water nor electricity. In short, it is very backward there.

2. 学生家长、老师、民间组织,总之,很多人都反对广告进入校园。

Parents, teachers, non-governmental organizations, in short, a lot of people opposed advertisements entering schools.

(12) A 是 B 的反映: A is the reflection of B

◆ 孩子的行为是社会思想的反映。

1. 有时候,孩子的道德水平就是家长道德水平的反映。

Sometimes children's moral levels can be a reflection of their parents' moral levels.

2. 在一定程度上,一个人的行为就是他所受的教育的反映。

To certain degree, a person's behavior is a reflection of his education.

(13) 谁知道⋯: who knows that…; no one expects that …

(a rhetorical sentence used to indicate something happens unexpectedly.)

◆ 谁知道讨论变成了辩论。

Unexpectedly, the discussion became a debate.

1. 我想组织大家去参观工厂,谁知道没有一个人有兴趣。

I planed to arrange a visit to the factory for all; to my surprise, nobody was interested.

2. 我以为他是个天真的孩子,谁知道他竟唯利是图。

I thought he was an innocent child. To my surprise, he cares about nothing but money.

(14) 则: (a conjunction used in second sentence or clause meaning "however.")

◆ 一方认为: 这个世界有比金钱更宝贵的东西。另一方则认为: 帮助别人就应该得到报酬。

One side thinks that there are things more precious than money in the world. However, the other side thinks that one should be rewarded when helping others.

1. "老夫少妻"越来越多，"老妻少夫"则不太常见。

   There are more and more "old husband young wife" marriages; however, "old wife young husband" marriages are still rare.

2. 老师多半认为考试是了解学生进步的好办法，而学生则多半讨厌考试。

   Most teachers think that it is effective to understand students' progress by testing; however, most students dislike tests.

(15) 既然…，就…: since …, then …

◆ 我既然付出劳动，就应该得到报酬。

Now that I worked for someone, I should get a reward.

1. 既然你没有空，我就自己去了。

   As you are busy, I will go without you.

2. 既然你已经决定了，我就不再说了。

   Now that you have already decided; I won't say anything anymore.

练习

I. Choose the correct answer.

1. 我再也不去那家商店了。那儿的服务员认为我是个穷学生，就对我 _____ 。

   a. 唯利是图　　b. 爱理不理　　c. 大惊小怪

2. 在这次讨论中，男生的看法 _____ 。

   a. 相反女生的看法　　b. 反对女生的看法

   c. 跟女生的看法相反

3. 结婚以前，两个人一定得 _____ 。

   a. 了解互相　　b. 知道互相　　c. 互相了解

4. 为了事业成功，他拼命工作，结果身体出了问题，得了很严重的病。他 _____ 的代价未免太高了。

a. 付出　b. 付钱　c. 付给

5. 儿童的心灵洁白如纸，很容易受到不良文化的影响。 _____ , 加强儿童的思想道德教育非常重要。

a. 所以　b. 总之　c. 而

6. 在火灾中，他不顾危险，救了邻居的孩子，受到了大家的_____。

a. 赞成　 b. 称赞　c. 同意

II. Choose the most appropriate word for each blank and fill in with its Chinese equivalent.

pride oneself on sth.　　　　beyond all expectations
make a fuss about nothing　　replace
to someone's face　　　　　　reluctantly

1. 要是你对他有意见，应该 _____ 跟他说。

2. 父母关心孩子是理所当然的，你不必 _____ 。

3. 北京的四合院被现代化的高楼 _____ 了，这是不可避免的现象。

4. 大家都以为这个电影里的男主角是英雄， _____ 的是他才是真正的坏人。

5. 他请我帮忙，虽然我自己忙得很，我还是 _____ 同意了。

6. 听到别人称赞他的儿子聪明，他心里很_____，可还是客气地说："哪里哪里！"

III.. Complete the following dialogues with patterns given.

1. A: 什么样的人是你的朋友?

B: _____。（谁…，谁…）

2. A: 我的同屋又懒又笨，我真讨厌他。

B: _____。（传到…的耳朵里，非…不可）

3. A: 美国人是不是都赞成把非法移民送回国呢?

B: _____（截然；有…的，有…的，有…的）

4. A: 那个老师那么年轻，一定教得不好。

B: _____。（以…来判断）

5. A: 我认为学外语对今后走入社会很有好处。

B: _____。（既然…就…）

IV. Complete the following sentences.

1. 房子失火了，情急之下，他 _____。

2. 因为我父母坚持，我只好勉强 _____。

3. 我起先认为他们都会同意，出人意料的是 _____。

4. 床太软，窗户太小，灯不够亮；总之，_____。

5. 我到了卖票的窗口，谁知道 _____。

6. 赞成这个行为的家长认为这样的孩子很聪明，反对的家长则认为
_____。

V. Rewrite the following sentences into a rhetorical sentence using the word given.

1. 英雄救人的时候，要是想到钱，就不会去救了。(还肯)

2. 你有偏食的不良习惯，身体当然不好。（还会）

3. 你把他的丑闻公布出来，他当然不高兴。（还会）

4. 要是没有重谢，没有多少失物能找回。（有多少…呢？）

5. 一个人最要紧的就是品德，至于有没有钱，没有什么关系。
（又有…呢？）

6. 要是连你都不帮我的忙，没有人会帮我的忙。（又有谁…呢？）

7. 我一出钱，就有人来帮助了。这说明钱很有用。（不是…吗？）

8. 现在的社会是一个金钱万能的社会。（不是…吗？）

VI. Composition

1. 你的随身听不见了，你要写一个寻物启事。这个寻物启事要包括：是在哪儿不见的，是什么样子的，是什么牌子的，为什么它对你很重要，报酬等等。

2. 现代社会是不是一个金钱万能的社会？

繁体字课文

（一）給錢才幫忙

學期剛結束，杭州勝利小學校長見到記者，談到學生的道德教育工作時，講起學期結束前發生的一場大討論。

事情非常簡單。有個男學生有三道數學題不會做，想請同學幫忙，可是從第一排問到最後一排，竟沒有一個同學願意教他。馬上就要交作業了，情急之下(1)，這位失望的男學生掏出五毛錢，說：“誰教我，我就給誰五毛錢(2)！”金錢馬上起了作用。一個女學生走過來，難題很快解開了。那個女生理所當然(3)得到了五毛錢。拿到了報酬，這位女學生得意地對同學說：“今後教同學都該這樣收錢。”這件事很快就傳到了班主任的耳朵裏(4)。“起先(5)我很生氣，”她說：“沒想到這個表現不錯的學生竟這麼自私。但事後一想，這件事不能簡單地以對或錯來(6)判斷。”她找這兩位學生談話。第二天，那位女學生勉强(7)把錢還給了那個男學生。

事情到此似乎也就結束了，然而(8)……

（二）該不該收錢？

幾天以後，班主任在家長會上講了這件事，希望家長配合學校，注意學生道德上的培養。出人意料(9)的是家長的反應竟截然不同：有對孩子行爲表示贊成，稱贊孩子聰明，長大了不會吃虧的(10)；有擔心孩子小小年紀就學會金錢交易，長大了會唯利是圖的。有家長說：孩子的心靈潔白如紙，過早的金錢意識會污染他們的天真；也有家長認爲錢該收，社會美德也該發揚，不必對這件事大驚小怪。

一位家長說:"老師搞家教可以收錢,學生爲什麼就不可以?讓學生從小學會通過勞動獲得報酬,這對他們今後走入社會很有好處。"也有家長認爲:五毛錢風波實際上是社會現象的反映。某些單位或機關給錢就辦事,不給錢就不辦事。這種現象很容易使孩子接受金錢萬能的觀念。總之(11),孩子的行爲是社會思想的反映(12),不能怪孩子。

會議結束了以後,班主任組織同學展開討論。誰知道(13)討論變成了辯論,同學們有兩種截然相反的意見。一方認爲:這個世界有比金錢更寶貴的東西。英雄救人的時候,如果想到錢,還肯去救嗎?要是同學之間互相幫助都要付錢,那麼這個世界除了金錢還有什麼?互相幫助是一種美德,不能讓金錢取代!另一方則(14)認爲:幫助別人就應該得到報酬。街上、電視上的尋物啓事不都說"當面重謝"嗎?沒有重謝,又有多少失物能找回呢?這五毛錢該收!錢是生活中的通行證!

這場風波的主角怎麼看這件事呢?那位男生說:"我沒出錢時,同學都愛理不理;我一出錢,就有同學來幫助了,這不是說明錢很有用嗎?今後我還是會這樣做的。"而那位女學生却不明白自己錯在哪裏。她說:"老師教學生是老師的義務,學生却沒有義務教同學。現在辦什麼事都要錢,我既然付出勞動,就(15)應該得到錢。我沒有錯!"

第十六课　浙江好学生杀母事件引起社会各界反思

　　一名十七岁中学生因无法(1)忍受学习的沉重压力而杀死亲生母亲，这个悲剧在浙江省引起社会各界对教育问题的深刻反思。

　　今年十七岁的徐力是浙江省金华市第四中学高二学生。他出生在一个普通的工人家庭。母亲吴凤仙是金华食品公司职工。由于父亲长期在外地火车站工作，徐力从小到大基本上(2)是在母亲的照顾下长大的。母亲吴凤仙工资不高，就帮别人织毛衣赚点儿钱供儿子读书。初中升高中时，徐力考进学校的重点班，但高一上半学期排名(3)全

浙江		Zhèjiāng	*n.*	Zhejiang Province, in southeast China
杀	殺	shā	*v.*	kill
事件		shìjiàn	*n.*	incident; event
各界		gèjiè	*n.*	all circles; all walks of life
反思		fǎnsī	*v.*	introspection; self-examination
无法	無法	wúfǎ	*adv.*	unable; incapable 无法了解/无法证明/无法判断
忍受		rěnshòu	*v.*	endure; bear
沉重		chénzhòng	*adj.*	heavy; weighty
亲生	親生	qīnshēng	*adj.*	one's own (children; parents)
悲剧	悲劇	bēijù	*n.*	tragedy
省	省	shěng	*n.*	province
深刻		shēnkè	*adj.*	profound; deep
徐力		Xú Lì	*n.*	personal name
金华市	金華市	Jīnhuáshì	*n.*	Jinhua City, Zhejiang Province

高二		gāo'èr	*n.*	second year in high school
出生		chūshēng	*v.*	be born
普通		pǔtōng	*adj.*	ordinary; common
工人		gōngrén	*v.*	labor worker
吴凤仙	吳鳳仙	Wú Fèngxiān	*n.*	personal name
食品		shípǐn	*n.*	food
职工	職工	zhígōng	*n.*	workers and staff members
长期	長期	chángqī	*n.*	long-term; over a long period of time
外地		wàidì	*n.*	place other than where one is; other places
火车站	火車站	huǒchēzhàn	*n.*	train station
从小到大	從小到大	cóng xiǎo dào dà	*phr.*	since one's childhood
基本上		jīběnshàng	*adv.*	basically; on the whole
照顾	照顧	zhào.gù	*v./n.*	look after; care for
长大	長大	zhǎngdà	*v.*	grow; grow up
织	織	zhī	*v.*	knit
毛衣		máoyī	*n.*	sweater
供		gōng	*v.*	support (financially); supply
儿子	兒子	ér.zi	*n.*	son
读书	讀書	dú//shū	*v.-o.*	attend school, read; study
初中		chūzhōng	*n.*	junior high school
升		shēng	*v.*	go up to a higher level in school
高中		gāozhōng	*n.*	senior high school
考进	考進	kǎo//jìn	*v.-c.*	enter a school by passing the entrance examination
重点班	重點班	zhòngdiǎn bān	*n.*	honors class; advanced class; tracked class for bright students
上半——		shàngbàn	*prefix*	first half (of a game, concert, period, etc.): 上半年/上半场比赛
排名		páimíng	*v.*	rank as; be ranked as

班倒数第二名。通过努力，高一下半学期，徐力进步到了第十名。吴凤仙喜出望外，要儿子以后每次期中、期末考试都排在全班前十名。然而，悲剧也就在这个时候埋下了种子。

去年十月底，吴凤仙参加家长会得知，徐力这学期期中考试的成绩排在全班第十八名。吴凤仙很生气，回家后狠狠(4)打了儿子一顿。徐力喜欢踢足球，吴凤仙就说："以后你再去踢足球，我就(5)把你的腿打断。"重压之下的徐力感到母亲对自己管得太严，而且为无法实现母亲提出的目标而深深感到委屈和压抑。

今年一月十七日，徐力从学校回家，吃完中饭后，想去看会儿电视，吴凤仙却提醒儿子期末考得考前十名。徐力说："很难考，不可能。"母子之间再次(6)为学习发生冲突。绝望中(7)，徐力从门口儿

倒数	倒數	dàoshǔ	v.	count from the end; count backwards
下半——		xiàbàn	prefix	second half (of a game, concert, period, etc.) 下半年/下半个月
喜出望外		xǐ chū wàng wài	idm.	be overjoyed (at an unexpected gain or good news）
期中		qīzhōng	n.	midterm
期末		qīmò	n.	end of semester
埋下		máixià	v.-c.	bury (here: plant)
种子	種子	zhǒng.zi	n.	seed (here: cause)

月底	月底	yuèdǐ	*n.*	end of the month
参加	參加	cānjiā	*v.*	attend (meeting, discussion, etc.)
得知		dézhī	*v.*	have learned of
狠狠		hěnhěn	*adv.*	ferociously
打		dǎ	*v.*	beat
顿	頓	dùn	*AN*	measure word for meals, occurrences, etc. 一天吃三顿饭。 打了他一顿/骂他一顿
踢		tī	*v.*	kick
足球		zúqiú	*n.*	football; soccer
打断	打斷	dǎ//duàn	*v.-c.*	break
重压	重壓	zhòngyā	*n.*	heavy pressure
…之下		zhīxià		under …
感到		gǎndào	*v.*	feel 感到非常高兴/感到寂寞
管		guǎn	*v.*	subject sb. to discipline; control (a child)
严	嚴	yán	*adj.*	strict; stern
实现	實現	shíxiàn	*v.*	realize; achieve; bring about
提出		tíchū	*v.*	put forward; pose; raise 提出意见/提出更高的要求
目标	目標	mùbiāo	*n.*	objective; target
深深		shēnshēn	*adv.*	profoundly; deeply
委屈		wěiqū	*adj.*	feel wronged
压抑	壓抑	yāyì	*adj.*	repressed; depressed
提醒		tíxǐng	*v.*	remind
再次		zàicì	*adv.*	once again; for the second time
冲突	衝突	chōngtū	*v.*	conflict
绝望	絕望	juéwàng	*n./v.*	hopelessness; despair, give up all hope
门口儿	門口儿	ménkǒur	*n.*	entrance; doorway; door; gate

拿起一把木柄榔头朝(8)母亲后脑砸去，把母亲活活砸死。

徐力杀母震惊(9)了社会。在徐力就读的金华四中，同学和老师反映，徐力平时一向(10)刻苦节俭，是个品学兼优的好学生。他性格文静，初中时期一直是三好学生，初二就入了团；进入高中以后，也一直努力学习，对集体活动很热心，也乐于助人。他们不懂，为什么这样的学生会干出这样的暴行？

当地有关专家认为，家长望子成龙心切，子女心理脆弱和缺乏法制观念，是导致(11)这出悲剧的主要原因。从徐力身上可以看到一个矛盾：他一方面似乎"训练有素"，杀死母亲后移尸灭迹，还写

把		bǎ	*AN*	measure word for things with handles or things to take hold of 一把椅子/一把伞/一把枪
木柄榔头	木柄榔頭	mùbǐng láng.tou	*n.*	a hammer with a wood shaft
朝		cháo	*prep.*	to; towards 朝南走/朝办公室走去/朝前看
后脑	後腦	hòunǎo	*n.*	back of the head
砸		zá	*v.*	smash
活活		huóhuó	*adv.*	while still alive
震惊	震驚	zhènjīng	*v.*	astonish; shock
就读	就讀	jiùdú	*v.*	attend (school) 他就读于第四中学。
反映	反映	fǎnyìng	*v.*	report; make known
平时	平時	píngshí	*n.*	ordinarily; in normal times
一向		yíxiàng	*adv.*	always; all the time
刻苦		kèkǔ	*adj.*	painstaking; hardworking
节俭	節儉	jiéjiǎn	*adj.*	frugal

品学兼优	品學兼優	pǐn xué jiān yōu	idm.	(of a student) of good character and scholarship
性格		xìnggé	n.	character; nature; disposition
文静		wénjìng	adj.	quiet and gentle
三好学生	三好學生	sānhǎo xuéshēng	n.	学习好、体育好、思想好的学生; students who are good in studying, in sports, and in thinking
入团	入團	rù//tuán	v.-o.	be admitted to the Communist Youth League
集体	集體	jítǐ	n./adj.	group, collective
热心	熱心	rèxīn	adj.	enthusiastic; zealous
乐于助人	樂於助人	lèyú zhùrén	phr.	be glad to help others
干	幹	gàn	v.	do
暴行		bàoxíng	n.	violent conduct; atrocities
当地	當地	dāngdì	adj.	local
有关	有關	yǒuguān	adj.	related; concerned; relevant;
专家	專家	zhuānjiā	n.	expert
望子成龙	望子成龍	wàng zǐ chéng lóng	idm.	wish for one's children to be successful (lit. "hope son becomes a dragon")
——心切		xīn qiè	adj.	eager; anxious 成功心切/出国心切/结婚心切
子女		zǐnǚ	n.	son and daughter; children
脆弱		cuìruò	adj.	fragile
缺乏		quēfá	v.	lack; be scanty of
法制		fǎzhì	n.	legality
导致	導致	dǎozhì	v.	give rise to; lead to
出	齣	chū	AN	measure word for dramatic pieces
矛盾		máodùn	n.	contradiction
训练有素	訓練有素	xùnliàn yǒu sù	idm.	be well trained
移尸灭迹	移尸滅迹	yí shī miè jì	phr.	remove the corpse and erase all trace

字条欺骗父亲说妈妈去杭州看病了，并居然照常⑿参加了考试；但另一方面他又十分脆弱，仅仅因为母亲对他学业上的压力就⒀杀了母亲。这说明他的心理很不健康，并且法制观念淡薄。

现在的青少年基本上是独生子女，从小就承受了很大的压力。家长对子女往往期望过高，子女考试不理想，就有一种对不起父母的感觉。结果，必然导致心理问题。而现在社会上凶杀、色情等读物泛滥，许多青少年受到不良文化的影响。因此，加强⒁对青少年思想道德教育和人格培养是非常重要的。

《人民日报》海外版 2000 年 2 月 15 日

字条	字條	zìtiáo	n.	brief note
欺骗	欺騙	qīpiàn	v.	cheat; dupe
看病		kàn//bìng	v.-o.	see a doctor
居然		jūrán	adv.	surprisingly; unexpectedly
照常		zhàocháng	adv.	(do something) as usual
十分		shífēn	adv.	extremely; very
仅仅	僅僅	jǐnjǐn	adv.	only; alone
学业	學業	xuéyè	n.	school work; one's study
并且	並且	bìngqiě	conj.	and; also, besides; moreover
淡薄		dànbó	adj.	be indifferent
承受		chéngshòu	v.	bear; sustain
期望		qīwàng	n.	hope; expectation
理想		lǐxiǎng	adj.	perfect; desirable; ideal
必然		bìrán	adv.	be bound to; inevitable
凶杀	兇殺	xiōngshā	n.	homicide; murder; manslaughter
色情		sèqíng	n.	pornography
读物	讀物	dúwù	n.	reading matter; reading material

泛滥	泛濫	fànlàn	v.	spread far and wide; spread unchecked
不良		bùliáng	adj.	harmful; unwholesome
加强		jiāqiáng	v.	enhance; reinforce
人格		réngé	n.	moral integrity

词语例句

(1) 无法 v. : unable; incapable

◆ 一名十七岁中学生因无法忍受学习的沉重压力而杀死亲生母亲。

A seventeen-year-old high school student killed his own mother because he couldn't bear the heavy pressure of study.

1. 这是一个无法解决的问题。

This is an insolvable problem.

2. 他的经验不够，无法做这项工作。

His experience is not sufficient to do this job.

(2)基本上：basically; on the whole

◆ 徐力从小到大基本上是在母亲的照顾下长大的。

Basically Xu Li grew up under the care of (only) his mother.

1. 我们的意见基本上是一样的。

Our opinions are on the whole the same.

2. 基本上学生都住在宿舍里，只有少数住在校外。

Basically all the students live in the dormitory; only a few live outside of the campus.

(3) 排名: rank as; be ranked as

◆ 徐力高一上半学期排名全班倒数第二名。

Xu Li ranked the second from the bottom of the class in the first semester of his first year of high school.

1. 这个学校的电脑系很有名，在美国排名第一。

This college has a very famous computer department; it ranks first in the United States.

2. 这次期中考，我在全班排名第二。

I ranked second in the class on this mid-term exam.

(4) 狠狠: ferociously

◆ 她很生气，狠狠打了儿子一顿。

She was very angry and gave her son a good beating.

1. 她因为逃学，被父母狠狠骂了一顿。

She was given a good scolding by her parents for cutting class.

2. 中国政府采取各种措施，狠狠打击盗版行为。

China's government took all kinds of vigorous measures to counter piracy.

(5) S.1 再 v., S.2 就…: If S.1 goes on v.-ing, S.2 would …

◆ 以后你再去踢足球，我就把你的腿打断。

If you go on playing soccer, I will break your leg.

1. 以后你再骗我，我就非把你告到法院不可。

If you keep on cheating me, I will definitely sue you.

2. 要是你再说谎，我就不跟你做朋友了。

If you keep on lying, I will stop being your friend.

(6) 再次: once more; the second time; once again

◆ 母子之间再次为学习发生冲突。

A conflict happened once again between the mother and the son because of the issue of study.

1. 下个月美国总统将再次访问中国。

The President of the United States will visit China for the second time next month.

2. 昨天他们夫妇再次为谁该做家务的问题发生争执。

Yesterday that couple had a quarrel again over who should do the household jobs.

(7)（在）…中: in (a certain situation)

◆ (在)绝望中，徐力拿起一把木柄榔头朝母亲后脑砸去。

In a fit of despair, Xu Li hit the back of his mother's head with a wood-shafted hammer.

1. 虽然在比赛中得到了胜利，他们并没有因此而骄傲。

Although they won in the competition, they didn't become arrogant because of it.

2. 你应该跟老师讨论一下学习中的一些困难。

You should discuss with your teacher about the difficulties in your study.

3. 在失望中，他还是很客气地说了一声"谢谢"，然后才离开。
   He politely said "thank you" in disappointment before he left.

(8) 朝: to; towards

◆ (在)绝望中，徐力拿起一把木柄榔头朝母亲后脑砸去。

1. 他朝他的办公室走去。
   He walked towards his office.

2. 要到邮局去，你得先朝南走，然后右转，就到了。
   You have to go south, make a right turn, and then you'll find the post office.

(9) 震惊: shock; astonish

◆ 徐力杀母，震惊了社会。
   All of society was shocked by the news that Xu Li killed his mother.

1. 徐力杀了母亲，老师和同学都很震惊。
   Xu Li's teachers and schoolmates were shocked by Xu Li's killing his mother.

2. 他被杀的消息令人震惊。
   The news of his murder was a shock to everyone.

(10) 一向: all along; consistently

◆ 徐力平时一向刻苦节俭。
   Xu Li had always been painstaking and frugal.

1. 他对学生一向很严格。
   He has always been very strict with his students.

2. 他父母一向反对他学哲学。
   His parents have consistently opposed his studying philosophy.

(11) 导致: give rise to; lead to (something undesirable)

◆ 家长望子成龙心切，子女心理脆弱和缺乏法制观念，是导致这出悲剧的主要原因。
   The fact that children could not live up to the high expectation of parents who eagerly want them to be successful, as well as their lack of the concept of law and order led up to this tragedy.

1. 这些事导致了第二次世界大战。
   These events led up to World War II.

2. 一次性产品的大量使用导致了严重的环境污染。
   The use of disposable products on a large scale leads up to serious environmental pollution.

⑿ 照常: as usual; as before

◆ 徐力杀死母亲后，写字条欺骗父亲说妈妈去杭州看病了，并照常参加考试。

　　After killed his mother, Xu Li wrote a note and tricked his father by saying that his mother went to Hongzhou to see a doctor, and he actually took the exam as usual.

1. 即使下雨，比赛也会照常进行。

　　The match will be played as scheduled even in the event of rain.

2. 这家商店假日也照常做生意。

　　This store is open even on holidays.

⒀ 仅仅…就…: only because…; merely for…

◆ 他十分脆弱，仅仅因为母亲对他学业上的压力就杀了母亲。

　　He is so weak that he killed his mother just because she put pressure on him to study.

1. 你不应该仅仅为了这件小事就要跟丈夫离婚。

　　You shouldn't divorce your husband just because of such a trivial matter.

2. 我们不能仅仅因为改革开放造成了竞争就反对改革开放。

　　We can't oppose the reform and open-up policy just because it causes competition.

3. 我仅仅花了一百块人民币，就买到了一件又漂亮又合身的旗袍。

　　With only one hundred *RMB*, I bought a *qipao* which is both pretty and fits me well.

⒁ 加强: enhance; reinforce

◆ 加强对青少年思想道德教育和人格培养是非常重要的。

　　It is very important to enhance the moral education and the cultivation of character of teenagers.

1. 美国总统来访问，是为了加强中美关系。

　　The purpose of this visit of the President of the United States is to enhance the Sino-American relationship.

2. 青少年犯罪率日益提高，加强法制观念是很有必要的。

　　Since the crime rate of teenagers is increasing day by day, it is necessary to enhance teenagers' legal knowledge.

练习

I. Choose the correct answer.

1. 高中学生杀死同学的事件_____ 美国全社会对青少年心理问题的讨论。

    a. 造成　b. 引起　c. 导致

2. 因为他 _____ ，结果身体出了问题。

    a. 成功心切　b. 心切成功　c. 成功得心切

3. 这位作家 _____ ，写出了很多关于纽约的作品。

    a. 生活在纽约长期　b. 生活长期在纽约　c. 长期生活在纽约

4. 在十四、五世纪的欧洲，要是一个人不相信上帝，他会被 _____ 烧死。

    a. 狠狠　b. 活活　c. 深深

II. Choose the most appropriate word for each blank and fill in with its Chinese equivalent.

cheat	one's own	as usual	put forward
feel wronged	endure; bear	wish for one's children to be successful	

1. 大部分的中国父母都有 _____ 的观念。他们常常给孩子_____ 很高的目标，比如考进最好的大学，考试排名第一等等。

2. 虽然今天下雨了，他还是 _____ 去跑步。

3. 他长大以后才知道自己并不是父母 _____ 的孩子。

4. 据说是因为无法 _____ 丈夫长期 _____ 她，她才离婚的。

III. Choose the phrase that is closest in meaning to the underlined phrase in the sentence.

1. 子女考试不理想，就觉得对不起父母，结果<u>必然</u>导致心理问题。

    a. 一定　b. 必须　c. 必要

2. 徐力杀了母亲以后，还<u>居然</u>参加了考试。

    a. 自然　b. 当然　c. 竟然

3. 徐力的老师们都说他是一个<u>品学兼优</u>的好学生。

    a. 性格和道德都好　b. 人品和成绩都好　c. 学习和运动都好

4. 因为她<u>减肥心切</u>，每天只喝水，吃点儿青菜，别的什么都不吃。
    a. 很希望减肥　　b. 很喜欢减肥　　c. 忙着减肥

5. 三年以后，他<u>再次</u>来到金华，发现那里有了很大的变化。
    a. 两次　　b. 第二次　　c. 下次

6. 一般来说，女人不大<u>乐于</u>回答关于他们年龄的问题。
    a. 愿意　　b. 幸福　　c. 快乐

IV. Make a sentence using the underlined expression.

1. 她参加家长会时<u>得知</u>，徐力期中考试的成绩排在全班第十八名。

2. 她说："以后你<u>再</u>去踢球，我<u>就</u>把你的腿打断。"

3. 他太脆弱，<u>仅仅</u>因为母亲对他学习上的压力，<u>就</u>杀了母亲。

4. 他对女儿的<u>期望</u>很高，<u>因此</u>花了很多钱让她学弹琴、跳舞、画画。

5. <u>通过</u>努力，高一下半学期，徐力进步到了第十名。

6. 徐力平时<u>一向</u>刻苦节俭，是个品学兼优的好学生。

7. 家长望子成龙心切、子女心理脆弱和缺乏法制观念，是<u>导致</u>这出悲剧的主要原因。

8. 子女考试不理想，就有一种对不起父母的感觉。结果，<u>必然</u>导致心理问题。

V. Composition

1. 徐力的同学和老师都很同情徐力。在他们看来，徐力是个品学兼优的好学生，他们想给报纸写一封信，为徐力辩护（defend）。你是徐力的同学，请你用下面的词，为他写一封辩护的信。

升学压力	忍受	过问	寂寞	忽视
过分	提醒	排名	重视	导致
心理障碍	脆弱	期望	情急之中	大惊小怪
培养	长期	提高	从小	承受
压抑	同情	值得	缺乏	震惊

2. 为什么徐力杀死了亲生母亲？请从下面几点分析：

a. 中国的升学考试制度和中国社会的情况

b. 父母和子女的关系

c. 不良文化的影响

VI. Answer the following questions.

1. 看了这个新闻以后，你同情谁？为什么？

2. 什么是"望子成龙"？你的父母有没有望子成龙的态度？这种态度和社会与文化有没有关系？

3. 近年来，在美国也发生过中学生开枪杀人的事件。他们杀人的原因跟中国学生杀人的原因一样不一样？这反映了什么？

繁体字课文

　　一名十七歲中學生因無法(1)忍受學習的沉重壓力而殺死親生母親，這個悲劇在浙江省引起社會各界對教育問題的深刻反思。

　　今年十七歲的徐力是浙江省金華市第四中學高二學生。他出生在一個普通的工人家庭。母親吳鳳仙是金華食品公司職工。由於父亲長期在外地火車站工作，徐力從小到大基本上(2)是在母親的照顧下長大的。母親吳鳳仙工資不高，就幫別人織毛衣賺點儿錢供兒子讀書。初中升高中時，徐力考進學校的重點班，但高一上半學期排名(3)全班倒數第二名。通過努力，高一下半學期，徐力進步到了第十名。吳鳳仙喜出望外，要兒子以後每次期中、期末考試都排在全班前十名。然而，悲劇也就在這個時候埋下了種子。

　　去年十月底，吳鳳仙參加家長會得知，徐力這學期期中考試的成績排在全班第十八名。吳鳳仙很生氣，回家後狠狠(4)打了兒子一頓。徐力喜歡踢足球，吳鳳仙就說：“以後你再去踢足球，我就(5)把你的腿打斷。”重壓之下的徐力感到母親對自己管得太嚴，而且爲無法實現母親提出的目標而深深感到委屈和壓抑。

　　今年一月十七日，徐力從學校回家，吃完中飯後，想去看會儿電視，吳鳳仙却提醒兒子期末考得考前十名。徐力說：“很難考，不可能。”母子之間再次(6)爲學習發生衝突。絕望中(7)，徐力從門口拿起一把木柄榔頭朝(8)母親後腦砸去，把母親活活砸死。

　　徐力殺母震驚(9)了社會。在徐力就讀的金華四中，同學和老師反映，徐力平時一向(10)刻苦節儉，是個品學兼優的好學生。他性格文靜，初中時期一直是三好學生，初二就入了團；進入高中以後，也一直努力學習，對集體活動很熱心，也樂於助人。他們不懂，爲什麼這樣的學生會幹出這樣的暴行？

當地有關專家認爲，家長望子成龍心切，子女心理脆弱和缺乏法制觀念，是導致(11)這齣悲劇的主要原因。從徐力身上可以看到一個矛盾：他一方面似乎"訓練有素"，殺死母親後移尸滅迹，還寫字條欺騙父親說媽媽去杭州看病了，並居然照常(12)參加了考試；但另一方面他又十分脆弱，僅僅因爲母親對他學業上的壓力就(13)殺了母親。這說明他的心理很不健康，並且法制觀念淡薄。

現在的青少年基本上是獨生子女，從小就承受了很大的壓力。家長對子女往往期望過高，子女考試不理想，就有一種對不起父母的感覺。結果，必然導致心理問題。而現在社會上凶殺、色情等讀物泛濫，許多青少年受到不良文化的影響。因此，加强(14)對青少年思想道德教育和人格培養是非常重要的。

附录

故意杀母案作出一审判决

新华社杭州 5 月 1 日电 浙江金华市中级人民法院昨天对震惊社会的"徐力杀母"案作出一审判决，以故意杀人罪判处⑴徐力有期徒刑十五年。

十七岁的徐力是浙江省金华市第四中学高二学生，母亲吴凤仙是金华食品公司职工。由于徐父长期在外地工作，徐力从小到大基本上是在母亲的照料下长大的。母亲吴凤仙工资不高，就帮别人织毛衣赚点儿钱供儿子读书。初中升高中时，徐力考进了学校的重点班，吴凤仙要求儿子每次期中、期末考试成绩都要排在班级前十名。重压之下的徐力感到母亲对自己管得太严，而且为母亲提出的目标无法实现而深感委屈和压抑。

今年 1 月 17 日中午，徐力放学回家吃过中饭后，因对母亲吴凤仙管教不满，便拿了一把铁榔头将母亲杀害。

法院认为，被告人徐力因对其母学习上的管束不满而使用铁榔头砸其母头部致死，非法剥夺了其母吴凤仙的生命，其行为依照《中华人民共和国刑法》第 232 条，已构成故意杀人罪。被告人徐

附录	附錄	fùlù	*n.*	appendix
故意		gùyì	*adv.*	deliberately; intentionally
一审	一審	yī shěn	*n.*	first trial

判决		pànjué	v.	court decision; judgment
新华社	新華社	Xīnhuáshè	n.	The China News Agency
电	電	diàn	n.	telex
中级	中級	zhōngjí	adj.	intermediate
杀人罪	殺人罪	shārénzuì	n.	manslaughter; murder
判处	判處	pànchǔ	v.	sentence; condemn
有期徒刑		yǒuqī túxíng	n.	set term of imprisonment
照料		zhàoliào	v.	take care of; care for
放学	放學	fàng//xué	v.-o.	classes are over; school is over
管教		guǎnjiào	v./n.	subject sb. to discipline
不满		bùmǎn	adj.	resentful; dissatisfied
便		biàn	conj.	then; 就
铁	鐵	tiě	n.	iron
将	將	jiāng	prep.	把
杀害	殺害	shāhài	v.	kill
被告人		bèigàorén	n.	defendant; the accused
其		qí	pron.	his; her; its
管束		guǎnshù	v./n.	restrain; control
头部	頭部	tóubù	n.	head
致死		zhìsǐ	v.	cause death; result in death
非法		fēifǎ	adj./ adv.	illegal, illegally
剥夺	剝奪	bōduó	v.	deprive of
生命		shēngmìng	n.	life
依照		yīzhào	prep.	according to
中华人民 共和国	中華人民 共和國	Zhōnghuá Rénmín Gònghéguó	n.	the People's Republic of China
刑法		xíngfǎ	n.	criminal law
条	條	tiáo	AN	measure word for clauses
构成	構成	gòuchéng	v.	constitute; compose

力犯罪时未满 18 周岁，依照《中华人民共和国刑法》第 17 条第 3 款，应当从(2)轻处罚。鉴于(3)本案具体情况，可依法酌情从轻处罚。为保护公民的人身权利不受非法侵犯，维护社会治安秩序，贯彻惩罚与教育相(4)结合的刑事政策，依照法律规定，以杀人罪判处被告人有期徒刑 15 年。

犯罪		fàn//zuì	v.-o.	commit a crime
未		wèi	adv.	not; not yet
满	滿	mǎn	v.	reach
周岁	周歲	zhōusuì	n.	one full year of life 一周歲/十八周歲
款		kuǎn	AN	measure word for clauses
应当	應當	yīngdāng	aux.	should
从轻	從輕	cóngqīng	adv.	settle a case (punishment, etc.) rather on the lenient side
处罚	處罰	chǔfá	v.	punish
鉴于	鑒於	jiànyú	prep.	in light of; seeing that; in consideration of
本		běn	pron.	this
具体	具體	jùtǐ	adj.	specific; concrete
依法		yīfǎ	adv.	according to law
酌情		zhuóqíng	adv.	take into consideration the circumstances
公民		gōngmín	n.	citizen
人身		rénshēn	adj.	personal
侵犯		qīnfàn	v.	infringe
维护	維護	wéihù	v.	defend; safeguard
治安		zhì'ān	n.	public security; public order
秩序		zhìxù	n.	law and order

贯彻	貫徹	guànchè	*v.*	carry out; implement
惩罚	懲罰	chéngfá	*v.*	punish
相结合	相結合	xiāng jiéhé	*v.*	combine; integrate
刑事		xíngshì	*adj.*	criminal; penal
政策		zhèngcè	*n.*	policy
规定	規定	guīdìng	*n.*	rule; regulations

词语例句

(1) 以···罪判处···： sentence sb. to …for …

◆ 浙江金华市中级人民法院以故意杀人罪判处徐力有期徒刑十五年。

The Intermediate People's Court of Jinhua of Zhejiang Province sentenced Xu Li to fifteen years' imprisonment for murder.

1. 他因为杀人被判了死刑。

　He was sentenced to death for murder.

2. 法院以贩毒罪判处他无期徒刑。

　The court sentenced him to life imprisonment for selling drugs.

(2) 从 adj. ： in a certain manner; according to a certain principle

◆ 被告人徐力犯罪时未满 18 周岁，依照《中华人民共和国刑法》第 17 条第 3 款，应当从轻处罚。

Xu Li, who committed the offense before he turned 18 years old, should be punished leniently, according to China's criminal law.

1. 他认为对于政府官员的贪污腐化，应当从严处理。

　He thinks that government officials who are guilty of corruption should be penalized harshly.

2. 你们是职业运动员，必须从严训练。

You are professional athletes; you must be trained with severity.

(3) 鉴于：seeing that; in light of

◆ 鉴于本案具体情况，可依法酌情从轻处罚。

In light of the particular circumstances of this case, Xu Li could be punished leniently according to the law.

1. 鉴于人口增长数量仍然很大，政府坚持实行一家一个孩子的政策。

   In light of the great amount of population increase, the government insists on implementing the one child one family policy.

2. 鉴于森林日益减少，政府决定采取保护森林的措施。

   Seeing the forest area decreasing day by day, the government decided to adopt some measures to protect it.

(4) A 跟 B 相 v.

◆ …贯彻惩罚与教育相结合的刑事政策。

…to implement criminal policy that combines punishment and education.

1. 这个节目既有意义，又有意思，可以说把娱乐和教育相结合得很好。

   This TV program is both interesting and meaningful; it can be called the perfect combination of entertainment and education.

2. 中国跟发达国家相比，还有很大差距。

   Compared with developed countries, China has a long way to go to catch up.

繁体字附录

新華社杭州 5 月 1 日電 浙江金華市中級人民法院昨天對震驚社會的
"徐力殺母"案作出一審判決，以故意殺人罪判處⑴徐力有期徒刑
十五年。

　　十七歲的徐力是浙江省金華市第四中學高二學生，母親吳鳳仙
是金華食品公司職工。由於徐父長期在外地工作，徐力從小到大基
本上是在母親的照料下長大的。母親吳鳳仙工資不高，就幫別人織
毛衣賺點儿錢供兒子讀書。初中升高中時，徐力考進了學校的重點
班，吳鳳仙要求兒子每次期中、期末考試成績都要排在班級前十
名。重壓之下的徐力感到母親對自己管得太嚴，而且為母親提出的
目標無法實現而深感委屈和壓抑。

　　今年 1 月 17 日中午，徐力放學回家吃過中飯後，因對母親吳
鳳仙管教不滿，便拿了一把鐵榔頭將母親殺害。

　　法院認為，被告人徐力因對其母學習上的管束不滿而使用鐵榔
頭砸其母頭部致死，非法剝奪了其母吳鳳仙的生命，其行為依照
《中華人民共和國刑法》第 232 條，已構成故意殺人罪。被告人徐
力犯罪時未滿 18 周歲，依照《中華人民共和國刑法》第 17 條第 3
款，應當從⑵輕處罰。鑒於⑶本案具體情況，可依法酌情從輕處罰。
為保護公民的人身權利不受非法侵犯，維護社會治安秩序，貫徹懲
罰與教育相⑷結合的刑事政策，依照法律規定，以殺人罪判處被告
人有期徒刑 15 年。

第十七课 中国大学生对性的态度

最近，北京医科大学公共卫生学院对北京市五所高校 1310 名在校本科大学生进行(1)了性观念的调查，其中男生占(2)63%，平均年龄 20 岁。

在对大学生婚前性行为的态度的调查中，半数以上(3)的被调查的学生（54%）认为在大学生中婚前性行为应该绝对禁止。同时，半数以上的学生同意在双方相爱、关系稳定、双方正准备结婚的情况下，婚前性行为是可以接受的。

研究者认为，这一结果表明受当今西方性自由思潮的影响，大学生对性的态度已经比过去开放多了。

在对大学生性行为调查中，27.7% 的男生和 34.4% 的女生表示目前他们有稳定的恋人。有过婚前性行为的，男生占 15%， 女生 13%。首次发生性关系的平均年龄，男生为 18.7 岁，女生为 19 岁左右(4)。女生更倾向于(5)和比她们年龄大的男生发生性关系。

另外，青少年的自我保护意识较差，当首次发生性关系时(6)，只有 42.2% 的人使用了保险套。

性		xìng	n.	sex
态度	態度	tài.du	n.	attitude
北京医科大学	北京醫科大學	Běijīng Yīkē Dàxué	n.	Beijing Medical University

公共卫生学院	公共衛生學院	Gōnggòng Wèishēng Xuéyuàn	n.	School of Public Health
高校		gāoxiào	n.	universities and colleges
在校		zàixiào	v.	be at school
本科		běnkē	n.	undergraduate
进行	進行	jìnxíng	v.	carry out; conduct
占		zhàn	v.	make up; account for
性行为	性行爲	xìng xíngwéi	n.	sexual intercourse; sexual behavior
半数	半數	bànshù	n.	half the number
以上		yǐshàng	n.	more than; over, the above; the above-mentioned
绝对	絕對	juéduì	adv.	absolutely
禁止		jìnzhǐ	v.	forbid; prohibit from
相爱	相愛	xiāng'ài	v.	be in love with each other 他们相爱十年了，还没结婚呢！
稳定	穩定	wěndìng	adj.	steady; stable
准备	準備	zhǔnbèi	v.	intend; plan, prepare
研究者		yánjiūzhě	n.	researcher
表明		biǎomíng	v.	demonstrate
当今	當今	dāngjīn	n.	now; at present; nowadays
自由		zìyóu	n.	freedom
思潮	思潮	sīcháo	n.	trend of thought
恋人	戀人	liànrén	n.	lover; sweetheart
首次		shǒucì	adv.	for the first time
为	為	wéi	v.	是; be
左右		zuǒyòu	n.	about; or so
倾向于	傾向於	qīngxiàngyú	v.	be inclined to; tend to
自我保护	自我保護	zìwǒ bǎohù	n.	self-protection
较	較	jiào	adv.	relatively; 比较
当…时	當…時	dāng…shí	conj.	when

研究人员分析认为，当今大学生对婚前性行为的态度正处于(7)混乱和危险的阶段。一方面，受我国传统文化、道德、价值观的影响，他们表现出传统的一面，认为婚前性行为应该绝对禁止，贞节对男女青年来说还是十分重要的。另一方面，受西方的性自由生活方式的影响，某些大学生的性观念和性态度已越来越自由化，如(8)调查中已有相当一部分学生对婚前性行为持宽容和认可的态度(9)。

从发生婚前性行为的大学生日益增多的现状来看(10)，出现这一现象的主要原因是因为缺少性健康教育，对婚前性行为后果的严重性缺少认识。这种现象实际上已经使部分大学生面临(11)未婚先孕、人工流产和性病等问题的威胁。这说明性教育在学校还需要加强。

《人民日报》1999 年 8 月 15 日

人员	人員	rényuán	n.	personnel; staff
处于	處於	chǔyú	v.	be (in a certain condition)
混乱	混亂	hùnluàn	adj.	disorderly; chaotic
阶段	階段	jiēduàn	n.	phase; stage
价值观	價值觀	jiàzhíguān	n.	value system
贞节	貞節	zhēnjié	n.	chastity or virginity
青年		qīngnián	n.	young people; youth
方式		fāngshì	n.	fashion; way; manner
自由化		zìyóuhuà	v.	liberalize
如		rú	prep.	for example; such as
相当	相當	xiāngdāng	adv.	quite; fairly; considerably 相当好/相当成功/相当长
持		chí	v.	hold (an opinion or an attitude)

宽容	寬容	kuānróng	*adj.*	tolerant
认可	認可	rènkě	*v.*	accept; approve
增多	增多	zēngduō	*v.*	grow in number; increase
现状	現狀	xiànzhuàng	*n.*	present situation
出现	出現	chūxiàn	*v.*	appear; arise; emerge
缺少		quēshǎo	*v.*	lack; be deficient in
后果	後果	hòuguǒ	*n.*	consequence
严重性	嚴重性	yánzhòngxìng	*n.*	seriousness; gravity
面临	面臨	miànlín	*n.*	be faced with; be confronted with
未婚先孕		wèihūn xiānyùn	*phr.*	get pregnant before marriage
人工流产	人工流產	rén'gōng liúchǎn	*n.*	induced abortion
威胁	威脅	weixié	*n./v.*	threat, threaten

词语例句

(1) 对⋯进行⋯ : make a ...on ...

◆ 最近北京医科大学对北京市五所高校1310名在校学生进行了性观念的调查。

Recently Beijing Medical University conducted a survey of thirteen hundred and ten students from five colleges in Beijing on their attitudes toward sex.

1. 最近政府对饭馆进行了调查，发现有些饭馆雇用非法移民。

Recently the government investigated some restaurants and found that some of them had illegally hired immigrants.

2. 在家长会上，家长们对帮助同学该不该收钱进行了激烈的讨论。

In the parents' meeting, the parents discussed actively whether one should collect money when helping one's classmates.

(2) 占: make up …

◆ …其中男生占 63%。

… Among them the male students account for 63%.

1. 女生占全校学生的一半。

Female students constitute half the school students.

2. 据报导，中国人花在食物上的钱占收入的一半。

It is reported that Chinese people spend half of their salaries on food.

(3) 以上: more than; over

◆半数以上的被调查的学生认为在大学生中婚前性行为应该绝对禁止。

More than half of the surveyed students are of the opinion that university students should absolutely be prohibited from sexual relations before they get married.

1. 半数以上的学生同意在双方相爱、关系稳定、双方正准备结婚的情况下，婚前性行为是可以接受的。

More than half of the students agreed that if the two people are in love, their relationship is stable, and they are ready to get married, premarital sexual relations are acceptable.

2. 在美国，21 岁以上的人才能买酒。

In America only people over 21 years old are allowed to buy alcohol.

(4) …左右: about …; … or so

◆首次发生性关系的平均年龄，男生为 18.7 岁，女生为 19 岁左右。

The average age of their first sexual relations is 18.7 years old for boys and 19 or so for girls.

1. 参加考试的学生有 2000 左右。

There are about 2000 students who attended this examination.

2. 我用了三个星期左右才把这本书看完。

It took me about three weeks to finish reading this book.

(5) 倾向于: be inclined to; prefer to

◆女生更倾向于和比她们年龄大的男生发生性关系。

The girl students are more inclined to have sexual relations with older male students.

1. 中国大学生毕业以后，倾向于在大城市找工作。

After graduation, college students tend to look for jobs in big cities.

2. 大多数的公司倾向于雇佣有经验的职工。

Most companies prefer to hire experienced staff.

(6) 当… 时: when …

◆ 当首次发生性关系时，只有 42.2% 的人使用了保险套。

Only 42.2% of them used condoms when they first had sex.

1. 当同学们听说徐力杀了母亲时，他们都非常震惊。

When Xu Li's friends heard that he killed his mother, they were simply shocked.

2. 当他住院时，许多朋友到医院去看他。

Many friends went to see him when he was hospitalized.

(7) 处于: be in the state of

◆ 当今大学生对婚前性行为的态度正处于混乱和危险的阶段。

The college students' attitudes toward sex are in a state of chaos and danger.

1. 由于长期的战争，这个国家的经济水平一直处于较低的水平。

The economy of this country had been at a comparatively low level owing to the long period of war.

2. 不少农村的家庭还处于贫困之中。

Quite a few families in the country are still in poverty.

(8) 如: for example; such as

◆ 某些大学生的性观念和性态度已越来越自由化，如调查中已有相当一部分学生对婚前性行为持宽容和认可的态度。

Some college students' concept of and attitude towards sex have become more and more liberal. For instance, in the survey there were a considerable number of students who held a tolerant and approving attitude towards premarital sexual behaviors.

1. 常见的一次性产品很多，如纸杯、纸盘、纸巾等等。

There are many common disposable products, such as paper cups, paper plates, and paper napkins.

2. 32% 的中小学生不同程度地存在心理异常，如讨厌上学、想出走等等。

Thirty-two percent of elementary and middle school students have abnormal psychological problems of varying degrees. For instance, some hate school and some want to run away from home.

(9) 持…态度: hold a … attitude

◆ 调查中已有相当一部分学生对婚前性行为持宽容和认可的态度。

1. 他对别人的好意总是持怀疑的态度。

He is always suspicious of others' good intentions.

2. 一个世纪以前，中国人对外来的文化持抵抗的态度。

A century ago, Chinese people resisted (lit. "held a resisting attitude toward") foreign culture.

(10) 从…来看: judging from; as can be seen from

◆ 从发生婚前性行为的大学生日益增多的现状来看，出现这一现象的主要原因是因为缺少性健康教育。

Judging by the current fact that the number of college students who have sexual relations before marriage increases day by day, one can see that the phenomenon appears because of a lack of sex education.

1. 学习外语的美国人日益增加，从这个状况来看，美国人越来越关心其他国家了。

The number of Americans who study foreign language is getting bigger day by day. Judging from this situation, Americans are concerned more and more about other countries.

2. 汽车已经进入了一般的中国家庭。从这个现象来看，中国人的生活水平的确提高了。

Cars have entered the common Chinese families. As we can see from this phenomenon, the Chinese people's living standard has indeed been raised.

(11) 面临: be faced with; be confronted with

◆ 部分大学生面临未婚先孕、人工流产和性病等问题的威胁。

A portion of college students are confronted with the threat of premarital pregnancy, induced abortion, and venereal disease.

1. 中国面临人口过多、资源不足的难题。

China is confronted with the problems of overpopulation and insufficiency of natural resources.

2. 这所大学面临经费缺乏的困难。

This university is faced with the problem of lacking funds.

练习

I. Choose the correct answer.

1. 上个星期我读了十本书，_____ 七本是关于中国历史的。

      a. 中间   b. 之间   c. 其中

2. 这所大学半数 _____ 的学生都是本州的学生。

      a. 部分   b. 多   c. 以上

3. 他们结婚十年了，_____。

      a. 他一直相爱她   b. 他们一直相爱   c. 他们一直相爱对方

4. A：一个人很能干，一个人很诚实，你会选谁当总统？

  B：我比较 _____ 选能干的人当总统。

      a. 倾向于   b. 宁可   c. 与其

5. 有些人的环境保护意识很差，换句话说，他们 _____ 。

      a. 没有钱保护环境   b. 没有保护环境的经验

      c. 不知道要保护环境

6. 他开车的时候心里一直想着别的事，_____ 出了车祸。

      a. 后果   b. 结果   c. 好在

II. Choose the most appropriate word for each blank and fill in with its Chinese equivalent.

        prohibit   be in a state of
        be faced with   gravity

1. 上个星期，美国总统选举正 _____ 最紧张的阶段。

2. 到了七十年代后期，中国政府才认识到人口过多的 _____ 。

3. 电影院、饭馆儿、教室，几乎所有的公共场所都 _____ 吸烟。

4. 四年级学生 _____ 的最大压力就是找工作和完成论文。

III. Translate into Chinese.

Survey — Sexual Behavior Before Marriage

    Young Chinese are adopting a more tolerant attitude towards premarital sex, love, and marriage, an urban study found recently.

    Only 35.1% of respondents voiced agreement with the traditional notion that "premarital sex is immoral and should not be permitted under any circumstance," according to the results of the study conducted by Beijing Medical University.

The survey also found men and women held different opinions, with 43.9% of female respondents, or 18.5% more than their male counterparts, pointing to the immorality of premarital sex.

Respondents with higher education levels voiced a great tolerance towards premarital sex, and individuals living in economically developed regions voiced greater tolerance than those in less-developed regions, the survey said.

The respondents attributed the increasing tolerance of young Chinese towards premarital sex to two main reasons. Firstly, Western culture has prompted the young generation to reflect on traditional culture. Secondly, greater tolerance towards premarital sex by the general public reduces the costs which young people must pay for more liberal behavior, they said.

IV. Make a sentence using the underlined expression.

1. 家长会后，老师组织学生对帮助别人应不应该给钱进行讨论。
2. 很多人认为在正准备结婚的情况下，婚前性行为是可以接受的。
3. 据调查，相当一部分美国人对禁止人民自由买卖枪持反对态度。
4. 在对婚前性关系的问题上，大多数中国人倾向于反对。
5. 全球环境的变化，使很多动物面临死亡的威胁。
6. 火灾后，整个大楼处于混乱状态。

V. Answer the following questions.

1. 在你看来，婚前性关系是不是不道德的行为？为什么？
2. 性观念的开放对整个社会来说是件好事还是坏事？
3. 中国大学生性观念的开放是受到西方的影响还是社会发展的必然
   结果？

繁体字课文

最近，北京醫科大學公共衛生學院對北京市五所高校 1310 名
在校本科大學生進行(1)了性觀念的調查，其中男生占(2)63%，平均年
齡 20 歲。

在對大學生婚前性行爲的態度的調查中，半數以上(3)的被調查的學生（54%）認爲在大學生中婚前性行爲應該絕對禁止。同時，半數以上的學生同意在雙方相愛、關係穩定、雙方正準備結婚的情況下，婚前性行爲是可以接受的。

研究者認爲，這一結果表明受當今西方性自由思潮的影響，大學生對性的態度已經比過去開放多了。

在對大學生性行爲調查中，27.7% 的男生和 34.4% 的女生表示目前他們有穩定的戀人。有過婚前性行爲的，男生占 15%， 女生 13%。首次發生性關係的平均年齡，男生為 18.7 歲，女生為 19 歲左右(4)。女生更傾向於(5)和比她們年齡大的男生發生性關係。

另外，青少年的自我保護意識較差，當首次發生性關係時(6)，只有 42.2%的人使用了保險套。

研究人員分析認為，當今大學生對婚前性行爲的態度正處於(7)混亂和危險的階段。一方面，受我國傳統文化、道德、價值觀的影響，他們表現出傳統的一面，認為婚前性行為應該絕對禁止，貞節對男女青年來說還是十分重要的。另一方面，受西方的性自由生活方式的影響，某些大學生的性觀念和性態度已越來越自由化，如(8)調查中已有相當一部分學生對婚前性行爲持寬容和認可的態度(9)。

從發生婚前性行爲的大學生日益增多的現狀來看(10)，出現這一現象的主要原因是因爲缺少性健康教育，對婚前性行爲後果的嚴重性缺少認識。這種現象實際上已經使部分大學生面臨(11)未婚先孕、人工流産和性病等問題的威脅。這說明性教育在學校還需要加强。

第十八课 暑假大学生在做什么?

七月的北京,各大高校放了暑假。大学生们是怎样过这个假期的呢?带着这个疑问,我们采访了一些大学生。

一些大学生选择了回家"避暑",大一的学生绝大多数属于(1)这种情况。一名对外经济贸易大学读大一的同学说:"北京这么热,不回家干嘛(2)?"

许多高校自己组织了一些社会实践活动,用这种特殊的形式来(3)使同学们与社会多接触,更重要的是加强对同学们思想上的教育,使同学们在科学文化和思想教育上有些收获。有的学校组织了一部分学生去陕西延安、河北平山县进行参观考察;还有的学校组织了一部分同学去毛主席纪念堂站岗值勤,维护秩序。

在留校的学生中,大部分人还是把学习放在第一位(4)。大一和

暑假		shǔjià	*n.*	summer vacation
放假		fàng//jià	*v.-o.*	have or be on (a holiday or vacation)
过	過	guò	*v.*	spend (time); pass (time)
假期		jiàqī	*n.*	vacation; holiday
疑问	疑問	yíwèn	*n.*	question; doubt
采访	採訪	cǎifǎng	*v.*	(of a journalist) have an interview with; cover (news)

避暑		bì//shǔ	*v.-o.* go away for summer; go to a summer resort; avoid summer heat
大一		dàyī	*n.* (college) freshman
绝大多数	絕大多數	jué dà duōshù	*n.* vast majority; overwhelming majority
属于	屬於	shǔyú	*v.* be part of; fall into the same category; belong to
对外经济贸易大学	對外經濟貿易大學	Duìwài Jīngjì Màoyì Dàxué	*n.* University of International Trade and Economics
干嘛	幹嘛	gànmá	*pron.* do what? (used in a rhetorical question)
组织	組織	zǔzhī	*v./n.* organize; arrange, organization
实践	實踐	shíjiàn	*v.* practice
特殊		tèshū	*adj.* special; particular
形式		xíngshì	*n.* form
接触	接觸	jiēchù	*v.* come into contact with
科学	科學	kēxué	*n.* scientific knowledge
收获	收穫	shōuhuò	*n.* gains; harvests
陕西	陝西	Shǎnxī	*n.* Shaanxi Province
延安		Yán'ān	*n.* Yan'an City
河北		Héběi	*n.* Hebei Province
平山县	平山縣	Píngshān xiàn	*n.* Pingshan County
考察		kǎochá	*v.* make an on-the-spot investigation; observe and study
毛主席纪念堂	毛主席紀念堂	Máozhǔxí Jìniàntáng	*n.* Chairman Mao's Memorial Hall
站岗	站崗	zhàn//gǎng	*v.-o.* stand guard; be on sentry
值勤		zhíqín	*v.-o.* be on duty (of police or military)
维护	維護	wéihù	*v.* defend; safeguard
秩序		zhìxù	*n.* order; law and order
留校		liú xiào	*v.-o.* stay at school

大二的学生忙着(5)参加各种英语辅导班；而在大三和大四的学生

中，考研和考 TOEFL、GRE 的则占了相当大的比例。这类辅导班虽然

收费不低，但仍吸引了大批的学生。像北京的新东方学校，聚集了

全国各大高校的学生。有许多在新疆、青海、云南、贵州、广东等

地上大学的同学，都不远千里赶到新东方上 TOEFL 和 GRE 辅导班。

据一些大学生介绍，新东方学校的 TOEFL 和 GRE 暑期班早在几个月

之前就(6)报满了。看来(7)，求学仍是许多当代大学生追求的主要目标。

　　许多高校自己成立了勤工俭学中心，帮助学生解决后顾之忧。

这些打工的同学在做些什么呢？家教、翻译、市场调查、网页制

大二		dà'èr	*n.*	(college) sophomore
辅导班	輔導班	fǔdǎobān	*n.*	auxiliary class; tutorial class
大三		dàsān	*n.*	(college) junior
大四		dàsì	*n.*	(college) senior
考研		kǎo yán	*v.-o.*	take a graduate school entrance exam
TOEFL			*n.*	Test of English as a Foreign Language
比例		bǐlì	*n.*	proportion; ratio
类	類	lèi	*n.*	class; category; kind; type
收费	收費	shōufèi	*n./v.*	charges; fees, charge
仍		réng	*adv.*	still
吸引		xīyǐn	*v.*	attract; draw
大批		dàpī	*adj.*	a large number of; great deal of 大批学生/大批观光客/大批机器
新东方	新東方	Xīndōng fāng	*n.*	New Oriental (name of a tutorial school)

聚集		jùjí	v.	gather; assemble
新疆		Xīnjiāng	n.	Xinjiang Province
青海		Qīnghǎi	n.	Qinghai Province
云南	雲南	Yúnnán	n.	Yunnan Province
贵州	貴州	Guìzhōu	n.	Guizhou Province
广东	廣東	Guǎngdōng	n.	Guangdong Province
地		dì	n.	place; 地方
不远千里	不遠千里	bù yuǎn qiānlǐ	idm.	without regarding a thousand miles as very distant - take the trouble of traveling a long distance
赶到	趕到	gǎn//dào	v.-c.	hurry to 赶到学校去/赶到飞机场
介绍	介紹	jièshào	v.	let know; brief; provide information; introduce
报	報	bào	v.	enroll; enlist; enter one's name; sign up; 报名
满	滿	mǎn	adj.	full; filled; (here used as a resultative complement)
看来	看來	kànlái	adv.	it seems; it looks as if
求学	求學	qiúxué	v.-o.	pursue one's studies; seek knowledge; attend school
当代	當代	dāngdài	n.	present age; contemporary era
追求		zhuīqiú	v.	pursue; seek
成立		chénglì	v.	establish; found
勤工俭学	勤工儉學	qíngōng jiǎnxué	n.	part-work and part-study program
中心		zhōngxīn	n.	center
后顾之忧	後顧之憂	hòu gù zhī yōu	n.	family considerations that cause delay in decision; trouble back at home
翻译	翻譯	fānyì	n./v.	translation, translate
网页	網頁	wǎngyè	n.	web page

213

作，或者给一些公司帮忙，报酬为每小时２０至１００元不等。许多大学生充分发挥自己的专业特长；如学计算机的就给中关村的一些电脑公司做网页，学外国语专业的就给一些大公司翻译各种文稿、手册，而学师范专业的就热衷于(8)当家教。这些同学每个月都能拿到２０００到３０００元，报酬相当可观。

　　但相比之下(9)，勤工俭学似乎不是太热。一名中国人民大学的学生认为，虽然外出打工可以丰富自己的社会经验，提高自己的能力，并且可以挣一些零花钱和生活费，但是就目前来说，考研和考TOEFL、GRE 大于(10)一切。否则(11)，毕业后很难有机会出国进修或者找到一份好的工作。

《光明日报》2000 年 7 月 26 日

制作	製作	zhìzuò	v./n.	make; manufacture
不等		bùděng	v.	vary; differ 大小不等/费用从50元至100元不等。
充分		chōngfèn	adv.	fully
发挥	發揮	fāhuī	v.	bring (skill, talent, etc.) into full play
专业	專業	zhuānyè	n.	major; specialized field or subjects
特长	特長	tècháng	n.	what one is skilled in; strong point; special skill; specialty
计算机	計算機	jìsuànjī	n.	computer 计算: count; compute
中关村	中關村	Zhōngguāncūn	n.	Zhongguancun; a district in Beijing

外国语	外國語	wàiguóyǔ	*n.*	foreign language
文稿		wéngǎo	*n.*	manuscript; draft
手册		shǒucè	*n.*	handbook; manual
师范	師範	shīfàn	*n.*	(study of) teaching; "normal"
热衷于	熱衷於	rèzhōngyú	*v.*	be fond of; be keen on 热衷于游泳/热衷于教育
当	當	dāng	*v.*	work as; serve as; be
可观	可觀	kěguān	*adj.*	considerable; impressive; sizable 数量很可观/损失可观
相比之下		xiāngbǐ zhī xià	*phr.*	by comparison; by contrast
热	熱	rè	*adj.*	popular
人民大学	人民大學	Rénmín Dàxué	*n.*	People's University
外出		wàichū	*v.*	go out (from one's home or hometown)
打工		dǎ//gōng	*v.-o.*	do part time job
丰富	豐富	fēngfù	*v./adj.*	enrich, abundant; ample
经验	經驗	jīngyàn	*n.*	experience
能力		nénglì	*n.*	ability
零花钱	零花錢	línghuāqián	*n.*	pocket money
生活费	生活費	shēnghuófèi	*n.*	living expenses
大于	大於	dàyú	*v.*	be more/bigger than
一切		yíqiè	*n.*	all; everything
否则	否則	fǒuzé	*conj.*	otherwise; if not
出国	出國	chū//guó	*v.-o.*	go abroad
进修	進修	jìnxiū	*v.*	engage in advanced studies
份		fèn	*AN*	measure word for job

词语例句

(1) 属于：be part of; fall into the category of …

◆ 一些大学生选择了回家"避暑"，大一的学生绝大多数属于这种情况。

Some college students choose going home to "avoid the heat." The vast majority of freshmen belong to this category.

1. 有些学生因忍受不了学习的沉重压力而杀人，徐力杀死母亲就属于这种情况。

Some students kill people because they can't bear the pressure of their studies; such is the case of Xu Li killing his mother.

2. 喝醉以后，有人唱歌，有人不停地说话，他属于哪种类型？

Having gotten drunk, some people sing, some people keep talking; which type is he?

(2) 干嘛：do what? (used in a rhetorical question)

◆ 北京这么热，不回家干嘛？

Beijing is so hot. What would I do if I don't go home?

1. 周末没什么事儿，不逛街干嘛？

I don't have anything to do on weekends. What would I do besides window-shopping?

2. 一个职业运动员一年能赚好几百万，上大学干嘛？

A professional athlete can make several millions a year. Why would one go to college?

(3) 用…来 v.：use …to…

◆ 许多高校自己组织了一些社会实践活动，用这种特殊的形式来使同学们与社会多接触。

Many universities organized events in which students offer service to society. They use this particular form of event to let students have more contact with society.

1. 中国政府用一家一个孩子的政策来控制人口的增长。

The Chinese government uses the policy of one child per family to control the increase of population.

2. 作者用这个例子来说明，在地位与金钱之间，人们往往更重视地位。

The author used this example to illustrate that people often care more about status than money.

(4) 把···放在第一位: put …first

◆ 大部分人还是把学习放在第一位。

Most people still put studying first.

    1. 目前中国政府把发展经济放在第一位。

    At this point, China's government is putting economic development first.

    2. 你是个学生，当然应该把学习放在第一位。

    You are a student. You should of course put studying first.

(5) 忙着 v. : busy with …

◆ 大一和大二的学生忙着参加各种英语辅导班。

Freshmen and sophomores are busy with attending various kinds of English tutorial classes.

    1. 即使在暑假，他还是忙着学习。

    Even during summer vacation, he is still busy with studying.

    2. 他这几天忙着写论文，你别去找他。

    He is busy finishing his thesis. Don't bother him.

(6) 早在··· 就 v. : have v.-ed as early as

◆ 新东方学校的 TOEFL 和 GRE 暑期班早在几个月之前就报满了。

The New Oriental School's GRE and TOEFL courses had been full for several months already.

    1. 早在二十年前，中国政府就开始了控制吸烟的工作。

    As early as twenty years ago, the Chinese government had launched an effort to control smoking.

    2. 早在他上大学的时候，他就对中美关系很感兴趣。

    As early as when he was in college, he was very interested in Sino-American relations.

(7) 看来: it seems that; it looks as if

◆ 看来，求学仍是许多当代大学生追求的主要目标。

It looks like pursuing one's studies is still the major objective of many college students nowadays.

    1. 这个辅导班的学生很多，看来他们的教法不错。

    This tutorial class has plenty of students. It seems that they have a very effective teaching method.

2. 参观故宫的人很多，看来故宫还是最吸引人的景点之一。

There are a lot of people who visit the Imperial Palace. It seems that it is still one of the most attractive scenic spots.

(8) 热衷于: be fond of; be keen on

◆ …而学师范专业的就热衷于当家教。

… , and those majoring in teacher training are very fond of being a tutor.

1. 目前大城市里的人们很热衷于学英语。

Nowadays people in big cities are crazy about learning English.

2. 最近几年，中国的中产阶级非常热衷于去欧洲旅游。

During the past few years, China's middle class has been very fond of going traveling in Europe.

(9) 相比之下: by comparison

◆ 相比之下，勤工俭学似乎不是太热。

By comparison, having a part-time job seemed not very popular.

1. 相比之下，农村人更喜欢便宜、容易使用的产品。

Unlike their urban counterparts, farmers prefer cheap and easy-to-handle goods.

2. 上课的时候，美国学生常常积极提问；相比之下，中国学生就显得安静得多。

American students tend to ask questions actively in class, while Chinese students seem much quieter by comparison.

(10) adj. 于: adj. than

◆ 就目前来说，考研和考 TOEFL、GRE 大于一切。

1. 对他来说，家庭重于事业。

For him, family is more important than his career.

2. 目前农村人口仍然多于城市人口。

At present, the rural population is still more than the urban population.

(11) 否则: otherwise; if not

◆ 就目前来说，考研和考 TOEFL、GRE 大于一切。否则，毕业后很难有机会出国进修或者找到一份好的工作。

For the time being, (college students regard) taking the graduate school entrance exam, the TOEFL, and the GRE as more important than anything else. Otherwise, it would be very difficult to go abroad for advanced study or find a good job after graduation.

1. 除非找到工资很高的工作，否则我宁可去上研究生院。

   Unless I find a job with very high pay, I prefer to go to graduate school.
2. 你一定得亲自去体验外国文化，否则不能深刻地理解它。

   You have to personally experience a foreign culture; otherwise, you can not understand it deeply.

练习

I. Choose the most appropriate word for each blank and fill in with its Chinese equivalent.

come into contact with   popular   gains   fond of
family considerations that cause delay in decision

1. 孩子有人照顾，父母上班工作的时候就没有 后顾之忧。

2. 他是一个记者，每天都 ___接触___ 到各种各样的人。 *yǔ jiēchù*

3. 我参加了辅导班，但是觉得并没有什么 收获。

4. 他喜欢看书，但是他的太太却 热衷于 参加各种晚会。

5. 目前最 __热__ 的专业就是计算机。 *zhōng*

II. Complete the following dialogues with the expressions provided.

A: 你对大学生打工有什么看法?

B: 我觉得大学生打工有好处也有坏处。

A: 有什么好处呢? *经验* *生活能力* *很多不同的人*

B: （赚，零花钱，丰富，提高，接触，有助于）*以后找工作*，但是我不打工。

A: 既然好处这么多，为什么你不打工呢?

B: 我不打工有两个原因。第一，大部分的工作跟我的专业没有关系，虽然…（可观，报酬，充分，发挥，特长）；第二，现在的社会，一个人要是没上过研究生院，很难有机会找到很好的工作，所以…（第一位，就目前来说，用…来v.，否则）*学习现在更重要。*

A: 有你这样想法的人多不多? *zhàn*

B: …（占，早就，满，主要目标）*大多数学生的主要目标是学习。*

III. Answer the following questions using the expressions provided.

1. 放暑假了，你为什么还打工呢? （不…干嘛?）*不挣钱那干嘛?*

2. 今年暑期，你回家避暑了吗? *我*（忙着v.）*打工呢。*

3. 你快毕业了，开始找工作了没有? （早在…就v.了）*找工作,去年就*

4. 60% 的中国大学生都参加了各种各样的暑期辅导班。（看来）

5. 网页制作和当家教，哪个工作比较好? （相比之下）

6. 把英语学好很重要吗? （否则）*很重要,否则不能去留学。*

7. 到中国去的观光客多吗? （不远千里）*外国*

比之下，网页挣的钱更多，但是 xiāng by zhǐ xià by comparison 应力中比较多。

8. 到美国来留学的学生多吗? (其中,占相当大的比例)

9. 他今年会不会出国进修? (后顾之忧, 除非…要不然)

10. 人口问题是不是美国最严重的问题? (就…来说, 才)

IV. Answer the following questions.

1. 比较中美大学生的暑假生活。有什么相同的地方和不同的地方?

2. 暑期打工,美国大学生比较热衷于做什么样的工作?

3. 中美大学生参加的社会实践活动有什么不同?

4. 你的大学用什么办法来让学生与社会多接触?

5. 学英语为什么这么热? 中文会不会取代英语成为最热的语言?

6. 参加辅导班和在大学上课有什么不同?

IV. Composition

一个难忘的暑假

繁体字课文

　　七月的北京，各大高校放了暑假。大學生們是怎樣過這個假期的呢？帶著這個疑問，我們採訪了一些大學生。

　　一些大學生選擇了回家"避暑"，大一的學生絕大多數屬於(1)這種情況。一名對外經濟貿易大學讀大一的同學說："北京這麼熱，不回家幹嘛(2)？"

　　許多高校自己組織了一些社會實踐活動，用這種特殊的形式來(3)使同學們與社會多接觸，更重要的是加強對同學們思想上的教育，使同學們在科學文化和思想教育上有些收穫。有的學校組織了一部分學生去陝西延安、河北平山縣進行參觀考察；還有的學校組織了一部分同學去毛主席紀念堂站崗值勤，維護秩序。

　　在留校的學生中，大部分人還是把學習放在第一位(4)。大一和大二的學生忙著(5)參加各種英語輔導班；而在大三和大四的學生中，考研和考 TOEFL、GRE 的則占了相當大的比例。這類輔導班雖然收費不低，但仍吸引了大批的學生。像北京的新東方學校，聚集了全國各大高校的學生。有許多在新疆、青海、雲南、貴州、廣東等地上大學的同學，都不遠千里趕到新東方上 TOEFL 和 GRE 輔導班。據一些大學生介紹，新東方學校的 TOEFL 和 GRE 暑期班早在幾個月之前就(6)報滿了。看來(7)，求學仍是許多當代大學生追求的主要目標。

　　許多高校自己成立了勤工儉學中心，幫助學生解決後顧之憂。這些打工的同學在做些什麼呢？家教、翻譯、市場調查、網頁製作，或者給一些公司幫忙，報酬爲每小時２０至１００元不等。許多大學生充分發揮自己的專業特長；如學計算機的就給中關村的一些電腦公司做網頁，學外國語專業的就給一些大公司翻譯各種文稿、手冊，而學師範專業的就熱衷於(8)當家教。這些同學每個月都能拿到２０００到３０００元，報酬相當可觀。

　　但相比之下(9)，勤工儉學似乎不是太熱。一名中國人民大學的學生認爲，雖然外出打工可以豐富自己的社會經驗，提高自己的能力，並且可以掙一些零花錢和生活費，但是就目前來說，考研和考TOEFL、GRE 大於(10)一切。否則(11)，畢業後很難有機會出國進修或者找到一份好的工作。

第十九课 考试的"枪手"问题

　　在北京大学的研究生楼前，我看到了这样的启事："诚聘（急）八月托福（TOEFL）男代考。价格面议。"大概因为心虚，启事下面还专门⑴用英文注明："对不起，只能用 e-mail (xx@yahoo.com) 联系。"同时，这类启事在北京其他著名大学也常能看到。

　　代考者又称⑵"枪手"，意思是专替他人达成目标的人。高额的酬劳无疑⑶是穷学生愿意充当这个角色的主要原因。同样毫无⑷疑问的是，学生们对这类事情的违规性质十分清楚。

枪手	槍手	qiāngshǒu	n.	one who sits for an examination in place of another person 枪: gun
北京大学	北京大學	Běijīng Dàxué	n.	Peking University
研究生		yánjiūshēng	n.	graduate student
研究生楼	研究生樓	yánjiūshēng lóu	n.	graduate student dormitory 楼: storied building
启事	啓事	qǐshì	n.	notice; announcement
诚聘	誠聘	chéng pìn	v.	(written) sincerely would like to hire
急		jí	adj./ adv.	urgent, urgently
托福		Tuōfú	n.	TOEFL, Test of English as a Foreign Language
代考		dàikǎo	n./v.	one who sits for an examination

				in place of another person, take an exam for somebody else
价格	價格	jiàgé	*n.*	price
面议	面議	miànyì	*v.*	discuss in person 面：当面 议：讨论
心虚	心虛	xīnxū	*adj.*	with a guilty conscience; afraid of being found out
专门	專門	zhuānmén	*adv.*	specially 专门为儿童写的故事/专门研究中国历史
注明		zhùmíng	*v.*	make a footnote; mark out
联系	聯繫	liánxì	*v.*	contact
著名		zhùmíng	*adj.*	famous; celebrated
称	稱	chēng	*v.*	call; be called
专	專	zhuān	*adv.*	especially; 专门
替		tì	*prep.*	for; on behalf of 替他担心/替他想个办法/替他做功课
他人		tārén	*n.*	another person; other people
达成	達成	dáchéng	*v.*	realize; achieve
高额	高額	gāoé	*adj.*	a large amount (of money)
酬劳	酬勞	chóuláo	*n.*	compensation; reward; payment
无疑	無疑	wúyí	*adv.*	undoubtedly
充当	充當	chōngdāng	*v.*	play the part of; act as
角色		juésè	*n.*	role; part
毫无——	毫無——	háowú	*adv.*	not at all; not in the least 毫无关系/毫无经验/毫无疑问
违规	違規	wéiguī	*v.-o.*	violate regulations 违：违反；violate 规：规定；stipulation; rule
性质	性質	xìngzhì	*n.*	nature; quality; character

教务处的老师并不否认这类事情的存在，他们还举出了去年发生的几起代考案。教务处表示，学校对代考的处理是非常严厉的。去年学校化学系一个女生为人代考托福，学校发现后毫不(5)留情地把她开除了。只要发现这种违规情形，不仅将学生的情况上网，而且在全校发布通告。

但当问起学校是否(6)有其他办法防止这类事件发生时，几位老师都认为，想在学校考试范围之外管住这种行为比较困难。首先(7)是考试不一定在校内进行，难以(8)查找；其次，即使在校内进行，也只是一部分，而且人数众多，10 多个考场，每个考场少则 30-40人，多则(9)60 人，没有那么多时间和精力去逐一查看；第三，现在假证件四处泛滥，曾经有过一人带有好几个身份证的事情出现，而

教务处	教務處	jiàowùchù	n.	Dean's office; office of teaching affairs
否认	否認	fǒurèn	v.	deny
举出	舉出	jǔchū	v.	give (an example); cite as an example
起		qǐ	AN	measure word for legal cases or occurrences
——案		àn	suffix	case
处理	處理	chǔlǐ	v./n.	handle; manage; settle
严厉	嚴厲	yánlì	adj.	stern; severe
化学	化學	huàxué	n.	chemistry
系		xì	n.	(of a university) department

毫不留情		háobù liúqíng	*phr.*	show no mercy whatsoever; absolutely without consideration for others
开除	開除	kāichú	*v.*	expel; discharge; fire
将	將	jiāng	*prep.*	把
发布	發布	fābù	*v.*	announce; issue
通告		tōnggào	*n.*	public notice; announcement
防止		fángzhǐ	*v.*	prevent
范围	範圍	fànwéi	*n.*	scope; range; extent
管住		guǎn//zhù	*v.-c.*	control
首先		shǒuxiān	*conj.*	first; firstly
校内		xiàonèi	*n.*	inside the university
进行	進行	jìnxíng	*v.*	carry on/out; conduct
难以——	難以——	nányǐ	*adv.*	difficult to
查找		cházhǎo	*v.*	seek
其次		qícì	*conj.*	second; secondly
人数	人數	rénshù	*n.*	number of people
众多	衆多	zhòngduō	*adj.*	multitudinous; numerous 人口众多
考场	考場	kǎochǎng	*n.*	examination hall or room
逐一		zhúyī	*adv.*	one by one 逐一检查/逐一解决/逐一分析
查看		chákàn	*v.*	look over; examine; check
假		jiǎ	*adj.*	fake
证件	證件	zhèngjiàn	*n.*	certificate; credentials; papers
四处	四處	sìchù	*n.*	all around; everywhere
曾经	曾經	céngjīng	*adv.*	once have v.-ed （The negative form is 不曾） 曾经去过/曾经参加过
身份证	身份證	shēnfèn zhèng	*n.*	identity card

且足以⑽以假乱真，老师们又怎么能一一识别？再说，张贴广告的人什么时候出现，广告贴在什么地方，学校不可能时时监督，而且学生在学习之外、校园之外做什么事情又不是学校管得了的。所以，事先采取有效措施制止这一行为几乎无法做到，只能在发现后给予⑾严厉制裁。同时，北大教务处还表示，解决这一问题不能光靠惩罚，还需要考试机制的改革。

　　这些高等院校的学生是国家最值得骄傲的精英，但却受金钱驱使，心甘情愿⑿充当他人的工具，做出违规的事情，不能不说是教育的缺陷、知识的悲哀。仅靠事后处罚挡得住金钱的诱惑吗？

《光明日报》2000 年 7 月 19 日

足以——		zúyǐ	adv.	enough; sufficiently
以假乱真	以假亂真	yǐ jiǎ luàn zhēn	idm.	pass fake imitations for genuine; mix the spurious with the genuine
一一		yīyī	adv.	one by one; one after another
识别	識別	shíbié	v.	discern; distinguish
张贴	張貼	zhāngtiē	v.	post; put up (poster, etc.)
贴	貼	tiē	v.	paste; glue; post
时时	時時	shíshí	adv.	constantly; often
管得了		guǎn.deliǎo	v.-c.	be able to interfere
事先		shìxiān	adv.	in advance; beforehand
采取	採取	cǎiqǔ	v.	adopt; take
有效		yǒuxiào	adj.	effective; valid
措施		cuòshī	n.	measure; step
制止		zhìzhǐ	v.	stop; put an end to
几乎	幾乎	jīhū	adv.	almost; nearly

给予	給予	jǐyǔ	v.	(written) give 给予同情/给予支持/对有困难者 给予帮助
光		guāng	adv.	only
惩罚	懲罰	chéngfá	v./n.	punish, punishment
机制	機制	jīzhì	n.	mechanism
高等		gāoděng	adj.	higher; advanced
院校		yuànxiào	n.	colleges and universities
精英		jīngyīng	n.	elite
驱使	驅使	qūshǐ	v.	prompt; urge
心甘情愿	心甘情願	xīn'gān qíngyuàn	idm.	be totally willing to; be perfectly happy to
工具		gōngjù	n.	tool; instrument
缺陷		quēxiàn	n.	flaw; defect
悲哀		bēiāi	n./adj.	sorrow, sad; sorrowful
处罚	處罰	chǔfá	v./n.	punish, punishment; penalty
挡得住	擋得住	dǎng.de zhù	v.-c.	be able to block; be able to keep off
诱惑	誘惑	yòuhuò	n./v.	temptation, tempt; seduce

词语例句

(1) 专门: specially

◆启事下面还专门用英文注明…

Under the notice it is specially noted in English that ….

1. 这家商店专门卖旅游方面的书籍。

This shop specializes in selling books on traveling.

2. 他专门到北京来参加英语辅导班。

He came to Beijing specifically to enroll in an English tutorial class.

(2) A 又称 B: A is also called B

◆ 代考者又称"枪手"。

People who take an examination in place of another person are also called "shooters."

1. 纽约又称"大苹果"。

New York is nicknamed "The Big Apple."

2. 电脑在中国又称"电子计算机"。

Computers are also called "electric calculating machines" in China.

(3) 无疑: beyond doubt; undoubtedly

◆ 高额的酬劳无疑是穷学生愿意充当这个角色的主要原因。

Doubtlessly the great amount of reward is the major reason that poor students are willing to play such a role.

1. 这无疑是他自己的错。

It was doubtlessly his own fault.

2. 保护人民的利益无疑是政府的责任。

Without a doubt it is the government's responsibility to protect the people's interests.

(4) 毫无 n. : no … at all; there is no … at all

◆ 毫无疑问的是，学生们对这类事情的违规性质十分清楚。

There is no doubt that college students know very well that this kind of business is against the university's regulations.

1. 他对找工作的事毫无信心。

He was not confident of finding a job at all.

2. 我不选历史课是因为我对历史毫无兴趣。

I don't take history courses because I am not interested in history at all.

(5) 毫不 v./adj. : not …at all

◆ 学校毫不留情地把她开除了。

The school expelled her without any mercy whatsoever.

1. 他很自私，对别人的事毫不关心。

   He is so selfish that he doesn't care about other people's concerns at all.

2. 考试以前他已经做了充分的准备，所以考试的时候毫不紧张。

   He was not nervous during the test at all because he had prepared sufficiently before the test.

(6) 是否: whether or not; whether; if

◆ 学校是否有其他办法防止这类事件发生？

Does the school have other ways to prevent this kind of thing from happening?

1. 这个政策是否有效很难判断。

   It is hard to judge if this policy is effective.

2. 我们并不知道是否每个大学都存在这样的问题。

   We don't know if this kind of problem exists in every university.

(7) 首先…，其次… : first … , second …

◆ 首先，考试不一定是在校内进行，难以查找；其次，人数众多，老师没有那么多时间和精力去逐一查看。

First, the examination does not necessarily take place on campus, so it is difficult to search (for "shooters"); secondly, the people taking the examination are numerous, so the teachers don't have enough energy or time to check them one by one.

1. 我认为小学生不应该做生意。首先，这样做会影响他们的学习成绩；其次，生意经也会使他们接受金钱万能的观念。

   I think primary school students should not do business because first, doing business will affect their academic grades; second, these tricks of business will also make them accept the concept of "money is omnipotent."

2. 在家长会上，老师首先向家长介绍了学生的情况，其次，希望家长配合老师注意学生的道德培养。

   During the parents' meeting, the teacher first gave the parents an introduction on how their kids behave; then, she asked that the parents would work with teachers to pay attention to students' moral development.

(8) 难以 v. : difficult to; hard to

◆考试不一定是在校内进行，难以查找。

The examination does not necessarily take place on campus, so it is difficult to search (for "shooters").

1. 他中文说得那么好，让人难以相信他只学了三个月。

He speaks Chinese so well that it is hard to believe that he has studied it for only three months.

2. 如果不是亲眼看到，真难以想像世界上还有那么落后的地方。

If I had not seen it with my own eyes, it would be hard to imagine that there were such backward places in this world.

(9) adj. 1 则…，adj. 2 则…:

◆ 考试的人太多，每个考场少则 30-40 人，多则 60 人。

There are too many people taking the test: even the less crowded testing halls had 30 to 40 people in them, while some had as many as 60.

1. 学校要是发现学生替人代考，轻则警告，重则开除。

As soon as the school found out students were taking exams in place of others, it gave light punishments like warnings and heavy ones like expulsions.

2. 他每年总要在纽约住一段时间，长则半年，短则一个月。

Every year he lives for a period of time in New York, sometimes as much as half a year, sometimes as little as a month.

(10) 足以 v. : enough to; sufficiently

◆ …，而且他的假身份证足以以假乱真。

…, moreover his fake identity card (is so real that it) can be taken for a genuine one.

1. 他挣钱不多，但是足以维持自己的生活。

He does not earn a large salary, but it is adequate to support himself.

2. 我才学了半年，我的中文水平还不足以看报纸。

I have studied for only half a year, so my Chinese level is still not high enough to read the newspaper.

(11) 给予 v. : give (usually take abstract noun as direct object)

◆ 所以，事先采取有效措施制止这一行为几乎无法做到，只能在发现后给予严厉制裁。

Therefore, there is almost no way to take effective action beforehand to prevent this kind of behavior; the only thing that can be done is to give offenders severe punishment after they are caught.

1. 每次我遇到困难的时候，家人和朋友总是给予我最大的帮助。

Every time I encounter difficulty, my family and friends always give me all the help they can.

2. 很多人希望政府能对儿童乞丐的问题给予充分的重视。

A lot of people hoped the government could pay ample attention to the issue of child beggars.

⑿ 心甘情愿: be totally willing to; be perfectly happy to

◆ 这些高等院校的学生是国家最值得骄傲的精英，但却受金钱驱使，心甘情愿充当他人的工具，做出违规的事情。

These students are the elites who are the pride of the nation, but they succumb to the temptation of money and are willing to serve as a tool of others to do things against the regulations.

1. 为了金钱和地位，她心甘情愿嫁给了一个老头儿。

She was totally willing to marry an old chap for money and status.

2. 虽然英语辅导班收费很高，但是许多学生为了学好英文心甘情愿付高额的学费。

Although the English training center's tuition is very high, many students are willing to pay a lot to study English.

练习

I. Answer the questions using the expressions provided.

1. 目前中国大学生追求的主要目标是什么？（无疑）
2. 你为什么不选电脑作为你的专业呢？（毫无 n.）
3. 学校真的会开除替人代考的学生吗？（毫不 v.）
4. 要减少环境污染，你认为应当怎么做？（首先…，其次…）
5. 大学的考试都是一个小时吗？ （adj.1 则…，adj. 2 则…）
6. 学校中存在枪手，说明学生的品德很差，不是吗？（不足以）
7. 中国的报纸也起监督政府的作用吗（是否）

II. Fill in the blank with the most appropriate word. Each word should be used only once.

心虚	否认	毫无疑问	时时
是否	难以	一一	防止

在公共汽车上，你的钱包被偷了。要想知道是谁偷的，有一个办法。虽然跟别人一样，小偷也①偷了钱包，可因为他②，不敢看你的眼睛，所以要是谁不愿意面对你，③他就是小偷。

可是，有时候由于车上人多，④⑤查看，很可能找不到小偷。所以⑥钱包被偷最好的办法就是⑦小心，查看钱包⑧还在身上。

III. Composition

你是美国某大学东亚系的系主任，要写一份"招聘启事"，聘请一位中文老师。请你想一想，这位老师应该有什么条件？请参考 (consult; refer to) 下面加州大学的招聘启事。

Chinese Lecturer
California State University, Long Beach

The Department of Asian and Asian American Studies invites applications for a full-time lectureship in Chinese for a three-year appointment. Ph.D or Ed.D in a field related to Chinese Language Studies/Education at the time of appointment and potential for effective teaching and scholarship required. Candidates must have native or near native language competency in Chinese, as well as substantial knowledge and appreciation of Chinese culture. Applicants should have the ability to communicate and work effectively with an ethnically and culturally diverse campus community. Desired qualifications include expertise in the field of second language acquisition or other related fields. Candidates with training experience or interest in heritage language teaching and learning will be given preference. Also preferred are candidates who have expertise in instructional technology or in writing grant proposals with a record of receiving grants. The selection process will commence on March 19, 2001, and continue until the position is filled. Send a letter of application, resume, official transcript, and 3 letters of recommendation to Dr. Smith, Search Committee Chair, Asian and Asian American Studies Department, CSULB, Long Beach, CA 90840-1002. An EEO/AA employer.

IV. Answer the following questions.

1. 在美国，为别人代考的事情普遍不普遍？一旦被发现，会受到什么惩罚？为什么在美国考试的枪手并不普遍？跟教育制度和社会情况有什么关系？

2. 托福考试在中国这么热，反映了什么问题？

3. 每年中国都有成千上万的大学毕业生到美国留学，这对中国有什么好处？有什么坏处？

4. 谈谈美国学校里"考试作弊" (zuòbì: cheat) 的情形。

繁体字课文

在北京大學的研究生樓前，我看到了這樣的啓事："誠聘（急）八月托福（TOEFL）男代考。價格面議。"大概因爲心虛，啓事下面還專門(1)用英文注明："對不起，只能用 e-mail (xx@yahoo.com) 聯繫。"同時，這類啓事在北京其他著名大學也常能看到。

代考者又稱(2)"槍手"，意思是專替他人達成目標的人。高額的酬勞無疑(3)是窮學生願意充當這個角色的主要原因。同樣毫無(4)疑問的是，學生們對這類事情的違規性質十分清楚。

教務處的老師並不否認這類事情的存在，他們還舉出了去年發生的幾起代考案。教務處表示，學校對代考的處理是非常嚴厲的。去年學校化學系一個女生爲人代考托福，學校發現後毫不(5)留情地把她開除了。只要發現這種違規情形，不僅將學生的情況上網，而且在全校發布通告。

但當問起學校是否(6)有其他辦法防止這類事件發生時，幾位老師都認爲，想在學校考試範圍之外管住這種行爲比較困難。首先(7)是考試不一定在校內進行，難以(8)查找；其次，即使在校內進行，也只是一部分，而且人數衆多，10 多個考場，每個考場少則 30-40 人，多則(9)60 人，沒有那麼多時間和精力去逐一查看；第三，現在假證件四處泛濫，曾經有過一人帶有好幾個身份證的事情出現，而且足以(10)以假亂真，老師們又怎麼能一一識別？再說，張貼廣告的人什麼時候出現，廣告貼在什麼地方，學校不可能時時監督，而且學生在學習之外、校園之外做什麼事情又不是學校管得了的。所以，事先採取有效措施制止這一行爲幾乎無法做到，只能在發現後給予(11)嚴厲制裁。同時，北大教務處還表示，解決這一問題不能光靠懲罰，還需要考試機制的改革。

這些高等院校的學生是國家最值得驕傲的精英，但却受金錢驅使，心甘情願(12)充當他人的工具，做出違規的事情，不能不說是教育的缺陷、知識的悲哀。僅靠事後處罰擋得住金錢的誘惑嗎？

第二十课　赡养老人是子女应尽的责任

　　我国《婚姻法》明确规定：成年子女有赡养老人的义务。但是，近年来人民法院受理的农村赡养老人案件有所⑴增加，有的地区约占民事案件的 10%。由此⑵看出，目前农村老年人的生活还存在一定的困难。

　　如果到我国北方农村走走，就会发现不少老人住在简陋的小房子里。据了解，造成这种状况的原因，有的是子女嫌弃⑶老人，不愿跟老人住在一起；有的是几个子女成家后已经把家产全部分光⑷，根本没有老人的份儿，老人被迫另建小房子住。

　　老年人失去劳动能力后，种地就成了一大难题。老年人只好求助于⑸子女，把土地分给子女耕种，秋后要粮食。少数子女分地时

赡养	贍養	shànyǎng	*v.*	support (parents); provide for (parents)
老人		lǎorén	*n.*	(here) one's aged parents or grandparents
应尽的	應盡的	yīngjìn.de	*adj.*	bounden (duty); obligatory
婚姻法		hūnyīnfǎ	*n.*	marriage law
明确	明確	míngquè	*adv./ adj.*	clearly, clear and definite
规定	規定	guīdìng	*v./n.*	stipulate; provide, stipulation; rule; provision
成年		chéngnián	*v.*	grow up; come of age
受理		shòulǐ	*v.*	accept and hear (a case)
农村	農村	nóngcūn	*n.*	rural area; countryside

案件		ànjiàn	n.	law case; legal case
地区	地區	dìqū	n.	area; district; region
约	約	yuē	adv.	approximately; 大约
民事		mínshì	adj.	relating to civil law; civil
由此		yóu cǐ	conj.	from this
一定		yídìng	adj.	certain
北方		běifāng	n.	north; northern part of the country
简陋	簡陋	jiǎnlòu	adj.	simple and crude
嫌弃	嫌棄	xiánqì	v.	dislike and avoid; cold-shoulder
成家		chéng//jiā	v.-o.	(of a man) get married; start a family
家产	家產	jiāchǎn	n.	family property
全部		quánbù	n./adj.	whole; complete; entire; total; all
分		fēn	v.	distribute; allot
——光		guāng	adj.	used up; with nothing left
份儿		fènr	n.	share; portion
被迫		bèipò	v.	be forced to; be compelled to 被迫搬到农村/被迫把钱还给同学/被迫离开
另		lìng	adv.	separately
建		jiàn	v.	build
失去		shīqù	v.	lose
种地	種地	zhòng//dì	v.-o.	cultivate land
难题	難題	nántí	n.	difficult problem; tough question
求助于	求助於	qiúzhùyú	v.	seek for help from; turn to sb. for help
土地		tǔdì	n.	land
耕种	耕種	gēngzhòng	v.	cultivate; plough and sow
秋后	秋後	qiūhòu	n.	after the autumn harvest
粮食	糧食	liáng.shi	n.	grain; cereals; food
少数	少數	shǎoshù	adj./n.	small number of; few, minority

嫌(6)少，给粮时怕多，使老人要粮食如同要饭一样(7)难。

一些子女忘记当年父母把自己养育成人的辛苦，眼看(8)父母已经步入老年人的行列(9)，需要子女的照顾，却互相推委，不愿赡养老人。

当今农村有一种习惯，就是随着(10)几个子女成家，父母的财产也被分光。子女不愿或没能力赡养老人，往往让老人轮流(11)到几个子女家中生活，有的甚至把老两口分开，一家养一个。这种方法看起来似乎合理，但因为老人没有一个固定的住处，心里很不踏实。他们并没有享受到子孙满堂的天伦之乐，伴随他们的却只有孤独和寂寞。

总之，由于各地经济条件、老人的性格、子女的道德修养等不一样，老年人的生活状况存在很大差异，尤其是农村中部分老年人的生活状况令人担忧。希望天下做子女的(12)都能让父母在清静和谐的环境中安度晚年。

《人民日报》1999 年 8 月 5 日

嫌		xián	v.	dislike; mind
如同		rútóng	v.	like; similar to
要饭	要飯	yào//fàn	v.-o.	beg (for food or money)
忘记	忘記	wàngjì	v.	forget
当年	當年	dāngnián	n.	in those years
养育	養育	yǎngyù	v.	bring up; rear; raise
成人		chéngrén	v.	grow up; become full-grown

辛苦		xīnkǔ	*n./adj.*	hardship, hard; laborious
眼看		yǎnkàn	*v.*	look on passively; watch helplessly
步入		bùrù	*v.*	walk into; step into
行列		hángliè	*n.*	ranks (of people, vehicles, etc.); procession
推委	推諉	tuīwěi	*v.*	shift responsibility onto others
随着	隨著	suí.zhe	*prep.*	along with; in the wake of
财产	財産	cáichǎn	*n.*	property; fortune
轮流	輪流	lúnliú	*adv.*	take turns; do sth. in turn 我们两个人轮流开车。
老两口儿		lǎoliǎngkǒur	*n.*	old couple
分开	分開	fēn//kāi	*v.-c.*	separate; part; split
固定		gùdìng	*adj.*	fixed; regular
住处	住處	zhùchù	*n.*	dwelling (place); residence
踏实	踏實	tā.shi	*adj.*	free from anxiety
享受		xiǎngshòu	*v.*	enjoy
子孙满堂	子孫滿堂	zǐsūn mǎntáng	*idm.*	(of a person) be blessed with many children and grandchildren
天伦之乐	天倫之樂	tiānlún zhī lè	*idm.*	family happiness; the happiness of a family reunion
伴随	伴隨	bànsuí	*v.*	accompany
孤独	孤獨	gūdú	*adj./n.*	lonely; solitary, loneliness
修养	修養	xiūyǎng	*n.*	self-cultivation
差异	差異	chāyì	*n.*	difference
担忧	擔憂	dānyōu	*v.*	worry
天下		tiānxià	*n.*	whole world; in the world
清静		qīngjìng	*adj.*	quiet; tranquil; secluded
安度		ān dù	*v.*	spend (one's remaining years) in happiness
晚年		wǎnnián	*n.*	old age; one's later years

词语例句

(1) 有所 v. : have v-ed to some extent

◆ 近年来人民法院受理的农村赡养老人案件有所增加。

During recent years the cases heard in the people's court of old people in rural areas not getting support from their children have increased to some extent.

1. 经过一段时间的学习，他的中文水平有所提高。

After a period of studying, his Chinese improved to some extent.

2. 最近两国的关系有所改善。

Recently the relations between these two countries have improved to some extent.

(2) 由此 : from this; by this

◆ 由此看出，目前农村老年人的生活还存在一定的困难。

Judging from this, there still exist certain difficulties in the lives of old people in rural areas.

1. 她的中文水平跟一个月以前完全不同了。由此看来，这个语言培训班的确有用。

Her Chinese is completely different from that of a month before. Judging from this, this language program is really effective.

2. 要是你一定要这么做，那由此产生的后果由你自己负责。

If you insist on doing it this way, you will be responsible for all the consequences afterwards.

(3) 嫌弃: dislike and avoid; give the cold-shoulder

◆ 有的子女嫌弃老人，不愿跟老人住在一起。

Some children dislike their parents and don't want to live together with them.

1. 无论你的父母多么贫穷，你都不应该嫌弃他们。

You should not dislike and avoid your parents no matter how poor they are.

2. 他做生意赔了钱，太太居然嫌弃他而跟他离婚了。

He lost a lot of money in business. Unexpectedly he was given the cold shoulder by his wife and got divorced.

(4) v. 光: v. it all up; consumed completely

◆ 有的子女成家后把家产分光，根本没有老人的份儿。

Some children allotted all the property between themselves and left nothing to their parents.

1. 只有很少的几个菜，很快就吃光了。

There are only few dishes, and they were eaten up in no time.

2. 两个星期过去，他们的钱都用光了。

Two weeks have passed. They have used up all their money.

(5) 求助于: turn to sb. for help

◆ 有的老年人只好求助于子女。

Some elderly people had to turn to their children for help.

1. 他们离婚的时候发生了严重的争执，只好求助于律师。

They had to turn to a lawyer for help because of their serious arguments when getting a divorce.

2. 要是你有困难，可以求助于老师。

Go to your teacher for help if you are having any difficulty.

(6) 嫌: dislike; mind; complain about

◆ 少数子女分地时嫌少，给粮时怕多。

A small number of children dislike receiving little when being given land, but worry about giving too much grain to their parents.

1. 我不想租这所房子，主要嫌它太旧，也离学校太远。

I don't feel like renting this house mainly because I find it too old and too far away from school.

2. 她的父母嫌她的男朋友是农村人，又没有钱。

Her parents dislike her boyfriend because he is from a rural area and has no money.

(7) 如同…一样 (+ adj.) : like; similar to

◆ 老人要粮食如同要饭一样难。

It is as difficult as a beggar asking for food when the parents ask for grain (from their children.)

1. 他们对待我们如同家人一样。

They treated us like their family.

2. 住在留学生宿舍如同住在旅馆一样，既舒服又方便。

Living in the foreign students' dormitory is just like living in a hotel; it is both comfortable and convenient.

(8) 眼看: look on passively; watch helplessly

◆ 一些子女眼看父母已经步入老年人的行列，需要子女的照顾，却互相推委。

While their parents grew old and began to need their care, they just looked on passively and pushed the responsibility onto each other.

1. 旁边的人眼看她的钱包被偷，却不说一句话。

People next to her just looked on passively and didn't say a word while her purse was stolen.

2. 你怎么能眼看那个乞丐饿死而不给他东西吃？

How could you watch that beggar dying of starvation and not to give him anything to eat?

(9) 步入…的行列: step into the ranks of

◆ 一些子女眼看父母已经步入老年人的行列，需要子女的照顾，却互相推委。

1. 中国早已步入发展中国家的行列。

China stepped into the ranks of developing countries a long time ago.

2. 我国发展的目标是步入工业国家的行列。

Our developing goal is to step into the ranks of industrial countries.

(10) 随着: along with…

◆ 随着几个子女成家，父母的财产也被分光。

Along with the children getting married, their parents' property is also all distributed to the children.

1. 随着科技的进步，人们的生活也不断改善。

Along with the advancement of science and technology, people's lives are also improving continuously.

2. 随着电子邮件的广泛使用，写信的人越来越少了。

Along with the extensive use of e-mail, there are fewer and fewer people who write letters.

(11) 轮流: take turns; do sth. in turn

◆ 子女不愿或没能力赡养老人，往往让老人轮流到几个子女家中生活。

Because some children are not willing to or unable to support their parents, they often let their parents move from one son's or daughter's house to another in turn.

1. 我们既然住在一起，就应该轮流做家务。

Since we live together, we should do the household jobs in turn.

2. 从华盛顿到波士顿远是远，但是两个人轮流开车就不会太累。

It is indeed far from Washington to Boston, but it wouldn't be too tiresome if two were to take turns driving.

⑿ 做 n.的: each and every one who is …

◆ 希望天下做子女的都能让父母在清静和谐的环境中安度晚年。
I wish that all the children would provide their parents with a quiet and harmonious environment for them to spend their remaining years in happiness.

1. 做老师的有责任帮助学习有困难的学生。
All teachers have the responsibility of helping those students with learning difficulties.

2. 做父母的当然关心自己的孩子，这是毫无疑问的。
It is doubtless that parents are concerned about their children.

练习

I. Choose the phrase that is closest in meaning to the underlined phrase in the sentence.

1. 近年来人民法院受理的农村赡养老人案件有所增加。
    a. 增加了很多　b. 增加了一些　c. 增加的很少

2. 老年人只好求助于子女。
    a. 请子女帮助他们　b. 帮助子女　c. 请别人帮助子女

3. 有些人不愿给父母粮食，使父母要粮食如同要饭一样难。
    a. 如果　b. 相同　c. 好像

4. 子女成家后，把家产分光，没有老人的份儿。
    a. 结婚　b. 长大　c. 养育成人

II. Complete the following sentences using the expression provided.

1. 我真没想到她居然……。（眼看）
2. 要是你不喜欢这份工作，我认为……。（另）
3. 有的孩子不愿意跟父母一块儿住，因为……。（嫌）
4. 现在在报上也能看到批评政府的文章了，……。（由此看出）

III. Make sentence using the underlined expression.

1. 我国婚姻法明确规定，子女有赡养老人的义务。

2. 在农村有不少老人孤独地住在简陋的小房子里。<u>据了解</u>，是因为有的子女嫌弃老人，不愿跟他们住在一起。

3. 老年人失去劳动能力<u>后</u>，种地就成了<u>一大难题</u>。

4. <u>随着</u>子女成家，父母的财产也被分光了。

IV. Read the following passage and summarize it in Chinese.

What is neglect of elders? Neglect can be intentional or unintentional. If a relative or caregiver deliberately fails to give an elder what he or she needs, this is intentional neglect, which is a crime. Either way, neglect means that an elder is suffering from deprivation or abandonment. Neglect can involve a failure to meet basic needs, such as food, housing, medicine, clothing, or physical aids. Sometimes caregivers fail to keep elders clean and comfortable. An elder who is being neglected may be left alone, even if he or she needs supervision to be safe. Elders can be deprived of essential medical services like doctor's appointments. This is also neglect.

V. Answer the following questions.

1. 中国一向是个重视孝道的社会，但从这篇文章来看，中国农村老人的生活是非常困难的。孩子们为什么不照顾老人的生活了？是不是孩子越来越自私了？

2. 要想改善中国老人的生活，应该采取哪些措施？提倡传统的孝顺是不是一个有效的方法？

3. 对老年人的生活，政府有没有责任？

4. 从这篇文章所看到的中国老年人的生活跟美国老年人的生活有什么不同？

繁体字课文

我國《婚姻法》明確規定：成年子女有贍養老人的義務。但是，近年來人民法院受理的農村贍養老人案件有所(1)增加，有的地區約占民事案件的 10%。由此(2)看出，目前農村老年人的生活還存在一定的困難。

如果到我國北方農村走走，就會發現不少老人住在簡陋的小房子裏。據瞭解，造成這種狀況的原因，有的是子女嫌棄(3)老人，不願跟老人住在一起；有的是幾個子女成家後已經把家產全部分光(4)，根本沒有老人的份儿，老人被迫另建小房子住。

老年人失去勞動能力後，種地就成了一大難題。老年人只好求助於(5)子女，把土地分給子女耕種，秋後要糧食。少數子女分地時嫌(6)少，給糧時怕多，使老人要糧食如同要飯一樣(7)難。

一些子女忘記當年父母把自己養育成人的辛苦，眼看(8)父母已經步入老年人的行列(9)，需要子女的照顧，却互相推諉，不願贍養老人。

當今農村有一種習慣，就是隨著(10)幾個子女成家，父母的財產也被分光。子女不願或沒能力贍養老人，往往讓老人輪流(11)到幾個子女家中生活，有的甚至把老兩口分開，一家養一個。這種方法看起來似乎合理，但因爲老人沒有一個固定的住處，心裏很不踏實。他們並沒有享受到子孫滿堂的天倫之樂，伴隨他們的却只有孤獨和寂寞。

總之，由於各地經濟條件、老人的性格、子女的道德修養等不一樣，老年人的生活狀況存在很大差異，尤其是農村中部分老年人的生活狀況令人擔憂。希望天下做子女的(12)都能讓父母在清靜和諧的環境中安度晚年。

第二十一课　　中国老人需要关怀

中国 1/5 的老人生活在空荡荡(1)的家中。子女到大城市寻找工作，而(2)父母却在空空的房子中孤独地生活着。

子女决定到其他城市寻找更好的就业机会时，没有几个(3)中国父母会感到高兴。在中国 1.2 亿 60 岁以上父母当中(4)，有 1/5 的人受到子女在外就业情况的影响。

在传统的中国社会，老人受到年轻人的尊敬。年轻人从师长和父母那里学到生活哲学的基本原则。但近几十年来，越来越多的退休老人生活在空荡荡的家中，尽管其中 60%的人更希望跟子女共同生活。最近一项调查结果表明，子女也希望能够照顾自己的父母。

大部分父母和子女都认为这种孤独的情况是暂时的。父母希望出门在外的子女回到故乡一家团聚，或者功成名就的子女将他们接到大城市生活。

有些年轻人企图通过给老人钱来弥补这种离弃的行为，但他们忘记了老人需要的是关心和照顾。

关怀	關懷	guānhuái	n./v.	warm solicitude, show loving care; show solicitude for
空荡荡	空蕩蕩	kōngdàng dàng	adj.	empty; deserted
寻找	尋找	xúnzhǎo	v.	look for; seek
空		kōng	adj.	empty

就业	就業	jiù//yè	v.-o.	obtain employment; take up an occupation; get a job
亿	億	yì		hundred million
当中	當中	dāngzhōng	prep.	among 在学生当中有15%的外国人。
在外		zàiwài		away from home
尊敬		zūnjìng	n./v.	respect
师长	師長	shīzhǎng	n.	teachers and elders
生活哲学	生活哲學	shēnghuó zhéxué	n.	philosophy of life
基本		jīběn	adj.	basic; fundamental
原则	原則	yuánzé	n.	principle
退休		tuìxiū	v.	retire
共同		gòngtóng	adv.	together; jointly 共同生活/共同努力
表明	表明	biǎomíng	v.	make known; make clear; state clearly; indicate
能够		nénggòu	aux.	can; be able to; be capable of
暂时	暫時	zànshí	adj./adv.	temporary; for the time being, temporarily
故乡	故鄉	gùxiāng	n.	native place; hometown
团聚	團聚	tuánjù	v.	reunite; family reunite
功成名就		gōngchéng míngjiù	idm.	(of a person's career) be successful and famous
接		jiē	v.	meet; welcome 去机场接朋友/把父母接到家里
企图	企圖	qǐtú	v.	attempt; seek; try 他企图找人代考。
弥补	彌補	míbǔ	v.	make up; remedy 弥补过错/弥补缺陷/弥补自己的短处
离弃	離棄	líqì	v.	abandon; desert
关心	關心	guānxīn	v./n.	be concerned about

在失去子女的情况下，有些老人开始创造自己的生活方式，上海和北京在 60 岁以上老人之间开展的"时间储蓄计划"就证明了这一点。

67 岁的寡妇郎淑珍在照顾着另一位 95 岁的孤独老人，帮她做饭、洗澡、买东西、打扫房间、陪她散步，无微不至(5)地照料着老人。

她的所有工作都记录在一个银行帐户上。帐户上记录的不是钱数而是时间：洗衣服 4 小时，买东西 2 小时，打扫房间 5 小时。

根据这个"时间储蓄计划"，郎淑珍日后无法生活自理的时候，她将有权(6)得到与现在"投资"的同等时间的照料和服务。

比起农村的老人来(7)，城市的情况要好些。农村的老人不得不(8)眼睁睁地看着(9)子女到大城市谋生，将他们孤零零地留在空荡荡的家中。

《参考消息》1999 年 7 月 5 日

创造	創造	chuàngzào	v.	create
开展	開展	kāizhǎn	v.	develop; launch
储蓄	儲蓄	chǔxù	v.	save; deposit
这一点	這一點	zhèi yī diǎn	n.	this point; this feature
寡妇	寡婦	guǎ.fu	n.	widow
郎淑珍		Láng Shūzhēn	n.	personal name
洗澡		xǐ//zǎo	v.	take a bath
打扫	打掃	dǎsǎo	v.	sweep; clean
陪		péi	v.	accompany

散步		sàn//bù	*v.-o.*	go for a walk
无微不至	無微不至	wú wēi bú zhì	*idm.*	considerate right down to the most trivial detail; take care of sb. in every possible way
照料		zhàoliào	*v.*	take care of; attend to
记录	記錄	jìlù	*v.*	record; write down
银行	銀行	yínháng	*n.*	bank
帐户	帳戶	zhànghù	*n.*	account
钱数	錢數	qiánshù	*n.*	amount of money
根据	根據	gēnjù	*prep.*	on the basis of; according to
日后	日後	rìhòu	*n.*	in days to come
自理		zìlǐ	*v.*	take care of or provide for oneself
将	將	jiāng	*adv.*	will; shall; be going to
投资	投資	tóuzī	*v.*	invest
同等		tóngděng	*adj.*	of the same class (rank; status); on an equal basis 同等重要/同等待遇/同等价值
服务	服務	fúwù	*n.*	service
不得不		bùdébù	*adv.*	have no choice but; cannot but
眼睁睁		yǎnzhēng zhēng	*adv.*	look on helplessly
谋生	謀生	móushēng	*v.*	make a living
孤零零		gūlínglíng	*adv.*	solitarily; lonely

词语例句

(1) 空荡荡: empty

◆ 中国 1/5 的老人生活在空荡荡的家中。

One fifth of Chinese seniors are now living in "empty homes."

1. 我真同情那些孤零零的老人。

I heartily sympathize with those lonely elderly people.

2. 屋子里黑乎乎的，我什么也看不见。

The room is quite dark, and I can't see anything.

(2) 而: while

◆ 子女到大城市寻找工作，而父母却在空空的房子中孤独地生活着。

Parents live lonely lives in the empty houses while their children go to big cities to look for job opportunities.

1. 中国老人喜欢遛鸟，而美国老人喜欢遛狗。

Elderly Chinese like to take their birds for a walk, while American old people like walking a dog.

2. 你喜欢运动，而我呢，比较喜欢看书。

You like sports while I'd rather read.

(3) 没有几个 S. ⋯ : very few S. …; not too many S. …

◆ 子女决定到其他城市寻找更好的就业机会时，没有几个中国父母会感到高兴。

When their children decided to look for better job opportunities in other cities, very few Chinese parents would feel happy.

1. 学英语的人很多，但是没有几个人真的能用英语跟外国人谈话。

There are a lot of people who study English, but very few of them could really talk with foreigners in English.

2. 很多人谈市场经济，但是没有几个人真正了解市场经济的意义。

Many people talk about market economy, but very few really understand the meaning of market economy.

(4) 在⋯当中: among; in the middle of

◆ 在中国 1.2 亿 60 岁以上父母当中，有 1/5 的人受到子女在外就业情况的影响。

One fifth of the hundred and twenty million Chinese parents over sixty years old have been affected by their children working in different places.

1. 在所有学过的课文当中，"老夫少妻"给我留下最深的印象。

   Of all the lessons I've learned, that of old husbands and young wives has make the deepest impression on me.

2. 据报导，每一百个美国人当中，就有一个人被抢劫过。

   One out of every hundred Americans have been robbed, according to the press.

(5) 无微不至: considerate right down to the most trivial detail; take care of sb. in every possible way

◆ 67 岁的寡妇郎淑珍无微不至地照料着一个 95 岁的孤独老人。

Sixty-seven-year-old widow Lang Shuzhen is taking care of a ninety-five-year-old woman who is living alone.

1. 因为他是独生子，父母对他照顾得无微不至。

   His parents take very good care of him because he is their only child.

2. 学校对学生的照顾可以说是无微不至。

   The school has been considerate to the students down to the most trivial detail.

(6) 有权 v. : have the right to

◆ 郎淑珍日后无法生活自理的时候，她将有权得到同等时间的照料和服务。

When Lang Shuzhen cannot take care of herself in the future, she will have the right to get the care and service of an equal amount of time.

1. 知识产权受到侵犯时有权要求赔偿。

   When one's intellectual property rights are infringed upon, one has the right to ask for compensation.

2. 学生有困难时有权要求帮助。

   The students have the right to ask for help when they have difficulty studying.

(7) 比起…来: when compared with

◆ 比起农村的老人来，城市的情况要好些。

When compared with the situation of elderly people in rural areas, that of seniors in urban areas is a little better.

1. 比起中国的大学生来，美国大学生独立得多。

   Compared with Chinese college students, American college students are much more independent.

2. 比起城市的人来，农村的农民比较保守。

   Compared with urban people, country people are more conservative.

(8) 不得不: have no choice but to

◆农村的老人不得不眼睁睁地看着子女到大城市谋生，将他们孤零零地留在空荡荡的家中。

The elderly in the countryside have no choice but to watch helplessly as their children going to make a living in big cities and leave them in their empty houses.

1. 我出门太晚，不得不坐出租车。

I left home too late so I had to take a taxi.

2. 他做了严重违规的事，学校不得不把他开除。

He did something seriously against the rules, so the school had no choice but to expel him.

(9) 眼睁睁地看着…: watch helplessly; look on passively

◆农村的老人不得不眼睁睁地看着子女到大城市谋生，…

1. 你怎么可以眼睁睁地看着他吃亏而不帮助他？

How could you watch him suffer losses and not help him?

2. 他们眼睁睁地看着房子被烧了，一点儿办法都没有。

They watched their house burn down and could do nothing.

练习

I. Choose the most appropriate word for each blank and fill in with its Chinese equivalent.

retire	make up	empty	lose
reunite	take extra-good care of sb.		take care of oneself

1. 春节的时候，中国人的传统是一家人 _____ 在一起，吃一顿很好的晚饭。

2. 中国政府规定，女性 55 岁就可以 _____ 。

3. 希望你能给我一个机会，让我 _____ 我所做的错事。

4. 自从他在战争中 _____ 双手以后，他的生活就不能 _____ ，幸亏妻子 _____ 地照顾他。

5. 自从儿子上大学以后，她每天没什么事可做，心里觉得_____的。

II. Make a sentence using the underlined expression.

1. 农村的老人只好<u>眼睁睁地看着</u>子女到大城市谋生，把自己留在空荡荡的家中。

2. 年轻人<u>从</u>师长和父母<u>那里学到了</u>生活哲学的基本原则。

3. 子女决定到其他城市寻找更好的工作机会时，<u>没有几个</u>父母会感到高兴。

4. <u>根据</u>这个"时间储蓄计划"，她以后有权得到同等时间的照料。

5. <u>在</u>中国 60 岁以上的父母<u>当中</u>，有 1/5 的人受到子女在外就业情况的影响。

6. <u>比起</u>农村的老人<u>来</u>，城市的情况要好些。

III. Choose the correct answer.

1. 保护环境和发展经济（同等，相同）重要。

2. 有些学生（关心，关怀）的不是学到了什么，而是成绩。

3. 在我所有的老师（之间，当中），我最喜欢的是总是带着笑容的那位。

IV. Answer the question using the expressions given.

什么是"时间储蓄计划"？

（在…情况下，在外，无法，之间，开展，打扫，买，陪，记录，账户，不是 A 而是 B, 日后，有权，照顾，服务，创造）

V. Answer the following questions.

1. 在你看来，这个"时间储蓄计划"会不会成功？

2. 英文里有 empty nest syndrome 这个词儿，请你说明这个词儿的意思。

3. 中国老年人越来越孤独寂寞了，这是做子女的责任吗？

4. 孩子不照顾老人，是经济问题还是道德问题？

5. 美国有什么样的老人问题？政府怎么解决这些问题？

6. 美国有很多养老院。这些养老院对老人的照顾都很好吗？

繁体字课文

中國 1/5 的老人生活在空蕩蕩(1)的家中。子女到大城市尋找工作，而(2)父母却在空空的房子中孤獨地生活著。

子女決定到其他城市尋找更好的就業機會時，沒有幾個(3)中國父母會感到高興。在中國 1.2 億 60 歲以上父母當中(4)，有 1/5 的人受到子女在外就業情況的影響。

在傳統的中國社會，老人受到年輕人的尊敬。年輕人從師長和父母那裏學到生活哲學的基本原則。但近幾十年來，越來越多的退休老人生活在空蕩蕩的家中，儘管其中 60%的人更希望跟子女共同生活。最近一項調查結果表明，子女也希望能够照顧自己的父母。

大部分父母和子女都認爲這種孤獨的情況是暫時的。父母希望出門在外的子女回到故鄉一家團聚，或者功成名就的子女將他們接到大城市生活。

有些年輕人企圖通過給老人錢來彌補這種離棄的行爲，但他們忘記了老人需要的是關心和照顧。

在失去子女的情況下，有些老人開始創造自己的生活方式，上海和北京在 60 歲以上老人之間開展的"時間儲蓄計劃"就證明了這一點。

67 歲的寡婦郎淑珍在照顧著另一位 95 歲的孤獨老人，幫她做飯、洗澡、買東西、打掃房間、陪她散步，無微不至(5)地照料著老人。

她的所有工作都記錄在一個銀行帳戶上。帳戶上記錄的不是錢數而是時間：洗衣服 4 小時，買東西 2 小時，打掃房間 5 小時。

　　根據這個“時間儲蓄計劃”，郎淑珍日後無法生活自理的時候，她將有權(6)得到與現在“投資”的同等時間的照料和服務。

　　比起農村的老人來(7)，城市的情況要好些。農村的老人不得不(8)眼睜睜地看著(9)子女到大城市謀生，將他們孤零零地留在空蕩蕩的家中。

第二十二课　老夫少妻为何增多？

　　三年前，二十七岁年轻活泼的方小姐嫁给了比她大二十岁的李先生。不少亲戚朋友对这个婚姻持否定态度，认为方小姐是图(1)李先生有钱有地位。有的甚至说，瞧着吧，不出三年，方小姐就(2)得闹离婚。三年过去了，现在的方小姐整天和李先生一起出出进进，与李先生的儿子也相处得很和睦。问起她嫁给"老夫"三年的感受，方小姐说："其实，当初(3)我也挺犹豫(4)，他不仅比我大二十岁，而且我一嫁过去就得给他十五岁的儿子当后妈。可李先生的才华、经济实力、办事能力让我特别倾心，而且知道怎么疼我。那些和我年龄差不多的男孩儿虽然也爱我，却并不懂得怎么爱护我。"

　　像方小姐、李先生这样"老夫少妻"的家庭近年来正逐渐增多。据报载，进入九十年代后，男比女大五岁的比例最高，达48%，男比女大十岁以上的比例也比 1987 年增加了 10%。

　　分析男女结婚年龄差距拉大的原因，首先是因为经济的缘故。

为何	為何	wèihé	conj.	why; 为什么 何：什么
活泼	活潑	huó.po	adj.	active; full of life; vivacious
方		Fāng	n.	a surname
李		Lǐ	n.	a surname
不少		bùshǎo	adj.	many; not few

亲戚	親戚	qīn.qi	n.	relative
否定		fǒudìng	adj.	negative
图	圖	tú	v.	seek; pursue
瞧着吧	瞧著吧	qiáo.zhe.ba	phr.	just wait and see
不出		bùchū	prep.	within
闹	鬧	nào	v.	make a big fuss in request for or in protest of (sth.)
过去	過去	guò.qu	v.	pass by; go by
整天		zhěngtiān	n.	all day; the whole day
出出进进	出出進進	chūchū jìnjìn	v.	going in and out
相处	相處	xiāngchǔ	v.	get along 我跟同屋相处得很好。
感受		gǎnshòu	n.	feeling; experience
当初	當初	dāngchū	n.	at the beginning; originally
犹豫	猶豫	yóuyù	v./adj.	hesitate; hesitant
后妈	後媽	hòumā	n.	stepmother
才华	才華	cáihuá	n.	brilliance of mind; genius
实力	實力	shílì	n.	strength
倾心	傾心	qīngxīn	v.	admire wholeheartedly
疼		téng	v.	love dearly
爱护	愛護	àihù	v.	care; cherish; take good care of 爱护儿童/爱护国家财产
逐渐	逐漸	zhújiàn	adv.	gradually; progressively
据报载	據報載	jù bào zǎi	phr.	according to newspaper's report
年代		niándài	n.	a decade of a century
达	達	dá	v.	reach (a place or a figure such as a price or quantity)
差距		chājù	n.	the difference (in distance; amount; progress, etc.) disparity; gap
拉大		lādà	v.	expand; enlarge
缘故	緣故	yuángù	n.	cause; reason

新中国成立以后，提倡妇女解放，女人从家庭走向社会，经济独立。男女同工同酬，收入差别不大。夫妻双方自食其力，谁也不靠谁(5)养活。在这样的经济环境下，男女自然选择年龄差不多的对象结婚。因此，六十年代至八十年代结婚的夫妻大多数年龄差距只有两三岁。

改革开放以后，人们的收入差距逐步拉大。一些事业成功的男人或(6)因为忙于(7)事业而未婚，或离婚准备再娶。这些男人虽然早已过了传统观念中结婚的年龄，但因为他们有较强的经济实力，往往成为年轻女性选择的目标。这与近年来金钱在价值观中所占分量(8)越来越重也有很大关系。

"老夫少妻"婚姻比例的增加固然与经济因素有直接关系，但现在社会里有相当一部分知识女性找比自己大很多的男性并不是为了钱，而是被年长、成熟的男人的学识、能力、体贴所(9)吸引。

除了以上这些因素以外，社会宽容度的增加也是促使"老夫少妻"增多的原因之一。现在大家觉得嫁什么人完全是个人的事，跟别人是没有关系的。"老夫少妻"的增加，表明社会允许多元化价值观的存在。

《人民日报》海外版 1999 年 11 月 5 日

妇女解放	婦女解放	fùnǚ jiěfàng	*phr.*	emancipation of women; women's liberation
走向		zǒu xiàng	*v.*	walk towards; go to
同工同酬		tónggōng tóngchóu	*phr.*	equal pay for equal work
差别		chābié	*n.*	difference; disparity
自食其力		zì shí qí lì	*idm.*	support oneself by one's own labor
养活	養活	yǎnghuó	*v.*	support; provide for
自然		zìrán	*adv.*	naturally
对象	對象	duìxiàng	*n.*	partner for marriage
至		zhì	*prep.*	to; till; until
大多数	大多數	dàduōshù	*n.*	great majority; at large
逐步		zhúbù	*adv.*	step by step; gradually
事业	事業	shìyè	*n.*	career; enterprise
忙于	忙於	mángyú	*v.*	be busy with
过	過	guò	*v.*	exceed; go beyond; surpass
分量		fènliàng	*n.*	weight; measure 分量给得不够/占很重的分量 他的话说得很有分量。
因素		yīnsù	*n.*	factor; element 决定因素/关键因素/主要因素
现实	現實	xiànshí	*adj.*	real; actual
知识女性	知識女性	zhī.shi nǚxìng	*n.*	educated women
男性	男性	nánxìng	*n.*	male sex; man
成熟		chéngshú	*adj.*	mature
学识	學識	xuéshí	*n.*	scholarly attainments; learned wisdom
宽容度	寬容度	kuānróngdù	*n.*	degree of tolerance
促使		cùshǐ	*v.*	cause; compel; urge
允许	允許	yǔnxǔ	*v.*	permit; allow
多元化		duōyuánhuà	*adj.*	diversified

词语例句

(1) 图: seek; pursue

◆ 他们认为方小姐是图李先生有钱有地位。
They believed that Miss Fang was solely going after Mr. Li's money and status.

1. 我跟你结婚，不图你的钱，是因为你老实，孝敬父母。
   I'm marrying you not for your money, but because you are honest and you respect your parents.

2. 这个房子又小又贵，住在这儿只图方便。
   This house is small and expensive. I'm only living here because it is convenient.

(2) 不出…就…: within

◆ 不出三年，方小姐就得离婚。
She will surely get a divorce within the next three years.

1. 我看书很快，不出三天就能把这本书看完。
   I read fast. I could finish reading this book in three days.

2. 在这儿吃饭很方便，不出十米，就有好几家饭馆儿。
   It is very convenient to eat here. There are several restaurants within ten meters.

(3) 当初: at the beginning; originally

◆ 其实，当初我也挺犹豫。
Actually I was quite hesitant at first.

1. 当初你就不该这么做。
   You should never have acted the way you did in the first place.

2. 当初政府打算在这儿建一幢大楼。
   Originally the government planned to put up a big building here.

(4) 犹豫: hesitate; hesitant

◆ 其实，当初我也挺犹豫。

1. 我请她看电影的时候，她犹豫了一下，然后同意了。
   When I asked her to a movie, she hesitated a moment and then accepted.

2. 中国的父母舍不得为自己花钱，可是为了孩子的教育，花钱的时候一点儿都不犹豫。
   Chinese parents are unwilling to spend money on themselves, but when it comes to their children's education, they don't hesitate at all.

(5) 谁也不 v. 谁: neither of them v. one another

◆ 夫妻双方自食其力，谁也不靠谁养活。

A husband and wife supported themselves independently; neither of them depended on the other to live.

1. 昨天他们大吵了一架，现在谁也不理谁。

They had a big fight yesterday, and now neither of them is talking to the other.

2. 表面上这两个人关系很好，其实，他们谁也不相信谁。

On the surface they have a good relationship, but in reality, neither of them trusts the other.

(6) 或…或…: or...or...

◆ 一些事业成功的男人或因为忙于事业未婚，或离婚准备再娶。

Some successful men are single because they have been busy with their careers or have divorced and plan to remarry.

1. 他们学习中文，或因为父母是中国人，或因为对中国的文化特别有兴趣。

They are taking Chinese because their parents are Chinese or because they are particularly interested in Chinese culture.

2. 以前，在美国的中国人或开饭馆或开洗衣店，而现在的中国人往往或做电脑程序员或做生意。

In the past, most Chinese in America ran a restaurant or a dry cleaner; nowadays, they are computer programmers or doing business.

(7) 忙于: busy with

◆ 一些事业成功的男人因为忙于事业而未婚。

1. 这个暑期他忙于上英语辅导班而完全没休息。

He was busy with attending the English tutorial class and had no rest at all.

2. 你不应该忙于工作而忽视你的家庭。

You should not care only about your work and neglect your family.

(8) 在…中所占的分量: the influential role played in …; the importance of sth. to

◆ 这与近年来金钱在价值观中所占的分量越来越重也有很大关系。

It is greatly related to the fact that in recent years the position of money among Chinese values has been rising.

1. 运动在美国人的生活中所占的分量很重。

Sports play an important role in Americans' lives.

2. 数学课在经济专业中所占的分量很重。

　　Mathematics is a great portion of the classes for an economic major.

(9) 被…所 v. : be v.-ed by

◆ 有相当一部分知识女性被年长、成熟的男人的学识、能力、体贴所吸引。

　　There are quite a lot of educated women who are attracted by the knowledge, ability, and consideration of older and mature men.

1. 有些失去劳动能力的老人被子女所离弃。

　　Some elders who lost their productive capacity were abandoned by their children.

2. 不少传统观念已经被现代化的价值观所取代。

　　A lot of traditional ideas have been replaced by modern values.

练习

I. Choose the correct answer.

1. 很多父母由于_____工作，忽视了孩子的心理问题。

　　　a.急于　　　b.忙于　　　　c.求助于

2. 我今年已经三十岁了，早就_____上大学的年龄了。

　　　a. 已经了　　b. 经过了　　c.过了

3. 最近我的邻居娶了一位_____。

　　　a.年轻小姐比他二十岁小

　　　b.比他小二十岁的小姐

　　　c.比他二十岁小的小姐

4. 我觉得跟年龄大一点儿的人结婚无所谓，可是给跟我年龄差不多的人_____后妈是不能接受的。

　　　a. 当　　b. 成为　　c.成了

5. 我读了他的几篇作品以后，就一直_____。

　　　a.对他很倾心　　　b.很倾心他　　　c.倾心

II. Rewrite the following sentence using the expression provided.

1. 在北京交通堵塞非常严重，司机不让行人，行人也不让司机。

　　　（谁也不…谁）

2. 这个考试这么容易，我看，所有的学生很快就能做完。

　　　（不出…就…）

3. 大学毕业后，他就自己养活自己了。（自食其力）

4. 他一直反对婚前同居。（持…态度）

5. 我之所以选这个工作是因为工资特别高。（被…所吸引）

6. 在他的生活中，家庭大于一切。（所占的分量）

III. Choose the most appropriate word for each blank and fill in with its Chinese equivalent.

　　　all day　　　originally　　　support oneself by one's own labor
　　　according to newspapers　　　diversified　　　expand　　　hesitate

1. 科技的发展不但没有缩短富国和贫国的差距，反而_____了它们之间的差距。

2. 学习固然重要，你也不要_____坐在图书馆里，应该运动运动。

3. 纽约的_____文化吸引了世界各地的人。

4. 要不是_____你帮了我的忙，我怎么会有今天的成绩？

5. 别_____了，机会一旦失去，就不会再来了。

6. _____，女人的平均寿命比男人长五岁。

7. 我希望毕业以后能_____，不要再依靠父母。

IV. Composition

　　　你的儿子爱上了一个比他大二十岁的有才华、有经济实力的女人。作为母亲，你有点担心，所以你要跟他谈一谈，请用下面的生词，准备五个问题，另外再写出你的看法和建议。

　　　为何，图，懂得，自然，固然，吸引，犹豫，
　　　差距，体贴，提醒，禁止，倾向于，持…态度

V. Answer the following questions.

1. 这篇文章说改革开放以前男女结婚年龄差不多；改革开放以后，因为有了竞争，男人在事业上比较成功，于是就出现了"老夫少妻"的情形，这是不是暗示(ànshì: imply)女人竞争不过男人，你同意不同意这个看法？

2. 你见过"老夫少妻"的婚姻吗？　为什么"老夫少妻"比"老妻少夫"多得多？

3. 在你看来，"老夫少妻"的增多反映妇女地位的上升还是下降？

繁体字课文

　　三年前，二十七歲年輕活潑的方小姐嫁給了比她大二十歲的李先生，不少親戚朋友對這個婚姻持否定態度，認為方小姐是圖(1)李先生有錢有地位，有的甚至說，瞧著吧，不出三年，方小姐就(2)得鬧離婚。三年過去了，現在的方小姐，整天和李先生一起出出進進，與李先生的兒子也相處得很和睦。問起她嫁給"老夫"三年的感受，方小姐說："其實，當初(3)我也挺猶豫(4)，他不僅比我大二十歲，而且我一嫁過去就得給他十五歲的兒子當後媽。可李先生的才華、經濟實力、辦事能力讓我特別傾心，而且知道怎麼疼我。那些和我年齡差不多的男孩儿雖然也愛我，卻並不懂得怎麼愛護我。"

　　像方小姐、李先生這樣"老夫少妻"的家庭近年來正逐漸增多。據報載,進入九十年代後,男比女大五歲的比例最高,達48%,男比女大十歲以上的比例也比1987年增加10%。

　　分析男女結婚年齡差距拉大的原因,首先是因為經濟的緣故。新中國成立以後,提倡婦女解放,女人從家庭走向社會,經濟獨立。男女同工同酬,收入差別不大。夫妻雙方自食其力,誰也不靠誰(5)養活,在這樣的經濟環境下,男女自然選擇年齡差不多的对象結婚。因此,六十年代至八十年代結婚的夫妻大多數年齡差距只有兩三歲。

　　改革開放以後,人們的收入差距逐步拉大,一些事業成功的男人或(6)因為忙於(7)事業未婚,或離婚準備再娶。這些男人雖然早已過了傳統觀念中結婚的年齡,但因為他們有較強的經濟實力,往往成為年輕女性選擇的目標。這與近年來金錢在價值觀中所占分量(8)越來越重也有很大關係。

　　"老夫少妻"婚姻比例的增加固然與經濟因素有直接關係,但現在社會裡有相當一部分知識女性找比自己大很多的男性並不是為了錢,而是被年長、成熟的男人的學識、能力、體貼所(9)吸引。

　　除了以上這些以外,社會寬容度的增加也是促使"老夫少妻"增多的原因之一。現在大家覺得嫁什麼人完全是個人的事,跟別人是沒有關係的。"老夫少妻"的增加,表明社會允許多元化價值觀的存在。

第二十三课　产品质量与社会道德

　　现在，一次性产品越来越多了，从饭馆儿里的碗筷到宾馆里的牙刷、牙膏、拖鞋，从医院里的注射器到路边儿穿羊肉串儿的竹签儿等等。

　　对这类产品，人们不会有过高的要求，用过一次就扔了。可是这种"一次性"常常也难以保证。有一回我到山东出差，住进宾馆时已经很晚了，又(1)有些累，准备洗洗澡上床休息。我穿着"一次性"拖鞋上卫生间，鞋底软得(2)让人受不了。刚走出了两步，一只鞋就(3)坏了。然后我拿起"一次性"牙膏，那牙膏硬得像(4)石头，怎么挤也(5)挤不出来。我拿起牙刷来，还没(6)刷两下，"啪"的一声断了。第二天早晨，我做的第一件事就是去买牙刷、牙膏，当然还有拖鞋。

　　一次性产品的优点是很明显的：卫生，不会传染疾病。但是这一点也难以保证。人们到饭馆吃饭，总是用"一次性"筷子，但一次性筷子不见得都那么干净。有一次在一家饭馆吃饭，我拿了一双"一次性"筷子，发现上面黑乎乎的，再拿了一双还是那样。老板见我在那

| 宾馆 | 賓館 | bīn'guǎn | *n.* | hotel |
| 牙刷 | | yáshuā | *n.* | toothbrush |

268

牙膏		yágāo	*n.*	toothpaste
拖鞋		tuōxié	*n.*	slippers
注射器		zhùshèqì	*n.*	syringe
路边儿	路邊儿	lùbiānr	*n.*	roadside; wayside
穿		chuān	*v.*	string together
羊肉串儿	羊肉串儿	yángròu chuànr	*n.*	mutton kebob
竹签儿	竹簽儿	zhúqiānr	*n.*	bamboo skewer
山东	山東	Shāndōng	*n.*	Shandong Province
出差		chū//chāi	*v.-o.*	go on a business trip 他到上海出差去了。 他最近到广东出了一趟差。
住进	住進	zhùjìn	*v.*	check in
又		yòu	*adv.*	on top of sth.
休息		xiū.xi	*v.*	have a rest; have a break
卫生间	衛生間	wèishēngjiān	*n.*	bathroom
鞋底		xiédǐ	*n.*	sole
软	軟	ruǎn	*adj.*	soft
受不了		shòu.buliǎo	*v.-c.*	cannot stand
步		bù	*AN*	measure word for step
硬		yìng	*adj.*	hard; stiff; tough
石头	石頭	shí.tou	*n.*	stone; rock
挤	擠	jǐ	*v.*	squeeze
刷		shuā	*v.*	brush
啪的一声	啪的一聲	pā.de yìshēng	*phr.*	with a cracking sound; with a bang
优点	優點	yōudiǎn	*n.*	strong point; merit 缺点: shortcoming; defect; weak point
明显	明顯	míngxiǎn	*adj.*	obvious; evident
疾病		jíbìng	*n.*	disease
老板		lǎobǎn	*n.*	boss; shopkeeper

里挑筷子，"嘿嘿"地一笑，那筷子和那笑声都让我觉得不舒服。

　　至于穿羊肉串儿的竹签儿，就更让人不放心了。我家门口有烤羊肉串儿的，经常有许多人在那里买了吃。有一天晚上，十一点多钟的时候，我路过那里，发现地上到处(7)都是竹签儿，烤羊肉串儿的人正在捡。一位邻居对我说："你看那卖羊肉串儿的人多缺德，他把竹签儿捡回去，也不知道洗不洗，明天照样(8)用它来穿羊肉串儿。"

　　一次性产品连一次都用不了，那是产品质量问题；可是一次性产品用过了再拿给人用，那是道德问题。

《人民日报》1998 年 8 月 17 日

挑		tiāo	*v.*	choose; pick; select
嘿嘿一笑		hēihēi yíxiào	*phr.*	laugh with a hehe sound
笑声	笑聲	xiàoshēng	*n.*	laugh; laughter
烤		kǎo	*v.*	barbecue; roast
路过	路過	lùguò	*v.*	pass through or by (a place)
到处	到處	dàochù	*n.*	everywhere; all over
邻居	鄰居	línjū	*n.*	neighbor
缺德	缺德	quēdé	*adj.*	mean; wicked
照样	照樣	zhàoyàng	*adv.*	same as before; all the same
用不了		yòng.bu liǎo	*v.*	cannot be used

词语例句

(1) 又: on top of sth.; in addition to sth.

◆ 我住进宾馆时已经很晚了，又有些累，准备洗洗澡上床休息。

It was very late when I checked in, and I was also quite tired, so all I wanted was to take a shower and go to sleep.

1. 天很黑，又下着雨，路更难走了。

On top of it being dark it rained, which made the going even tougher.

2. 天气那么热，屋里又没有空调，很不舒服。

It is hot, and there is no air conditioner in the room, so it is very uncomfortable.

(2) adj. 得… : so adj. that…

◆ 鞋底软得让人受不了。

The soles are so soft that I can't stand it.

1. 那个学生累得上课的时候就睡着了。

That student was so exhausted that he fell asleep in class.

2. 他紧张得一句话也不说出来。

He is too nervous to utter even one word.

(3) 刚 v., 就…: no sooner…than…

◆ 刚走出两步，一只鞋就坏了。

No sooner had I walked a few steps than one of the slippers broke.

1. 他们刚认识一个礼拜就结婚了。

They got married just a week after they met.

2. 我刚写完最后一个字，时间就到了。

I had just finished writing the last character when the time was up.

(4) adj.得像…: as adj. as

◆ 那牙膏硬得像石头。

That toothpaste is as hard as a rock.

1. 这个校园大得像一个公园。

This campus is as big as a park.

2. 这个教室冷得像冰箱。

The classroom is as cold as a refrigerator.

(5) 怎么 v. 也不…: no matter how…, still can not…

◆ （牙膏）我怎么挤也挤不出来。

However hard I tried, I couldn't squeeze the toothpaste out.

1. 我怎么学也学不会。

However hard I worked, I just couldn't learn it.

2. 我怎么劝他他也不听。

I tried my best to persuade him, but he wouldn't listen to me.

3. 我怎么睡也睡不着。

However hard I tried, I just couldn't fall asleep.

(6) 还没 v. , (就)… : not even v.-ed yet, …(indicate something happens too soon)

◆ 我拿起牙刷来，还没刷两下，"啪"的一声断了。

I took the brush, and before I really brushed my teeth, it broke with a cracking sound.

1. 我跟他还没说两句话，他就说他得走了。

Before I said anything, he said that he had to go.

2. 他还没学两天，就说太难而不学了。

He said that it was too hard and quit studying after just a few days.

(7) 到处: everywhere; in every place

◆ 地上到处都是竹签儿。

There were bamboo skewers everywhere.

1. 即使在美国，中国菜也很热。到处都有中国饭馆儿。

Chinese food is very popular even in America. You can find a Chinese restaurant anywhere.

2. 地上到处都是垃圾，实在太脏了。

There was garbage everywhere. This place is too dirty.

(8) 照样: same as before

◆ 明天照样用它来穿羊肉串儿。

The next day he used the same skewers to string mutton kebobs as usual.

1. 他每天十点睡觉，即使大考的时候，也是照样十点上床。

He goes to sleep at ten every day. Even during finals he still goes to bed at ten as usual.

2. 谁看电影都得买票，美国总统也得照样买票。

Whoever wants to see a movie has to buy a ticket, even the President of the

United States of America.

练习

I. Choose the correct answer.

1. 他正在洗澡的时候，突然听见"啪的一声"，灯（损失；危害；坏）了。

2. 他在美国住了十年还不会说英文，真令人难以（信；想；相信）。

3. 看你的手，黑(乎乎；嘿嘿；荡荡) 的，快洗洗吧！

4. 这牙刷的质量真差，我刚用了两天(才；连；就) 断了。

II. Fill in each blank with the most appropriate word.

　　卫生　　照样　　缺德　　出差　　传染

1. 谁这么 ＿＿＿，竟然把我的新衣服弄成这样！

2. 我的邻居总是把电视的声音开得很大。每次我跟他说，他总是说对不起，可是下次还是 ＿＿＿ 开得那么大声。

3. 由于工作的关系，他常常去外国 ＿＿＿＿。

4. 你最好离我远一点儿，我正在感冒，不想 ＿＿＿＿ 给你。

5. 街上的烤羊肉串儿好吃是好吃，就是有点不 ＿＿＿＿。

III. Rewrite the sentence using the expression given.

1. 今天的数学题真难，我用了各种办法也解不开。(怎么 v. 也…)

2. 太不像话了，食堂的馒头那么硬，简直可以当榔头了。

　　　　　　　　　　　　　　　　　　　　(adj.得…)

3. 你的记性(jìxìng: memory) 太差了，我两分钟以前告诉你的事，现在你怎么就忘了呢？　(刚 v. 就…)

4. 未婚先孕的意思就是结婚以前生孩子。（还没 v. 就…）

IV. Complete the following sentences.

1. 无论什么事都可以告到法院去，从……到……，……

2. 一次性产品的质量难以保证，因为……

3. 到了中国以后，我做的第一件事就是……

4. 这支笔的质量太差了，我还没……

5. 这个学生的优点是很明显的，……

6. 饭馆儿的饭菜都很干净，至于……

7. 他真缺德，居然……

V. Answer the following questions.

1. 一次性产品存在的两个问题：质量问题、道德问题，哪个比较严重？

2. 把一次性产品像塑料刀叉或者竹签儿洗干净再用，不是节省资源的做法吗？

3. 在你看来，宾馆应该不应该为客人提供牙刷、牙膏、拖鞋、毛巾等东西？为什么？

繁体字课文

現在，一次性產品越來越多了，從飯館儿裏的碗筷到賓館裏的牙刷、牙膏、拖鞋，從醫院裏的注射器到路邊儿穿羊肉串儿的竹籤儿等等。

對這類產品，人們不會有過高的要求，用過一次就扔了。可是這種"一次性"常常也難以保證。有一回我到山東出差，住進賓館時已經很晚了，又(1)有些累，準備洗洗澡上床休息。我穿著"一次性"拖鞋上衛生間，鞋底軟得(2)讓人受不了。剛走出了兩步，一隻鞋就(3)壞了。然後我拿起"一次性"牙膏，那牙膏硬得像(4)石頭，怎麼擠也(5)擠不出來。我拿起牙刷來，還沒(6)刷兩下，"啪"的一聲斷了。第二天早晨，我做的第一件事就是去買牙刷、牙膏，當然還有拖鞋。

　　一次性產品的優點是很明顯的：衛生，不會傳染疾病。但是這一點也難以保證。人們到飯館吃飯，總是用"一次性"筷子，但一次性筷子不見得都那麼乾淨。有一次在一家飯館吃飯，我拿了一雙"一次性"筷子，發現上面黑乎乎的，再拿了一雙還是那樣。老闆見我在那裏挑筷子，"嘿嘿"地一笑，那筷子和那笑聲都讓我覺得不舒服。

　　至於穿羊肉串儿的竹簽儿，就更讓人不放心了。我家門口有烤羊肉串儿的，經常有許多人在那裏買了吃。有一天晚上，十一點多鐘的時候，我路過那裏，發現地上到處(7)都是竹簽儿，烤羊肉串儿的人正在撿。一位鄰居對我說："你看那賣羊肉串儿的人多缺德，他把竹簽儿撿回去，也不知道洗不洗，明天照樣(8)用它來穿羊肉串儿。"

　　一次性產品連一次都用不了，那是產品品質問題；可是一次性產品用過了再拿給人用，那是道德問題。

第二十四课　餐桌上的文明与野蛮

饮食文化作为(1)中华文明的特色之一，早已(2)世界闻名。然而近年来，在我国一些地方，这种文明却越来越带着野蛮的味道(3)。

不顾(4)法令的禁止，不顾舆论的批评，一些餐馆几乎成了野生动物"博物馆"。"孔雀全宴"、"天鹅全宴"、"纸包鸵鸟肉"、"红烧果子狸"、"清炖蛇龟鹰"、"香炸鳄鱼条"、"红烧五脚金龙（巨蜥）"……这是一个记者不久前在广西南宁市一些餐馆中看到的菜名。在那里，你还可以看到许多平常不容易看到的稀有动物都成了餐桌上的食物。珍稀野生动物作为一道"主菜"，

餐桌		cānzhuō	n.	dining table
野蛮	野蠻	yěmán	adj.	barbarous; cruel
作为	作為	zuòwéi	prep.	as
中华	中華	Zhōnghuá	n.	the Chinese nation
特色		tèsè	n.	distinguishing feature
早已		zǎoyǐ	adv.	long ago; for a long time
世界闻名	世界聞名	shìjiè wénmíng	adj.	world-famous
闻名	聞名	wénmíng	adj.	renowned; well-known 全国闻名/全校闻名
味道		wèi.dao	n.	flavor; smell
不顾	不顧	búgù	v.	disregard
法令		fǎlìng	n.	law and decrees
舆论	輿論	yúlùn	n.	public opinion
批评	批評	pīpíng	v./n.	criticize, criticism

餐馆	餐館	cānguǎn	*n.*	restaurant
野生		yěshēng	*adj.*	wild; uncultivated
动物	動物	dòngwù	*n.*	animal
博物馆	博物館	bówùguǎn	*n.*	museum
孔雀		kǒngquè	*n.*	peacock
——宴		yàn	*suffix*	banquet; dinning party
天鹅		tiān'é	*n.*	swan
包		bāo	*v.*	wrap
鸵鸟	鴕鳥	túoniǎo	*n.*	ostrich
红烧	紅燒	hóngshāo	*v.*	braise in soy sauce
果子狸		guǒ.zilǐ	*n.*	masked civet
清炖	清燉	qīngdùn	*v.*	boiled in clear soup (without soy sauce)
蛇		shé	*n.*	snake
龟	龜	guī	*n.*	tortoise; turtle
鹰		yīng	*n.*	hawk; eagle
香		xiāng	*adj.*	appetizing; fragrant
炸		zhá	*v.*	deep-fry
鳄鱼	鱷魚	èyú	*n.*	crocodile
条	條	tiáo	*n.*	strip
金		jīn	*n.*	gold
龙	龍	lóng	*n.*	dragon
巨蜥		jùxī	*n.*	huge lizard
不久前		bùjiǔqián	*n.*	not long ago; recently
广西	廣西	Guǎngxī	*n.*	Guangxi Province
南宁市	南寧市	Nánníng Shì	*n.*	Nanning City
稀有		xīyǒu	*adj.*	rare; unusual
食物		shíwù	*n.*	food; eatables; edibles
珍稀		zhēnxī	*adj.*	precious; rare
道		dào	*AN*	measure word for dishes
主菜		zhǔcài	*n.*	main dish

在一些场合甚至成为某种规格、待遇的象征。

　　这种情况，实在令人震惊和忧虑。著名生物学家杨雄里说：

"在南方某些地方，一些人为了补脑，竟然用绳子捆住猴子，再用

硬物敲开猴子的脑壳吃里面的猴脑。这种行为实在愚昧之极(5)、野

蛮之至！"他甚至用"没人性"这样的词句，来表达他对此类行为

的愤慨。前不久，上海有八位科学家联名发出"不吃野生动物，提

倡文明生活"的倡议，他们说："为了给子孙后代留下一个完整美

好的世界，千万别把我们的餐桌变成野生动物的屠宰场！"

　　据报道，在近 1600 年中，已有 700 多种有史料记载的动物灭

场合	場合	chǎnghé	n.	occasion; situation
规格	規格	guīgé	n.	standard; norm; specification
待遇		dàiyù	n.	treatment
象征	象徵	xiàngzhēng	n.	symbol; token
实在	實在	shízài	adv.	really; certainly; truly
生物学家	生物學家	shēngwù xuéjiā	n.	biologist
杨雄里	楊雄里	Yáng Xiónglǐ	n.	name of a person
南方		nánfāng	n.	south
补脑	補腦	bǔ//nǎo	v.-o.	nourish the brain
绳子	繩子	shéng.zi	n.	rope
捆住		kǔn//zhù	v.-c.	bind; tie
猴子		hóu.zi	n.	monkey

硬物		yìngwù	*n.*	hard objects
敲开	敲開	qiāo//kāi	*v.-c.*	strike open
脑壳	腦殼	nǎoké	*n.*	skull
脑	腦	nǎo	*n.*	brain
愚昧		yúmèi	*adj.*	ignorant; benighted
——之极	之極	zhījí	*adv.*	extremely
——之至		zhīzhì	*adv.*	extremely
人性		rénxìng	*n.*	human nature
词句	詞句	cíjù	*n.*	words and sentences (here: expression)
表达	表達	biǎodá	*v.*	express
愤慨	憤慨	fènkǎi	*adj./ n.*	be indignant (toward an injustice), (righteous) indignation 对…感到非常愤慨
前不久		qiánbùjiǔ	*n.*	not long ago
科学家	科學家	kēxuéjiā	*n.*	scientist
联名	聯名	liánmíng	*adv.*	jointly sign; jointly
发出	發出	fāchū	*v.*	put forward; raise
倡议	倡議	chàngyì	*v./n.*	propose; proposal
子孙	子孫	zǐsūn	*n.*	descendants 孙：孙子；grandson
后代	後代	hòudài	*n.*	descendants; posterity
留下		liúxià	*v.*	leave behind
完整		wánzhěng	*adj.*	intact; complete
美好		měihǎo	*adj.*	beautiful; fine; glorious
屠宰场	屠宰場	túzǎichǎng	*n.*	slaughterhouse
报道	報道	bàodào	*n.*	news report; 报导
近		jìn	*adj.*	recent
史料		shǐliào	*n.*	historical data/ materials
记载	記載	jìzǎi	*n./v.*	record, put down in writing
灭绝	滅絕	mièjué	*v.*	become extinct

绝。在国际公认(6)的 640 个面临灭绝的野生动物物种中，我国就占了
156 个。保护野生动物已成为我们的严峻课题(7)。

　　地球是人类及其他生物的共有家园。人与野生动物本是共生关系，这是我们越来越深切感受到的现实。餐桌上的野蛮再一次警告人们：保护野生动物，人人有责。

《人民日报》2000 年 7 月 21 日

国际	國際	guójì	*adj.*	international
公认	公認	gōngrèn	*v.*	be generally acknowledged
物种	物種	wùzhǒng	*n.*	species
严峻	嚴峻	yánjùn	*adj.*	stern; severe; grim (punishment)
课题	課題	kètí	*n.*	task; problem; question for study
地球		dìqiú	*n.*	the earth; the globe
人类	人類	rénlèi	*n.*	human kind
及		jí	*conj.*	and; 跟
生物		shēngwù	*n.*	living beings; living things
共有		gòngyǒu	*v.*	jointly possesses
家园	家園	jiāyuán	*n.*	home; homeland
本		běn	*adv.*	it goes without saying; of course
共生		gòngshēng	*n.*	(mutualistic) symbiosis; mutualism
深切		shēnqiè	*adv.*	deeply; keenly; thoroughly
现实	現實	xiànshí	*n.*	reality; facts
警告		jǐnggào	*v.*	warn
责	責	zé	*n.*	duty; responsibility; 责任

词语例句

(1) 作为: as

◆ 饮食文化作为中华文明的特色之一早已世界闻名。

Chinese food culture, as one of the features of Chinese civilization, has long since been world famous.

1.作为你的老师，我有责任指出你的错误。

As your teacher it is my responsibility to point out your faults.

2.珍稀野生动物作为一道主菜，在一些场合甚至成为某种规格、待遇的象征

On some occasions serving a rare and wild animal as a main course has even become a symbol of (high) standards and (good) treatment.

(2) 早已: long since

◆ 饮食文化作为中华文明的特色之一早已世界闻名。

1.他早已做了决定。

He made up his mind long ago.

2.你要的东西，我早已给你买来了。

I've long since bought all the things you want.

(3) 味道: flavor; hint

◆ 这种文明越来越带着野蛮的味道。

This kind of civilization is increasingly coming to have a hint of the savage.

1.她的话有点儿讽刺的味道。

There is a touch of sarcasm in her remarks.

2.看到自己的女朋友跟最好的朋友结婚，他心里有说不出的味道。

He had an indescribable feeling when he saw his girlfriend marrying his best friend. *flavor*

(4) 不顾: regardless; disregard

◆不顾法令的禁止，不顾舆论的批评，一些餐馆几乎成了野生动物"博物馆"。

Some restaurants almost became "museums of wild animals," regardless of the prohibition by law and the criticism of the public.

1.这个人真自私，从来不顾别人的感受。

This person is so selfish—he never cares about others' feelings.

2. 他不顾父母的反对，坚决要去外国念书。

He is determined to go study abroad in spite of his parents' disapproval.

(5) …之至；…之极: extremely

◆ 这种行为实在是愚昧之极，野蛮之至。

This kind of behavior really is extremely ignorant and uncivilized.

1. 让你等了那么久，真是抱歉之至。

I'm terribly sorry to have kept you waiting for such a long time.

2. 我对她的帮助感激之至。

I'm extremely grateful for her help.

3. 战争发生之后，这个地区的秩序可以说是混乱之极。

The order in this area may be described as extremely chaotic after the war began.

(6) 公认: generally acknowledge

◆ 在国际公认的 640 个面临灭绝的野生动物物种中，我国就占了 156 个。

Among the internationally acknowledged 640 wild animals that are on the brink of extinction, 156 are from China.

1. 一国的内政不容外国干涉，这是国际公认的原则。

The internal affairs of a country tolerate no interference from foreign countries. This is an internationally acknowledged principle.

2. 大家公认他是个品学兼优的好学生。

It is generally acknowledged that he is a student of good character and scholarship.

(7) 严峻课题: serious problem; serious challenge

◆ 保护野生动物已成为我们的严峻课题。

Protecting wild animals has become a serious challenge for us.

1. 和平和发展是当前世界的两大严峻课题。

Peace and development are two major issues in the world today.

2. 中国把缩短贫富差距作为政府的严峻课题。

China has taken narrowing the gap between the rich and the poor as the government's serious challenge.

练习

I. Choose the most appropriate word for each blank and fill in with its Chinese equivalent.

> warn   as   disregard   world-famous   jointly sign
> become extinct   record   be sure not to

1. 北京_____中国最古老的城市之一，有很多_____的名胜古迹。

2. 教务处_____学生，替人代考一定会受到严厉的惩罚。

3. 这种鳄鱼在世界别的地区已经_____了，只有在中国的长江地区还剩下不到 100 只。

4. 他_____危险跳进湖水里去救那个小孩儿。

5. 这本书详细地_____了第一次世界大战发生的原因。

6. 最近亚洲十二个国家_____发起"让毒品远离人类"的活动。

7. _____别在那条河里游泳，那条河里的水受到了严重的污染。

II. Choose the correct answer.

1. 保护环境是地球上每个人的（责任，责）。

2. 社会学家建议家长们挤出时间，多（关心，顾）孩子的心理情况。

3. 虽然中国的人口增长速度已经放慢，但是中国的人口状况还是十分（严厉，严峻）。

4. 80 年代，中国政府发出了少生孩子的（提倡，倡议）。

5. （我，各个高校）公认必须加强学生的性健康教育。

III. Make a sentence using the underlined expression.

1. 一些人为了补脑，竟然用硬物敲开猴子的脑袋吃猴脑，这种行为实在野蛮之至。

2. 饮食文化作为中华文明的特色之一，早已世界闻名，然而近年来，在我国一些地方，这种文明却越来越带着野蛮的味道。

3. 不顾法令的禁止，不顾舆论的批评，一些餐馆几乎成了野生动物"博物馆"。

4. 人与野生动物本是共生关系，这是我们越来越深切感受到的现实。

5. 餐桌上的野蛮<u>再一次</u>警告人们：保护野生动物，人人有责。

（手写批注：我 再一次 给他打电话 他还是没 Tie？ 第一次 他没回还）

IV. Composition

最近上海八名科学家联名向社会发出"不吃野生动物，提倡文明生活"的倡议。请你为他们写这份倡议。

繁体字课文

飲食文化作為(1)中華文明的特色之一，早已(2)世界聞名。然而近年來，在我國一些地方，這種文明卻越來越帶著野蠻的味道(3)。

不顧(4)法令的禁止，不顧輿論的批評，一些餐館幾乎成了野生動物"博物館"。"孔雀全宴"、"天鵝全宴"、"紙包鴕鳥肉"、"紅燒果子狸"、"清燉蛇龜鷹"、"香炸鱷魚條"、"紅燒五腳金龍（巨蜥）"……這是一個記者不久前在廣西南寧市一些餐館中看到的菜名。在那裏，你還可以看到許多平常不容易看到的稀有動物都成了餐桌上的食物。珍稀野生動物作為一道"主菜"，在一些場合甚至成為某種規格、待遇的象徵。

這種情況，實在令人震驚和憂慮。著名生物學家楊雄里說："在南方某些地方，一些人為了補腦，竟然用繩子捆住猴子，再用硬物敲開猴子的腦殼吃裏面的猴腦。這種行為實在愚昧之極(5)、野蠻之至！"他甚至用"沒人性"這樣的詞句，來表達他對此類行為的憤慨。前不久，上海有八位科學家聯名發出"不吃野生動物，提倡文明生活"的倡議，他們說："為了給子孫後代留下一個完整美好的世界，千萬別把我們的餐桌變成野生動物的屠宰場！"

據報導，在近 1600 年中，已有 700 多種有史料記載的動物滅絕。在國際公認(6)的 640 個面臨滅絕的野生動物物種中，我國就占了 156 個。保護野生動物已成為我們的嚴峻課題(7)。

地球是人類及其他生物的共有家園。人與野生動物本是共生關係，這是我們越來越深切感受到的現實。餐桌上的野蠻再一次警告人們：保護野生動物，人人有責。

第二十五课　杭州街头设置安全套自售机引起争议

今年 6 月 3 日，杭州市在街上设置了两个安全套自动售货机。20 多天来，销售平稳，但同时也发生了一些令人不愉快的事，有一位店主竟用挂历纸把自售机封上，只留下一个投币口。

用挂历纸把自售机封上的是一家发廊的店主。虽然自售机装在发廊隔壁的饮食店门口，但是这位店主还是嫌它碍眼。现在这部机器已经被计划生育站撤回。计划生育站的负责人说，由于在居民区找一个合适的装机点儿不容易，这台机器暂时还没有重新(1)装回去。

杭州市计划生育站负责人认为，杭州是华东地区第一个推行安全套自售机的城市。一些居民由于传统观念的影响，存在"这种东西见不得人(2)"、"设在自家门口不雅观"等思想。除此之外(3)，自

街头	街頭	jiētóu	n.	street; street corner
设置	設置	shèzhì	v.	install; fit; set up
安全套		ānquántào	n.	condom; 保险套
自售机	自售機	zìshòujī	n.	automatic vending machine; 自动售货机
争议	爭議	zhēngyì	n.	dispute; debate; contention
销售	銷售	xiāoshòu	n./v.	sale, sell
平稳	平穩	píngwěn	adj.	stable; smooth
愉快		yúkuài	adj.	delightful; pleasant
店主		diànzhǔ	n.	owner of a store
挂历	掛曆	guàlì	n.	wall calendar

封上		fēng//shàng	v.-c.	seal
投币口	投幣口	tóubìkǒu	n.	coin slot
发廊	髮廊	fàláng	n.	hair salon
装		zhuāng	v.	install
碍眼	礙眼	àiyǎn	adj.	be unpleasant to look at
部		bù	AN	measure word for machine 一部汽车/一部洗衣机
机器	機器	jīqì	n.	machine
计划生育	計劃生育	jìhuà shēngyù	n.	family planning; birth control
站		zhàn	n.	center; station 医疗站/服务站/销售站
撤回		chè//huí	v.-c.	withdraw; take back
负责人	負責人	fùzérén	n.	person in charge
居民区	居民區	jūmínqu	n.	residential district
合适	合適	héshì	adj.	suitable; appropriate
装机点儿	裝機點儿	zhuāngjī diǎnr	n.	place to install vending machine
台		tái	AN	measure word for engine, machine, etc. 一台电视/一台洗衣机
重新		chóngxīn	adv.	again; anew; re-
华东	華東	Huádōng	n.	Eastern China
推行		tuīxíng	v.	try to carry out (a policy, etc.)
居民		jūmín	n.	resident; inhabitant
见不得人	見不得人	jiàn.budé rén	phr.	not fit to be seen or revealed; unpresentable; shameful
设	設	shè	v.	establish
自家		zìjiā	pron	(dialect) oneself
不雅观	不雅觀	bù yǎguān	adj.	offensive to the eye; disagreeable to the sight
除此之外		chú cǐ zhī wài	conj.	besides; in addition; 除了这个以外

售机的设置还引起一部分市民的担心，认为自售机在方便育龄妇女的同时(4)，也给某些违法活动提供了方便。但计划生育部门的同志跟社会学家在接受记者采访时表示，这种忧虑是不必要的，因为安全套在各大药房都有，街头自售机与违法活动没有关系。

据了解，杭州市计划生育部门这次在西湖区等六个地方设置了一百多个自动售货机，所覆盖人口超过三十万。这种投币一元就可以吐套的二十四小时自动售货机比起商店来，有方便、可靠和免于(5)不好意思的优点。自动售货机设置以来(6)，平均每天吐套五百个。大部分杭州市民对这种销售方式已经有科学认识并持欢迎态度。

有关负责人在接受采访时表示，自售机是现代化城市文明的一种标志。尽管有观念上的争议，但杭州市仍然把它列为(7)计划生育优质服务的一项重要内容，大力(8)推行。今年下半年，杭州市各区都将设置安全套自售机，总量将达一千五百台左右。随着人民经济水平和对生活质量要求的提高，自售机也应该成为人民接受并爱护的一项公物，因为它终究(9)关系着⑽广大人民的健康。

《文汇报》1999 年 6 月 30 日

育龄妇女	育齡婦女	yùlíng fùnǚ	n.	woman of childbearing age
违法	違法	wéifǎ	adj.	lawless; illegal
提供		tígōng	v.	provide
部门	部門	bùmén	n.	department of a large organization

同志		tóngzhì	*n.*	comrade
社会学家	社會學家	shèhuìxué jiā	*n.*	sociologist
必要		bìyào	*adj.*	necessary
药房	藥房	yàofáng	*n.*	pharmacy
西湖区	西湖區	Xīhúqū	*n.*	Xihu District, Hangzhou City
覆盖	覆蓋	fùgài	*v.*	cover
投币	投幣	tóu bì	*v.-o.*	drop money (into a vending machine); drop a coin
吐		tǔ	*v.*	(here) dispense (lit. "spit out")
可靠		kěkào	*adj.*	reliable
免于	免於	miǎnyú	*v.*	avoid; avert
不好意思		bùhǎoyì.si	*v.*	feel embarrassed
…以来		yǐlái	*prep.*	since
欢迎	歡迎	huānyíng	*v.*	welcome; favorably receive 这种新产品受到大家的欢迎。
标志	標誌	biāozhì	*n.*	sign; mark; symbol
仍然		réngrán	*adv.*	still; 仍
列为	列為	lièwéi	*v.*	rank as; list as
优质	優質	yōuzhì	*n.*	high quality; high grade
内容		nèiróng	*n.*	content
大力		dàlì	*adv.*	energetically; vigorously; with great exertion
总量	總量	zǒngliàng	*n.*	total
公物		gōngwù	*n.*	public property
终究	終究	zhōngjiū	*adv.*	eventually; in the end; in the long run
关系着	關係著	guān.xi.zhe	*v.*	affect; have a bearing on; have to do with
广大	廣大	guǎngdà	*adj.*	numerous 广大工人/广大青少年/受到广大人民的支持

词语例句

(1) 重新: again; anew; re-

◆ 由于在居民区找一个合适的装机点儿不容易，这台机器暂时还没有重新装回去。

Since it is not easy to find a suitable place to install the machine in the residential district, this machine has not yet been reinstalled.

1. 我不小心把名字写错了，我能不能重新再填一张表？

   I wrote my name wrong. Can I refill a new form?

2. 因为两位总统候选人的票数太接近，美国政府只好重新数佛罗里达州的选票。

   Since the two presidential candidates' votes were too close, the American government had to recount the ballots in Florida.

(2) 见不得人: not fit to be seen; shameful; cannot bear the light of the day

◆ 一些市民存在"这种东西见不得人"的思想。

Some city residents have it in their mind that this kind of thing would be embarrassing if exposed.

1. 二十年以前，婚外关系还是很见不得人的事情。可是，现在很多人都觉得没有什么大不了的。

   Twenty years ago, extramarital relationships were kept hidden, but nowadays a lot of people think they are not a big deal.

2. 在有些人看来，离婚并不是见不得人的事，相反，他们还以此为荣。

   Some people are not ashamed to get a divorce; on the contrary, they are proud of it.

(3) 除此之外: besides; in addition

◆ 除此之外，自售机的设置还引起一部分市民的担心。

In addition, the installment of the automatic vending machine aroused some citizens' worries.

1. 家庭是培养孩子的美德的主要地方。除此之外，老师的影响也不小。

   Family is the main place for nurturing children's moral excellence. In addition, teachers also have some influence on it.

2. 大量使用一次性产品肯定会浪费资源。除此之外，也会对环境造成严重的污染。

Using a large amount of disposable products will definitely waste natural resources. Besides, it will also pollute the environment seriously.

(4) 在…的同时: while doing …

◆ 他们认为自售机在方便育龄妇女的同时，也给某些违法活动带来方便。

They thought that while the vending machine brings convenience to women of childbearing age, it will also make it easier for some unlawful activities to occur.

1. 政府在发展经济的同时，还很重视教育。

　　While the government focuses on the economy, at the same time they also pay a lot of attention to education.

2. 家长在重视孩子成绩的同时，也得关心孩子的心理健康。

　　Parents should be concerned about their children's psychological health while also paying attention to their grades.

(5) 免于 v. : avoid; avert

◆ 这种自动售货机有方便、可靠和免于不好意思的优点。

This kind of vending machine has the advantage of being convenient, reliable, and avoiding embarrassment.

1. 最近有许多人感冒了。你得常洗手才能免于被传染。

　　Many people caught colds recently. You have to wash your hands often in order not to be infected.

2. 免于贫穷是最基本的人权。

　　Averting poverty is the most basic human right.

(6) （自从）…以来: since

◆ 自动售货机设置以来，平均每天吐套五百个。

Since the vending machine was installed, it has sold an average of 500 condoms every day.

1. （自从）改革开放以来，人们的价值观发生了很大的变化。

　　Since the reform and open-up, people's values have changed tremendously.

2. 我上大学以来，每个暑假都打工。

　　I worked every summer since I went to college.

(7) 把…列为…: to list sth. as …

◆ 杭州市把它列为计划生育优质服务的一项重要内容。

Hangzhou City lists it as an important component of first-rate service for family planning.

1. 政府把减少污染列为最重要的课题之一。

The government lists reducing pollution as one of the most important issues.

2. 我把搞好英语列为上大学期间最主要的目标。

I consider studying English as the major goal during college years.

(8) 大力 v. : v. energetically; v. vigorously

◆ 杭州市把它列为计划生育的一项重要内容，大力推行。

Hangzhou City lists it as one of the most important components of family planning and carries it out energetically.

1. 政府大力推行新的教育政策。

The government vigorously carries out new education policies.

2. 这些工厂正在大力开展技术革新。

These factories are making technical innovations on a big scale.

(9) 终究: eventually; in the end

◆ ……， 因为它终究关系着广大人民的健康。

……， for it plays a great part in people's health after all.

1. 靠别人生活终究不是一个长久的法子。

It is not a permanent solution to rely on other people for a living.

2. 他一定会原谅你，终究他是你父亲。

He will forgive you in the end; after all, he is your father.

(10) A 关系着 B: affect; have a bearing on; have to do with

◆ 它终究关系着广大人民的健康。

1. 政府非重视交通建设不可，因为它关系着每个人的日常生活。

The government has to pay attention to transportation because it has a bearing on everyone's daily life.

2. 农业关系着国家的经济，不容忽视。

Agriculture is of vital importance to the nation's economy and cannot be neglected.

练习

I. Make a sentence using the underlined expression.

1. 他们认为自售机<u>在</u>方便育龄妇女的<u>同时</u>，<u>也</u>给某些违法活动带来方便。

2. <u>随着</u>人民对生活质量要求的提高，自售机也应该成为人民接受并爱护的一项公物。

3. 这种自售机<u>比起</u>商店来，<u>有</u>方便、可靠<u>的优点</u>。

4. 发廊的主人嫌自售机碍眼，<u>就</u>把自售机用挂历封上了。

5. 人们最终还是会接受安全套自售机的，因为它<u>终究</u>关系着人民的健康。

II. Choose the correct answer.

1. 找一位有名的人写推荐信(tuījiànxìn: letter of recommendation)非常重要，因为这_____着你能不能找到一个好工作。

    a. 有关   b. 关于   c. 关系

2. 我打算明年_____这个大学，去别的国家旅行。

    a. 留下   b. 剩下   c. 离开

3. 我住的城市很安全，你真的_____为我担心。

    a. 没必要 b. 不必须 c. 不一定

4. 一些市民_____在街上设置安全套自售机会方便一些违法活动。

    a. 忧虑   b. 不放心 c. 担心

III. Complete the following dialogues using the expressions provided.

1. A：对一个人来说，婚姻很重要吗？

  B：＿＿＿＿＿＿＿＿＿＿＿＿＿＿＿＿＿＿＿＿。（A 关系着 B）

2. A：对不起，你刚才说的我没听清楚。

  B：好吧!＿＿＿＿＿＿＿＿＿＿＿＿＿＿＿＿＿＿。（重新 v.）

3. A：在美国，自售机都卖些什么东西？

  B：＿＿＿＿＿＿＿＿＿＿＿＿＿＿＿＿＿＿＿＿。（除此之外）

4. A：他父母搬到北京来了吗？

B： _____。（由于，暂时）

5. A: 听说许多学生对新的考试制度持反对态度。

B： _____。（尽管）

IV. Answer the following questions.

1. 比较香烟自售机和安全套自售机对社会道德和健康的影响。
2. 如果你是一个店主，你愿意不愿意在你的商店里放一个安全套自售机？为什么？
3. 在你看来，那个店主有没有权利把安全套自售机用挂历纸封上？为什么？
4. 报道中所说的"违法活动"说的到底是什么？
5. 普遍设置安全套自售机会不会鼓励婚前和婚外的性关系？

繁体字课文

今年 6 月 3 日，杭州市在街上設置了兩個安全套自動售貨機。20 多天來，銷售平穩，但同時也發生了一些令人不愉快的事，有一位店主竟用掛曆紙把自售機封上，只留下一個投幣口。

用掛曆紙把自售機封上的是一家髮廊的店主。雖然自售機裝在髮廊隔壁的飲食店門口，但是這位店主還是嫌它礙眼。現在這部機器已經被計劃生育站撤回。計劃生育站的負責人說，由於在居民區找一個合適的裝機點儿不容易，這台機器暫時還沒有重新(1)裝回去。

杭州市計劃生育站負責人認為，杭州是華東地區第一個推行安全套自售機的城市。一些居民由於傳統觀念的影響，存在"這種東西見不得人(2)”、“設在自家門口不雅觀”等思想。除此之外(3)，自售機的設置還引起一部分市民的擔心，認為自售機在方便育齡婦女的同時(4)，也給某些違法活動提供了方便。但計劃生育部門的同志跟社會學家在接受記者採訪時表示，這種憂慮是不必要的，因為安全套在各大藥房都有，街頭自售機與違法活動沒有關係。

據瞭解，杭州市計劃生育部門這次在西湖區等六個地方設置了一百多個自動售貨機，所覆蓋人口超過三十萬。這種投幣一元就可以吐套的二十四小時自動售貨機比起商店來，有方便、可靠和免於(5)不好意思的優點。自動售貨機設置以來(6)，平均每天吐套五百個。大部分杭州市民對這種銷售方式已經有科學認識並持歡迎態度。

有關負責人在接受採訪時表示，自售機是現代化城市文明的一種標誌。儘管有觀念上的爭議，但杭州市仍然把它列為(7)計劃生育優質服務的一項重要內容，大力(8)推行。今年下半年，杭州市各區都將設置安全套自售機，總量將達一千五百台左右。隨著人民經濟水平和對生活質量要求的提高，自售機也應該成為人民接受並愛護的一項公物，因為它終究(9)關係著(10)廣大人民的健康。

第二十六课　男人有没有生育权？

男人有要求妻子生育孩子的权利吗？

最近，重庆一个市民因妻子擅自(1)做堕胎手术而告到法庭。这是又一个发生在夫妻之间的关于生育权的纠纷案件。

33 岁的杨先生结婚 4 年，妻子一直不想生育。急于(2)要孩子的杨先生就用维生素片代替避孕药给妻子服食。3 个月后，妻子怀孕，但她很快决定要去堕胎。杨先生坚决反对。情急之下，他无意中(3)说出了怀孕的缘故。知道真相的妻子认为杨先生的行为不可原谅，第二天就去医院堕了胎，并要跟杨先生离婚。理由很简单：杨先生侵犯了她的生育权，是变相强迫她生育子女。律师告诉杨先生，如果妻子真的起诉他，他绝对败诉。

我国的现行法律中，对男性是否有生育权没有任何规定。那么，男人是否也应该有生育权？

有的专家认为，男人应该有生育权。生育权反映的是夫妻关系的一种权利，假如(4)这种权利单单(5)只有夫妻中的一方享有，在法理上存在问题。也有专家认为《妇女儿童保障法》中保障的是妇女身

| 生育 | | shēngyù | v. | give birth; bear |
| 重庆 | 重慶 | Chóngqìng | n. | Chongqing City, Sichuan Province |

擅自	擅自	shànzì	adv.	(do sth.) without authorization
堕胎	墮胎	duò//tāi	v.-o.	perform an abortion; abortion
手术	手術	shǒushù	n.	surgery
法庭	法庭	fǎtíng	n.	court
纠纷	糾紛	jiūfēn	n.	dispute; quarrel
杨	楊	Yáng	n.	a surname
急于	急於	jíyú	v.	be eager/anxious to do sth.
维生素片	維生素片	wéishēng sù piàn	n.	vitamin pills
代替		dàitì	v.	replace; substitute for
药	藥	yào	n.	medicine
服食		fúshí	v.	take (medicine)
怀孕	懷孕	huái//yùn	v.-o.	become pregnant
坚决	堅決	jiānjué	adv.	firmly; resolutely
反对	反對	fǎnduì	v.	oppose; be against
无意中	無意中	wúyìzhōng	adv.	accidentally; inadvertently
真相		zhēnxiàng	n.	truth; the actual state of affairs
原谅	原諒	yuánliàng	v.	forgive; excuse
侵犯		qīnfàn	v.	infringe on (one's rights)
变相	變相	biànxiàng	adv.	in disguised form; covertly 变相贪污/变相侵犯人权
强迫	強迫	qiǎngpò	v.	force; compel
起诉	起訴	qǐsù	v.	sue; bring a suit against sb.; bring an action against sb.; file a lawsuit
败诉	敗訴	bàisù	v.	lose a lawsuit
现行	現行	xiànxíng	adj.	currently in effect; in force; active
假如		jiǎrú	conj.	if; supposing; in case
单单	單單	dāndān	adv.	only
享有		xiǎngyǒu	v.	enjoy (rights, prestige, etc.) 享有平等的权利/享有公民权
法理		fǎlǐ	n.	legal principle; theory of law
保障		bǎozhàng	v.	guarantee; safeguard; protect

处弱者地位时的权利，意思就是说妻子不能在实现自己不生育的自由时，剥夺丈夫繁衍后代的权利。孩子是夫妻两人的。谁也不能单方面决定他的命运。怀孕以后孩子的去留问题应该是双方共同协商后决定的。所以专家建议在法律中加入有关规定，已婚妇女的流产手术必须经(6)丈夫同意，才可以进行。

而一名妇联干部却认为：法律没有必要为丈夫加进生育的条款。如果法律赋予(7)男性生育权的话，那么他就有权要求妻子生育，女性的不生育权就无法保证了。

另一位女士认为，真如男人所愿，给一半生育权，最终将会导致法律的紊乱。以重庆杨先生为例(8)，妻子不生，有生育自由保护；丈夫让妻子怀孕，也以生育权作为(9)借口。如果保护丈夫的权利，那么就侵犯了妻子的权利；保护了妻子的权利，则侵犯了丈夫的权利。如此下去，光讨论是否生育子女就(10)够法官忙的(11)了，这是不现实的。更有人认为解决丈夫生育权的问题，应该是在家里，而不是在法庭上。换句话说(12)，这是一个道德伦理或习俗范围里的问题，不应该由(13)法律来处理。　　《人民日报》2000 年 4 月 21 日

身处	身處	shēnchǔ	v.	be situated in; be in a certain condition
弱者		ruòzhě	n.	the weak
剥夺	剝奪	bōduó	v.	deprive; expropriate
繁衍	繁衍	fányǎn	v.	multiply; produce
单方面	單方面	dān fāngmiàn	n./adv. /adj.	one side, one-sidedly, unilateral 单方面的决定/单方面决定

命运	命運	mìngyùn	n.	fate
去留		qùliú	n.	"go or stay"(here: get an abortion or give birth)
协商	協商	xiéshāng	v.	talk things over; consult
建议	建議	jiànyì	v./n.	suggest; advise, suggestion
法规	法規	fǎguī	n.	law and regulation; code
加入		jiārù	v.	add; put in
已婚		yǐhūn	adj.	married
流产	流產	liúchǎn	n./v.	abortion, miscarry; miscarriage
经	經	jīng	prep.	through; after
妇联	婦聯	Fùlián	n.	short for 妇女联合会; The Woman's Federation
干部	幹部	gànbù	n.	cadre
加进	加進	jiājìn	v.	add; to put in; append
条款	條款	tiáokuǎn	n.	clause; article; provisions
赋予	賦予	fùyǔ	v.	give; endow; entrust
女士		nǚshì	n.	lady; Madam
如···所愿	如···所願	rú...suǒyuàn	phr.	as one wished
最终	最終	zuìzhōng	adv.	finally; ultimately
紊乱	紊亂	wěnluàn	n./adj.	disorderliness; confusion; chaos, disorder; chaotic
以···为例	以···為例	yǐ...wéi lì	phr.	take ... as an example
以···作为	以···作為	yǐ...zuòwéi	phr.	take ... as ...
借口	藉口	jièkǒu	n.	excuse
如此下去		rúcǐ xià.qu	phr.	if it keeps going on in this way
法官		fǎguān	n.	judge
现实	現實	xiànshí	adj.	realistic; practical
换句话说	換句話說	huàn jù huà shuō	phr.	in other words
伦理	倫理	lúnlǐ	n.	ethics
习俗	習俗	xísú	n.	custom
由		yóu	prep.	by

词语例句

(1) 擅自：(do sth.) without authorization

◆ 最近，重庆一个市民因为妻子擅自做堕胎手术而告到法庭。

　Recently, a Chongqing citizen brought a lawsuit against his wife because she had an abortion without consulting with him.

　1. 那个护士上班的时候擅自离开病房，导致病人的死亡。

　　That nurse left the ward without authorization while she was on duty, and this caused the patient's death.

　2. 要是有什么事情发生，等我回来，你不能擅自做决定。

　　If something happens, wait until I come back; don't make any decisions yourself.

(2)　adj 于 v.：be adj. to v.

◆ 急于要孩子的杨先生就用维生素片代替避孕药给妻子服食。

So Mr. Yang, who was anxious to have a baby, replaced his wife's contraceptive pills with vitamin pills.

　1. 下班之后他急于去学校接孩子，所以一般不跟别人聊天儿。

　　He usually doesn't chat with other people after work because he is anxious to go to pick up his child at school.

　2. 因为最近忙于写毕业论文，所以没有时间给朋友打电话。

　　I've been busy with my thesis, so I have no time to call my friends.

　3. 请你留下你的地址和电话，这样便于我们跟你联系。

　　Please leave your address and phone number so that it is easy for us to contact you.

(3) 无意中：accidentally; inadvertently

◆ 他无意中说出了怀孕的缘故。

　He inadvertently told the truth about making her pregnant.

　1. 今天我迟到是因为昨天我无意中把闹钟关掉了，所以今天早上睡过头了。

　　I was late because I turned off my alarm clock by accident yesterday, and so I overslept this morning.

2.牛顿坐在树下，无意中看见一个苹果从树上掉下来，这个现象引起了他的注意。

　　Sitting under the tree, Newton happened to see an apple dropping from the tree; this drew his attention.

(4) 假如: if; supposing; in case

◆ 假如这种权利单单只有夫妻中的一方享有，在法理上存在问题。

　　If only one side of a couple can enjoy this kind of right, it causes problems in the (theory of) law.

1.假如你丈夫不同意，你还要堕胎吗?

　　If your husband disagrees, will you still want the abortion?

2.假如我忘了，请提醒我一下。

　　Remind me in case I forget.

(5) 单单: only; solely

◆ 假如这种权利单单只有夫妻中的一方享有，在法理上存在问题。

1.那只狗为什么不咬人，单单只咬你? 一定是你先踢了它。

　　Why did that dog only bite you, of all people? You must have kicked it first.

2.别人都来了，单单他没来。

　　Everybody has arrived except him.

(6) 经… v. : after v.-ed by; after v.-ed through

◆已婚妇女的流产手术必须经丈夫同意，才可以进行。

　　The abortion of a married woman can be done only after the husband has agreed.

1.经中学老师的建议，我进了这所大学。

　　Based upon my high school teacher's proposal, I entered this university.

2.任何学生都需要经考试才能进入大学。

　　Students may only be admitted upon examination.

(7) 赋予: give; endow; entrust

◆ 如果法律赋予男性生育权的话，那么他就有权要求妻子生育，女性的不生育权就无法保证了。

　　If the law gives the male reproductive rights, the male would have the right to ask his wife to bear children; then the female's freedom of not bearing children would not be ensured in such a case.

1. 总统的权力是人民赋予的，所以应该为人民服务。

   A president's power comes from the people; therefore he should serve the people.

2. 人权是 天赋 予的，是不可剥夺的。

   Human rights, which are endowed by ~~God~~ Heaven must not be taken away.

(8) 以…为例: take...for example

◆另一位女士认为，真如男人所愿，给一半生育权，最终将会导致法律的紊乱。以重庆杨先生为例，妻子不生，有生育自由保护；丈夫让妻子怀孕，也以生育权作为借口。

Another woman believed that if men were given half of the authority to (make women) have babies as they wished, it would eventually lead to chaos in the law. Take Mr. Yang in Chongqing as an example. His wife was protected by reproductive rights to not have a baby while the husband also used the same right as an excuse to force his wife to get pregnant.

1. 美国的大学都很重视运动。以我的大学为例，每星期都有各种各样的运动比赛。

   All American universities pay a lot of attention to sports. Take my university as an example. There are various kinds of sports competitions every week.

2. 大城市的交通堵塞都很严重。以北京为例，上下班时间汽车简直走不动。

   The traffic jams in big cities are all very serious. Take Beijing as an example; the cars simply cannot move during rush hours.

(9) 以/把…作为…: take ...as ...

◆丈夫让妻子怀孕，也以生育权作为借口。

When the husband forces the wife to get pregnant, he also uses reproductive rights as an excuse.

1. 中国政府以/把发展经济作为主要的工作目标。

   The Chinese government takes developing the economy as its major goal.

2. 做子女的应该以/把赡养老年的父母作为自己应尽的义务。

   All children should consider supporting aged parents as their obligatory duty.

(10) 光…就…: only; merely

◆ 如此下去，光讨论是否生育子女就够法官忙的了。

If this keeps going on, judges will have no time to do anything but discuss whether women or men should have the right to have babies.

1. 这个学校太贵了，每年光学费就四万多。

This school is too expensive. Tuition alone costs forty thousand dollars a year!

2. 你不必告诉我他是谁，光听笑声我就知道是张先生。

You don't need to tell me who that is; I know it's Mr. Zhang just by his laughter.

(11) 够（人）忙的了: enough to make sb. busy

◆ 如此下去，光讨论是否生育子女就够法官忙的了。

1. 光做功课就够我忙的了，哪儿有时间去看电影呢！

I'm busy enough doing homework, I simply don't have time for a movie!

2. 四门课就够你忙的了，你千万别选五门课！

Four courses will make you busy enough. By all means, don't take five courses!

(12) 换句话说: in other words

◆ 换句话说，这是一个道德伦理或习俗范围里的问题，不应该由法律来处理。

In other words, this is a problem within the range of morals, ethics, or customs; it should not be handled by law.

1. 尽管有许多人同情徐力，但他犯的是杀人罪。换句话说，他不能不受到法律的制裁。

Even though many people sympathized with Xu Li, what he committed was a murder. In other words, he must be punished by law.

2. 解决污染问题光靠政府是不够的。换句话说，保护环境，人人有责。

Relying entirely on the government to solve the problem of pollution is not enough. In other words, protecting the environment is everybody's responsibility.

(13) 由 sb./sth. v. : by means of; be v.-ed by sb./sth.

◆ 换句话说，这是一个道德伦理或习俗范围里的问题，不应该由法律来处理。

1. 美国总统是由全国人民选举出来的。

The president of America is elected by Americans.

2. 这个钱该由我来付。

This money should be paid by me.

练习

I. Fill in the blank with the most appropriate word.

经　　震惊　侵犯　绝对　　因...而...

擅自　坚决　深刻　告

　　　最近在纽约，一位华裔(huáyì: American of Chinese descent)女高中生____杀死亲生父母____被____到法庭。事情的原因是这位女学生交了一个男朋友，而父母____反对。父母认为，她还是个高中学生，未____父母同意，不可以____交男朋友，他们也说____不允许她上高中时跟人谈恋爱。女儿觉得自由和权利受到了____，绝望中，就跟男朋友一起把父母杀死。这件事____了纽约的华人社会，引起了华人父母的____反思。

II. Choose the correct answer.

1. 在中国现行的法律中，没有男人有没有生育权的（有关；关于）规定。

2. 有些法律专家认为没有（必要；必须）给男人生育权。

3. 给不给男人生育权并不（被；由）妇联决定。

4. 在战争中，很多人（被迫；强迫）离开自己的家。

5. 在有些地方，妻子被看作是为丈夫（生育；出生）子女的工具。

6. 他的学费、生活费都是父母（赋予，给）的。

III. Complete the following sentences with the expressions provided.

1. 我昨天在饭馆儿里要吃鸡肉，可是服务员怎么也听不懂我的话。
_____。（情急之下，只好）

2. 我不是故意要听你们两人的私事，只是_____。(无意中)

3. 所有的事情都有好的一面的坏的一面，_____。（以…为例）

4. 有些妇女认为，法律特别保护妇女和儿童其实是____。（变相）

5. A：怎么你那么生气?

　　B: 因为我的同屋_____。（擅自）

6. 杨先生的行为是不可原谅的，_____。（换句话说）

7. 住在像纽约这样的大城市里，生活费用非常高，＿＿＿＿＿。（单单）

8. 杨先生欺骗太太的办法就是＿＿＿＿＿＿＿。（用 A 代替 B，让）

9. 我哪儿有时间谈恋爱啊? ＿＿＿＿＿＿。（光…就够…忙的了）

IV. Answer the following questions.

1. 你认为男人应该不应该有生育权? 可能不可能男人跟女人共同享有生育权? 男人享有生育权会不会侵犯女人的生育权利?

2. 如果不能男人和女人共同享有生育权，谁应该享有? 为什么?

3. 在这个事件中，你对杨先生和他的爱人的行为有什么看法?

4. 你觉得应该怎么解决这个问题?

5. 有哪些事情是属于道德伦理或习俗范围而不应该由法律来处理?

繁体字课文

男人有要求妻子生育孩子的權利嗎？

最近，重慶一個市民因妻子擅自(1)做墮胎手術而告到法庭。這是又一個發生在夫妻之間的關於生育權的糾紛案件。

33 歲的楊先生結婚 4 年，妻子一直不想生育。急於(2)要孩子的楊先生就用維生素片代替避孕藥給妻子服食。3 個月後，妻子懷孕，但她很快決定要去墮胎。楊先生堅決反對。情急之下，他無意中(3)說出了懷孕的緣故。知道真相的妻子認為楊先生的行為不可原諒，第二天就去醫院墮了胎，並要跟楊先生離婚。理由很簡單：楊先生侵犯了她的生育權，是變相強迫她生育子女。律師告訴楊先生，如果妻子真的起訴他，他絕對敗訴。

我國的現行法律中，對男性是否有生育權沒有任何規定。那麼，男人是否也應該有生育權？

有的專家認為，男人應該有生育權。生育權反映的是夫妻關係的一種權利，假如(4)這種權利單單(5)只有夫妻中的一方享有，在法理上存在問題。也有專家認為《婦女兒童保障法》中保障的是婦女身處弱者地位時的權利，意思就是說妻子不能在實現自己不生育的自由時，剝奪丈夫繁衍後代的權利。孩子是夫妻兩人的。誰也不能單方面決定他的命運。懷孕以後孩子的去留問題應該是雙方共同協商後決定的。所以專家建議在法律中加入有關規定，已婚婦女的流產手術必須經(6)丈夫同意，才可以進行。

　　而一名婦聯幹部卻認為：法律沒有必要為丈夫加進生育的條款。如果法律賦予(7)男性生育權的話，那麼他就有權要求妻子生育，女性的不生育權就無法保證了。

　　另一位女士認為，真如男人所願，給一半生育權，最終將會導致法律的紊亂。以重慶楊先生為例(8)，妻子不生，有生育自由保護；丈夫讓妻子懷孕，也以生育權作為(9)藉口。如果保護丈夫的權利，那麼就侵犯了妻子的權利；保護了妻子的權利，則侵犯了丈夫的權利。如此下去，光討論是否生育子女就(10)夠法官忙的(11)了，這是不現實的。更有人認為解決丈夫生育權的問題，應該是在家裏，而不是在法庭上。換句話說(12)，這是一個道德倫理或習俗範圍裏的問題，不應該由(13)法律來處理。

第二十七课　　尊重人格尊严

（一）人格尊严受到侵害

近年来，经常在报上看到侵害人格尊严的案件。去年，两位小学六年级的老师为了抬高毕业班总成绩，就哄骗成绩较差的学生假装(1)成弱智学生，并开出弱智证明，把学生推上求学无门的绝路(2)。

还是去年，四川一个小学老师因为几个学生违反课堂纪律又都不敢承认(3)，就强迫全班 80 多名学生集体在教室里下跪。

今年，一名 17 岁的女孩儿在武汉市一个超市偷了两包食品，商店的工作人员用白底红字牌写了"偷"字挂在她的胸前，强迫她站在店门前示众。

尊重		zūnzhòng	v.	respect; esteem
人格		réngé	n.	moral integrity
尊严	尊嚴	zūnyán	n.	dignity
抬高		táigāo	v.-c.	raise; increase
毕业班	畢業班	bìyèbān	n.	graduating class
总	總	zǒng	adj.	total; overall
总成绩	總成績	zǒng chéngjì	n.	overall score
哄骗	哄騙	hǒngpiàn	v.	trick; cheat
假装	假裝	jiǎzhuāng	v.	pretend; feign

弱智		rùozhì	*adj.*	mentally retarded
开	開	kāi	*v.*	write out (a certificate) 医生给他开了一个生病的 证明。
证明	證明	zhèngmíng	*n.*	certificate; testimonial
推		tuī	*v.*	push
无门	無門	wúmén	*v.-o.*	have no way (of doing sth.)
绝路	絕路	juélù	*n.*	road to ruin; impasse 走上了绝路/被推上了绝路
四川		Sìchuān	*n.*	Sichuan Province
违反	違反	wéifǎn	*v.*	violate
课堂	課堂	kètáng	*n.*	classroom
纪律	紀律	jìlù	*n.*	discipline; morale
承认	承認	chéngrèn	*v.*	confess
强迫	強迫	qiǎngpò	*v.*	force (sb. to do sth.) 强迫他把所有的菜吃完
集体	集體	jítǐ	*adv.*	collectively
下跪		xià//guì	*v.-o.*	kneel
武汉	武漢	Wǔhàn	*n.*	Wuhan City, Hubei Province
超市		chāoshì	*n.*	supermarket; 超级市场
包		bāo	*AN*	measure word for wrapped things
工作人员	工作人員	gōngzuò rényuán	*n.*	staff
底		dǐ	*n.*	background
牌（子）		pái(.zi)	*n.*	plate; tablet
挂	掛	guà	*v.*	hang
胸		xiōng	*n.*	chest
示众	示眾	shìzhòng	*v.*	publicly expose (as a punishment)

在上述行为中，侵权的具体方式虽然各有不同，但都有一个共同的特点，这就是使受害人的人格尊严受到严重的损害。

（二）保护人格尊严

上述行为，都严重地侵害了人格尊严，都是违反法律的侵权行为。但是不仅实施侵害行为的教师不知道这侵害了人格尊严，就是在实施侵权行为之后，受害人自己及其监护人也都不知道受害人的人格尊严受到了严重的侵害，有权要求赔偿。

我国法律早就确认了人格尊严。《宪法》中明文规定(4)："中华人民共和国公民的人格尊严不受侵犯。"

1991 年 12 月 23 日，两个女青年到北京一个超级市场购买商品。在她们交完钱准备离开时，超级市场的两名男保安将二人拦住，并将二人推进一间仓库，强行(5)要求她们摘下帽子，解开衣服，打开包，进行检查。检查后发现二人并没有偷窃行为，才让她们走。

这一事件，正是典型的侵犯人格尊严的案例。它引起了公众的愤怒。

特点	特點	tèdiǎn	n.	characteristic; trait
受害人	受害人	shòuhàirén	n.	victim
损害	損害	sǔnhài	n./v.	harm; damage
侵权行为	侵權行為	qīnquán xíngwéi	n.	tort

实施	實施	shíshī	v.	(here: legal term) do, put into effect; implement
其		qí	*pron.*	his or her
监护人	監護人	jiānhùrén	n.	guardian
赔偿	賠償	péicháng	v./n.	compensate; pay for; indemnification
确认	確認	quèrèn	v.	confirm; recognize
宪法	憲法	xiànfǎ	n.	constitution; charter
明文规定	明文規定	míngwén guīdìng	v.	stipulate in explicit terms
公民		gōngmín	n.	citizen
购买	購買	gòumǎi	v.	buy
商品		shāngpǐn	n.	goods; merchandise
交（钱）	交（錢）	jiāo	v.	pay
离开	離開	líkāi	v.	leave
保安		bǎoān	n.	sccurity personnel
拦住	攔住	lán//zhù	v.-c.	hold back; stop
推进	推進	tuī//jìn	v.-c.	push into
仓库	倉庫	cāngkù	n.	warehouse; storehouse
强行	強行	qiángxíng	adv.	(do sth.) by force
摘下		zhāi//xià	v.-c.	take off (hat, glasses, etc.)
解开	解開	jiě//kāi	v.-c.	unbutton; untie
打开	打開	dǎ//kāi	v.-c.	open
包		bāo	n.	bag; sack
检查	檢查	jiǎnchá	v.	examine; check; inspect
走		zǒu	v.	leave; go away
正		zhèng	adv.	precisely; exactly
典型		diǎnxíng	adj.	typical
案例	案例	ànlì	n.	case
公众	公眾	gōngzhòng	n.	the public; the community
愤怒	憤怒	fènnù	adj./n.	indignant, angry

目前重要的是，从理论上和实践上都要加强对人格尊严的研究和宣传，使更多的法律专业人士和群众熟悉并掌握这一法律赋予的权利，更好地保护他人，保护自己。

《人民日报》2000 年 7 月 19 日

理论	理論	lǐlùn	*n.*	theory
实践	實踐	shíjiàn	*n./v.*	practice
研究		yánjiū	*v./n.*	study; research
宣传	宣傳	xuānchuán	*v./n.*	give publicity to; advertisement
专业人士	專業人士	zhuānyè rénshì	*n.*	professionals
群众	群眾	qúnzhòng	*n.*	the masses
熟悉		shúxī	*n.*	know sb./sth. well; be familiar with 我对北京的交通规则不太熟悉。
掌握		zhǎngwò	*v.*	grasp; master

词语例句

(1) 假装: pretend; feign

◆ 去年，两位小学六年级的老师哄骗成绩较差的学生假装成弱智学生。

Last year, two teachers teaching sixth grade in an elementary school tricked students with lower scores into pretending to be mentally retarded.

1. 他假装生病。

   He faked illness.

2. 他假装成中国人。

   He pretended to be a Chinese.

(2) 把···推上绝路: put···to a road to ruin

◆ 两名小学老师哄骗成绩较差的学生假装成弱智学生，并开出弱智证明，把学生推上求学无门的绝路。

Two teachers tricked students into pretending to be mentally retarded and wrote out certificates which confirmed they were mentally retarded, making it impossible for them to continue their education.

1. 母亲给他的沉重的学习压力和脆弱的心理状态把徐力推上了绝路。

   The heavy pressure from Xu Li's mother and his fragile mentality put him onto the road to ruin.

2. 不公平的社会制度把他推上了绝路。

   It was the unfair social system that left him at a dead end.

(3) 承认: admit; confess

◆ 几个学生违反了课堂纪律又不敢承认。

Severl students violated the class rules and dared not admit it.

1. 克林顿不得不承认他有了婚外关系。

   Clinton had no choice but to confess that he had an extramarital relationship.

2. 我承认是我打破了窗户。

   I admit to breaking the window.

(4) 明文规定: stipulate explicitly; expressly provide

◆ 《宪法》中明文规定：中华人民共和国公民的人格尊严不受侵犯。

The constitution expressly provides that the human dignity of citizens of the People's Republic of China must not be violated.

1. 政府明文规定，电视上不能出现烟草广告。

The government stipulates in explicit terms that tobacco advertisements are prohibited on TV.

2. 学校当局明文规定，学生打工每周不得超过十八个钟头。

The university authorities expressly stipulate that university students must not work more than eighteen hours per week.

(5) 强行: forcefully

◆ （男保安）强行要求她们摘下帽子，解开衣服，打开包，进行检查。

The security guards forcefully asked them to take off their hats, unbutton their clothes, and open their purses for inspection.

1. 尽管大多数人反对这个议案，他们还是强行通过了。

They forced the bill through even though the majority opposed it.

2. 警察强行进入她的家，把她的丈夫带走了。

The police forcefully entered her house and took her husband away.

练习

I. Choose the most appropriate word for each blank and fill in with its Chinese equivalent.

pretend to	write out a certificate	typical
kneel (down)	publicly expose	compensate

1. 如果你真的生病，不能考试，得请医生给你_____。

2. 100 年前，要是一个中国女人有了婚外关系，一定会受到严厉的惩罚，轻则_____，重则被杀死。

3. 他在父母面前_____，请父母原谅他的错。

4. 要是航空公司把你的行李弄丢了，你绝对有权要求_____。

5. 苹果馅饼(apple pie)可以说是最_____的美国甜点(pastry)了。

6. 当路边的乞丐向行人要钱时，大部分的行人都 ＿＿＿＿＿ 没听见或没看见。

II. Make a sentence using the underlined expression.

1. 两个小学老师<u>为了</u>抬高毕业班总成绩，<u>就</u>哄骗成绩较差的学生假装成弱智学生。

2. 在上述行为中，侵权的具体方式<u>虽然各有不同，但都有一个共同的特点</u>，这就是使受害人的人格尊严受到严重的损害。

3. 但是<u>不仅</u>实施侵害行为的教师不知道这侵害了人格尊严，<u>就是</u>受害人自己及其监护人<u>也</u>不知道。

4. 宪法中<u>明文规定</u>：中华人民共和国公民的人格尊严不受侵犯。

5. 目前重要的是：使更多的法律专业人士和群众熟悉和掌握法律赋予的权利，<u>更好地</u>保护他人，保护自己。

III. Answer the following questions.

1. 在这篇报道中，哪一件事让你最愤怒？为什么？

2. 在超市中，假如有人偷窃商品，工作人员应该怎么处理才合理？

3. 怎么样才可以防止损害人格尊严？

4. 在美国你听过类似这样的损害人格尊严的事吗？说说你的经验。

5. 举几个例子说明美国社会尊重人格尊严的做法。

繁体字课文

（一）人格尊嚴受到侵害

近年來，經常在報上看到侵害人格尊嚴的案件。去年，兩位小學六年級的老師為了抬高畢業班總成績，就哄騙成績較差的學生假裝(1)成弱智學生，並開出弱智證明，把學生推上求學無門的絕路(2)。

還是去年，四川一個小學老師因為幾個學生違反課堂紀律又都不敢承認(3)，就強迫全班 80 多名學生集體在教室裏下跪。

今年，一名 17 歲的女孩儿在武漢市一個超市偷了兩包食品，商店的工作人員用白底紅字牌寫了"偷"字掛在她的胸前，強迫她站在店門前示眾。

在上述行為中，侵權的具體方式雖然各有不同，但都有一個共同的特點，這就是使受害人的人格尊嚴受到嚴重的損害。

（二）保護人格尊嚴

上述行為，都嚴重地侵害了人格尊嚴，都是違反法律的侵權行為。但是不僅實施侵害行為的教師不知道這侵害了人格尊嚴，就是在實施侵權行為之後，受害人自己及其監護人也都不知道受害人的人格尊嚴受到了嚴重的侵害，有權要求賠償。

我國法律早就確認了人格尊嚴。《憲法》中明文規定(4)："中華人民共和國公民的人格尊嚴不受侵犯。"

1991 年 12 月 23 日，兩個女青年到北京一個超級市場購買商品。在她們交完錢準備離開時，超級市場的兩名男保安將二人攔住，並將二人推進一間倉庫，強行(5)要求她們摘下帽子，解開衣服，打開包，進行檢查。檢查後發現二人並沒有偷竊行為，才讓她們走。

這一事件，正是典型的侵犯人格尊嚴的案例。它引起了公眾的憤怒。

目前重要的是，從理論上和實踐上都要加強對人格尊嚴的研究和宣傳，使更多的法律專業人士和群眾熟悉並掌握這一法律賦予的權利，更好地保護他人，保護自己。

第二十八课　　儿童乞丐

（一）不给钱就不"放行"

在北京过街天桥、地铁出入口或商店门口，常常可以看到一些不到(1)10 岁的小孩儿截住过往行人，不给钱就"不放行"。尽管这种沿街要钱的小孩儿很少，但他们的行为却给城市带来了一种不愉快。这种不劳而获的谋生方式更会对孩子的人格产生非常不好的影响。

一位朋友不久前告诉记者，她在北京某过街天桥被几个看上去(2)农村模样(3)的小孩儿"围攻"，不给钱就"不放行"，给每人一角两角也不让走。最后，每个小孩儿都得到五角钱之后才"放行"。"这些孩子长大后怎么办？"

记者也曾在过街天桥上见过 3 个不到 10 岁的小孩儿向(4)行人要钱，不给钱就"不放行"，而小孩儿后面跟着两个带外地口音的妇女。这两个妇女手上拎着一个过时的提包，假装行人跟在小孩儿后面不远的地方。

记者注意到北京动物园儿过街天桥、西单过街天桥、地铁出入口这些外地游客多、行人多的繁华地段，一些结伴的小孩儿不断地向行人要钱。在动物园儿过街天桥，三个小孩儿一边儿喝着易拉罐儿饮

过街天桥	過街天橋	guòjiē tiānqiáo	n.	overhead walkway

出入口		chūrùkǒu	*n.*	exit and entrance; 出口 and 入口
不到		búdào	*v.*	less than
截住		jié//zhù	*v.-c.*	stop; intercept
过往	過往	guòwǎng	*v.*	coming and going
放行		fàngxíng	*v.*	let sb. pass (by an authority)
沿街		yánjiē	*adv.*	along the street
产生	產生	chǎnshēng	*v.*	produce 产生了很好的结果/产生重大影响
看上去		kàn.shang.qu	*v.*	look like
模样	模樣	múyàng	*n.*	appearance; look
围攻	圍攻	wéigōng	*v.*	attack from all sides
向…要钱	向…要錢	xiàng…yào qián	*phr.*	beg money from
外地		wàidì	*n.*	place other than where one is
口音		kǒuyīn	*n.*	accent 他说话时带着一点儿南方口音。
拎	拎	līn	*v.*	hold something by the arm 他拎着那么多东西，你去帮帮忙吧！
过时	過時	guòshí	*adj.*	out of fashion
提包		tíbāo	*n.*	handbag
动物园儿	動物園儿	dòngwùyuánr	*n.*	zoo
游客		yóukè	*n.*	tourist
繁华	繁華	fánhuá	*adj.*	prosperous
地段		dìduàn	*n.*	area
结伴	結伴	jié//bàn	*v.-o.*	join company with sb. 我跟你结伴到车站去吧！ 我们两个人总是结伴回家。
不断	不斷	búduàn	*adv.*	continuously; constantly

料，一边儿(5)观察行人。一位打扮入时的姑娘走过天桥，三个小孩儿就突然出现在这位姑娘面前，吓了她一跳。低头一看，一个小孩儿抱住她的腿正在"哭"；另一个小孩儿硬(6)拉着她的花裙子不放；第三个小孩儿站在她的面前，双手伸开，意思是不给钱就不能走。姑娘刚开始还试图逃走，后来可能是怕小孩儿把她的裙子撕破，于是打开了钱包；她以为这就解决了问题，谁知道其中一个孩子得到的钱和另外两个孩子的钱数不一样。这个小孩儿非要姑娘"补足"，姑娘不得不满足这个小孩儿的要求。姑娘走后，小孩儿们又高兴地喝起易拉罐儿来了。

（二）让人担心的问题

记者发现，在什么地段要钱，向什么人要钱，用什么方法要钱，这些 10 岁左右的小孩儿都很清楚。在热闹繁华的地段，最能截住行人的地方是天桥、地铁出入口或商店门口，因为行人通过这些地段时，一般会自然放慢速度，加上地段狭窄，行人简直没有地方躲闪。记者观察到，小孩儿知道哪些人可能会给钱——打扮入时的姑

一边儿…一边儿…	一邊儿…一邊儿…	yìbiānr...yì biānr...		do A while doing B; do A and B at the same time
饮料	飲料	yǐnliào	*n.*	drinks
观察	觀察	guānchá	*v.*	observe; survey
打扮		dǎbàn	*v./n.*	dress up; make up, attire

入时	入時	rùshí	*adj.*	fashionable; trendy
姑娘		gū.niang	*n.*	girl; young lady
面前		miànqián	*n.*	in front of sb.
吓一跳	嚇一跳	xià yí tiào	*v.*	startle or scare sb. 他突然站起来，吓了我一大跳。 他竟然哭了起来，使我吓了一 跳。
低头	低頭	dī//tóu	*v.-o.*	hang one's head　低下头/低着头
抱住		bào//zhù	*v.-c.*	hold with both arms tightly; embrace
哭		kū	*v.*	cry
硬		yìng	*adv.*	obstinately
拉		lā	*v.*	pull
花裙子		huāqún.zi	*n.*	floral skirt
不放		búfàng	*v.*	not release; not let go one's hold
双手	雙手	shuāng shǒu	*n.*	both hands
伸开	伸開	shēn//kāi	*v.-c.*	stretch; extend
试图	試圖	shìtú	*v.*	try; attempt
撕破	撕破	sī//pò	*v.-c.*	tear
钱包	錢包	qiánbāo	*n.*	wallet; purse
非要		fēiyào	*adv.*	simply must; 非要…不可
补足	補足	bǔ//zú	*v.-c.*	make up the difference
满足	滿足	mǎnzú	*v.*	satisfy
热闹	熱鬧	rè.nao	*adj.*	bustling with noise and excitement ; lively 大街上热闹得很。 热闹的饭馆儿/热闹的市场
通过	通過	tōngguò	*v.*	pass by
放慢		fàngmàn	*v.*	slow down
狭窄	狹窄	xiázhǎi	*adj.*	narrow
躲闪	躲閃	duǒshǎn	*v.*	dodge; evade; get out of the way

娘、成对的青年男女、看上去和善以及看上去有钱的人，都是小孩儿们要钱的主要对象。

记者想知道这些小孩儿的有关问题：他们是从什么地方来的？在北京住在哪里？由什么人带出来的？家里究竟(7)穷不穷？为什么不上学？即使记者答应给他们很多钱，这些小孩儿都不回答，而且躲得远远的。显然这些孩子是受过训练的，知道要钱时应该注意什么！

行人对这些小孩儿的行为怎么看呢？曾在西单过街天桥被"围攻"过的一对青年男女笑着对记者说："他们哪里是在讨钱，明明(8)是在抢钱！碰到抢劫犯还可以报警或搏斗搏斗，被这些小孩儿截住，骂不得打不得，还真没有办法。"其他被截过的行人，嘴里不停地说："这些小孩儿的大人呢？"看热闹的人也说："这些小孩儿不应该跑到北京来讨钱，该上学。"

儿童向行人要钱令人担心。一般来说，儿童要钱的原因有三点：首先，从全社会来讲，社会发生变化之后，一定比例的家庭处于贫困状态；同时，也有一些家庭并不贫困，但是却要小孩儿出门讨钱；最后一个原因可能是父母带小孩儿来北京讨钱是为了"致富"。尽管沿街要钱的小孩儿人数很少，但是他们毕竟(9)是小孩儿，应

成对	成對	chéngduì	adj.	in a pair
和善		héshàn	adj.	kind and gentle; genial
对象	對象	duìxiàng	n.	target; object

究竟		jiūjìng	*adv.*	(used in a question) actually; exactly
上学	上學	shàng//xué	*v.-o.*	attend school; go to school; be at school
				六岁以上的孩子都应该上学。
				他今天早上 7 点钟就上学去了。
答应	答應	dāyìng	*v.*	promise; comply with, agree; consent
				他答应马上办这件事。
				我不能答应你的要求。
躲		duǒ	*v.*	hide
显然	顯然	xiǎnrán	*adv.*	obviously; clearly
讨钱	討錢	tǎo//qián	*v.-o.*	beg for money
明明		míngmíng	*adv.*	clearly; evidently
抢	搶	qiǎng	*v.*	rob; loot
碰到		pèng//.dào	*v.*	run into; encounter
抢劫	搶劫	qiǎngjié	*v.*	rob; loot; plunder
抢劫犯	搶劫犯	qiǎngjiéfàn	*n.*	robber; mugger
报警	報警	bào//jǐng	*v.-o.*	report (an incident) to police
				我已經打 911 电话报了警了。
搏斗	搏鬥	bódòu	*v.*	fight; wrestle; engage in hand-to-hand combat
v. 不得		.bu.de	*v.-c.*	must not v.; may not v.
				买不得/去不得/做不得
骂	罵	mà	*v.*	scold; abuse
不停地		bùtíng.de	*adv.*	continuously
大人		dàrén	*n.*	(here) parents; elder member of a family
看热闹	看熱鬧	kàn rè.nao	*v.-o.*	watch the fun; watch the excitement
贫困	貧困	pínkùn	*adj.*	impoverished; poor
致富		zhìfù	*v.*	get rich
毕竟	畢竟	bìjìng	*adv.*	after all

该在学校读书的。现在问题是，这个问题究竟要如何解决？又应该由哪些部门来解决呢？

《光明日报》1998 年 7 月 13 日

如何	*rúhé*	*pron.*	how; 怎么

词语例句

(1) 不到: less than; under

◆ 一些不到 10 岁的小孩儿截住过往行人。
Some kids under 10 years old stopped the pedestrian traffic.

1. 不到一个小时她就把考试做完了。
She completed the test in less than one hour.

2. 公立学校的学费比较便宜，一年不到两万块钱。
The tuition of public school is relatively inexpensive; it is less than twenty thousand per year.

(2) 看上去: looks like; appears

◆ 她在北京某过街天桥被几个看上去农村模样的小孩儿"围攻"。
On an overpass in Beijing she "came under attack from all sides" by a few kids who looked like they were from the countryside.

1. 他看上去还是个中学生。
He looks like a high school student.

2. 这件事看上去在短时间内解决不了。
It looks that this cannot be solved in a short period of time.

(3) …模样: with the appearance of …

◆ 她在北京某过街天桥被几个看上去农村模样的小孩儿"围攻"。

　1. 那个老师模样的人走进了教室。

　　The man who looks like a teacher entered the classroom.

　2. 儿子的模样很像父亲。

　　The son takes after his father.

(4) 向… v. : v. from

◆ 3 个不到 10 岁的小孩儿向行人要钱。

Three kids under 10 years old asked for money from the pedestrians.

　1. 许多中国人喜欢向外国老师学习英语。

　　Many Chinese like to learn English from a foreign teacher.

　2. 每年中国都向外国公司购买大量的飞机。

　　Every year China purchased many airplanes from foreign companies.

(5) 一边儿…, 一边儿…: doing v. 1 while doing v. 2 at the same time

◆ 三个小孩儿一边儿喝着易拉罐儿饮料，一边儿观察行人。

　The three kids drank from the pop-top can while surveying the pedestrians.

　1. 我喜欢跟朋友一边喝茶, 一边聊天。

　　I enjoy chatting with friends over a cup of tea.

　2. 他们一边工作一边学习。

　　They learn and work at the same time.

(6) 硬 v. : v. obstinately

◆ 另一个小孩儿硬拉着她的花裙子不放。

　Another child firmly pulled on her skirt and wouldn't let go.

　1. 她明明很累，可是硬说不累。

　　She clearly looked tired, but she insisted that she wasn't.

　2. 我对中文没什么兴趣，可使父母硬要我学。

　　I'm not interested in learning Chinese, but my parents (obstinately) want me to study it anyway.

(7) 究竟: (used in a question) actually; exactly

◆ 他们家里究竟穷不穷?

Are their families actually poor or not?

　1. 你们究竟要什么?

What exactly do you want?

2. 这些孩子究竟是从哪儿来的?

Where did these kids come from exactly?

(8) 明明: obviously; undoubtedly; plainly

◆ 他们哪里是在讨钱, 明明是在抢钱!

They are not begging, they are obviously robbing!

1. 你明明没懂, 为什么要假装懂了呢?

Obviously you didn't understand. Why would you pretend that you've understood already?

2. 这话明明是她说的, 我怎么会骗你呢!

It is undoubtedly she who has said that. Why would I lie to you?

(9) 毕竟: after all; at least

◆ 但他们毕竟是小孩儿, 现在应该在学校读书。

After all, they are still kids and are supposed to study in school now.

1. 虽然他很聪明, 可是毕竟刚来, 对工作还不熟悉。

Although he is smart, after all, he is new to the work and isn't good at it yet.

2. 他虽然不好, 可是毕竟是我弟弟, 我得照顾他。

Although he did misbehave, he is my brother after all; I have to take care of him.

练习

I. Choose the correct answer.

1. 当孩子告诉父母他不继续上学了, _____。

      a. 孩子吓了一跳　b.父母吓了一跳　c.父母吓了孩子一跳

2. 我不认识路, 请你走在前面, _____。

      a. 我跟在你后面　b.你跟在我后面　c.你跟着我

3. 你说得太快了, 我听不懂, 请你_____。

      a.说得慢　b.慢速度　c.放慢速度

4. 我上大学时靠奖学金过日子, 很少_____父母要钱。

      a.从　b.由　c.向

5. 我们中学的电脑都是_____那家公司免费提供的。

      a.由　b.给　c.被

II. Make a sentence using the underlined expressions.

1. 姑娘以为给了钱就能走, <u>谁知道</u>因为孩子们的钱数不一样, 他们非要她补足。

2. 你<u>哪里</u>是来帮我的, <u>明明</u>是来给我找麻烦的。

3. 第三个孩子站在她的前面, 双手伸开, <u>意思是</u>不给钱就不能走。

4. <u>即使</u>记者答应给他们很多钱, 这些孩子都不回答。

5. <u>尽管</u>要钱的小孩儿人数很少, <u>可是</u>他们<u>毕竟</u>是小孩儿, 应该在学校里读书。

6. 在北京过街天桥、地铁出入口或商店门口, 常常可以看到一些<u>不到</u> 10 岁的小孩儿截住过往行人。

7. 他们家里<u>究竟</u>穷不穷?

III. Choose the most appropriate word for each blank and fill in with its Chinese equivalent.

      accent   pretend   stop   reap without sowing
      tear   obstinately   prosperous

1. "快 _____ 那个人, 他抢了我的钱包! "一个老人大声喊着。

2. 你的南方 _____那么重, 别人一听就听出来了。

3. 这是新书，你看的时候小心一点儿，别 _____ 了。

4. 昨天我本来很不想看电影，可是女朋友 _____ 要我去，结果我在电影院里睡了一个多小时。

5. 有些年轻人不想努力工作，却总想过 _____ 的生活。

6. 年轻人多半喜欢住在 _____ 的大城市里。

7. 他的脾气真好，即使别人当面笑他，他也 _____ 听不懂。

IV. Answer the question using the expressions provided.

1. 哪些人是儿童乞丐要钱的主要对象？为什么？

　　（看上去，模样，入时，成对，和善，训练，往往，怕，即使）

2. 为什么有时候儿童乞丐会让人觉得很不愉快？

　　（突然，面前，吓一跳，抱住，拉住，非要，要不然，甚至，抢，满足）

V. Answer the following questions.

1. 从社会安全、孩子的人格发展、孩子的将来等方面谈谈儿童做乞丐有什么坏处？

2. 中国乞丐跟美国乞丐有什么不同吗？

3. 你遇到乞丐以后怎么办？你同情不同情他们？

4. 给儿童乞丐钱是不是帮助他们最好的办法？为什么？

繁体字课文

（一）不給錢就不"放行"

在北京過街天橋、地鐵出入口或商店門口，常常可以看到一些不到(1)10 歲的小孩儿截住過往行人，不給錢就"不放行"。儘管這種沿街要錢的小孩儿很少，但他們的行為卻給城市帶來了一種不愉快。這種不勞而獲的謀生方式更會對孩子的人格產生非常不好的影響。

一位朋友不久前告訴記者，她在北京某過街天橋被幾個看上去(2)農村模樣(3)的小孩儿"圍攻"，不給錢就"不放行"，給每人一角兩角也不讓走。最後，每個小孩儿都得到五角錢之後才"放行"。"這些孩子長大後怎麼辦？"

記者也曾在過街天橋上見過 3 個不到 10 歲的小孩儿向(4)行人要錢，不給錢就"不放行"，而小孩儿後面跟著兩個帶外地口音的婦女。這兩個婦女手上拎著一個過時的提包，假裝行人跟在小孩儿後面不遠的地方。

記者注意到北京動物園儿過街天橋、西單過街天橋、地鐵出入口這些外地遊客多、行人多的繁華地段，一些結伴的小孩儿不斷地向行人要錢。在動物園儿過街天橋，三個小孩儿一邊儿喝著易拉罐儿飲料，一邊儿(5)觀察行人。一位打扮入時的姑娘走過天橋，三個小孩儿就突然出現在這位姑娘面前，嚇了她一跳。低頭一看，一個小孩儿抱住她的腿正在"哭"；另一個小孩儿硬(6)拉著她的花裙子不放；第三個小孩儿站在她的面前，雙手伸開，意思是不給錢就不能走。姑娘剛開始還試圖逃走，後來可能是怕小孩儿把她的裙子撕破，於是打開了錢包；她以為這就解決了問題，誰知道其中一個孩子得到的錢和另外兩個孩子的錢數不一樣。這個小孩儿非要姑娘"補足"，姑娘不得不滿足這個小孩儿的要求。姑娘走後，小孩儿們又高興地喝起易拉罐儿來了。

（二）讓人擔心的問題

記者發現，在什麼地段要錢，向什麼人要錢，用什麼方法要錢，這些 10 歲左右的小孩儿都很清楚。在熱鬧繁華的地段，最能截住行人的地方是天橋、地鐵出入口或商店門口，因為行人通過這些地段時，一般會自然放慢速度，加上地段狹窄，行人簡直沒有地方躲閃。記者觀察到，小孩儿知道哪些人可能會給錢——打扮入時的姑娘、成對的青年男女、看上去和善以及看上去有錢的人，都是小孩儿們要錢的主要對象。

記者想知道這些小孩儿的有關問題：他們是從什麼地方來的？在北京住在哪裏？由什麼人帶出來的？家裏究竟(7)窮不窮？為什麼不上學？即使記者答應給他們很多錢，這些小孩儿都不回答，而且躲得遠遠的。顯然這些孩子是受過訓練的，知道要錢時應該注意什麼！

行人對這些小孩儿的行為怎麼看呢？曾在西單過街天橋被"圍攻"過的一對青年男女笑著對記者說："他們哪裏是在討錢，明明(8)是在搶錢！碰到搶劫犯還可以報警或搏鬥搏鬥，被這些小孩儿截住，罵不得打不得，還真沒有辦法。"其他被截過的行人，嘴裏不停地說："這些小孩儿的大人呢？"看熱鬧的人也說："這些小孩儿不應該跑到北京來討錢，該上學。"

儿童向行人要錢令人擔心。一般來說，儿童要錢的原因有三點：首先，從全社會來講，社會發生變化之後，一定比例的家庭處於貧困狀態；同時，也有一些家庭並不貧困，但是卻要小孩儿出門討錢；最後一個原因可能是父母帶小孩儿來北京討錢是為了"致富"。儘管沿街要錢的小孩儿人數很少，但是他們畢竟(9)是小孩儿，應該在學校讀書的。現在問題是，這個問題究竟要如何解決？又應該由哪些部門來解決呢？

第二十九课　　中国要控制吸烟率上升趋势

　　今天是世界卫生组织发起(1)的第 12 个世界无烟日。中国副总理李岚清发表书面讲话，表示要把控制吸烟作为政府的职责，采取更有效的措施控制吸烟率上升的趋势。

　　李岚清在讲话中指出，中国政府从 1979 年以来一直大力提倡控制吸烟的工作，成绩显著。但全国的吸烟率，特别是青少年和妇女的吸烟率仍在持续上升，因为吸烟得病和死亡的人数也在上升，中国控制吸烟的任务仍然很艰巨。

　　中国现有 3.2 亿人吸烟。1996 年的调查表明，与 1984 年相比(2)，中国人吸烟率上升了 3.74%，开始吸烟的年龄提前(3)了 3 岁，吸烟者每日平均吸烟量增加了 2 支，青少年吸烟率上升明显。近年来中国因肺癌而死亡的人数每年以 4.5%的速度增加。

　　中国在 20 年前开始正式展开控制吸烟的工作，包括吸烟危害健康的教育，立法以及在公共场所禁止吸烟等措施。卫生部部长张

控制		kòngzhì	v.	control
吸烟	吸煙	xī//yān	v.-o.	smoke
上升		shàngshēng	v.	rise; ascend
趋势	趨勢	qūshì	n.	trend
世界卫生组织	世界衛生組織	Shìjiè Wèishēng Zǔzhī	n.	World Health Organization
发起	發起	fāqǐ	v.	initiate; sponsor

世界无烟日	世界無煙日	Shìjiè Wúyānrì	n.	No Smoking Day
副——		fù	prefix	vice-
总理	總理	zǒnglǐ	n.	premier; prime minister
李岚清	李嵐清	Lǐ Lánqīng	n.	personal name
发表	發表	fābiǎo	v.	deliver; issue; announce
书面	書面	shūmiàn	adj.	in written form; in writing
讲话	講話	jiǎnghuà	n.	speech
职责	職責	zhízé	n.	duty; responsibility
显著	顯著	xiǎnzhù	adj.	notable; remarkable; outstanding
持续	持續	chíxù	v.	continue
得病		dé//bìng	v.-o.	fall ill; be ill 得了病/得了严重的病
死亡		sǐwáng	v.	die; be dead
任务	任務	rènwù	n.	mission; assignment; task; duties
艰巨	艱巨	jiānjù	adj.	extremely difficult; arduous
现（在）	現（在）	xiàn (zài)	n.	now
相比		xiāngbǐ	v.	compared with
提前		tíqián	v.	shift to an earlier date/time
支		zhī	AN	measure word for long and narrow objects
肺癌	肺癌	fèiái	n.	lung cancer
正式		zhèngshì	adv. /adj.	formally; officially, formal
包括		bāokuò	v.	include
危害		wēihài	v.	harm; endanger
立法		lìfǎ	v.-o.	enact law; legislate
以及		yǐjí	conj.	as well as; along with
公共场所	公共場所	gōnggòng chǎngsuǒ	n.	public places
卫生部	衛生部	Wèishēngbù	n.	Ministry of Health
部长	部長	bùzhǎng	n.	minister

333

文康说，全国已有 85 个城市颁布在公共场所禁止吸烟的规定；自 1991 年起(4)逐步取消新闻媒体上的烟草广告，北京等 10 个城市首先成为"无烟草广告城市"；1997 年还在北京成功地举办了第 10 届世界烟草与健康大会。

但他强调，中国必须认识到控制吸烟工作面临的巨大考验和挑战，"特别是有些发达国家的烟草商因为在国内受到限制和责难，就转向中国等发展中国家推销香烟，诱惑青少年吸洋烟。"

张文康要求继续开展"无烟学校"等活动，使全国 2 亿多学生逐步摆脱烟草危害；同时倡导公务人员、教师带头(5)不吸烟，不敬烟，主动(6)戒烟，并宣传吸烟危害健康的知识。

今年世界无烟日的主题是"戒烟"，口号是"放弃香烟"。这一主题的目的是使人们提高对吸烟危害健康的认识(7)，强调戒烟工作的重要性。

《人民日报》海外版 1999 年 6 月 1 日

张文康	張文康	Zhāng Wénkāng	n.	a person's name
颁布	頒佈	bānbù	v.	promulgate; issue
取消		qǔxiāo	v.	abolish; cancel
新闻媒体	新聞媒體	xīnwén méitǐ	n.	news media
烟草	煙草	yāncǎo	n.	tobacco

举办	舉辦	jǔbàn	*v.*	hold (a meeting , exhibition, etc)
届		jiè	*AN*	measure word for session of a conference, year of graduation
巨大		jùdà	*adj.*	tremendous
挑战	挑戰	tiǎozhàn	*n.*	challenge
发达国家	發達國家	fādá guójiā	*n.*	developed country
烟草商	煙草商	yāncǎo shāng	*n.*	tobacco businessman
国内	國內	guónèi	*n.*	internal; domestic; home
限制		xiànzhì	*v.*	restrict; confine
责难	責難	zénàn	*v.*	censure; criticize
转向	轉向	zhuǎnxiàng	*v.*	turn to
发展中国家	發展中國家	fāzhǎn zhōng guójiā	*n.*	developing country
推销	推銷	tuīxiāo	*v.*	promote sale
洋——		yáng	*prefix*	foreign 洋烟/洋酒/洋文
继续	繼續	jìxù	*v.*	continue
摆脱	擺脫	bǎituō	*v.*	shake off; get rid of
倡导	倡導	chàngdǎo	*v.*	initiate; propose
公务人员	公務人員	gōngwù rényuán	*n.*	government employees
带头	帶頭	dàitóu	*v.*	take the lead; be the first
敬烟	敬煙	jìng//yān	*v.-o.*	offer a cigarette politely
主动	主動	zhǔdòng	*adv.*	take the initiative
戒烟	戒煙	jiè//yān	*v.-o.*	give up smoking
主题	主題	zhǔtí	*n.*	theme
口号	口號	kǒuhào	*n.*	slogan
放弃	放棄	fàngqì	*v.*	give up; abandon
目的		mùdì	*n.*	purpose; goal; objective

335

词语例句

(1) 发起: initiate; sponsor

◆ 今天是世界卫生组织发起的第十二个世界无烟日。

　Today is the twelfth "No Smoking Day" initiated by the World Health Organization.

　1. 这次会议是由十四个国家发起的。

　　Fourteen countries are sponsoring this conference.

　2. 为了让全社会都认识到校园暴力的严重性，他发起了这次反暴力的集会。

　　He initiated this anti-violence rally in order to make all of society know the seriousness of campus violence.

(2) 与…相比: compared with

◆ 与 1984 年相比，中国人吸烟率上升了百分之三点四。

　Compared with that of 1984, the number of Chinese smokers has increased by 3.4 percent.

　1. 这两个根本不能相比。

　　There is no comparison between the two.

　2. 中国与先进国家相比，还有很大差距。

　　China still has a long way to go to catch up with developed countries.

(3) 提前: shift to an earlier date/time; in advance; ahead of time

◆ 开始吸烟的年龄提前了三岁。

　The age at which people start smoking is three years earlier than it used to be.

　1. 要是谁不能参加星期五的考试，请提前通知我。

　　If any of you can't take the exam on Friday, please notify me in advance.

　2. 由于他在监狱里表现很好，所以被提前释放了。

　　He was released before his sentence expired due to his good behavior in jail.

(4) 自/从…起: starting …

◆ 政府自 1991 年起逐步取消新闻媒体上的烟草广告。

　Starting in 1991, the government gradually canceled the cigarette advertisements in news media.

　1. 从今天起，我要天天运动。

　　I want to exercise every day starting today.

2. 自八十年代起，中国政府开始推行独生子女政策。

Starting with the 80s, the Chinese government carried out the one-child-per-family policy.

(5) 带头: take the lead; be the first

◆ ⋯，同时倡导公务人员、教师带头不吸烟、不敬烟。

…, at the same time, they advocate that all government employees and teachers take the lead in not smoking and not offering cigarettes.

1. 这个学生总是准备得很好，常常带头回答问题。

This student is always well prepared and often the first to answer a question.

2. 要养成孩子的良好习惯，家长应该起带头作用。

The parents should play a leading role in helping the children form good habits.

(6) 主动: on one's own initiative

◆ ⋯主动戒烟并宣传吸烟危害健康的知识。

(He wants them) to quit smoking of their own accord and popularize the knowledge that smoking does harm to one's health.

1. 他每天放学回来都主动帮母亲做家务。

He helped his mother with her housework after school without being asked.

2. 这个人对别人很冷淡，从来不主动跟别人说话。

He is a cold-natured person and never talks to other people of his own accord.

(7) 提高对⋯的认识: be more aware of

◆ 这一主题的目的是使人们提高对吸烟危害健康的认识。

The purpose of this topic is to raise people's awareness that smoking is harmful to one's health.

1. 这个电影的目的是使人们提高对爱滋病的认识。

The purpose of this movie is to make people become more aware of AIDS.

2. 他写这篇文章是为了提高人们对环境保护的认识。

In order to make people more aware of the importance of protecting the environment, he wrote this article.

练习

I. Choose the correct answer.

1. 新年前夕，学校为全校学生_____了一次很大的晚会。

    a. 开展   b.进行   c.举行

2. 这次帮助无家可归者的活动是由一个学生组织_____的。

    a. 发起   b. 发表   c.颁布

3. 由于传统习惯的影响，中国的女孩子一般不会_____跟不认识的
人谈话。

    a. 动手   b. 主动   c.发起

4. 政府的_____应该是保护人民，为人民服务，而不是控制人民。

    a. 职责   b. 主要   c.趋势

5. 昨天新总统在电视上_____讲话，表示他会努力提高人民的生活
水平，改善人民的生活环境。

    a.展开   b. 发表   c.颁布

6. 这家饭馆的生意相当好，得_____好几天才能订到位子。

    a. 提前   b. 上升   c.提高

7. 自这个培训班成立以来，学生人数_____八年超过一百人。

    a. 继续   b. 持续   c.一向

8. 很多乞丐把外国游客_____要钱的主要对象。

    a. 成为   b. 作为   c.认为

9. 一旦吸毒，就很难_____毒品的诱惑。

    a. 摆脱   b. 取消   c.禁止

II. Fill in the blank with the most appropriate word.

    大力   强调   显著   面临   限制   挑战   实行   艰巨

    中国总理在最近的讲话中说，近二十年来，由于中国政府
_____提倡并_____计划生育政策，人口增长率_____下降
了。同时，他也_____，中国的人口工作还_____巨大的
_____，"特别是农村地区，由于在当地生孩子受到_____，

有些人就跑到城里来偷偷地生。"所以控制人口工作的任务还很

__艰巨__。
jiān jù

III. Make a sentence using the underlined expression.

1. 中国政府表示要__把__控制吸烟__作为__政府的职责。

2. 中国政府从1979年以来__一直__大力提倡控制吸烟的工作，__成绩显著__。

3. 中国控制吸烟的任务__仍然__很艰巨。

4. __与__1984年__相比__，中国人吸烟率上升了3%。

5. 近年来中国因肺癌而死亡的人数每年__以__4.5%__的速度__增加。

6. 这一主题的目的是使人们__提高__对吸烟危害健康的__认识__。

7. 中国控制吸烟的工作__包括__宣传、教育__以及__立法。

8. 控制吸烟工作面临巨大考验和挑战。

IV. Read the following article and summarize it into Chinese.

NO SMOKING, PLEASE

At present about 38% of the Chinese population smoke. Eighty-nine percent of smokers are male. Every year, millions of smokers die because of illnesses that are caused by smoking tobacco.

The Chinese government receives a lot of money from sales of tobacco; in 1989 it received about 24 billion *yuan*. But in the same year, cigarette smoking cost the government even more money, about 28 billion *yuan*. Smokers cost the government a lot of money for two reasons. First, money is spent looking after people with illnesses, which have been caused by smoking. Second, many fires are caused by smokers. People who smoke in bed often fall asleep while they are smoking. The bedclothes catch fire and the whole house may be burnt down.

China produces one third of the world's cigarettes. Each day, about 220 million packets of cigarettes are smoked by Chinese. This is good news for the tobacco companies, but bad news for the health of the nation. Every year, tobacco companies must persuade new people to start smoking cigarettes. This is because each year millions of smokers die from this habit.

In Britain, which has a population of only 58 million people, 110,000 people die from smoking each year. The chance is that one smoker in four will die from smoking.

In Britain, sales of cigarettes have fallen by 30% in the last ten years. Just under a third of the population now smokes, about 17 million people. In the 16-19 age group, 32% of women smoke, compared to 28% of men. The problem is that 300 people are dying each day from illnesses caused by smoking. Therefore, if the tobacco companies want to remain in business, they have to encourage young people to start smoking.

V. Answer the following questions

1. 美国政府采取哪些措施控制青少年吸烟?

2. 在美国社会里，吸烟的情况从 50 年代到现在有什么改变?

3. 请你分析一下为什么青少年和妇女的吸烟率在上升?

4. 政府控制吸烟是不是侵犯人民的权利?

5. 课文中所谈到的几个降低吸烟率的措施，你认为那个最有效? 为什么?

繁体字课文

今天是世界衛生組織發起(1)的第 12 個世界無煙日。中國副總理李嵐清發表書面講話，表示要把控制吸煙作為政府的職責，採取更有效的措施控制吸煙率上升的趨勢。

李嵐清在講話中指出，中國政府從 1979 年以來一直大力提倡控制吸煙的工作，成績顯著。但全國的吸煙率，特別是青少年和婦女的吸煙率仍在持續上升，因為吸煙得病和死亡的人數也在上升，中國控制吸煙的任務仍然很艱巨。

中國現有 3.2 億人吸煙。1996 年的調查表明，與 1984 年相比(2)，中國人吸煙率上升了 3.74%，開始吸煙的年齡提前(3)了 3 歲，吸煙者每日平均吸煙量增加了 2 支，青少年吸煙率上升明顯。近年來中國因肺癌而死亡的人數每年以 4.5% 的速度增加。

　　中國在 20 年前開始正式展開控制吸煙的工作，包括吸煙危害健康的教育，立法以及在公共場所禁止吸煙等措施。衛生部部長張文康說，全國已有 85 個城市頒佈在公共場所禁止吸煙的規定；自 1991 年起(4)逐步取消新聞媒體上的煙草廣告，北京等 10 個城市首先成為 "無煙草廣告城市"；1997 年還在北京成功地舉辦了第 10 屆世界煙草與健康大會。

　　但他強調，中國必須認識到控制吸煙工作面臨的巨大考驗和挑戰，"特別是有些發達國家的煙草商因為在國內受到限制和責難，就轉向中國等發展中國家推銷香煙，誘惑青少年吸洋煙。"

　　張文康要求繼續開展 "無煙學校" 等活動，使全國 2 億多學生逐步擺脫煙草危害；同時宣導公務人員、教師帶頭(5)不吸煙，不敬煙，主動(6)戒煙，並宣傳吸煙危害健康的知識。

　　今年世界無煙日的主題是 "戒煙"，口號是 "放棄香煙"。這一主題的目的是使人們提高對吸煙危害健康的認識(7)，強調戒煙工作的重要性。

第三十课 中国强烈谴责分裂中国的议案

中国全国人大外事委员会负责人今天发表谈话，强烈谴责美国国会少数议员提出的分裂中国的议案。

这位负责人说，美国国会众议院少数议员 7 月 29 日向众议院国际关系委员会提交了一份明目张胆(1)地主张"一中一台"、"台湾独立"的议案。这是对中国主权、领土完整的严重侵犯和对国际关系准则的粗暴干涉，也与美国历届政府奉行的一个中国的政策背道而驰(2)。对此，我们坚决反对，强烈谴责。

他指出，世界上只有一个中国，中华人民共和国是代表全中国唯一的合法政府，台湾是中国领土不可分割的一部分，这是包括美

强烈	強烈	qiángliè	*adv.*	vehemently; strongly
谴责	譴責	qiǎnzé	*v.*	condemn; blame; denounce
分裂		fēnliè	*v.*	split; disunite; disrupt
议案	議案	yìàn	*n.*	proposal; motion; bill
人大		Réndà	*n.*	short for 全国人民代表大会; National People's Congress
外事		wàishì	*n.*	foreign affairs
委员会	委員會	wěiyuánhuì	*n.*	committee; council
谈话	談話	tánhuà	*n.*	statement; talk
国会	國會	guóhuì	*n.*	Congress
议员	議員	yìyuán	*n.*	senator
提出		tíchū	*v.*	submit; propose

众议院	眾議院	zhòngyì yuàn	n.	House of Representatives
提交		tíjiāo	v.	submit; file
份		fèn	AN	measure word for documents, papers, etc.
明目张胆	明目張膽	míng mù zhāng dǎn	idm.	do evil things openly and unscrupulously; have the impudence to do sth.
主张	主張	zhǔzhāng	v./n.	advocate; maintain, proposal; opinion; assertion
一中一台		yì Zhōng yì Tái	n.	a China and a Taiwan
主权	主權	zhǔquán	n.	sovereignty
领土	領土	lǐngtǔ	n.	territory
国际关系	國際關係	gúojì guān.xi	n.	international relation
准则	準則	zhǔnzé	n.	norm; standard
粗暴		cūbào	adj./ adv.	rude; rough; brutal, brutally; wantonly
历届	歷屆	lìjiè	n.	all previous (sessions, government, etc.)
奉行		fèngxíng	v.	pursue (a policy)
背道而驰	背道而馳	bèi dào ér chí	v.	run in the opposite direction; run counter to
对此	對此	duì cǐ		in regards to this; regarding this
反对	反對	fǎnduì	v.	oppose; be against
代表		dàibiǎo	v.	represent
唯一的		wéiyī.de	adj.	sole; the only one
合法		héfǎ	adj.	legal
台湾	臺灣	Táiwān	n.	Taiwan
分割		fēn'gē	v.	cut apart; separate
包括…在内		bāokuò...zài nèi	v.	include

国政府在内(3)的国际社会普遍公认的事实。台湾问题完全是中国的内政。在一个中国的原则下，正式结束两岸敌对状态，通过谈判实现"和平统一"、"一国两制"是我们解决台湾问题的基本方针，是中国各族人民的共同心愿和强烈要求，也完全符合台湾同胞的愿望。

我们也希望美国国会议员先生们，应该充分认识到支持"台独"、分裂中国的严重性和危险性。中国人民热爱和平，但中国的主权、领土完整决不(4)容许侵犯。我们将不惜(5)付出任何代价来捍卫祖国的主权和领土完整。中国的统一一定要实现，也一定能够实现。任何企图分裂中国的作法都只能搬起石头砸自己的脚，是注定(6)要失败的。

《光明日报》1999 年 8 月 5 日

内政		nèizhèng	n.	internal affairs
两岸	兩岸	liǎng'àn	n.	two sides of the strait
敌对	敵對	díduì	adj.	hostile; antagonistic
谈判	談判	tánpàn	n.	negotiation
和平		hépíng	n.	peace
统一	統一	tǒngyī	v./n.	unify; unite; integrate, integration; unification
一国两制	一國兩制	yìguó liǎngzhì	phr.	one country two systems
方针	方針	fāngzhēn	n.	policy; guiding principle
各族		gè zú	n.	all ethnicities; every ethnicity

心愿	心願	xīnyuàn	n.	cherished desire; wish
符合		fúhé	v.	accord with; conform to
同胞		tóngbāo	n.	fellow countryman
愿望	願望	yuànwàng	n.	aspiration; desire
支持		zhīchí	v.	support
台独	台獨	Táidú	n.	short for "台湾独立"; Taiwan's Independence
决不	決不	juébù	adv.	definitely not; under no circumstance
容许	容許	róngxǔ	v.	tolerate; allow
不惜		bùxī	v.	not hesitate to (do sth.); not spare
捍卫	捍衛	hànwèi	v.	defend; guard; protect
祖国	祖國	zǔguó	n.	homeland; motherland
搬起		bānqǐ	v.	lift
搬起石头砸自己的脚	搬起石頭砸自己的腳	bānqǐ shí.tou zá zìjǐ.de jiǎo	idm.	lift a rock only to drop it on one's own feet; hurt oneself by one's own doing 实行这种政策, 只能是搬起石头砸自己的脚。
注定		zhùdìng	v.	be doomed; be destined

词语例句

(1) 明目张胆: do evil things openly and unscrupulously

◆ 美国国会众议院少数议员明目张胆地主张"一中一台"、"台湾独立"。

A small number of the representatives of the U. S. House of Representatives in Congress openly and wantonly maintain "A China and a Taiwan" and "the independence of Taiwan."

1. 真没想到她居然明目张胆地在教室里吸烟。

   Surprisingly she smoked in the classroom before everybody's eyes.

2. 在中国，谁也不敢明目张胆地主张不赡养父母。

   In China, nobody dares openly and unscrupulously hold the opinion that one should not support one's parents.

(2) A 与 B 背道而驰: run in opposite directions; run counter to

◆ 这与美国历届政府奉行的一个中国的政策背道而驰。

This goes against the "one China" policy that all previous U. S. government administrations pursued.

1. 这种保守的态度与现代化的思潮背道而驰。

   This conservative attitude runs counter to the modern trend of thought.

2. 台独的主张是与中国人民的愿望背道而驰的。

   The Taiwan independence proposition is against the Chinese people's wish.

(3) 包括…在内: including…

◆ 这是包括美国政府在内的国际社会普遍公认的事实。

   This is a fact generally acknowledged by the international community including the U. S. government.

1. 中国所谓的"中国领土"，包括台湾在内。

   The term "Chinese territory" used by China includes Taiwan.

2. 这个考试的范围不包括上个学期的课文在内。

   This examination doesn't include the texts of last semester.

(4) 决不 v. : definitely not

◆ 中国的主权、领土完整决不容许侵犯。

China's sovereignty over her territory should never be interfered with.

1. 他总是不达到目的决不放弃。

   He never gives up until the goal has been reached.

2. 中国在任何情况下决不首先使用核子武器。

Under no circumstances will the Chinese government use nuclear weapons first.

(5) 不惜: not hesitate to

◆ 我们将不惜任何代价来捍卫祖国的主权和领土完整。

We will defend the motherland's integrity of sovereignty and territory at any cost.

1. 为了帮助丈夫，她不惜放弃自己的事业。

To help her husband, she is even willing to give up her own career.

2. 要是美国帮助台湾独立，中国政府会不惜使用武力。

If the United States helps Taiwan to gain independence, the Chinese government will not hesitate to use military force.

(6) 注定: be doomed; be destined to

◆分裂中国的企图是注定要失败的。

The attempt to split China is doomed to failure.

1. 你又懒又不负责，注定这辈子找不到工作。

You are lazy and irresponsible, so you are doomed to be unemployed.

2. 按照马克思理论，帝国主义是注定要灭亡的。

According to Marxism's theory, imperialism is doomed to extinction.

练习

1. Choose the correct answer.

1. 现在的社会太不像话了，居然有人在街上明目张胆地_____。

    a.抢钱　　b.投票　　c.认识吸烟的危害

2. 第二次世界大战后，德国_____成东德和西德。。

    a.分开　　b.分裂　　c.分光

3. 他是家里_____的男孩子，所以父母和祖父母把他惯坏了。

    a.只有　　b.只一个　　c.唯一

4. 这三千块钱只是学费，并不_____。

    a.在内保险费　　b.包括在内保险费　　c.包括保险费在内

5. 大部分家长都认为小孩子不应该在学校做生意，不过也有_____家长觉得做生意对他们有好处。

     a.少   b.少数   c.没有几个

II. Complete the following sentences using the underlined expression.

1. 中国的主权和领土完整<u>决不容许</u>侵犯。

     a. 我的家庭非常保守，……。

     b. 在没有新闻自由的社会里，……。

2. 我们也希望美国议员<u>充分</u>认识到支持台独的危险性。

     a. 他之所以考试考得这么好，……。

     b. 这次去了中国，……。

3. 我们将<u>不惜</u>任何代价来捍卫祖国的主权和领土完整。

     a. 为了追求金钱和财富，……。

     b. 她为了让孩子进好大学，……。

4. 任何企图分裂中国的做法都是<u>注定</u>要失败的。

     a. 平时不上课，考试以前又不准备，你……。

     b. 他又不好看，性格又奇怪……。

III. Answer the following questions.

1. 中国政府为什么要统一台湾？中国政府希望怎么统一台湾？

2. 美国政府对台湾地位的看法是怎么样的？美国人对台湾独立的看法呢？对这个问题，中国老百姓的看法是什么？台湾老百姓的态度怎么样？

IV. Composition

1. "搬起石头砸自己的脚"是说自己主动做了一件事情，可是结果却对自己有害。中国人用这句话来形容一个人做了一件笨事。请你写一件你或者别人做过的这样的事。

2. 请你分别采访大陆和台湾的以下的这些人：大学生、汽车司机、政府官员、商人。也采访美国的中国问题专家和老百姓。请他们谈谈对台湾独立的看法。

繁体字课文

中國全國人大外事委員會負責人今天發表談話，強烈譴責美國國會少數議員提出的分裂中國的議案。

這位負責人說，美國國會眾議院少數議員 7 月 29 日向眾議院國際關係委員會提交了一份明目張膽(1)地主張"一中一台"、"臺灣獨立"的議案。這是對中國主權、領土完整的嚴重侵犯和對國際關係準則的粗暴干涉，也與美國歷屆政府奉行的一個中國的政策背道而馳(2)。對此，我們堅決反對，強烈譴責。

他指出，世界上只有一個中國，中華人民共和國是代表全中國唯一的合法政府，臺灣是中國領土不可分割的一部分，這是包括美國政府在内(3)的國際社會普遍公認的事實。臺灣問題完全是中國的内政。在一個中國的原則下，正式結束兩岸敵對狀態，通過談判實現"和平統一"、"一國兩制"是我們解決臺灣問題的基本方針，是中國各族人民的共同心願和強烈要求，也完全符合臺灣同胞的願望。

我們也希望美國國會議員先生們，應該充分認識到支持"台獨"、分裂中國的嚴重性和危險性。中國人民熱愛和平，但中國的主權、領土完整決不(4)容許侵犯。我們將不惜(5)付出任何代價來捍衛祖國的主權和領土完整。中國的統一一定要實現，也一定能夠實現。任何企圖分裂中國的作法都只能搬起石頭砸自己的腳，是注定(6)要失敗的。

第三十一课　　中国人口结构发生转变

　　自 70 年代初中国开始实行计划生育以来，我国人口增长过快得到了有效控制。按(1)1970 年的生育水平推算，近 30 年来，全国累计少出生 3 亿人。我国城市地区人口完成了从"高出生、高死亡、高增长"向"低出生、低死亡、高增长"的转变；农村地区正在转变过程中(2)。

　　据统计，到 1998 年底，我国人口自然增长率已经降到 9.53‰（千分之九点五三），自 70 年代以来第一次降到 10‰（千分之十）以下，其中上海已经连续(3) 7 年实现人口负增长；全国育龄妇女生育率从 1970 年的人均 5.8 下降到 2.0 个左右。按国际通用标准，我国已经进入低生育率国家行列。

　　控制数量的同时，人口素质也稳步提高。由于经济发展、生活改善和各种优生优育措施的实行，我国初生婴儿死亡率由(4)建国前的 200‰下降到目前的 33‰。

结构	結構	jiégòu	n.	structure; composition
转变	轉變	zhuǎnbiàn	n.	transition; shift; change
自…以来	自…以來	zì...yǐlái	prep.	since
初		chū	n.	at the beginning of; in the early part of 八月初/年初

实行	實行	shíxíng	*v.*	put into practice; implement
增长	增長	zēngzhǎng	*v.*	increase; rise; grow
按		àn	*prep.*	according to
推算		tuīsuàn	*v.*	calculate; predict
累计	累計	lěijì	*v./n.*	add up, accumulative total; grand total
完成		wánchéng	*v.*	complete; finish
过程	過程	guòchéng	*n.*	process; course
统计	統計	tǒngjì	*n./v.*	statistics, add up; count
年底		niándǐ	*n.*	the end of the year
自然增长率	自然增長率	zìrán zēngzhǎng lǜ	*n.*	natural population growth rate
降		jiàng	*v.*	drop; descend
以下		yǐxià	*n.*	below; under 7岁以下的儿童/摄氏零度以下
连续	連續	liánxù	*adv.*	continuously; successively
负增长	負增長	fù zēngzhǎng	*v.*	negative growth (used only for statistics)
人均		rénjūn	*n.*	per capita
通用		tōngyòng	*adj.*	commonly used
数量	數量	shùliàng	*n.*	quantity; amount; number
稳步	穩步	wěnbù	*adv.*	with steady steps; steadily 稳步上升/稳步改善
优生优育	優生優育	yōushēng yōuyù	*n.*	give a good birth and good care; sound child rearing
婴儿	嬰兒	yīng'ér	*n.*	infant
初生婴儿	初生嬰兒	chūshēng yīngér	*n.*	newborn infant; an infant who is within hours, days, or up to a few weeks from birth
由		yóu	*prep.*	from; 从
建国	建國	jiànguó	*v.*	found a state; establish a state, (here) the establishment of the PRC in 1949

更深刻的变化表现在人的思想上。随着教育水平的提高和计划生育观念的建立，"多子多福"、"传宗接代"的看法已经越来越淡薄了，"少生优生"正在成为人们的自觉追求。在经济富裕的农村，许多夫妇自愿放弃生育第二个孩子，走上"少生快富"的道路。

国家计划生育委员会强调，由于人口基数较大，在未来几十年内(5)，我国人口的年净增量将保持在约 1200 万左右。如何在满足新增人口需求的同时，妥善处理人口、资源、环境之间的矛盾，保持经济、社会的可持续发展，是摆在我们面前(6)的一个十分重要的问题。

《人民日报》1999 年 7 月 20 日

变化	變化	biànhuà	n.	change
建立		jiànlì	v.	establish
多子多福		duō zǐ duō fú	idm.	the more children you have, the more lucky you will be
传宗接代	傳宗接代	chuán zōng jiē dài	idm.	have a son to carry on the family line
自觉	自覺	zìjué	adv.	consciously; of one's own initiative; of one's own free will
富裕		fùyù	adj.	abundant; well-to-do; well-off
自愿	自願	zìyuàn	adv.	of one's own free will
基数	基數	jīshù	n.	base; base number; cardinal number
未来	未來	wèilái	n.	future

净增量	淨增量	jìngzēng liàng	*n.*	net increase; net growth
保持		bǎochí	*v.*	keep; hold; retain; maintain; preserve 保持传统/保持健康/保持联系/保持新鲜/保持原来的样子
满足	滿足	mǎnzú	*v.*	satisfy; meet 满足需要/满足要求
需求		xūqiú	*n.*	needs; demand; requirement
妥善		tuǒshàn	*adv.*	properly; carefully and skillfully
可持续发展	可持續發展	kěchíxù fāzhǎn	*n.*	sustainable growth
摆	擺	bǎi	*v.*	place; put 把书摆在桌子上/把东西摆好

词语例句

(1) 按: according to

◆ 按 1970 年的生育水平推算，……
Calculated from the 1970 birth rate, ...

1. 按国际通用标准，中国已经进入低生育率国家行列。
   According to international standards, China has joined the ranks of those countries with low birth rate.

2. 按中国的大学规定，体育考试不及格的学生不能毕业。
   According to the regulations of universities in China, students who fail in physical education can not graduate from university.

3. 按目前的情况判断，这个地区的污染很难短期内解决。
   According to the current situation, the pollution in this area couldn't be solved in a short time.

(2) 在⋯过程中: in the course of ...

◆ 农村地区的人口状况正在转变过程中。
The population situation in rural area is in the course of changing.

1. 在现代化的过程中，出现困难是免不了的。
   It is inevitable to encounter problems during the course of modernization.

2. 在学习的过程中，他的表现一直很好。
   His performance is excellent in the course of study.

(3) 连续: continuous; successive

◆其中上海已经连续七年实现人口负增长。
The population growth rate of Shanghai has been decreasing for seven continuous years.

1. 已经连续下了三天雨了。
   It has been raining for three successive days.

2. 为了准备考试，他连续两天没有睡觉了。
   He didn't get any sleep for three continuous days because he was preparing for the examination.

(4) 由⋯v.: v. from

◆ 我国初生婴儿死亡率由建国前的 200‰ 下降到目前的 33‰。
The newborn infant mortality rate has been reduced to the current 33‰ from 200‰ before the People's Republic was established.

1. 城市地区的人口状况已经由高出生、高死亡转变到低出生、低死亡。

The population situation in urban areas has changed from high birth rate and high mortality to low birth rate and low mortality.

2. 中国大学生的性观念已经由保守变到相当开放。

The Chinese college students' attitude towards sex has turned to being fairly liberal from being conservative.

3. 中国的改革开放是由八十年代开始的。

The reform and open-up started in the 80s.

(5)（在）time duration 内: in (certain) time

◆ 在未来几十年内，我国人口的年净增量将保持在约1200万左右。

During the next few decades, the annual net increase of our nation's population will be kept at around 12,000,000.

1. 他计划（在）三年内把大学念完。

He planned to finish college in three years.

2.（在）未来的一两年内，海峡两岸的情况大概不会发生重大变化。

The situation of the two sides of the strait probably will have no tremendous change in the coming one or two years.

(6) 摆在（人）的面前: be put in front of us; needed to be faced squarely

◆ 如何妥善处理人口、资源、环境之间的矛盾是摆在我们面前的一个十分重要的问题。

How to deal properly with the conflict between population, natural resources and the environment is a very important task confronting us.

1. 普及教育是摆在中国政府面前的一个重要课题。

The popularization of education is an important task that the Chinese government is facing.

2. 这个问题摆在我们面前，不容忽视。

This problem is right in front of us and allows no neglect.

练习

I. Translate into Chinese.

1. According to sociologists at Harvard University, modern marriage is becoming more about romance than about child rearing and family. At the end of the 19th century, 75% of American households included children under the age of 18. By the 1960s only 48.7% of families had kids living at home, and by 1998 that number had dropped to 33.9%.
2. In 1989 the natural growth rate of China's population was 14‰, in 1995 the natural growth rate was 10.5‰. Because of the enactment of family planning, between 1989 and 1995 the decrease in the number of births nationwide was 13 million. According to the latest statistics, the total population of China was 1.25 billion by the end of 1997.

II. Rewrite the following sentence using the expressions given.

1. 十年前他当总统的时候，国家的经济开始快速增长，现在还是这样。（自…以来，一直）

2. 虽然她从来不告诉别人自己的年龄，可是因为她 1985 年大学毕业，所以我想她大概 50 岁左右了。（按…推算）

3. 越来越多的人接受"老夫少妻"这样的婚姻，说明社会的宽容度真是增加了。（表现在…上）

4. 新政府面临的最严重的问题是如何降低失业率。（摆在…面前）

5. 自从十年前韩国人的年平均收入超过 8000 美元，韩国就成了一个发达国家。（进入…行列）

III. Make sentence using the expression provided.

1. 自 70 年代初中国开始实行计划生育以来，我国人口增长过快<u>得到</u>了有效控制。

2. 农村地区的人口状况<u>正在</u>转变<u>过程中</u>。

3. 控制数量<u>的同时</u>，人口素质<u>也</u>稳步提高。

4. <u>随着</u>教育水平的提高和计划生育观念的建立，"多子多福"、"传宗接代"的看法已经<u>越来越</u>淡薄了。

5. 在经济富裕的农村，许多夫妇<u>自愿</u>放弃生育第二个孩子。

6. <u>在</u>未来几十年<u>内</u>，我国人口的年净增量将保持在约 1200 万左右。

IV. Read the following passage and summarize it in Chinese.

China at 2050

Since the establishment of the People's Republic in 1949, China has gone through some of the most dramatic changes in its history. Analysts believe the next 50 years will bring another series of radical shifts in China, affecting its people, its government, and the world. Population is one of the major issues challenging China in the next half-century.

"In the next 50 years, China will have to face three population peaks," said Mr. Wang, a professor at Beijing University. Wang said that in 2020 China's working population, age 15 to 64, will total around 1 billion. "That means we will have to create a lot of new jobs," he said.

By 2030 China's population is expected to reach 1.6 billion, prompting concerns about food supply. And, Wang said, the third peak will be in 2040, when about 320 million Chinese will be 60 or older.

"People who are 20 now will be 60 and ready to retire in 2040," said Wang, "During the 40 years in between, they will have to accumulate wealth for their retirement, so it is urgent for them to start planning now."

China's population also is expected to become more urbanized in the next 50 years. "Eighty percent of the population will move to urban areas," Wang predicated. "They will not rely on agriculture for their livelihood. That's a fundamental change in society: 500 million people will move, changing their lives, changing culture, and changing values."

繁体字课文

　　自 70 年代初中國開始實行計劃生育以來，我國人口增長過快得到了有效控制。按⑴1970 年的生育水平推算，近 30 年來，全國累計少出生 3 億人。我國城市地區人口完成了從"高出生、高死亡、高增長"向"低出生、低死亡、高增長"的轉變；農村地區正在轉變過程中⑵。

　　據統計，到 1998 年底，我國人口自然增長率已經降到 9.53‰（千分之九點五三），自 70 年代以來第一次降到 10‰（千分之十）以下，其中上海已經連續⑶ 7 年實現人口負增長；全國育齡婦女生育率從 1970 年的人均 5.8 下降到 2.0 個左右。按國際通用標準，我國已經進入低生育率國家行列。

　　控制數量的同時，人口素質也穩步提高。由於經濟發展、生活改善和各種優生優育措施的實行，我國初生嬰兒死亡率由⑷建國前的 200‰下降到目前的 33‰。

　　更深刻的變化表現在人的思想上。隨著教育水平的提高和計劃生育觀念的建立，"多子多福"、"傳宗接代"的看法已經越來越淡薄了，"少生優生"正在成為人們的自覺追求。在經濟富裕的農村，許多夫婦自願放棄生育第二個孩子，走上"少生快富"的道路。

　　國家計劃生育委員會強調，由於人口基數較大，在未來幾十年內⑸，我國人口的年淨增量將保持在約 1200 萬左右。如何在滿足新增人口需求的同時，妥善處理人口、資源、環境之間的矛盾，保持經濟、社會的可持續發展，是擺在我們面前⑹的一個十分重要的問題。

第三十二课　　中国对核裁军的立场

　　为期(1)三天的 1999 年禁止原子弹国际会议 3 日在日本广岛开幕。中国代表在会上发表讲话，重申了中国在核裁军问题上的立场。

　　中国代表说："中国在核裁军问题上始终(2)采取负责任的态度。"这就是：

　　第一，中国从拥有核武器的第一天起就郑重声明，中国在任何时候、任何情况下都不首先使用核武器。

　　第二，中国从未在境外部署过核武器，也从未对别国使用或威胁使用核武器。

　　第三，中国在发展核武器方面历来(3)采取最克制的态度。中国进行的核试验、拥有的核武器的数量十分有限。在印度和巴基斯坦进行核试验后，中国方面明确表示无意(4)恢复核试验。

核裁军	核裁軍	hé cáijūn	n.	nuclear disarmament
立场	立場	lìchǎng	n.	position; stand (point)
为期	為期	wéi qī	v.	last for (a certain time); (to be completed) by a definite date
原子弹	原子彈	yuánzǐdàn	n.	atomic bomb

广岛	廣島	Guǎngdǎo	n.	Hiroshima, Japan
开幕	開幕	kāimù	v.-o.	(of a meeting, exhibition, etc.) open; inaugurate
代表		dàibiǎo	n.	delegate; representative
重申		chóngshēn	v.	reiterate
始终	始終	shǐzhōng	adv.	from beginning to end; all along; throughout
拥有	擁有	yōngyǒu	v.	possess; own 拥有大量财富/拥有很大的权力 拥有原子弹
核武器		hé wǔqì	n.	nuclear weapon
武器		wǔqì	n.	weapon
郑重	鄭重	zhèngzhòng	adv.	solemnly; seriously
声明	聲明	shēngmíng	v.	declare
从未	從未	cóng wèi	adv.	have never; 从來沒 v. 过 从未欺骗过他人/从未做过违法的事
境外		jìngwài	n.	outside the border
部署		bùshǔ	v.	deploy; dispose (troops)
别国	別國	biéguó	n.	other countries; 别的国家
历来	歷來	lìlái	adv.	always; all through the ages; all along
克制		kèzhì	v.	restrain; exercise restraint 克制愤怒/克制自己
核试验	核試驗	hé shìyàn	n.	nuclear test
有限		yǒuxiàn	adj.	limited; a little; not much 经验有限/能力有限
巴基斯坦		Bājīsītǎn	n.	Pakistan
无意	無意	wúyì	adv.	have no intention (of doing sth.); have no interest in 无意干涉/无意过问
恢复	恢復	huīfù	v.	resume

第四，中国一贯(5)积极支持全面禁止和彻底销毁核武器。

他说："中国的国防政策具有自卫性质。中国不谋求霸权，不进行扩张，不在外国驻军，不搞军事同盟，不参加军备竞赛，中国军费开支一直处于较低水平。"

他在驳斥所谓的"中国威胁论"时说："中国是维护亚洲和世界和平的重要力量。中国一心一意(6)地从事(7)和平建设。中国的发展只会增强世界的和平，促进各国共同发展。中国不发展，长期处于贫穷落后状态，对人类才是威胁。"

《光明日报》1999 年 8 月 3 日

一贯	一貫	yíguàn	adv.	consistently; from beginning to end; all along
积极	積極	jījí	adv.	actively; positively 积极参加/积极工作
全面		quánmiàn	adv.	comprehensively; all-around; entirely 全面检查/全面发展
彻底	徹底	chèdǐ	adv./ adj.	thoroughly; totally, thorough
销毁	銷毁	xiāohuǐ	v.	destroy by burning or melting
国防	國防	guófáng	n.	national defense
具有		jùyǒu	v.	have; possess; be provided with 具有责任心/具有历史意义/具有中国特色
自卫	自衛	zìwèi	n./v.	self-defense; self-protection; be in self-defense
谋求	謀求	móuqiú	v.	seek; try to get; try for 谋求解决办法/谋求和平解决/谋

求稳定的发展

霸权	霸權	bàquán	*n.*	hegemony; supremacy
扩张	擴張	kuòzhāng	*v.*	extend; expand 扩张领土/扩张势力
驻军	駐軍	zhù//jūn	*v.-o.*	station troops 军：军队；troops; army
军事	軍事	jūnshì	*n.*	military affairs
同盟		tóngméng	*n.*	alliance; league
军备	軍備	jūnbèi	*n.*	armament; arms
竞赛	競賽	jìngsài	*n.*	contest; competition; race
军费	軍費	jūnfèi	*n.*	military expenditure
开支	開支	kāizhī	*n.*	expenses; expenditure
驳斥	駁斥	bóchì	*v.*	refute; denounce
——论	——論	lùn	*suffix*	theory; - ism 进化论: theory of revolution 唯物论: materialism
中国威胁论	中國威脅論	Zhōngguó Wēixiélùn	*n.*	"China Threat" theory
维护	維護	wéihù	*v.*	maintain; safeguard; defend
亚洲	亞洲	Yàzhōu	*n.*	Asia
力量		lì.liang	*n.*	strength; power; force
一心一意		yì xīn yí yì	*adv.*	wholeheartedly; single-mindedly; pay undivided attention to
从事	從事	cóngshì	*v.*	be engaged in
建设	建設	jiànshè	*n./v.*	construction; development, build; construct; develop
增强	增強	zēngqiáng	*v.*	reinforce; strengthen
促进	促進	cùjìn	*v.*	promote; help advance 促进相互的了解/促进友好关系
贫穷	貧窮	pínqióng	*adj.*	impoverished; destitute; needy
落后	落後	luòhòu	*adj.*	backward; less developed

词语例句

(1) 为期: (to be completed) by a definite date; lasting (a certain amount of time)

◆ 为期三天的 1999 年禁止原子弹国际会议 3 日在日本广岛开幕。

The three-day 1999 International Conference on the Prohibition of Atomic Bombs was inaugurated in Hiroshima on the 3rd (of this month).

1. 这个语言培训班为期两个月。

This language program is scheduled to last two months.

2. 为期半个月的奥林匹克运动会今天结束了。

The Olympic Games, which lasted half a month, finished today.

(2) 始终: from beginning to end; all along

◆ 中国在核裁军问题上始终采取负责任的态度。

The Chinese government has taken a responsible position on nuclear disarmament all along.

1. 虽然试验已经失败了很多次，可是他始终没有失去信心。

Although his experiments failed many times, he didn't lose his faith.

2. 在手术过程中，病人始终是清醒的。

The patient remained conscious throughout the operation.

(3) 历来: always; all through the ages; all along

◆ 中国在发展核武器方面历来采取最克制的态度。

The Chinese government has always assumed great restraint as far as the development of nuclear weapons is concerned.

1. 中国人历来认为孝顺是最基本的道德。

Chinese have always maintained that filial piety is the most basic moral.

2. 中国历来是一个人治的社会。

China has always been a society ruled by man.

(4) 无意: have no intention to

◆ 中国方面明确表示无意恢复核试验。

The Chinese government clearly said that they had no intention of resuming nuclear experiments.

1. 我只是路过，无意要偷听你们的秘密。

I was just passing by and had no intention of eavesdropping.

2. 他公开表示无意参加总统竞选。

He openly stated that he had no intention to enter the presidential election.

(5) 一贯: consistently; all along

◆ 中国一贯积极支持全面禁止和彻底销毁核武器。

The Chinese government has consistently and enthusiastically supported the complete and thorough destruction of nuclear weapons.

1. 他对人一贯诚实。

He is always honest in his attitude towards others.

2. 中国政府一贯主张国家不分大小，一律平等。

The Chinese government has always held that all nations, big or small, are equal.

(6) 一心一意: wholeheartedly

◆ 中国一心一意从事和平建设。

China is wholeheartedly working for peace.

1. 自从她结婚后，就辞去工作，一心一意做起家庭主妇来。

After getting married, she quit her job, and wholeheartedly worked as a housewife.

2. 他一心一意要上名牌大学。

He was dead set on going to a famous university.

(7) 从事: be engaged in

◆ 中国一心一意从事和平建设。

1. 他从事政治已有三十多年了。

He has been engaged in politics for more than thirty years.

3. 他一直在从事科学研究工作。

He has always been engaged in scientific research.

练习

I. Make a sentence using the underlined expression.

1. 中国<u>从</u>拥有核武器的<u>第一天起</u>就郑重声明在任何时候都不首先使用核武器。

2. 中国<u>从未</u>在境外部署过核武器，<u>也从未</u>对别国使用或威胁使用核武器。

3. 中国<u>在</u>发展核武器方面<u>历来</u>采取最克制的态度。

4. 中国不发展，长期<u>处于</u>贫穷落后<u>状态</u>，对人类才是威胁。

5. 中国在核裁军问题上<u>始终</u>采取负责任的态度。

6. 中国<u>在任何时候、任何情况下都</u>不首先使用核武器。

7. 中国进行的核试验、拥有的核武器的数量<u>十分有限</u>。

8. 中国的发展只会增强世界的和平；中国不发展，长期处于贫穷落后状态，对人类<u>才</u>是威胁。

II. Choose the most appropriate word for each blank and fill in with its Chinese equivalent.

have no intention of (doing sth.)		promote; help advance
have	develop; construct	possess	responsible
resume	ally; alliance	wholeheartedly	outside the border

1. 这个工作很重要，我们应该把它交给_____的人去做。

2. 最近五年去 _____ 旅游的中国人显著增加。

3. 对学校组织的任何活动，她都表示 _____ 参加。

4. 无论在政治上、军事上，英国一向是美国的 _____。

5. 这两个国家曾经中断过外交关系，可是很快就 _____ 了。

6. 中国 _____ 十三亿人口，九百六十万平方公里土地。

7. 这种自动售货机 _____ 方便可靠的优点。

8. 他的妻子死了十年了，可是他还 _____ 地想着她。

9. 中国总理访问美国将 _____ 两国之间的友好与合作。

10. 中国政府决定中国当前最主要的任务是发展经济，把中国 _____ 成社会主义的现代化强国。

III. Answer the following questions.

1. 有人说，核武器是世界不安全的原因；也有人说，核武器正是世界安全的原因，你同意哪种说法？为什么？

2. "中国在发展核武器方面历来采取最克制的态度。"这句话是什么意思？

3. 美国对核武器的立场与中国的有什么不同？

4. 这篇报道说："中国的国防政策具有自卫性质。" 美国的国防政策是否也是如此？

5. 为什么西方国家有所谓的"中国威胁论"？ 在你看来，中国会成为世界和平的威胁吗？

6. "中国不发展，长期处于贫穷落后状态，对人类才是威胁。"你同意这句话吗？为什么？

繁体字课文

　　為期(1)三天的 1999 年禁止原子彈國際會議 3 日在日本廣島開幕。中國代表在會上發表講話，重申了中國在核裁軍問題上的立場。

　　中國代表說：“中國在核裁軍問題上始終(2)採取負責任的態度。”這就是：

　　第一，中國從擁有核武器的第一天起就鄭重聲明，中國在任何時候、任何情況下都不首先使用核武器。

　　第二，中國從未在境外部署過核武器，也從未對別國使用或威脅使用核武器。

　　第三，中國在發展核武器方面歷來(3)採取最克制的態度。中國進行的核試驗、擁有的核武器的數量十分有限。在印度和巴基斯坦進行核試驗後，中國方面明確表示無意(4)恢復核試驗。

　　第四，中國一貫(5)積極支持全面禁止和徹底銷毀核武器。

　　他說：“中國的國防政策具有自衛性質。中國不謀求霸權，不進行擴張，不在外國駐軍，不搞軍事同盟，不參加軍備競賽，中國軍費開支一直處於較低水平。”

　　他在駁斥所謂的“中國威脅論”時說：“中國是維護亞洲和世界和平的重要力量。中國一心一意(6)地從事(7)和平建設。中國的發展只會增強世界的和平，促進各國共同發展。中國不發展，長期處於貧窮落後狀態，對人類才是威脅。”

Pinyin Index

拼音索引

chā, 插, *v.*, stick in; insert, L. 10, p. 106

chābié, 差别, *n.*, difference; disparity, L. 22, p. 261

chājù, 差距, *n.*, the difference (in distance; amount; progress, etc.) disparity; gap, L. 22, p. 259

chāyì, 差异, *n.*, difference, L. 20, p. 241

chájué, 察觉, *v.*, be conscious of; become aware of; perceive, L. 14, p. 149

chákàn, 查看, *v.*, look over; examine; check, L. 19, p. 227

cházhǎo, 查找, *v.*, seek, L. 19, p. 227

chà, 差, *adj.*, poor; bad; not up to standard, L. 5, p. 54

chà.buduō, 差不多, *adj.*, about the same; similar, L. 1, p. 6

chà.buduō, 差不多, *adv.*, almost, L. 9, p. 97

chǎnpǐn, 产品, *n.*, product, L. 5, p. 54

chǎnshēng, 产生, *v.*, produce, L. 28, p. 319

Chángchéng, 长城, *n.*, the Great Wall, L. 1, p. 3

chángqī, 长期, *n.*, long-term; over a long period of time, L. 16, p. 179

chángshí, 常识, *n.*, common knowledge, L. 10, p. 109

chǎng, 场, *AN*, measure word for games, performance, etc., L. 15, p. 163

chǎnghé, 场合, *n.*, occasion; situation, L. 24, p. 278

chàngdǎo, 倡导, *v.*, initiate; propose, L. 29, p. 335

chàngyì, 倡议, *v./n.*, propose; proposal, L. 24, p. 279

chāoguò, 超过, *v.*, exceed; surpass, L. 6, p. 68

chāojí shìchǎng, 超级市场, *n.*, supermarket, L. 4, p. 44

chāoshì, 超市, *n.*, supermarket; 超级市场, L. 27, p. 309

cháo, 朝, *prep.*, to; towards, L. 16, p. 182

chēhuò, 车祸, *n.*, car accident, L. 3, p. 30

chě//zhù, 扯住, *v.-c.*, pull and hold tight, L. 7, p. 74

chè//huí, 撤回, *v.-c.*, withdraw; take back, L. 25, p. 287

chèdǐ, 彻底, *adv./adj.*, thoroughly; totally, thorough, L. 32, p. 362

chénzhòng, 沉重, *adj.*, heavy; weighty, L. 16, p. 178

chēng, 称, *v.*, call; be called, L. 19, p. 225

chēngzàn, 称赞, *v.*, praise; acclaim, L. 15, p. 165

chéng, 成, *v.*, become, L. 9, p. 99

chéngdù, 程度, *n.*, degree; extent, L. 14, p. 148

chéngduì, 成对, *adj.*, in a pair, L. 28, p. 322

chéngfá, 惩罚, *v./n.*, punish, punishment, L. 16 附录, p. 197/L. 19, p. 229

chénggōng, 成功, *v./n.*, succeed, success, L. 7, p. 77

chéngguǒ, 成果, *n.*, achievement; fruit; gain; positive result, L. 14, p. 153

chéngjì, 成绩, *n.*, results (of work or study); achievement; grade, L. 13, p. 143

chéng//jiā, 成家, *v.-o.*, (of a man) get married; start a family, L. 20, p. 239

chénglì, 成立, *v.*, establish; found, L. 18, p. 213

chéngnián, 成年, *v.*, grow up; come of age, L. 20, p. 238

chéng pìn, 诚聘, *v.*, (written) sincerely would like to hire, L. 19, p. 224

chéngqiáng, 城墙, *n.*, city wall, L. 1, p. 4

chéngrén, 成人, *v.*, grow up; become full-grown, L. 20, p. 240

chéngrèn, 承认, *v.*, confess, L. 27, p. 309

chéngshí, 诚实, *adj.*, honest, L. 11, p. 121

chéngshì, 城市, *n.*, city, L. 14, p. 151

chéngshòu, 承受, *v.*, bear; sustain, L. 16, p. 184

chéngshú, 成熟, *adj.*, mature, L. 22, p. 261

chī//kuī, 吃亏, *v.-o.*, suffer losses; in an unfavorable situation, L. 15, p. 165

chí, 持, *v.*, hold (an opinion or an attitude), L. 17, p. 202

chíxù, 持续, *v.*, continue, L. 29, p. 333

chōngdāng, 充当, *v.*, play the part of; act as, L. 19, p. 225

chōngfèn, 充分, *adv.*, fully, L. 18, p. 214

chōngmǎn, 充满, *v.*, be full of, L. 7, p. 77

chōngtū, 冲突, *v.*, conflict, L. 16, p. 181

chóngfù, 重复, *v./adv.*, repeat, repeatedly; again and again, L. 5, p. 55

Chóngqìng, 重庆, *n.*, Chongqing City, Sichuan Province, L. 26, p. 296

chóngshēn, 重申, *v.*, reiterate, L. 32, p. 361

chóngxīn, 重新, *adv.*, again; anew; re-, L. 25, p. 287

chóuláo, 酬劳, *n.*, compensation; reward; payment, L. 19, p. 225

chǒu, 丑, *adj.*, ugly, L. 10, p. 107

chǒuwén, 丑闻, *n.*, scandal, L. 11, p. 119

chū, 出, *AN*, measure word for dramatic pieces, L. 16, p. 183

chū, 出, *v.*, pay; contribute (money), L. 3, p. 33

chū, 初, *n.*, at the beginning of; in the early part of, L. 31, p. 350

chū//chāi, 出差, *v.-o.*, go on a business trip, L. 23, p. 269

chū//guó, 出国, *v.-o.*, go abroad, L. 18, p. 215

chū chēhuò, 出车祸, *v.-o.*, get into a car accident, L. 3, p. 30

chūchū jìnjìn, 出出进进, *v.*, going in and out, L. 22, p. 259

chū//mén, 出门, *v.-o.*, go out; leave home, L. 9, p. 98

chū//qián, 出钱, *v.-o.*, put forth money; offer money, L. 15, p. 168

chū rén yìliào, 出人意料, *phr.*, come as a surprise, L. 15, p. 165

chūrùkǒu, 出入口, *n.*, exit and entrance; 出口 and 入口, L. 28, p. 319

chūshēng, 出生, *v.*, be born, L. 16, p. 179

chūshēng yīngér, 初生婴儿, *n.*, newborn infant, L. 31, p. 351

chū//shìr, 出事儿, *v.-o.*, meet with a mishap; have an accident, L. 2, p. 16

chūxiàn, 出现, *v.*, appear; arise; emerge, L. 17, p. 203

chūyī, 初一, *n.*, first year in junior high school, L. 13, p. 141

chū//yuàn, 出院, *v.-o.*, be discharged from hospital, L. 3, p. 33

dàiyù, 待遇, *n.*, treatment, L. 24, p. 278

dāndān, 单单, *adv.*, only, L. 26, p. 297

dān fāngmiàn, 单方面, *n./adv./adj.*, one side, one-sidedly, unilateral, L. 26, p. 298

dānwèi, 单位, *n.*, work unit, L. 6, p. 67/L. 8, p. 87

dānwù, 耽误, *v.*, delay; hold up, L. 3, p. 33

dānxīn, 担心, *v.*, worry; feel anxious, L. 3, p. 33

dānyōu, 担忧, *v.*, worry, L. 20, p. 241

dànbó, 淡薄, *adj.*, be indifferent , L. 16, p. 184

dāng, 当, *v.*, work as; serve as; be, L. 18, p. 215

dāng...shí, 当…时, *conj.*, when, L. 17, p. 201

dāngchū, 当初, *n.*, at the beginning; originally, L. 22, p. 259

dāngdì, 当地, *adj.*, local, L. 16, p. 183

dāngdài, 当代, *n.*, present age; contemporary era, L. 18, p. 213

dāngjīn, 当今, *n.*, now; at present; nowadays, L. 17, p. 201

dāng//miàn, 当面, *adv.*, to somebody's face; in somebody's presence, L. 15, p. 167

dāngnián, 当年, *n.*, in those years, L. 20, p. 240

dāngrán, 当然, *adv.*, certainly; of course, L. 2, p. 17

dāng.zhe ....de miàn, 当着…的面, *adv.*, in one's presence; face to face, L. 11, p. 120

dāngzhōng, 当中, *prep.*, among, L. 21, p. 249

dàng, 档, *n.*, grade of consumer goods, L. 2, p. 17

dǎng.de zhù, 挡得住, *v.-c.*, be able to block; be able to keep off, L. 19, p. 229

dāochā, 刀叉, *n.*, knife and fork, L. 4, p. 41

dǎozhì, 导致, *v.*, give rise to; lead to, L. 16, p.183

dào, 盗, *n.*, theft; burglary; 盗窃, L. 6, p. 67

dào, 道, *AN*, measure word for a question in a test or assignment, L. 15, p. 163

dào, 道, *AN*, measure word for dishes, L. 24, p. 277

dàochù, 到处, *n.*, everywhere; all over, L. 23, p. 270

dàodé, 道德, *n.*, morality, L. 12, p. 131

dàolù, 道路, *n.*, road; way; path, L. 8, p. 89

dàoshǔ, 倒数, *v.*, count from the end; count backwards, L. 16, p. 180

dé//bìng, 得病, *v.-o.*, fall ill; be ill, L. 29, p. 333

dédào, 得到, *v.*, gain; get, L. 8, p. 88

déyì, 得意, *adj.*, proud of oneself; pleased with oneself, L. 15, p. 163

dézhī, 得知, *v.*, have learned of, L. 16, p. 181

děng, 等, *v.*, wait , L. 1, p. 3

děngděng, 等等, , and so on; etc, L. 14, p. 149

dī//tóu, 低头, *v.-o.*, hang one's head , L. 28, p. 321

díduì, 敌对, *adj.*, hostile; antagonistic, L. 30, p. 344

dǐ, 底, *n.*, background, L. 27, p. 309

dì, 地, *n.*, place; 地方, L. 18, p. 213

dìbù, 地步, *n.*, extent; stage, L. 12, p. 132

dìduàn, 地段, *n.*, area, L. 28, p. 319

dìqū, 地区, *n.*, area; district; region, L. 20, p. 239

dìqiú, 地球, *n.*, the earth; the globe, L. 24, p. 280

dìtiě, 地铁, *n.*, subway, L. 2, p. 15

dìtiě zhàn, 地铁站, *n.*, subway station, L. 2, p. 15

dìwèi, 地位, *n.*, (social) status, L. 10, p. 109

diǎnxíng, 典型, *adj.*, typical, L. 27, p. 311

diàn, 店, *n.*, shop; store, L. 2, p. 19

diàn, 电, *n.*, telex, L. 16 附录, p. 195

diànnǎo, 电脑, *n.*, computer, L. 9, p. 97

diànzhǔ, 店主, *n.*, owner of a store, L. 25, p. 286

diànzǐ, 电子, *n.*, electronic, L. 9, p. 96

diànzǐ yóujiàn, 电子邮件, *n.*, electronic mail, L. 9, p. 96

diàochá, 调查, *n./v.*, investigation; survey, investigate, L. 14, p. 151

dǐngduō, 顶多, *adv.*, at (the) most, L. 6, p. 67

dìngzuò, 定做, *v.*, have sth. made to order; tailored-made , L. 4, p. 41

diū, 丢, *v.*, discard, L. 5, p. 55

diū//liǎn, 丢脸, *v.-o.*, lose face; be disgraced, L. 11, p. 118

dōngběi, 东北, *n.*, Northeastern China, L. 14, p. 148

Dōngjīng, 东京, *n.*, Tokyo, Japan, L. 1, p. 3

dǒng, 懂, *v.*, understand, L. 1, p. 4

dǒng.de, 懂得, *v.*, understand; know, L. 14, p. 153

dòngwù yuánr, 动物园儿, *n.*, zoo, L. 28, p. 319

dòngwù, 动物, *n.*, animal, L. 24, p. 277

dòu.fu, 豆腐, *n.*, bean curd, L. 4, p. 44

dòuzhēng, 斗争, *n.*, struggle, L. 11, p. 121

dú, 读, *v.*, attend (school, class, etc.), L. 13, p. 141

dúlìxìng, 独立性, *n.*, ability to be independent, L. 14, p. 152

dúshēng zǐnǚ, 独生子女, *n.*, the only child, L. 14, p. 151

dú//shū, 读书, *v.-o.*, attend school, read; study, L. 16, p. 179

dúwù, 读物, *n.*, reading matter; reading material, L. 16, p. 184

dù, 度, *n.*, degree for temperature, L. 1, p. 6

duǎn, 短, *adj.*, short (in length, duration, height), L. 10, p. 109

duàn, 断, *v.*, break (used for something long and thin, e.g. thread, rope, or sticks), L. 5, p. 55

duànliàn, 锻炼, *v.*, exercise (the body), L. 2, p. 17

duì cǐ, 对此, , in regards to this; regarding this, L. 30, p. 343

duìxiàng, 对象, *n.*, partner for marriage, L. 22, p. 261

duìxiàng, 对象, *n.*, target; object , L. 28, p. 322

Duìwài Jīngjì Màoyì Dàxué, 对外经济贸易大学, *n.*, University of International Trade and Economics, L. 18, p. 211

dùn, 顿, *AN*, measure word for meals, occurrences, etc., L. 2, p. 15/L. 16, p. 181

duōyuánhuà, 多元化, *adj.*, diversified, L. 22, p. 261

duō zǐ duō fú, 多子多福, *idm.*, the more children you have, the more lucky you will be, L. 31, p. 352

duǒ, 躲, *v.*, hide, L. 28, p. 323

fènliàng, 分量, *n.*, weight; measure, L. 22, p. 261

fènnù, 愤怒, *adj./n.*, indignant, angry, L. 27, p. 311

fēng, 封, *AN*, measure word for letters, L. 9, p. 97

fēngbō, 风波, *n.*, disturbance (lit. "wind and wave'), L. 15, p. 167

fēngfù, 丰富, *v./adj.*, enrich, abundant; ample, L. 18, p. 215

fēngjǐng, 风景, *n.*, scenery, L. 5, p. 58

fēngjǐngqū, 风景区, *n.*, scenic spot, L. 5, p. 58

fēngqì, 风气, *n.*, common practice, L. 8, p. 89

fēng//shàng, 封上, *v.-c.*, seal, L. 25, p. 287

fèngxíng, 奉行, *v.*, pursue (a policy), L. 30, p. 343

fǒudìng, 否定, *adj.*, negative, L. 22, p. 259

fǒurèn, 否认, *v.*, deny, L. 19, p. 226

fǒuzé, 否则, *conj.*, otherwise; if not, L. 18, p. 215

fūfù, 夫妇, *n.*, husband and wife; 夫妻, L. 10, p. 107

fūqiǎn, 肤浅, *adj.*, (of one's understanding of a subject or issue) superficial; shallow, L. 1, p. 5

fū.rén, 夫人, *n.*, Lady; Madam; Mrs., L. 11, p. 119

fúhé, 符合, *v.*, accord with; conform to, L. 30, p. 345

fúshí, 服食, *v.*, take (medicine), L. 26, p. 297

fúwù, 服务, *n.*, service, L. 21, p. 251

fúwùyuán, 服务员, *n.*, waiter, L. 5, p. 55

fúzhuāng, 服装, *n.*, clothing; costume, L. 4, p. 41

fǔdǎobān, 辅导班, *n.*, auxiliary class; tutorial class, L. 18, p. 212

fǔhuà, 腐化, *v./n.*, become corrupt, corruption, L. 11, p. 119

fù, 付, *v.*, pay, L. 2, p. 19

fù, 副——, *prefix*, vice-, L. 29, p. 333

fù//chū, 付出, *v.-c.*, pay, L. 15, p. 168

fùdān, 负担, *n.*, burden, L. 7, p. 77/L. 14, p. 150

fùgài, 覆盖, *v.*, cover, L. 25, p. 289

Fùlián, 妇联, *n.*, The Woman's Federation; short for 妇女联合会, L. 26, p. 299

fùlù, 附录, *n.* appendix, L. 16, p. 194

fùmǔ, 父母, *n.*, parents, L. 1, p. 5/L. 10, p. 109

fùnǚ, 父女, *n.*, father and daughter, L. 10, p. 107

fùnǚ jiěfàng, 妇女解放, *phr.*, emancipation of women; women's liberation, L. 22, p. 261

fùyǔ, 赋予, *v.*, give; endow; entrust, L. 26, p. 299

fùyù, 富裕, *adj.*, abundant; well- to-do; well-off, L. 31, p. 352

fùzé, 负责, *v.*, be responsible for; be in charge of, L. 3, p. 31

fùzérén, 负责人, *n.*, person in charge, L. 25, p. 287

fù zérèn, 负责任, *adj.*, responsible, L. 7, p. 76

fù zēngzhǎng, 负增长, *v.*, negative growth (used only for statistics), L. 31, p. 351

G

gāi, 该, *aux.*, should; ought to, 应该, L. 12, p. 131

gǎibiàn, 改变, *n./v.*, change; transformation, change; transform, L. 9, p. 97

gǎigé kāifàng, 改革开放, *n.*, the economic reform and open up policy that began in 1979, L. 7, p. 78/L. 12, p. 131

gǎiliáng, 改良, *v./n.*, improve; reform, L. 4, p. 44

gǎishàn, 改善, *v.*, improve, L. 9, p. 99

gānshè, 干涉, *v.*, interfere; intervene; meddle, L. 10, p. 110

gǎn//dào, 赶到, *v.-c.*, hurry to, L. 18, p. 213

gǎndào, 感到, *v.*, feel, L. 16, p. 181

gǎnjué, 感觉, *n.*, feeling, L. 9, p. 97

gǎnmào, 感冒, *v./n.*, catch cold, cold, L. 4, p. 43

gǎnshòu, 感受, *n.*, feeling; experience, L. 22, p. 259

gǎnxiè, 感谢, *v.*, thank; be grateful, L. 5, p. 58

gàn, 干, *v.*, do, L. 14, p. 152/L. 16, p. 183

gànbù, 干部, *n.*, cadre, L. 26, p. 299

gànmá, 干嘛, *pron.*, do what? (used in a rhetorical question) , L. 18, p. 211

gāng, 刚, *adv.*, just, L. 1, p. 3

gāodàng, 高档, *adj.*, (of the quality of things) first rate; high-class, L. 4, p. 43

gāoděng, 高等, *adj.*, higher; advanced, L. 19, p. 229

gāoé, 高额, *adj.*, a large amount (of money), L. 19, p. 225

gāo'èr, 高二, *n.*, second year in high school, L. 16, p. 179

gāoxiào, 高校, *n.*, universities and colleges, L. 17, p. 201

gāozhōng, 高中, *n.*, senior high school, L. 16, p. 179

gǎo, 搞, *v.*, do; be engaged in, L. 15, p. 166

gào, 告, *v.*, sue; accuse, L. 8, p. 87

gébì, 隔壁, *n.*, next door, L. 10, p. 107

gèjiè, 各界, *n.*, all circles; all walks of life , L. 16, p. 178

gèrén, 个人, *n.*, individual (person), L. 7, p. 76/L. 8, p. 87/L. 10, p. 109

gètǐ, 个体, *n.*, individual, L. 3, p. 33

gèzhǒng, 各种, *adj.*, various kinds, L. 2, p. 17

gè zú, 各族, *n.*, all ethnicities; every ethnicity, L. 30, p. 344

gěi, 给, *prep.*, (here) passive marker, same as 被, L. 3, p. 31

gēn, 跟, *v.*, follow, L. 1, p. 3

gēnběn, 根本, *adv.*, at all; simply, L. 9, p. 97

gēnjù, 根据, *prep.*, on the basis of; according to, L. 21, p. 251

gēngzhòng, 耕种, *v.*, cultivate; plough and sow, L. 20, p. 239

gèngjiā, 更加, *adv.*, even more, L. 14, p. 153

gōng, 供, *v.*, support (financially); supply, L. 16, p. 179

gōngbù, 公布, *v.*, make public; announce; promulgate, L. 11, p. 119

gōngchéng míngjiù, 功成名就, *idm.*, (of a person's career) be successful and famous, L. 21, p. 249

gōnggòng chǎngsuǒ, 公共场所, *n.*, public places, L. 29, p. 333

gōnggòng qìchē, 公共汽车, *n.*, public bus, L. 2, p. 14

Gōnggòng Wèishēng Xuéyuàn, 公共卫生学院, *n.*, School of Public Health, L. 17, p. 201

gōngjiāochē, 公交车, *n.*, public bus; 公共汽车, L. 2, p. 15

gōngjīn, 公斤, *AN*, measure word for weight; kilograms, L. 2, p. 17

gōngjù, 工具, *n.*, tool; instrument, L. 19, p. 229

gōngkuài, 公筷, *n.*, a pair of chopsticks that is shared by all for the purpose of picking up food from the main platter, L. 4, p. 43

gōngmín, 公民, *n.*, citizen, L. 16 附录, p. 196/L. 27, p. 311

gōngpíng, 公平, *adj.*, fair, L. 7, p. 75/L. 10, p. 109

gōngrén, 工人, *v.*, labor worker, L. 16, p. 179

gōngrèn, 公认, *v.*, be generally acknowledged, L. 24, p. 280

gōngsháor, 公勺儿, *n.*, serving spoon , L. 4, p. 43

gōngsī, 公司, *n.*, company, L. 3, p. 33

gōngwù, 公物, *n.*, public property, L. 25, p. 289

gōngwù rényuán, 公务人员, *n.*, government employees, L. 29, p. 335

gōngzhòng, 公众, *n.*, the public; the community, L. 27, p. 311

gōngzī, 工资, *n.*, wages; pay, L. 7, p. 77

gōngzuò rényuán, 工作人员, *n.*, staff, L. 27, p. 309

gòngshēng, 共生, *n.*, (mutualistic) symbiosis; mutualism, L. 24, p. 280

gòngtóng, 共同, *adv.*, together; jointly, L. 21, p. 249

gòngyǒu, 共有, *v.*, jointly possesses, L. 24, p. 280

gòuchéng, 构成, *v.*, constitute; compose, L. 16 附录, p. 195

gòumǎi, 购买, *v.*, buy, L. 27, p. 311

gūdú, 孤独, *adj./n.*, lonely; solitary, loneliness, L. 20, p. 241

gūlínglíng, 孤零零, *adv.*, solitarily; lonely, L. 21, p. 251

gū.niang, 姑娘, *n.*, girl; young lady, L. 28, p. 321

gǔdài, 古代, *n.*, ancient times, L. 1, p. 5

gǔlì, 鼓励, *v.*, encourage, L. 7, p. 75/L. 12, p. 131

gǔlǎo, 古老, *adj.*, ancient; old, L. 1, p. 4

gǔ.tou, 骨头, *n.*, bone, L. 3, p. 31

gùdìng, 固定, *adj.*, fixed; regular, L. 20, p. 241

Gùgōng, 故宫, *n.*, the Imperial Palace, L. 1, p. 3

gùrán, 固然, *conj.*, it is true; no doubt, L. 6, p. 67

gùxiāng, 故乡, *n.*, native place; hometown, L. 21, p. 249

gùyì, 故意, *adv.*, deliberately; intentionally, L. 16 附录, p. 194

guǎfù, 寡妇, *n.*, widow, L. 21, p. 250

guà, 挂, *v.*, hang, L. 27, p. 309

guàlì, 挂历, *n.*, wall calendar, L. 25, p. 286

guài, 怪, *v.*, blame, L. 15, p. 167

guānchá, 观察, *v.*, observe; survey, L. 28, p. 320

guānguāng kè, 观光客, *n.*, tourist, L. 1, p. 5

guānhuái, 关怀, *n./v.*, warm solicitude, show loving care; show solicitude for, L. 21, p. 248

guānjiàn, 关键, *adj.*, crucial; key; very important, L. 13, p. 142

guānniàn, 观念, *n.*, sense; idea; concept, L. 15, p. 167

guān.si, 官司, *n.*, lawsuit, L. 8, p. 86

guān.xi, 关系, *n.*, relation, L. 11, p. 120

guān.xi.zhe, 关系着, *v.*, affect; have a bearing on; have to do with, L. 25, p. 289

guānxīn, 关心, *v./n.*, be concerned about, L. 21, p. 249

guānyú, 关于, *prep.*, about; concerning; regarding, L. 14, p. 149

guǎn, 管, *v.*, subject sb. to discipline; control (a child), L. 16, p. 181

guǎn.deliǎo, 管得了, *v.-c.*, be able to interfere, L. 19, p. 228

guǎnjiào, 管教, *v./n.*, subject sb. to discipline, L. 16 附录, p. 195

guǎnshù, 管束, *v./n.*, restrain; control, L. 16 附录, p. 195

guǎn//zhù, 管住, *v.-c.*, control, L. 19, p. 227

guànchè, 贯彻, *v.*, carry out; implement, L. 16 附录, p. 197

guāng, 光, *adj.*, used up; with nothing left, L. 20, p. 239

guāng, 光, *adv.*, only, L. 19, p. 229

guǎngdà, 广大, *adj.*, numerous, L. 25, p. 289

Guǎngdǎo, 广岛, *n.*, Hiroshima, Japan, L. 32, p. 361

Guǎngdōng, 广东, *n.*, Guangdong Province, L. 18, p. 213

guǎngfàn, 广泛, *adj./adv.*, extensive; wide-ranging, extensively; widely, L. 9, p. 97

guǎnggào, 广告, *n.*, advertisement, L. 5, p. 57

Guǎngxī, 广西, *n.*, Guangxi Province, L. 24, p. 277

guī, 龟, *n.*, tortoise; turtle, L. 24, p. 277

guīdìng, 规定, *n.*, rule; regulations, L. 16 附录, p. 197/ L. 20, p. 238

guīgé, 规格, *n.*, standard; norm; specification, L. 24, p. 278

guīzé, 规则, *n.*, rule; regulation, L. 2, p. 15

Guìzhōu, 贵州, *n.*, Guizhou Province, L. 13, p. 140/L. 18, p. 213

guófáng, 国防, *n.*, national defense, L. 32, p. 362

guóhuì, 国会, *n.*, Congress, L. 30, p. 342

guójì, 国际, *adj.*, international, L. 24, p. 280

guójì guān.xi, 国际关系, *n.*, international relation, L. 30, p. 343

guójiā, 国家, *n.*, country; nation, L. 5, p. 57

guónèi, 国内, *n.*, internal; domestic; home, L. 29, p. 335

guǒ.zilǐ, 果子狸, *n.*, masked civet, L. 24, p. 277

guò, 过, *v.*, cross; pass, L. 3, p. 31

guò, 过, *adv.*, excessively; over-, L. 14, p. 150

guò, 过, *v.*, spend (time); pass (time), L. 18, p. 210

guò, 过, *v.*, exceed; go beyond; surpass, L. 22, p. 261

guòchéng, 过程, *n.*, process; course, L. 31, p. 351

guòcuò, 过错, *n.*, fault; mistake, L. 7, p. 76

gùojiē tiānqiáo, 过街天桥, *n.*, overhead walkway, L. 28, p. 318

gùo.qu, 过去, *v.*, pass by; go by, L. 22, p. 259

guòshí, 过时, *adj.*, out of fashion, L. 28, p. 319

gùowǎng, 过往, *v.*, coming and going, L. 28, p. 319

guòwèn, 过问, *v.*, make inquiry about; concern oneself with; take an interest in, L. 11, p. 119

H

hái, 还, *adv.*, even more; 更, L. 1, p. 3

hái.zi, 孩子, *n.*, child; children; kids, L. 9, p. 97

hài, 害, *v.*, harm; impair; cause trouble to, L. 7, p. 75

hàipà, 害怕, *v.*, fear, L. 7, p. 77

Hán'guó, 韩国, *n.*, Korea, L. 14, p. 151

hànwèi, 捍卫, *v.*, defend; guard; protect, L. 30, p. 345

hángliè, 行列, *n.*, ranks (of people, vehicles, etc.); procession, L. 20, p. 241

hángyè, 行业, *n.*, profession, L. 8, p. 87

Hángzhōu, 杭州, *n.*, Hangzhou; capital city of Zhejiang Province, L. 15, p. 162

háobù liúqíng, 毫不留情, *phr.*, show no mercy whatsoever; absolutely without consideration for others, L. 19, p. 227

háowú, 毫无, *adv.*, not at all; not in the least, L. 19, p. 225

hǎo.chu, 好处, *n.*, advantage, L. 5, p. 56

hǎohāor, 好好儿, *adj./adv.*, in perfectly good condition, nicely; well; to one's heart's content, L. 7, p. 75

hǎojǐ, 好几, *adj.*, quite a few, L. 8, p. 87

hǎowánr, 好玩儿, *adj.*, fun; amusing; interesting, L. 1, p. 6

hǎoxiàng, 好像, *v.*, seem to be, L. 4, p. 41

hǎozài, 好在, *adv.*, luckily; fortunately, L. 3, p. 31

hē, 喝, *v.*, drink, L. 4, p. 43

hē//chá, 喝茶, *v.-o.*, drink tea, L. 7, p. 77

Héběi, 河北, *n.*, Hebei Province, L. 18, p. 211

hé cáijūn, 核裁军, *n.*, nuclear disarmament, L. 32, p. 360

héfǎ, 合法, *adj.*, legal, L. 30, p. 343

hélǐ, 合理, *adj.*, reasonable; equitable, L. 7, p. 75

hémù, 和睦, *adj.*, harmonious, L. 14, p. 152

hépíng, 和平, *n.*, peace, L. 30, p. 344

héshàn, 和善, *adj.*, kind and gentle; genial, L. 28, p. 322

héshēn, 合身, *adj.*, (of clothes) fitting, L. 4, p. 41

héshì, 合适, *adj.*, suitable; appropriate, L. 25, p. 287

hé shìyàn, 核试验, *n.*, nuclear test, L. 32, p. 361

hé wǔqì, 核武器, *n.*, nuclear weapon, L. 32, p. 361

héxié, 和谐, *n./adj.*, harmony, harmonious, L. 8, p. 89

hēi, 黑, *adj.*, black; dark, L. 5, p. 55

hēiàn, 黑暗, *adj.*, dark, L. 11, p. 119

hēihēi yíxiào, 嘿嘿一笑, *phr.*, laugh with a hehe sound, L. 23, p. 270

hěnhěn, 狠狠, *adv.*, ferociously, L. 16, p. 181

hèn.bu.de, 恨不得, *v.*, very anxious to; itch to; how one wishes one could, L. 11, p. 121

hóngshāo, 红烧, *v.*, braise in soy sauce, L. 24, p. 277

hǒngpiàn, 哄骗, *v.*, trick; cheat, L. 27, p. 308

hóu.zi, 猴子, *n.*, monkey, L. 24, p. 278

hòudài, 后代, *n.*, descendants; posterity, L. 24, p. 279

hòu gù zhī yōu, 后顾之忧, *n.*, family considerations that cause delay in decision; trouble back at home, L. 18, p. 213

hòuguǒ, 后果, *n.*, consequence, L. 17, p. 203

hòumā, 后妈, *n.*, stepmother, L. 22, p. 259

hòunǎo, 后脑, *n.*, back of the head, L. 16, p. 182

hūshì, 忽视, *v.*, overlook; neglect; ignore, L. 14, p. 149

húshuō, 胡说, *v.*, talk nonsense, L. 12, p. 133

hùliánwǎng, 互联网, *n.*, Internet, L. 9, p. 98

hùxiāng, 互相, *adv.*, mutually; each other; one another, L. 15, p. 167

huāfèi, 花费, *v.*, spend, L. 14, p. 153

huāqún.zi, 花裙子, *n.*, floral skirt, L. 28, p. 321

huá.bùlái, 划不来, *v.-c.*, not worth it, L. 2, p. 17

huá.delái, 划得来, *v.-c.*, worth it, L. 2, p. 17

Huádōng, 华东, *n.*, Eastern China, L. 25, p. 287

Huáshì, 华氏, *n.*, Fahrenheit, L. 1, p. 6

huà, 化, *suffix*, - ize; -ify, L. 1, p. 5

huàtí, 话题, *n.*, topic of conversation, L. 11, p. 121

huàxué, 化学, *n.*, chemistry, L. 19, p. 226

huáiyí, 怀疑, *v.*, suspect; doubt, L. 7, p. 77/L. 10, p. 109

huái//yùn, 怀孕, *v.-o.*, become pregnant, L. 26, p. 297

huài.chu, 坏处, *n.*, disadvantage, L. 5, p. 56

huānyíng, 欢迎, *v.*, welcome; favorably receive, L. 25, p. 289

huán, 还, *v.*, return; give back, L. 15, p. 165

huánjìng, 环境, *n.*, environment, L. 5, p. 55

huàn, 换, *v.*, change, L. 5, p. 55

huàn jù huà shuō, 换句话说, *phr.*, in other words, L. 26, p. 299

huángdì, 皇帝, *n.*, emperor, L. 1, p. 4

huīfù, 恢复, *v.*, resume, L. 32, p. 361

huí, 回, *AN*, measure word for occurrences; 次, L. 11, p. 119

huídá, 回答, *v.*, answer; reply, L. 13, p. 141

huíshōu, 回收, *v.*, recycle; retrieve; reclaim, L. 5, p. 55

huìbào, 汇报, *v.*, report; give an account of, L. 6, p. 68

huìyì, 会议, *n.*, meeting; conference, L. 15, p. 167

hūnqián, 婚前, *n.*, before getting married, L. 12, p. 131

hūnwài, 婚外, *adj.*, out of marriage, L. 12, p. 131

hūnyīn, 婚姻, *n.*, marriage, L. 10, p. 107

hūnyīnfǎ, 婚姻法, *n.*, marriage law, L. 20, p. 238

hùn, 混, *v.*, mix, L. 5, p. 57

hùnluàn, 混乱, *adj.*, disorderly; chaotic, L. 17, p. 202

huódòngliàng, 活动量, *n.*, amount of physical activity, L. 14, p. 150

huóhuó, 活活, *adv.*, while still alive, L. 16, p. 182

huó.po, 活泼, *adj.*, active; full of life; vivacious, L. 22, p. 258

huǒ, 火, *n.*, fire, L. 6, p. 67

huǒchēzhàn, 火车站, *n.*, train station, L. 16, p. 179

huǒzāi, 火灾, *n.*, fire disaster, L. 6, p. 67

huò, 或, *conj.*, 或者; or, L. 6, p. 67

huòdé, 获得, *v.*, obtain; gain, L. 15, p. 166

J

jīběn, 基本, *adj.*, basic; fundamental, L. 21, p. 249

jīběnshàng, 基本上, *adv.*, basically; on the whole, L. 16, p. 179

jīchǎng, 机场, *n.*, airport, L. 1, p. 3

jīguān, 机关, *n.*, government work unit, L. 15, p. 167

jīhū, 几乎, *adv.*, almost; nearly, L. 19, p. 228

jīhuì, 机会, *n.*, opportunity; chance, L. 1, p. 5

jījí, 积极, *adv.*, actively; positively, L. 32, p. 362

jīliè, 激烈, *adj.*, intense; fierce, L. 14, p. 153

jīqì, 机器, *n.*, machine, L. 25, p. 287

jīshù, 基数, *n.*, base; base number; cardinal number, L. 31, p. 352

jīzhì, 机制, *n.*, mechanism, L. 19, p. 229

jí, 及, *conj.*, and; 跟, L. 24, p. 280

jí, 急, *adj./adv.*, urgent, urgently, L. 19, p. 224

jíbìng, 疾病, *n.*, disease, L. 23, p. 269

jíshǐ, 即使, *conj.*, even; even if; even though, L. 10, p. 109

jítǐ, 集体, *adv.*, collectively, L. 27, p. 309

jítǐ, 集体, *n./adj.*, group, collective, L. 16, p. 183

jíyú, 急于, *v.*, be eager/anxious to do sth., L. 26, p. 297

jǐ, 挤, *v.*, squeeze, L. 23, p. 269

jǐ, 挤, *v./adj.*, jostle; push against, crowded, L. 2, p. 15

jǐ//chū, 挤出, *v.-c.*, squeeze, L. 14, p. 153

jǐ//jìn, 挤进, *v.-c.*, squeeze in; push one's way in; join eagerly, L. 14, p. 153

jǐyǔ, 给予, *v.*, (written) give, L. 19, p. 228

jìhuà, 计划, *v./n.*, plan to, plan, L. 1, p. 5

jìhuà shēngyù, 计划生育, *n.*, family planning; birth control, L. 25, p. 287

jìlù, 记录, *v.*, record; write down, L. 21, p. 251

jìlǜ, 纪律, *n.*, discipline; morale, L. 27, p. 309

jìmò, 寂寞, *adj.*, lonely; lonesome, L. 14, p. 148

jìrán, 既然, *conj.*, since; as; now that, L. 2, p. 15

jìsuàn, 计算, *v.*, count; compute, L. 18, p. 214

jìsuànjī, 计算机, *n.*, computer, L. 18, p. 214

jìxù, 继续, *v.*, continue, L. 29, p. 335

jìzǎi, 记载, *n./v.*, record, put down in writing, L. 24, p. 279

jìzhě, 记者, *n.*, reporter; journalist, L. 11, p. 120

jiā, 夹, *v.*, press from both sides; (here) pick up (with chopsticks), L. 4, p. 43

jiāchǎn, 家产, *n.*, family property, L. 20, p. 239

jiājiào, 家教, *n.*, private tutoring, L. 15, p. 166

jiājìn, 加进, *v.*, add; to put in; append, L. 26, p. 299

jiāqiáng, 加强, *v.*, enhance; reinforce, L. 16, p. 185

jiārù, 加入, *v.*, add; put in, L. 26, p. 299

jiāshàng, 加上, *conj.*, moreover; in addition, L. 3, p. 33

jiātíng, 家庭, *n.*, family; household, L. 14, p. 149

jiāwù, 家务, *n.*, household chores; housework, L. 14, p. 151

jiāyuán, 家园, *n.*, home; homeland, L. 24, p. 280

jiāzhǎng, 家长, *n.*, parents or guardian of a child, L. 14, p. 149

jiāzhǎnghuì, 家长会, *n.*, parents' meeting, L. 15, p. 165

jiǎ, 假, *adj.*, fake, L. 19, p. 227

jiǎrú, 假如, *conj.*, if; supposing; in case, L. 26, p. 297

jiǎzhuāng, 假装, *v.*, pretend; feign, L. 27, p. 308

jià, 嫁, *v.*, (of a woman) marry, L. 10, p. 107

jiàgé, 价格, *n.*, price, L. 19, p. 225

jiàqī, 假期, *n.*, vacation; holiday, L. 18, p. 210

jiàzhíguān, 价值观, *n.*, value system, L. 17, p. 202

jiān, 间, *AN*, measure word for rooms, L. 3, p. 33

jiānchí, 坚持, *v.*, persist in; insist on, L. 4, p. 41

jiāndū, 监督, *v.*, keep watch on and to supervise, L. 11, p. 121

jiānhùrén, 监护人, *n.*, guardian, L. 27, p. 311

jiānjù, 艰巨, *adj.*, extremely difficult; arduous, L. 29, p. 333

jiānjué, 坚决, *adv.*, firmly; resolutely, L. 26, p. 297

jiǎn, 捡, *v.*, pick up; collect; gather, L. 5, p. 57

jiǎnchá, 检查, *v.*, examine; check; inspect, L. 27, p. 311

jiǎndān, 简单, *adj.*, simple; uncomplicated, L. 4, p. 41

jiǎnlòu, 简陋, *adj.*, simple and crude, L. 20, p. 239

jiǎnpǔ, 俭朴, *adj.*, thrifty and simple; economical, L. 14, p. 152

jiǎnshǎo, 减少, *v.*, reduce; cut down, L. 12, p. 133

jiǎnzhí, 简直, *adv.*, simply; virtually, L. 4, p. 43

jiàn, 件, *AN*, measure word for matters in general, L. 10, p. 109

jiàn, 建, *v.*, build, L. 20, p. 239

jiàn.budé rén, 见不得人, *phr.*, not fit to be seen or revealed; unpresentable; shameful, L. 25, p. 287

jiànguó, 建国, *v.*, found a state; establish a state, (here) the establishment of the PRC in 1949, L. 31, p. 351

jiànjiàn, 渐渐, *adv.*, gradually, L. 8, p. 88

jiànkāng, 健康, *adj.*, healthy, L. 14, p. 149

jiànlì, 建立, *v.*, establish, L. 31, p. 352

jiànshè, 建设, *n./v.*, construction; development, build; construct; develop, L. 32, p. 363

jiànyì, 建议, *v./n.*, suggest; advise, suggestion, L. 26, p. 299

jiànyú, 鉴于, *prep.*, in light of; seeing that; in consideration of, L. 16 附录, p. 196

jiànzhù, 建筑, *n.*, building; structure; architecture, L. 1, p. 4

jiāng, 将, *adv.*, will; shall; be going to, L. 21, p. 251

jūmínqū, 居民区, *n.*, residential district, L. 25, p. 287

jūrán, 居然, *adv.*, surprisingly; unexpectedly, L. 16, p. 184

jǔbàn, 举办, *v.*, hold (a meeting , exhibition, etc), L. 29, p. 335

jǔchū, 举出, *v.*, give (an example); cite as an example, L. 19, p. 226

jù, 据, *prep.*, according to; on the ground of, L. 1, p. 3

jù bào zǎi, 据报载, *phr.*, according to newspaper's report, L. 22, p. 259

jùdà, 巨大, *adj.*, tremendous, L. 29, p. 335

jùjí, 聚集, *v.*, gather; assemble, L. 18, p. 213

jùshuō, 据说, *v.*, it is said, L. 3, p. 33

jùtǐ, 具体, *adj.*, specific; concrete, L. 16 附录, p. 196

jùxī, 巨蜥, *n.*, huge lizard, L. 24, p. 277

jùyǒu, 具有, *v.*, have; possess; be provided with, L. 32, p. 362

juébù, 决不, *adv.*, definitely not; under no circumstance, L. 30, p. 345

jué dà duōshù, 绝大多数, *n.*, vast majority; overwhelming majority, L. 18, p. 211

juéduì, 绝对, *adv.*, absolutely, L. 17, p. 201

juélù, 绝路, *n.*, road to ruin; impasse, L. 27, p. 309

juésè, 角色, *n.*, role; part, L. 19, p. 225

juéwàng, 绝望, *n./v.*, hopelessness; despair, give up all hope, L. 16, p. 181

jūnbèi, 军备, *n.*, armament; arms, L. 32, p. 363

jūnduì, 军队, *n.*, troops; army, L. 32, p. 363

jūnfèi, 军费, *n.*, military expenditure, L. 32, p. 363

jūnshì, 军事, *n.*, military affairs, L. 32, p. 363

K

kāfēi, 咖啡, *n.*, coffee, L. 8, p. 87

kāi, 开, *v.*, write out (a certificate), L. 27, p. 309

kāichú, 开除, *v.*, expel; discharge; fire, L. 19, p. 227

kāifàng, 开放, adj., open-minded; liberal, L. 10, p. 110

kāimù, 开幕, *v.-o.*, (of a meeting, exhibition, etc.) open; inaugurate , L. 32, p. 361

kāishǐ, 开始, *v.*, begin; start, L. 4, p. 44

kāitōng, 开通, *adj.*, open-minded; liberal, L. 12, p. 131

kāi/xué, 开学, *v.-o.*, start school; begin a term, L. 2, p. 19

kāizhǎn, 开展, *v.*, develop; launch, L. 21, p. 250

kāizhī, 开支, *n.*, expenses; expenditure, L. 32, p. 363

kàn//bào, 看报, *v.-o.*, read newspaper, L. 7, p. 77

kàn//bìng, 看病, *v.-o.*, see a doctor, L. 16, p. 184

kàn.buqǐ, 看不起, *v.-c.*, look down upon, L. 10, p. 109

kànlái, 看来, *adv.*, it seems; it looks as if, L. 7, p. 77/L. 18, p. 213

kàn rè.nao, 看热闹, *v.*, watch the fun; watch the excitement, L. 28, p. 323

kàn.shang.qu, 看上去, *v.*, look like, L. 28, p. 319

kǎo, 烤, *v.*, barbecue; roast, L. 23, p. 270

kǎochá, 考察, *v.*, make an on-the-spot investigation; observe and study, L. 18, p. 211

kǎochǎng, 考场, *n.*, examination hall or room, L. 19, p. 227

kǎo//jìn, 考进, *v.-c.*, enter a school by passing the entrance examination, L. 16, p. 179

kǎoyán, 考研, *v.-o.*, take a graduate school entrance exam, L. 18, p. 212

kǎoyàn, 考验, *n.*, test; trial, L. 1, p. 7

kào, 靠, *prep.*, keep to; get near, L. 2, p. 16

kào, 靠, *v.*, rely on; depend on, L. 5, p. 57

kào...wéi shēng, 靠…为生, *n.*, make a living by, L. 5, p. 57

kējì, 科技, *n.*, science and technology, L. 9, p. 98

kēxué, 科学, *n.*, scientific knowledge, L. 18, p. 211

kēxuéjiā, 科学家, *n.*, scientist, L. 24, p. 279

kěchíxù fāzhǎn, 可持续发展, *n.*, sustainable growth, L. 31, p. 353

kěguān, 可观, *adj.*, considerable; impressive; sizable, L. 18, p. 215

kěkào, 可靠, *adj.*, reliable, L. 25, p. 289

kěnéng, 可能, *adv./adj.*, probably; maybe, possible; probable; may, L. 6, p. 68

kěnéng, 可能, *n.*, possibility, L. 10, p. 109

kèkǔ, 刻苦, *adj.*, painstaking; hardworking, L. 16, p. 182

Kèlíndùn, 克林顿, *n.*, Bill Clinton, L. 11, p. 122

kètí, 课题, *n.*, task; problem; question for study, L. 24, p. 280

kètáng, 课堂, *n.*, classroom, L. 27, p. 309

kèzhì, 克制, *v.*, restrain; exercise restraint, L. 32, p. 361

kěn, 肯, *aux.*, be willing to, L. 15, p. 167

kěndìng, 肯定, *adv.*, definitely; surely, L. 9, p. 97

kōng, 空, *adj.*, empty, L. 21, p. 248

kōngdàngdàng, 空荡荡, *adj.*, empty; deserted, L. 21, p. 248

kōngtiáo, 空调, *n.*, air conditioning; air conditioner, L. 1, p. 7

kǒngquè, 孔雀, *n.*, peacock, L. 24, p. 277

Kǒngzǐ, 孔子, *n.*, Confucius, L. 12, p. 133

kòngzhì, 控制, *v.*, control, L. 29, p. 332

kǒuhào, 口号, *n.*, slogan, L. 29, p. 335

kǒuyīn, 口音, *n.*, accent, L. 28, p. 319

kū, 哭, *v.*, cry, L. 28, p. 321

kù.zi, 裤(子), *n.*, pants, L. 5, p. 57

kuài.zi, 筷子, *n.*, chopsticks, L. 4, p. 41

kuānróng, 宽容, *adj.*, tolerant, L. 17, p. 203

kuānróngdù, 宽容度, *n.*, degree of tolerance, L. 22, p. 261

kuǎn, 款, *AN*, measure word for clauses, L. 16 附录, p. 196

kuàngquánshuǐ, 矿泉水, *n.*, mineral water, L. 5, p. 58

kǔn//zhù, 捆住, *v.-c.*, bind; tie, L. 24, p. 278

kuòzhāng, 扩张, *v.*, extend; expand, L. 32, p. 363

L

lā, 拉, *v.*, pull, L. 28, p. 321

pà, 怕, *v.*, be afraid of; fear, L. 2, p. 15

pái, 排, *n.*, row, L. 15, p. 163

pái(.zi), 牌（子）, *n.*, plate; tablet, L. 27, p. 309

pái//duì, 排队, *v.-o.*, stand in line; form a line, L. 2, p. 15

páimíng, 排名, *v.*, rank as; be ranked as, L. 16, p. 179

pán.zi, 盘子, *n.*, plate; tray, L. 4, p. 43

pànchǔ, 判处, *v.*, sentence; condemn, L. 16 附录, p. 195

pànduàn, 判断, *v.*, judge, L. 15, p. 164

pànjué, 判决, *v.*, court decision; judgment, L. 16 附录, p. 195

pàng, 胖, *adj./v.*, fat, get fat; put on weight, L. 2, p. 17

pǎo, 跑, *v.*, run, L. 6, p. 67

pǎo//bù, 跑步, *v.-o.*, jog, L. 6, p. 67

péi, 赔, *v.*, compensate; pay for, L. 8, p. 87

péi, 陪, *v.*, accompany, L. 21, p. 250

péicháng, 赔偿, *v./n.*, compensate; pay for; indemnification, L. 27, p. 311

péiyǎng, 培养, *v.*, foster; develop; educate; cultivate, L. 13, p. 142

pèihé, 配合, *v.*, work with; cooperate, L. 15, p. 165

pèng, 碰, *v.*, encounter; run into, L. 6, p. 68

pèng//.dào, 碰到, *v.*, run into; encounter, L. 28, p. 323

pīpíng, 批评, *v./n.*, criticize, criticism, L. 24, p. 276

piānshí, 偏食, *v.*, be partial to a limited variety of food, L. 14, p. 151

pián.yi, 便宜, *adj.*, cheap, L. 2, p. 17

piào.liang, 漂亮, *adj.*, beautiful, L. 4, p. 41

pīnmìng, 拼命, *adv.*, do something desperately; with all one's might, L. 14, p. 153

pínfù bùjūn, 贫富不均, *phr.*, large gap between the rich and the poor, L. 7, p. 75

pínkùn, 贫困, *adj.*, impoverished; poor, L. 28, p. 323

pínqióng, 贫穷, *adj.*, impoverished; destitute; needy, L. 32, p. 363

pǐndé, 品德, *n.*, (moral) character; morals, L. 13, p. 143/ L. 14, p. 153

pǐn xué jiān yōu, 品学兼优, *idm.*, (of a student) of good character and scholarship, L. 16, p. 183

píngjūn, 平均, *adj.*, average, L. 10, p. 109

Píngshān Xiàn, 平山县, *n.*, Pingshan County, L. 18, p. 211

píngshí, 平时, *n.*, ordinarily; in normal times, L. 16, p. 182

píngwěn, 平稳, *adj.*, stable; smooth, L. 25, p. 286

píng.zi, 瓶子, *n.*, bottle, L. 5, p. 58

pǔbiàn, 普遍, *adj.*, common; prevalent, L. 10, p. 107

pǔtōng, 普通, *adj.*, common; ordinary, L. 3, p. 33/L. 16, p. 179

Q

qījiān, 期间, *n.*, time; period, L. 13, p. 142

qīmò, 期末, *n.*, end of semester, L. 16, p. 180

qīpiàn, 欺骗, *v.*, cheat; dupe, L. 16, p. 184

qīwàng, 期望, *n.*, hope; expectation, L. 16, p. 184

qīzhōng, 期中, *n.*, midterm, L. 16, p. 180

qī.zi, 妻子, *n.*, wife, L. 10, p. 107

qí, 其, *pron.*, his or her, L. 16 附录, p. 195/L. 27, p. 311

qí, 骑, *v.*, ride (a bicycle, a horse, etc.), L. 2, p. 15

qícì, 其次, *conj.*, second; secondly, L. 19, p. 227

qípáo, 旗袍, *n.*, qipao, ("long gown"), a traditional Chinese costume for women, L. 4, p. 40

qíshí, 其实, *adv.*, actually; in fact, L. 1, p. 6

qítā, 其他, *adj.*, other, L. 3, p. 33

qízhōng, 其中, *n.*, among (which, them, etc.), L. 7, p. 74

qǐ, 起, *AN*, measure word for legal cases or occurrences, L. 19, p. 226

qǐgài, 乞丐, *n.*, beggar, L. 7, p. 74

qǐshì, 启事, *n.*, notice; announcement, L. 19, p. 224

qǐsù, 起诉, *v.*, sue; bring a suit against sb.; bring an action against sb.; file a lawsuit, L. 26, p. 297

qǐtú, 企图, *v.*, attempt; seek; try, L. 21, p. 249

qǐxiān, 起先, *adv.*, at first; in the beginning, L. 15, p. 164

qǐ zuòyòng, 起作用, *v.-o.*, take effect, L. 11, p. 121

qiān, 千, *n.*, thousand, L. 1, p. 4

qiānwàn, 千万, *adv.*, be sure to; must, L. 3, p. 33

qiánbāo, 钱包, *n.*, wallet; purse, L. 28, p. 321

qiánbùjiǔ, 前不久, *n.*, not long ago, L. 24, p. 279

qiánshù, 钱数, *n.*, amount of money, L. 21, p. 251

qiánxī, 前夕, *n.*, eve, L. 13, p. 142

qián xiē rì.zi, 前些日子, *n.*, few days ago, L. 13, p. 140

qiǎnzé, 谴责, *v.*, condemn; blame; denounce, L. 30, p. 342

qiāng, 枪, *n.*, gun, L. 19, p. 224

qiāngshǒu, 枪手, *n.*, one who sits for an examination in place of another person, L. 19, p. 224

qiáng, 墙, *n.*, wall, L. 1, p. 4

qiáng, 强, *adj.*, strong, L. 14, p. 152

qiángdiào, 强调, *v.*, emphasize; stress, L. 11, p. 121

qiángliè, 强烈, *adv.*, vehemently; strongly, L. 30, p. 342

qiángxíng, 强行, *adv.*, (do sth.) by force, L. 27, p. 311

qiǎng, 抢, *v.*, rob; loot, L. 28, p. 323

qiǎng, 抢, *v.*, scramble for, L. 2, p. 15

qiǎngjié, 抢劫, *v.*, rob; loot; plunder, L. 28, p. 323

qiǎngjiéfàn, 抢劫犯, *n.*, robber; mugger, L. 28, p. 323

qiǎngpò, 强迫, *v.*, force (sb. to do sth.), L. 26, p. 297/L. 27, p. 309

qiāo//kāi, 敲开, *v.-c.*, strike open, L. 24, p. 279

qiáo, 瞧, *v.*, look at; see, L. 7, p. 75

qiáo.zhe.ba, 瞧着吧, *phr.*, just wait and see, L. 22, p. 259

qīnfàn, 侵犯, *v.*, infringe on (one's rights), L. 16 附录, p. 196/L. 26, p. 297

qīnhài, 侵害, *v.*, encroach upon; infringe upon, L. 8, p. 88/L. 11, p. 121

qīn.qi, 亲戚, *n.*, relative, L. 22, p. 259

qīnquán xíngwéi, 侵权行为, *n.*, tort, L. 27, p. 310

Pinyin Index

qīnshēng, 亲生, *adj.*, one's own (children; parents), L. 16, p. 178

qíngōng jiǎnxué, 勤工俭学, *n.*, part-work and part-study program, L. 18, p. 213

qínláo, 勤劳, *adj.*, diligent; hardworking, L. 14, p. 152

qīng, 轻, *adj.*, slight; not serious; light, L. 3, p. 31

Qīng Cháo, 清朝, *n.*, the Qing Dynasty (1644-1911), L. 4, p. 41

qīngdùn, 清炖, *v.*, boiled in clear soup (without soy sauce), L. 24, p. 277

Qīnghǎi, 青海, *n.*, Qinghai Province, L. 18, p. 213

qīngjìng, 清静, *adj.*, quiet; tranquil; secluded, L. 20, p. 241

qīngnián, 青年, *n.*, young people; youth, L. 17, p. 202

qīngshàonián, 青少年, *n.*, teenager, L. 13, p. 142

qīngxiàngyú, 倾向于, *v.*, be inclined to; tend to, L. 17, p. 201

qīngxīn, 倾心, *v.*, admire wholeheartedly, L. 22, p. 259

qíngjí zhī xià, 情急之下, *phr.*, in a moment of desperation, L. 15, p. 163

qióng, 穷, *adj.*, (financially) poor; poverty-stricken, L. 7, p. 76/L. 10, p. 109

qiūhòu, 秋后, *n.*, after the autumn harvest, L. 20, p. 239

qiúshēng, 求生, *v.*, seek to survive, L. 1, p. 6

qiúxué, 求学, *v.-o.*, pursue one's studies; seek knowledge; attend school, L. 18, p. 213

qiúzhùyú, 求助于, *v.*, seek for help from; turn to sb. for help, L. 20, p. 239

qū, 区, *n.*, area; region, L. 5, p. 58

qūshǐ, 驱使, *v.*, prompt; urge, L. 19, p. 229

qūshì, 趋势, *n.*, trend, L. 29, p. 332

qǔ, 娶, *v.*, (of men) marry, take (a wife), L. 10, p. 109

qǔdài, 取代, *v.*, replace; substitute, L. 4, p. 43/L. 15, p. 167

qǔxiāo, 取消, *v.*, abolish; cancel, L. 29, p. 334

qùliú, 去留, *n.*, "go or stay"(here: give birth or get an abortion), L. 26, p. 299

quānr, 圈儿, *AN*, measure word for rounds, L. 2, p. 19

quán, 全, *adj.*, whole; entire, L. 5, p. 55

quán, 权, *suffix*, right, L. 11, p. 121

quánbù, 全部, *n./adj.*, whole; complete; entire; total; all, L. 20, p. 239

quánlì, 权利, *n.*, right, L. 10, p. 110

quánmiàn, 全面, *adv.*, comprehensively; all-around; entirely, L. 32, p. 362

quàn, 劝, *v.*, urge; persuade; exhort, L. 5, p. 57

quēdé, 缺德, *adj.*, mean; wicked, L. 23, p. 270

quēdiǎn, 缺点, *n.*, shortcoming; defect; weak point, L. 23, p. 269

quēfá, 缺乏, *v.*, lack; be scanty of, L. 16, p. 183

quēshǎo, 缺少, *v.*, lack; be deficient in, L. 17, p. 203

quēxiàn, 缺陷, *n.*, flaw; defect, L. 19, p. 229

què, 却, *adv.*, but; yet, L. 4, p. 43

quèrèn, 确认, *v.*, confirm; recognize, L. 27, p. 311

quèshí, 确实, *adv.*, indeed; really, L. 10, p. 110

qún, 群, *AN*, measure word for groups or flocks, L. 7, p. 74

qúnzhòng, 群众, *n.*, the masses, L. 27, p. 312

qún.zi, 裙子, *n.*, skirt, L. 7, p. 75

R

rán'ér, 然而, *conj.*, however, L. 15, p. 165

ràng, 让, *v.*, yield; allow, L. 3, p. 31

rè, 热, *adj.*, popular, L. 18, p. 215

rè'ài, 热爱, *v.*, love fervently, L. 14, p. 152

rè.nao, 热闹, *adj.*, bustling with noise and excitement; lively, L. 28, p. 321

rèxīn, 热心, *adj.*, enthusiastic; zealous, L. 16, p. 183

rèzhōngyú, 热衷于, *v.*, be fond of; be keen on , L. 18, p. 215

Réndà, 人大, *n.*, short for 全国人民代表大会; National People's Congress, L. 30, p. 342

réngé, 人格, *n.*, moral integrity , L. 16, p. 185/L. 27, p. 308

rén'gōng liúchǎn, 人工流产, *n.*, induced abortion, L. 17, p. 203

rénjūn, 人均, *n.*, per capita, L. 31, p. 351

rénkǒu, 人口, *n.*, population, L. 5, p. 55

rénlèi, 人类, *n.*, human kind, L. 24, p. 280

rénmín, 人民, *n.*, people, L. 14, p 149

Rénmín Dàxué, 人民大学, *n.*, People's University, L. 18, p. 215

Rénmín Rìbào, 人民日报, *n.*, the People's Daily, L. 13, p. 140

rénpǐn, 人品, *n.*, moral standing; moral quality; character, L. 11, p. 119

rénquán, 人权, *n.*, human rights, L. 8, p. 87

rénshēn, 人身, *adj.*, personal, L. 16 附录, p. 196

rénshēng, 人生, *n.*, life, L. 13, p. 142

rénshù, 人数, *n.*, number of people, L. 19, p. 227

rénxìng, 人性, *n.*, human nature, L. 24, p. 279

rényuán, 人员, *n.*, personnel; staff, L. 17, p. 202

rénzhì, 人治, *n.*, rule by man; rule of man, L. 8, p. 89

rěnshòu, 忍受, *v.*, endure; bear, L. 16, p. 178

rènhé, 任何, *adj.*, any, L. 7, p. 76/L. 9, p. 98

rènkě, 认可, *v.*, accept; approve, L. 17, p. 203

rèn.shi, 认识, *n.*, understanding, L. 14, p. 151

rènwéi, 认为, *v.*, think that; believe that, L. 4, p. 42

rènwù, 任务, *n.*, mission; assignment; task; duties, L. 29, p. 333

rēng, 扔, *v.*, throw away; throw; toss, L. 5, p. 55

réng, 仍, *adv.*, still, L. 18, p. 212

réngrán, 仍然, *adv.*, still; 仍, L. 25, p. 289

rìcháng, 日常, *adj.*, daily; day-to-day, L. 4, p. 44

rìhòu, 日后, *n.*, in days to come, L. 21, p. 251

rìyì, 日益…, *adv.*, increasingly; day by day, L. 14, p. 153

róngxǔ, 容许, *v.*, tolerate; allow, L. 30, p. 345

shuō.budìng, 说不定, *adv.*, perhaps; maybe, L. 12, p. 133

shuō//huǎng, 说谎, *v.-o.*, tell a lie, L. 11, p. 121

shuōmíng, 说明, *v.*, show; illustrate, explain, L. 4, p. 43

sīcháo, 思潮, *n.*, trend of thought, L. 17, p. 201

sīfǎ, 司法, *adj.*, judicial, L. 8, p. 88

sījī, 司机, *n.*, driver, L. 3, p. 31

sī//pò, 撕破, *v.-c.*, tear, L. 28, p. 321

sīxiǎng, 思想, *n.*, thought; thinking, L. 12, p. 131

sǐ, 死, *v.*, die, L. 6, p. 67

sǐwáng, 死亡, *v.*, die; be dead, L. 29, p. 333

sìchù, 四处, *n.*, all around; everywhere, L. 19, p. 227

Sìchuān, 四川, *n.*, Sichuan Province , L. 27, p. 309

sìhū, 似乎, *adv.*, it seems that; it appears that; it appears as if, L. 14, p. 151

sùdù, 速度, *n.*, speed; pace, L. 9, p. 99

sùliào, 塑料, *n.*, plastics, L. 5, p. 57

sùshè, 宿舍, *n.*, dormitory, L. 2, p. 17

sùzhì, 素质, *n.*, quality, L. 14, p. 149

suíbiàn, 随便, *adv.*, carelessly; willfully, L. 12, p. 131

suíshí suídì, 随时随地, *adv.*, at any time and any place, L. 12, p. 132

suíshēntīng, 随身听, *n.*, walkman, L. 13, p. 140

suí.zhe, 随着, *prep.*, along with; in the wake of, L. 20, p. 241

sǔnhài, 损害, *n./v.*, harm; damage, L. 27, p. 310

sǔnshī, 损失, *n./v.*, loss, lose, L. 6, p. 68

suōduǎn, 缩短, *v.*, shorten, L. 9, p. 99

suǒ, 所, *AN*, measure word for houses, institutions, etc., L. 14, p. 148

suǒ, 锁, *v./n.*, lock (up), lock, L. 6, p. 67

suǒwèi, 所谓, *adj.*, so-called, L. 7, p. 75

T

tā, 它, *pron.*, it, L. 9, p. 97

tārén, 他人, *n.*, another person; other people, L. 19, p. 225

tā.shi, 踏实, *adj.*, free from anxiety, L. 20, p. 241

tái, 台, *AN*, measure word for engine, machine, etc., L. 25, p. 287

Táidú, 台独, *n.*, short for "台湾独立"; Taiwans's Independence, L. 30, p. 345

táigāo, 抬高, *v.-c.*, raise; increase, L. 27, p. 308

Táiwān, 台湾, *n.*, Taiwan, L. 30, p. 343

tài.du, 态度, *n.*, attitude, L. 7, p. 76/ L. 14, p. 151/L. 17, p. 200

tānwū, 贪污 , *v./n.*, embezzle; practice graft, embezzlement, L. 11, p. 119

tán, 谈, *v.*, talk; negotiate, L. 1, p. 3

tándào, 谈到, *v.-c.*, speak about or of; mention, L. 15, p. 163

tánhuà, 谈话, *n.*, statement; talk, L. 30, p. 342

tán liàn'ài, 谈恋爱, *v.-o.*, be in love, L. 11, p. 122

tánpàn, 谈判, *n.*, negotiation, L. 30, p. 344

tāng, 汤, *n.*, soup, L. 4, p. 43

tàng, 趟, *AN*, measure word for trip, L. 1, p. 3

tàng, 烫, *adj./v.*, very hot; scalding, burn; scald, L. 8, p. 87

tāo//chū, 掏出, *v.-c.*, take out; fish out; draw out, L. 15, p. 163

táotài, 淘汰, *v.*, eliminate through selection or competition, L. 4, p. 42

tǎolùn, 讨论, *n./v.*, discussion, discuss, L. 15, p. 163

tǎo//qián, 讨钱, *v.-o.*, beg for money, L. 28, p. 323

tǎoyàn, 讨厌, *v.*, dislike; loathe, L. 5, p. 54

tào.zi, 套子, *n.*, cover; case; (here) condom, L. 12, p. 131

tèbié, 特别, *adv.*, especially, L. 2, p. 19

tècháng, 特长, *n.*, what one is skilled in; strong point; special skill; specialty, L. 18, p. 214

tèdiǎn, 特点, *n.*, characteristic; trait, L. 27, p. 310

tèsè, 特色, *n.*, distinguishing feature, L. 24, p. 276

tèshū, 特殊, *adj.*, special; particular, L. 18, p. 211

téng, 疼, *v.*, love dearly, L. 22, p. 259

tī, 踢, *v.*, kick, L. 16, p. 181

tí, 题, *n.*, question in a test or assignment, L. 15, p. 163

tíbāo, 提包, *n.*, handbag, L. 28, p. 319

tíchàng, 提倡, *v.*, advocate; promote, L. 5, p. 57

tíchū, 提出, *v.*, put forward; pose; raise, L. 16, p. 181

tíchū, 提出, *v.*, submit; propose, L. 30, p. 342

tígāo, 提高, *v.*, raise; increase; heighten, L. 11, p. 122

tígōng, 提供, *v.*, provide, L. 25, p. 288

tíjiāo, 提交, *v.*, submit; file, L. 30, p. 343

tíqián, 提前, *v.*, shift to an earlier date/time, L. 29, p. 333

tíxǐng, 提醒, *v.*, remind, L. 16, p. 181

tǐyàn, 体验, *v.*, learn through one's personally experience; experience (life), L. 1, p. 5

tì, 替, *prep.*, for; on behalf of, L. 19, p. 225

tiān'é, 天鹅, *n.*, swan, L. 24, p. 277

tiānlún zhī lè, 天伦之乐, *idm.*, family happiness; the happiness of a family reunion, L. 20, p. 241

tiānqì, 天气, *n.*, weather, L. 1, p. 6

tiānshù, 天数, *n.*, number of days, L. 2, p. 19

Tiāntán, 天坛, *n.*, Temple of Heaven, L. 2, p. 14

tiānxià, 天下, *n.*, under the heaven, L. 9, p. 98

tiānxià, 天下, *n.*, whole world; in the world, L. 20, p. 241

tiānxiàshì, 天下事, *n.*, things in the world, L. 9, p. 98

tiānzhēn, 天真, *adj.*, innocent, L. 15, p. 165

tiāo, 挑, *v.*, choose; pick; select, L. 23, p. 270

tiáo, 条, *AN*, measure word for clauses, L. 16 附录, p. 195

tiáo, 条, *AN*, measure word for long, narrow things, L. 7, p. 75

tiáo, 条, *n.*, strip, L. 24, p. 277

tiáojiàn, 条件, *n.*, condition; requirement; prerequisite; term, L. 5, p. 57/L. 13, p. 143

tiáokuǎn, 条款, *n.*, clause; article; provisions, L. 26, p. 299

zhěngtiān, 整天, *n.*, all day; the whole day, L. 22, p. 259

zhèng, 正, *adv.*, precisely; exactly, L. 27, p. 311

zhèngcè, 政策, *n.*, policy, L. 16 附录, p. 197

zhèngjiàn, 证件, *n.*, certificate; credentials; papers, L. 19, p. 227

zhèngmíng, 证明, *n.*, certificate; testimonial, L. 27, p. 309

zhèngmíng, 证明, *n./v.*, proof, prove, L. 12, p. 131

zhèng//qián, 挣钱, *v.-o.*, make money; 赚钱, L. 14, p. 153

zhèngshì, 正式, *adv /adj.*, formally; officially, formal, L. 29, p. 333

zhèngzhì, 政治, *n.*, politics, L. 11, p. 121

zhèngzhòng, 郑重, *adv.*, solemnly; seriously, L. 32, p. 361

zhī, 支, *AN*, measure word for long and narrow objects, L. 29, p. 333

zhī, 织, *v.*, knit, L. 16, p. 179

zhīchí, 支持, *v.*, support, L. 30, p. 345

zhījí, 之极, *adv.*, extremely, L. 24, p. 279

zhī.shi, 知识, *n.*, knowledge, L. 14, p. 149

zhī.shi chǎnquán, 知识产权, *n.*, intellectual property right, L. 8, p. 88

zhī.shi nǚxìng, 知识女性, *n.*, educated women, L. 22, p. 261

zhīxià, …之下, , under …, L. 16, p. 181

…zhīyī, …之一, one of …, L. 8, p. 87

zhīzhì, 之至, *adv.*, extremely, L. 24, p. 279

zhí.dé, 值得, *v.*, deserve; be worth, L. 4, p. 41

zhífēi, 直飞, *v.*, fly directly , L. 1, p. 3

zhígōng, 职工, *n.*, workers and staff members, L. 16, p. 179

zhíjiē, 直接, *adj.*, direct; immediate, L. 14, p. 152

zhíqín, 值勤, *v.-o.*, be on duty (of police or military), L. 18, p. 211

zhíyè, 职业, *n.*, occupation, L. 8, p. 87

zhízé, 职责, *n.*, duty; responsibility, L. 29, p. 333

zhǐbēi, 纸杯, *n.*, paper cup, L. 5, p. 57

zhǐchū, 指出, *v.*, point out, L. 4, p. 43

zhǐgù, 只顾, *adv.*, be preoccupied solely with, L. 14, p. 153

zhǐhǎo, 只好, *adv.* , have to; be forced to, L. 2, p. 15

zhǐjīn, 纸巾, *n.*, paper towel; tissue paper, L. 5, p. 57

zhǐyào, 只要, *conj.*, so long as, L. 1, p. 6

zhǐzé, 指责, *v.*, censure; criticize; find fault with, L. 14, p. 153

zhì, 至, *prep.*, to; till; until, L. 22, p. 261

zhì'ān, 治安, *n.*, public security; public order, L. 16 附录, p. 196

zhìcái, 制裁, *v.*, sanction; punish, L. 11, p. 119

zhìfù, 致富, *v.*, get rich, L. 28, p. 323

zhìliàng, 质量, *n.*, quality, L. 5, p. 54

zhìshǎo, 至少, *adv.*, at least, L. 9, p. 97

zhìsǐ, 致死, *v.*, cause death; result in death, L. 16 附录, p. 195

zhìxù, 秩序, *n.*, order; law and order, L. 16 附录, p. 196/ L. 18, p. 211

zhìyú, 至于, *prep.*, as for, L. 11, p. 121

zhìzhǐ, 制止, *v.*, stop; put an end to, L. 19, p. 228

zhìzuò, 制作, *v./n.*, make; manufacture, L. 18, p. 214

zhōngchǎn jiējí, 中产阶级, *n.*, middle class, L. 14, p. 153

zhōngdàng, 中档, *adj.*, (of the quality of things) of second rate, L. 2, p. 17

Zhōngguāncūn, 中关村, *n.*, Zhongguancun; a district in Beijing , L. 18, p. 214

Zhōngguóhuà, 中国化, *v.*, "sinicize"; become Chinese, L. 1, p. 5

Zhōngguó Wēixiélùn, 中国威胁论, *n.*, "China Threat" theory , L. 32, p. 363

Zhōnghuá, 中华, *n.*, the Chinese nation, L. 24, p. 276

Zhōnghuá Rénmín Gònghéguó, 中华人民共和国, *n.*, the People's Republic of China, L. 16 附录, p. 195

zhōngjí, 中级, *adj.*, intermediate, L. 16 附录, p. 195

zhōngjiū, 终究, *adv.*, eventually; in the end; in the long run, L. 25, p. 289

zhōng xiǎo xuéshēng, 中小学生, *n.*, middle school and primary school students, L. 13, p. 140

zhōngxīn, 中心, *n.*, center, L. 18, p. 213

zhǒng.zi, 种子, *n.*, seed (here: cause), L. 16, p. 180

zhòng, 重, *adj.*, heavy, L. 14, p. 150

zhòng//dì, 种地, *v.-o.*, cultivate land, L. 20, p. 239

zhòngdiǎnbān, 重点班, *n.*, honors class; advanced class; tracked class for bright students, L. 16, p. 179

zhòngduō, 众多, *adj.*, multitudinous; numerous, L. 19, p. 227

zhòngshì, 重视, *v.*, take something seriously; value, L. 11, p. 121

zhòngxiè, 重谢, *v.*, present a grand reward, L. 15, p. 167

zhòngyā, 重压, *n.*, heavy pressure, L. 16, p. 181

zhòngyào, 重要, *adj.*, important, L. 6, p. 67

zhòngyìyuàn, 众议院, *n.*, House of Representatives, L. 30, p. 343

zhōumò, 周末, *n.*, weekend, L. 1, p. 7

zhōusuì, 周岁, *n.*, one full year of life, L. 16 附录, p. 196

zhú(.zi), 竹（子）, *n.*, bamboo, L. 5, p. 55

zhúbù, 逐步, *adv.*, step by step; gradually, L. 22, p. 261

zhújiàn, 逐渐, *adv.*, gradually; progressively, L. 22, p. 259

zhúqiānr, 竹签儿, *n.*, bamboo skewer, L. 23, p. 269

zhúyī, 逐一, *adv.*, one by one, L. 19, p. 227

zhǔ.yì, 主意, *n.*, idea, L. 2, p. 17

zhǔcài, 主菜, *n.*, main dish, L. 24, p. 277

zhǔdòng, 主动, *adv.*, take the initiative, L. 29, p. 335

zhǔjué, 主角, *n.*, main character; leading role, L. 15, p. 168

zhǔquán, 主权, *n.*, sovereignty, L. 30, p. 343

zhǔtí, 主题, *n.*, theme, L. 29, p. 335

English Index

英文索引

English Index

amount of money, 钱数, qiánshù, *n.*, L. 21, p. 251

amount of physical activity, 活动量, huódòngliàng, *n.*, L. 14, p. 150

analysis, analyze, 分析, fēnxī, *n./v.*, L. 14, p. 149

ancient times, 古代, gǔdài, *n.*, L. 1, p. 5

ancient; old, 古老, gǔlǎo, *adj.*, L. 1, p. 4

and; also, besides; moreover, 并且, bìngqiě, *conj.*, L. 16, p. 184

and; 跟, 与, yǔ, *conj.*, L. 12, p. 131

and; 跟, 及, jí, *conj.*, L. 24, p. 280

and so on; etc, 等等, děngděng, , L. 14, p. 149

animal, 动物, dòngwù, *n.*, L. 24, p. 277

announce; declare, 宣布, xuānbù, *v.*, L. 11, p. 119

announce; issue, 发布, fābù, *v.*, L. 19, p. 227

another person; other people, 他人, tārén, *n.*, L. 19, p. 225

answer; reply, 回答, huídá, *v.*, L. 13, p. 141

any, 任何, rènhé, *adj.*, L. 9, p. 98

any; whatever, 任何, rènhé, *adj.*, L. 7, p. 76

apart from, 离, lí, *v.*, L. 2, p. 15

aphrodisiacs; drugs that induce sexual desire, 春药, chūnyào, *n.*, L. 12, p. 133

appear; arise; emerge, 出现, chūxiàn, *v.*, L. 17, p. 203

appearance; look, 模样, múyàng, *n.*, L. 28, p. 319

appendix, 附录, fùlù, *n.* L. 16, p. 194

appetizing; fragrant, 香, xiāng, *adj.*, L. 24, p. 277

approve of; be in favor of, 赞成, zànchéng, *v.*, L. 15, p. 165

approximately; 大约, 约, yuē, *adv.*, L. 20, p. 239

area, 地段, dìduàn, *n.*, L. 28, p. 319

area; district; region, 地区, dìqū, *n.*, L. 20, p. 239

area; region, 区, qū, *n.*, L. 5, p. 58

armament; arms, 军备, jūnbèi , *n.*, L. 32, p. 363

as, 作为, zuòwéi, *prep.*, L. 24, p. 276

as far as possible; to the best of one's ability, 尽可能, jǐn kěnéng, *adv.*, L. 14, p. 153

as for, 至于, zhìyú, *prep.*, L. 11, p. 121

as one wished, 如…所愿, rú…suǒ yuàn, *phr.*, L. 26, p. 299

as usual, 照常, zhàocháng, *adv.*, L. 16, p. 184

as well as; along with, 以及, yǐjí, *conj.*, L. 29, p. 333

Asia, 亚洲, Yàzhōu, *n.*, L. 32, p. 363

aspiration; desire, 愿望, yuànwàng, *n.*, L. 30, p. 345

association; relationship, have an association with, 交往, jiāowǎng, *n./v.*, L. 15, p. 162

astonish; shock, 震惊, zhènjīng, *v.*, L. 16, p. 182

at a very young age, 小小年纪, xiǎoxiǎo niánjì, *phr.*, L. 15, p. 165

at all; simply, 根本, gēnběn, *adv.*, L. 9, p. 97

at any time and any place, 随时随地, suíshí suídì, *adv.*, L. 12, p. 132

at first; in the beginning, 起先, qǐxiān, *adv.*, L. 15, p. 164

at least, 至少, zhìshǎo, *adv.*, L. 9, p. 97

at (the) most, 顶多, dǐngduō, *adv.*, L. 6, p. 67

at once; right away, 马上, mǎshàng, *adv.*, L. 15, p. 163

at present; at the moment, 目前, mùqián, *n.*, L. 5, p. 55

at the beginning of; in the early part of, 初, chū, *n.*, L. 31, p. 350

at the beginning; originally, 当初, dāngchū, *n.*, L. 22, p. 259

at the same time; in the mean time, 同时, tóngshí, *conj.*, L. 14, p. 153

atomic bomb, 原子弹, yuánzǐdàn, *n.*, L. 32, p. 360

attack from all sides, 围攻, wéigōng, *v.*, L. 28, p. 319

attempt; seek; try, 企图, qǐtú, *v.*, L. 21, p. 249

attend (meeting, discussion, etc.) , 参加, cānjiā, *v.*, L. 16, p. 181

attend (school), 就读, jiùdú, *v.*, L. 16, p. 182

attend (school, class, etc.), 读, dú, *v.*, L. 13, p. 141

attend school; go to school; be at school, 上学, shàng//xué, *v.-o.*, L. 28, p. 323

attend school, read; study, 读书, dú//shū, *v.-o.*, L. 16, p. 179

attend to; take care of; manage, 料理, liàolǐ, *v.*, L. 14, p. 151

attitude, 态度, tài.du, *n.*, L. 7, p. 76/L. 14, p. 151/L. 17, p. 200

attract; draw, 吸引, xīyǐn, *v.*, L. 18, p. 212

automatic vending machine; 自动售货机, 自售机, zìshòujī, *n.*, L. 25, p. 286

automatic, 自动, zìdòng, *adj.*, L. 12, p. 131

auxiliary class; tutorial class, 辅导班, fǔdǎobān, *n.*, L. 18, p. 212

average, 平均, píngjūn, *adj.*, L. 10, p. 109

avoid; avert, 免于, miǎnyú, *v.*, L. 25, p. 289

away from home, 在外, zàiwài, , L. 21, p. 249

B

back of the head, 后脑, hòunǎo, *n.*, L. 16, p. 182

background, 底, dǐ, *n.*, L. 27, p. 309

backward; less developed, 落后, luòhòu, *adj.*, L. 32, p. 363

bad; harmful, 不良, bùliáng, *adj.*, L. 14, p. 151

bag; sack, 包, bāo, *n.*, L. 27, p. 311

bag; sack, 袋（子）, dài(.zi), *n.*, L. 5, p. 57

bamboo, 竹（子）, zhú(.zi), *n.*, L. 5, p. 55

bamboo skewer, 竹签儿, zhúqiānr, *n.*, L. 23, p. 269

bank, 银行, yínháng, *n.*, L. 21, p. 251

banquet; dinning party, 宴, yàn, *suffix*, L. 24, p. 277

barbarous; cruel, 野蛮, yěmán, *adj.*, L. 24, p. 276

barbecue; roast, 烤, kǎo, *v.*, L. 23, p. 270

base; base number; cardinal number, 基数, jīshù, *n.*, L. 31, p. 352

basic; fundamental, 基本, jīběn, *adj.*, L. 21, p. 249

English Index

compensation; reward; payment, 酬劳, chóuláo, *n.*, L. 19, p. 225

competition, compete, 竞争, jìngzhēng, *n./v.*, L. 7, p. 77

complete; finish, 完成, wánchéng, *v.*, L. 31, p. 351

complete; perfect (not to be used for people), *adj.*, L. 11, p. 119

completely, 完全, wánquán, *adv.*, L. 1, p. 5

completely different, 截然不同, jiérán bùtóng, *adj.*, L. 15, p. 165

comprehensively; all-around; entirely, 全面, quánmiàn, *adv.*, L. 32, p. 362

computer, 电脑, diànnǎo, *n.*, L. 9, p. 97

computer, 计算机, jìsuànjī, *n.*, L. 18, p. 214

comrade, 同志, tóngzhì, *n.*, L. 25, p. 289

condemn; blame; denounce, 谴责, qiǎnzé, *v.*, L. 30, p. 342

condition; requirement; prerequisite; term, 条件, tiáojiàn, *n.*, L. 5, p. 57/L. 13, p. 143

condition; situation, 状况, zhuàngkuàng, *n.*, L. 14, p. 149

condom, 保险套, bǎoxiǎntào, *n.*, L. 12, p. 131

condom; 保险套, 安全套, ānquántào, *n.*, L. 25, p. 286

confess, 承认, chéngrèn, *v.*, L. 27, p. 309

confidence, 信心, xìnxīn, *n.*, L. 8, p. 88

confirm; recognize, 确认, quèrèn, *v.*, L. 27, p. 311

conflict, 冲突, chōngtū, *v.*, L. 16, p. 181

Confucius, 孔子, Kǒngzǐ, *n.*, L. 12, p. 133

Congress, 国会, gúohuì, *n.*, L. 30, p. 342

consciously; of one's own initiative; of one's own free will, 自觉, zìjué, *adv.*, L. 31, p. 352

consequence, 后果, hòuguǒ, *n.*, L. 17, p. 203

consequently; hence; thereupon, 于是, yúshì, *conj.*, L. 8, p. 87

conservative, 保守, bǎoshǒu, *adj.*, L. 4, p. 41

considerable; impressive; sizable, 可观, kěguān, *adj.*, L. 18, p. 215

considerate right down to the most trivial detail; take care of sb. in every possible way, 无微不至, wú wēi bú zhì, *idm.*, L. 21, p. 251

consistently; from beginning to end; all along, 一贯, yíguàn, *adv.*, L. 32, p. 362

constantly; often, 时时, shíshí, *adv.*, L. 19, p. 228

constitute; compose, 构成, gòuchéng, *v.*, L. 16 附录, p. 195

constitution; charter, 宪法, xiànfǎ, *n.*, L. 27, p. 311

construction; development, build; construct; develop, 建设, jiànshè, *n./v.*, L. 32, p. 363

contact, 联系, liánxì, *v.*, L. 19, p. 225

content, 内容, nèiróng, *n.*, L. 25, p. 289

contest; competition; race, 竞赛, jìngsài, *n.*, L. 32, p. 363

continue, 持续, chíxù, *v.*, L. 29, p. 333

continue, 继续, jìxù, *v.*, L. 29, p. 335

continuously, 不停地, bùtíng.de, *adv.*, L. 28, p. 323

continuously; constantly, 不断, búduàn, *adv.*, L. 28, p. 319

continuously; successively, 连续, liánxù, *adv.*, L. 31, p. 351

contradiction, 矛盾, máodùn, *n.*, L. 16, p. 183

contribute to; be conducive to, 有助于, yǒuzhùyú, *v.*, L. 14, p. 152

control, 控制, kòngzhì, *v.*, L. 29, p. 332

control, 管住, guǎn//zhù, *v.-c.*, L. 19, p. 227

could it be that...? (used in a rhetorical question to make it more forceful), 难道, nándào, *adv.*, L. 5, p. 56

count; compute, 计算, jìsuàn, *v.*, L. 18, p. 214

count from the end; count backwards, 倒数, dàoshǔ, *v.*, L. 16, p. 180

country; nation, 国家, guójiā, *n.*, L. 5, p. 57

court, 法庭, fǎtíng, *n.*, L. 26, p. 297

court, 法院, fǎyuàn, *n.*, L. 8, p. 87

court decision; judgment, 判决, pànjué, *v.*, L. 16 附录, p. 195

cover, 覆盖, fùgài, *v.*, L. 25, p. 289

cover; case; (here) condom, 套子, tào.zi, *n.*, L. 12, p. 131

cow dung, 牛粪, niúfèn, *n.*, L. 10, p. 106

create, 创造, chuàngzào, *v.*, L. 21, p. 250

criminal; penal, 刑事, xíngshì, *adj.*, L. 16 附录, p. 197

criminal law, 刑法, xíngfǎ, *n.*, L. 16 附录, p. 195

criticize, criticism, 批评, pīpíng, *v./n.*, L. 24, p. 276

crocodile, 鳄鱼, èyú, *n.*, L. 24, p. 277

cross; pass, 过, guò, *v.*, L. 3, p. 31

crucial; key; very important, 关键, guānjiàn, *adj.*, L. 13, p. 142

cruel, 残酷, cánkù, *adj.*, L. 7, p. 77

cry, 哭, kū, *v.*, L. 28, p. 321

cultivate; plough and sow, 耕种, gēngzhòng, *v.*, L. 20, p. 239

cultivate land, 种地, zhòng//dì, *v.-o.*, L. 20, p. 239

culture, 文化, wénhuà, *n.*, L. 4, p. 42

currently in effect; in force; active, 现行, xiànxíng, *adj.*, L. 26, p. 297

custom, 习俗, xísú, *n.*, L. 26, p. 299

cut apart; separate, 分割, fēn'gē, *v.*, L. 30, p. 343

D

daily; day-to-day, 日常, rìcháng, *adj.*, L. 4, p. 44

dangerous, 危险, wēixiǎn, *adj.*, L. 2, p. 15

dark, 黑暗, hēi'àn, *adj.*, L. 11, p. 119

daughter, 女儿, nǚ.er, *n.*, L. 13, p. 141

Dean's office; office of teaching affairs, 教务处, jiàowùchù, *n.*, L. 19, p. 226

debate; argument, debate, 辩论, biànlùn, *n./v.*, L. 15, p. 167

decade of a century, 年代, niándài, *n.*, L. 22, p. 259

declare, 声明, shēngmíng, *v.*, L. 32, p. 361

deep; profound, 深刻, shēnkè, *adj.*, L. 1, p. 3

deep-fry, 炸, zhá, *v.*, L. 24, p. 277

English Index

deeply; keenly; thoroughly, 深切, shēnqiè, *adv.*, L. 24, p. 280

defend; guard; protect, 捍卫, hànwèi, *v.*, L. 30, p. 345

defend; safeguard, 维护, wéihù, *v.*, L. 16 附录, p. 196/ L. 18, p. 211

defendant; the accused, 被告人, bèigàorén, *n.*, L. 16 附录, p. 195

definitely; surely, 肯定, kěndìng, *adv.*, L. 9, p. 97

definitely not; under no circumstance, 决不, juébù, *adv.*, L. 30, p. 345

degree; extent, 程度, chéngdù, *n.*, L. 14, p. 148

degree for temperature, 度, dù, *n.*, L. 1, p. 6

degree of tolerance, 宽容度, kuānróngdù, *n.*, L. 22, p. 261

delay; hold up, 耽误, dānwù, *v.*, L. 3, p. 33

delegate; representative, 代表, dàibiǎo, *n.*, L. 32, p. 361

deliberately; intentionally, 故意, gùyì, *adv.*, L. 16 附录, p. 194

delightful; pleasant, 愉快, yúkuài, *adj.*, L. 25, p. 286

deliver; issue; announce, 发表, fābiǎo, *v.*, L. 29, p. 333

demonstrate; make clear, 表明, biǎomíng, *v.*, L. 14, p. 149/L. 17, p. 201

deny, 否认, fǒurèn, *v.*, L. 19, p. 226

department (of a university), 系, xì, *n.*, L. 19, p. 226

department of a large organization, 部门, bùmén, *n.*, L. 25, p. 288

deploy; dispose (troops), 部署, bùshǔ, *v.*, L. 32, p. 361

deposit, 押金, yājīn, *n.*, L. 2, p. 19

deprive of; expropriate, 剥夺, bōduó, *v.*, L. 16 附录, p. 195/L. 26, p. 298

descend; drop off; decrease, 下降, xiàjiàng, *v.*, L. 14, p. 150

descendants, 子孙, zǐsūn, *n.*, L. 24, p. 279

descendants; posterity, 后代, hòudài, *n.*, L. 24, p. 279

describe, 形容, xíngróng, *v.*, L. 9, p. 98

deserve; be worth, 值得, zhí.dé, *v.*, L. 4, p. 41

deservedly; as a matter of fact; be natural and right, 理所当然, lǐ suǒ dāng rán, *idm.*, L. 15, p. 163

destroy by burning or melting, 销毁, xiāohuǐ, *v.*, L. 32, p. 362

develop; cultivate; form (habit), 养成, yǎngchéng, *v.*, L. 7, p. 75

develop; launch, 开展, kāizhǎn, *v.*, L. 21, p. 250

develop; promote; carry forward; carry on (the object is always a abstract noun), 发扬, fāyáng, *v.*, L. 15, p. 165

developed; advanced; prosperous, 发达, fādá, *adj.*, L. 14, p. 149

developed country, 发达国家, fādá guójiā, *n.*, L. 29, p. 335

developing country, 发展中国家, fāzhǎn zhōng guójiā, *n.*, L. 29, p. 335

die, 死, sǐ, *v.*, L. 6, p. 67

die; be dead, 死亡, sǐwáng, *v.*, L. 29, p. 333

difference, 差异, chāyì, *n.*, L. 20, p. 241

difference; disparity, 差别, chābié, *n.*, L. 22, p. 261

difference (in distance; amount; progress, etc.) disparity; gap, 差距, chājù, *n.*, L. 22, p. 259

difficult problem; tough question, 难题, nántí, *n.*, L. 15, p. 163/L. 20, p. 239

difficult question, 难题, nántí, *n.*,

difficult to, 难以, nányǐ, *adv.*, L. 19, p. 227

dignity, 尊严, zūnyán, *n.*, L. 27, p. 308

diligent; hardworking, 勤劳, qínláo, *adj.*, L. 14, p. 152

dining table, 餐桌, cānzhuō, *n.*, L. 24, p. 276

direct; immediate, 直接, zhíjiē, *adj.*, L. 14, p. 152

direction, 方向, fāngxiàng, *n.*, L. 5, p. 55

disadvantage, 坏处, huài.chu, *n.*, L. 5, p. 56

disappear, 不见, bújiàn, *v.*, L. 13, p. 141

disappointed, 失望, shīwàng, *adj.*, L. 15, p. 163

discard, 丢, diū, *v.*, L. 5, p. 55

discern; distinguish, 识别, shíbié, *v.*, L. 19, p. 228

discipline; morale, 纪律, jìlǜ, *n.*, L. 27, p. 309

discuss in person, 面议, miànyì, *v.*, L. 19, p. 225

discussion, discuss, 讨论, tǎolùn, *n./v.*, L. 15, p. 163

disease, 疾病, jíbìng, *n.*, L. 23, p. 269

disgusting; feel like vomiting, 恶心, ěxīn, *adj.*, L. 4, p. 43

dislike; loathe, 讨厌, tǎoyàn, *v.*, L. 5, p. 54

dislike; mind, 嫌, xián, *v.*, L. 20, p. 240

dislike and avoid; cold-shoulder, 嫌弃, xiánqì, *v.*, L. 20, p. 239

disorderliness; confusion; chaos, disorder; chaotic, 紊乱, wěnluàn, *n./adj.*, L. 26, p. 299

disorderly; chaotic, 混乱, hùnluàn, *adj.*, L. 17, p. 202

dispense (lit. "spit out"), 吐, tǔ, *v.*, L. 25, p. 289

dispute; be at odds with, dispute, 争执, zhēngzhí, *n./v.*, L. 8, p. 87

dispute; debate; contention 争议, zhēngyì, *n.*, L. 25, p. 286

dispute; quarrel, 纠纷, jiūfēn, *n.*, L. 26, p. 297

disregard, 不顾, búgù, *v.*, L. 24, p. 276

distinguishing feature, 特色, tèsè, *n.*, L. 24, p. 276

distribute; allot, 分, fēn, *v.*, L. 20, p. 239

disturbance (lit. "wind and wave'), 风波, fēngbō, *n.*, L. 15, p. 167

diversified, 多元化, duōyuánhuà, *adj.*, L. 22, p. 261

do, 干, gàn, *v.*, L. 14, p. 152/L. 16, p. 183

do; be engaged in, 搞, gǎo, *v.*, L. 15, p. 166

do (legal term), put into effect; implement 实施, shíshī, *v.*, L. 27, p. 311

do A while doing B; do A and B at the same time, 一边儿…一边儿…, yìbiānr...yìbiānr..., L. 28, p. 320

do business, 做生意, zuò shēng.yi, *v.-o.*, L. 13, p. 140

do evil things openly and unscrupulously; have the impudence to do sth., 明目张胆, míng mù zhāng dǎn, *idm.*, L. 30, p. 343

405

even; even to the point that; so much so that, 甚至于, shènzhìyú, *conj.*, L. 5, p. 57/L. 8, p. 87

even more, 更加, gèngjiā, *adv.*, L. 14, p. 153

even more; 更, 还, hái, *adv.*, L. 1, p. 3

even though; despite, 尽管, jǐnguǎn, *conj.*, L. 5, p. 55

eventually; in the end; in the long run, 终究, zhōngjiū, *adv.*, L. 25, p. 289

everywhere; all over, 到处, dàochù, *n.*, L. 23, p. 270

examination hall or room, 考场, kǎochǎng, *n.*, L. 19, p. 227

examine; check; inspect, 检查, jiǎnchá, *v.*, L. 27, p. 311

example; case; instance, 例子, lì.zi, *n.*, L. 4, p. 44/L. 10, p. 109

exceed; go beyond; surpass, 过, guò, *v.*, L. 22, p. 261

exceed; surpass, 超过, chāoguò, *v.*, L. 6, p. 68

excessively; over-, 过, guò, *adv.*, L. 14, p. 150

exchange (each other's experiences, view, etc.), 交流, jiāoliú, *v.*, L. 4, p. 42

exciting, 刺激, cìjī, *adj.*, L. 1, p. 6

excuse, 借口, jièkǒu, *n.*, L. 26, p. 299

exercise (the body), 锻炼, duànliàn, *v.*, L. 2, p. 17

exist; be, 存在, cúnzài, *v.*, L. 14, p. 148

exit and entrance; 出口 and 入口, 出入口, chūrùkǒu, *n.*, L. 28, p. 319

expand; enlarge, 拉大, lādà, *v.*, L. 22, p. 259

expel; discharge; fire, 开除, kāichú, *v.*, L. 19, p. 227

expense; cost, 费用, fèiyòng, *n.*, L. 3, p. 31

expenses; expenditure, 开支, kāizhī, *n.*, L. 32, p. 363

experience, 经验, jīngyàn, *n.*, L. 18, p. 215

expert, 专家, zhuānjiā, *n.*, L. 16, p. 183

express, 表达, biǎodá, *v.*, L. 24, p. 279

extend, expand, 扩张, kuòzhāng, *v.*, L. 32, p. 363

extend; stretch, 伸, shēn, *v.*, L. 4, p. 43

extensive; wide-ranging, extensively; widely, 广泛, guǎngfàn, *adj./adv.*, L. 9, p. 97

extent; stage, 地步, dìbù, *n.*, L. 12, p. 132

extremely difficult; arduous, 艰巨, jiānjù, *adj.*, L. 29, p. 333

extremely, 之极, zhījí, *adv.*, L. 24, p. 279

extremely, 之至, zhīzhì, *adv.*, L. 24, p. 279

extremely; very, 十分, shífēn, *adv.*, L. 16, p. 184

F

fact, 事实, shìshí, *n.*, L. 14, p. 152

factor; element, 因素, yīnsù, *n.*, L. 22, p. 261

Fahrenheit, 华氏, Huáshì, *n.*, L. 1, p. 6

fail; lose, 失败, shībài, *v.*, L. 7, p. 76

fair, 公平, gōngpíng, *adj.*, L. 7, p. 75/L. 10, p. 109

fake, 假, jiǎ, *adj.*, L. 19, p. 227

fall ill; be ill, 得病, dé//bìng, *v.-o.*, L. 29, p. 333

familiar, 熟, shú, *adj.*, L. 2, p. 15

family; household, 家庭, jiātíng, *n.*, L. 14, p. 149

family considerations that cause delay in decision; trouble back at home, 后顾之忧, hòu gù zhī yōu, *n.*, L. 18, p. 213

family happiness; the happiness of a family reunion, 天伦之乐, tiānlún zhī lè, *idm.*, L. 20, p. 241

family planning; birth control, 计划生育, jìhuà shēngyù, *n.*, L. 25, p. 287

family property, 家产, jiāchǎn, *n.*, L. 20, p. 239

famous; celebrated, 著名, zhùmíng, *adj.*, L. 19, p. 225

Fang, a surname, 方, Fāng, *n.*, L. 22, p. 258

far, 远, yuǎn, *adj.*, L. 2, p. 15

fashion; way; manner, 方式, fāngshì, *n.*, L. 17, p. 202

fashionable; trendy, 入时, rùshí, *adj.*, L. 28, p. 321

fat, get fat; put on weight, 胖, pàng, *adj./v.*, L. 2, p. 17

fat; corpulent; obese, 肥胖, féipàng, *adj.*, L. 14, p. 150

fate, 命运, mìngyùn, *n.*, L. 26, p. 299

father and daughter, 父女, fùnǚ, *n.*, L. 10, p. 107

fault; mistake, 过错, guòcuò, *n.*, L. 7, p. 76

fear, 害怕, hàipà, *v.*, L. 7, p. 77

feel, 感到, gǎndào, *v.*, L. 16, p. 181

feel embarrassed, 不好意思, bùhǎoyì.si, *v.*, L. 25, p. 289

feel wronged, 委屈, wěiqū, *adj.*, L. 16, p. 181

feeling, 感觉, gǎnjué, *n.*, L. 9, p. 97

feeling; experience, 感受, gǎnshòu, *n.*, L. 22, p. 259

fellow countryman, 同胞, tóngbāo, *n.*, L. 30, p. 345

ferociously, 狠狠, hěnhěn, *adv.*, L. 16, p. 181

few days ago, 前些日子, qián xiē rì.zi, *n.*, L. 13, p. 140

fight; wrestle; engage in hand-to-hand combat, 搏斗, bódòu, *v.*, L. 28, p. 323

fight a battle; go to war, 打仗, dǎ//zhàng, *v.-o.*, L. 11, p. 122

finally; ultimately, 最终, zuìzhōng, *adv.*, L. 26, p. 299

find out; discover, 发现, fāxiàn, *v.*, L. 13, p. 141

fire, 火, huǒ, *n.*, L. 6, p. 67

fire disaster, 火灾, huǒzāi, *n.*, L. 6, p. 67

firmly; resolutely, 坚决, jiānjué, *adv.*, L. 26, p. 297

first; firstly, 首先, shǒuxiān, *conj.*, L. 19, p. 227

first half (of a game, concert, period, etc.), 上半, shàngbàn, *prefix*, L. 16, p. 179

first rate; high-class, 高档, gāodàng, *adj.*, L. 4, p. 43

first trial, 一审, yī shěn, *n.*, L. 16 附录, p. 194

first year in junior high school, 初一, chūyī, *n.*, L. 13, p. 141

fitting (of clothes), 合身, héshēn, *adj.*, L. 4, p. 41

fixed; regular, 固定, gùdìng, *adj.*, L. 20, p. 241

flavor; smell, 味道, wèi.dao, *n.*, L. 24, p. 276

flaw; defect, 缺陷, quēxiàn, *n.*, L. 19, p. 229

floral skirt, 花裙子, huāqún.zi, *n.*, L. 28, p. 321

fly directly, 直飞, zhífēi, *v.*, L. 1, p. 3

follow, 跟, gēn, *v.*, L. 1, p. 3

food, 食品, shípǐn, *n.*, L. 4, p. 44/L. 16, p. 179

lose a lawsuit, 败诉, bàisù, v., L. 26, p. 297

lose face; be disgraced, 丢脸, diū//liǎn, v.-o., L. 11, p. 118

loss, lose, 损失, sǔnshī, n./v., L. 6, p. 68

lost and found notice, 寻物启事, xúnwù qǐshì, n., L. 15, p. 167

lost items, 失物, shīwù, n., L. 15, p. 167

love, 爱, ài, v., L. 9, p. 99

love dearly, 疼, téng, v., L. 22, p. 259

love fervently, 热爱, rè'ài, v., L. 14, p. 152

lover; sweetheart, 恋人, liànrén, n., L. 17, p. 201

luckily; fortunately, 好在, hǎozài, adv., L. 3, p. 31

lung cancer, 肺癌, fèiái, n., L. 29, p. 333

M

machine, 机器, jīqì, n., L. 25, p. 287

magazine, 杂志, zázhì, n., L. 13, p. 142

mail; postal items, 邮件, yóujiàn, n., L. 9, p. 96

main character; leading role, 主角, zhǔjué, n., L. 15, p. 168

main dish, 主菜, zhǔcài, n., L. 24, p. 277

main entrance, 大门, dàmén, n., L. 6, p. 67

mainly, 主要, zhǔyào, adv., L. 6, p. 68

maintain; safeguard; defend, 维护, wéihù, v., L. 32, p. 363

major; specialized field or subjects, 专业, zhuānyè, n., L. 18, p. 214

make, 弄, nòng, v., L. 7, p. 75

make; enable; cause, 使, shǐ, v., L. 9, p. 98

make; manufacture, 制作, zhìzuò, v./n., L. 18, p. 214

make a big fuss in request for or in protest of (sth.), 闹, nào, v., L. 22, p. 259

make a big fuss over a trifle; make a mountain out of a molehill, 小题大做, xiǎotí dàzuò, idm., L. 11, p. 119

make a footnote; mark out, 注明, zhùmíng, v., L. 19, p. 225

make a living by, 靠…为生, kào...wéi shēng, n., L. 5, p. 57

make a living, 谋生, móushēng, v., L. 21, p. 251

make a right turn; turn to the right, 右转, yòuzhuǎn, v., L. 3, p. 31

make an on-the-spot investigation; observe and study, 考察, kǎochá, v., L. 18, p. 211

make contact with, 打交道, dǎ jiāodào, v.-o., L. 1, p. 5

make great efforts; try hard; exert oneself, 努力, nǔlì, adv., L. 14, p. 153

make hand gestures, 比划, bǐ.hua, v., L. 12, p. 131

make inquiry about; concern oneself with; take an interest in, 过问, guòwèn, v., L. 11, p. 119

make known; make clear; state clearly; indicate, 表明, biǎomíng, v., L. 21, p. 249

make money; gain money, 赚钱, zhuàn//qián, v.-o., L. 14, p. 153

make money; 赚钱, 挣钱, zhèng//qián, v.-o., L. 14, p. 153

make people feel…, 令人…, lìngrén, v., L. 14, p. 149

make public; announce; promulgate, 公布, gōngbù, v., L. 11, p. 119

make sense, 有道理, yǒu dàolǐ, v., L. 7, p. 77

make things convenient, 方便, fāngbiàn, v., L. 12, p. 132

make up; account for, 占, zhàn, v., L. 17, p. 201

make up; remedy, 弥补, míbǔ, v., L. 21, p. 249

make up the difference, 补足, bǔ//zú, v.-c., L. 28, p. 321

male sex; man, 男性, nánxìng, n., L. 22, p. 261

manslaughter; murder, 杀人罪, shārénzuì, n., L. 16 附录, p. 195

manuscript; draft, 文稿, wéngǎo, n., L. 18, p. 215

many; not few, 不少, bùshǎo, adj., L. 22, p. 258

mao, ten cents, 毛, máo, , L. 15, p. 163

market economy; market-oriented economy, 市场经济, shìchǎng jīngjì, n., L. 13, p. 142

marriage, 婚姻, hūnyīn, n., L. 10, p. 107

marriage law, 婚姻法, hūnyīnfǎ, n., L. 20, p. 238

married, 已婚, yǐhūn, adj., L. 26, p. 299

marry; take (a wife), 娶, qǔ, v., L. 10, p. 109

marry (of a woman), 嫁, jià, v., L. 10, p. 107

masked civet, 果子狸, guǒ.zilí, n., L. 24, p. 277

masses, 群众, qúnzhòng, n., L. 27, p. 312

mathematics, 数学, shùxué, n., L. 15, p. 163

matter; affair; business, 事情, shì.qing, n., L. 11, p. 119

mature, 成熟, chéngshú, adj., L. 22, p. 261

McDonald's, 麦当劳, Màidāngláo, n., L. 8, p. 87

mean; wicked, 缺德, quēdé, adj., L. 23, p. 270

means; way, 法子, fǎ.zi, n., L. 2, p. 17

measure; step, 措施, cuòshī, n., L. 19, p. 228

measure word for a question in a test or assignment, 道, dào, AN, L. 15, p. 163

measure word for clauses, 条, tiáo, AN, L. 16 附录, p. 195

measure word for clauses, 款, kuǎn, AN, L. 16 附录, p. 196

measure word for dishes, 道, dào, AN, L. 24, p. 277

measure word for documents, papers, etc., 份, fèn, AN, L. 30, p. 343

measure word for dramatic pieces, 出, chū, AN, L. 16, p. 183

measure word for engine, machine, etc., 台, tái, AN, L. 25, p. 287

measure word for games, performance, etc., 场, chǎng, AN, L. 15, p. 163

measure word for group or flock, 群, qún, AN, L. 7, p. 74

measure word for houses, institutions, etc., 所, suǒ, AN, L. 14, p. 148

measure word for items, clauses, etc., 项, xiàng, AN, L. 14, p. 148

measure word for job, 份, fèn, AN, L. 18, p. 215

measure word for legal cases or occurrences, 起, qǐ, AN, L. 19, p. 226

thrifty and simple; economical, 俭朴, jiǎnpǔ, *adj.*, L. 14, p. 152

through; after, 经, jīng, *prep.*, L. 26, p. 299

throw away; throw; toss, 扔, rēng, *v.*, L. 5, p. 55

time; period, 期间, qījiān, *n.*, L. 13, p. 142

times; age; era, 时代, shídài, *n.*, L. 10, p. 109

to; till; until, 至, zhì, *prep.*, L. 22, p. 261

to; towards, 朝, cháo, *prep.*, L. 16, p. 182

to a great degree; extremely; greatly, 远远, yuǎnyuǎn, *adv.*, L. 6, p. 68

to somebody's face; in somebody's presence, 当面, dāng//miàn, *adv.*, L. 15, p. 167

to the fullest (amount, degree, etc.), 尽量, jǐnliàng, *adv.*, L. 1, p. 5

tobacco, 烟草, yāncǎo, *n.*, L. 29, p. 334

tobacco businessman, 烟草商, yāncǎoshāng, *n.*, L. 29, p. 335

TOEFL, Test of English as a Foreign Language, 托福, Tuōfú, *n.*, L. 19, p. 224

together; jointly, 共同, gòngtóng, *adv.*, L. 21, p. 249

Tokyo, Japan, 东京, Dōngjīng, *n.*, L. 1, p. 3

tolerant, 宽容, kuānróng, *adj.*, L. 17, p. 203

tolerate; allow, 容许, róngxǔ, *v.*, L. 30, p. 345

tool; instrument, 工具, gōngjù, *n.*, L. 19, p. 229

toothbrush, 牙刷, yáshuā, *n.*, L. 23, p. 268

toothpaste, 牙膏, yágāo, *n.*, L. 23, p. 269

topic of conversation, 话题, huàtí, *n.*, L. 11, p. 121

tort, 侵权行为, qīnquán xíngwéi, *n.*, L. 27, p. 310

tortoise; turtle, 龟, guī, *n.*, L. 24, p. 277

total; overall, 总, zǒng, *adj.*, L. 27, p. 308

total, 总量, zǒngliàng, *n.*, L. 25, p. 289

tourism; tour, 旅游, lǚyóu, *n./v.*, L. 1, p. 5

tourist, 游客, yóukè, *n.*, L. 28, p. 319

tourist, 观光客, guānguāng kè, *n.*, L. 1, p. 5

toward; in the direction of, 往, wǎng, *prep.*, L. 4, p. 43

trade; deals; business, 交易, jiāoyì, *n.*, L. 15, p. 165

tradition, 传统, chuántǒng, *n.*, L. 4, p. 41

traffic, 交通, jiāotōng, *n.*, L. 2, p. 15/L. 8, p. 87

tragedy, 悲剧, bēijù, *n.*, L. 16, p. 178

train station, 火车站, huǒchēzhàn, *n.*, L. 16, p. 179

transition; shift; change, 转变, zhuǎnbiàn, *n.*, L. 31, p. 350

translation, translate, 翻译, fānyì, *n./v.*, L. 18, p. 213

transmit; deliver; transfer, transmission, 传递, chuándì, *v./n.*, L. 9, p. 97

treatment, 待遇, dàiyù, *n.*, L. 24, p. 278

trees; wood, 树木, shùmù, *n.*, L. 5, p. 57

tremendous, 巨大, jùdà, *adj.*, L. 29, p. 335

trend, 趋势, qūshì, *n.*, L. 29, p. 332

trend of thought, 思潮, sīcháo, *n.*, L. 17, p. 201

trick; cheat, 哄骗, hǒngpiàn, *v.*, L. 27, p. 308

troops; army, 军队, jūnduì, *n.*, L. 32, p. 363

true; real; authentic, 真实, zhēnshí, *adj.*, L. 9, p. 97

truth; the actual state of affairs, 真相, zhēnxiàng, *n.*, L. 26, p. 297

try, 试, shì, *v.*, L. 2, p. 19

try; attempt, 试图, shìtú, *v.*, L. 28, p. 321

try to carry out (a policy, etc.), 推行, tuīxíng, *v.*, L. 25, p. 287

turn into; become, 变成, biànchéng, *v.*, L. 7, p. 77

turn to, 转向, zhuǎnxiàng, *v.*, L. 29, p. 335

turn to the left, 左转, zuǒzhuǎn, *v.*, L. 3, p. 31

two sides of the strait, 两岸, liǎng'àn, *n.*, L. 30, p. 344

type; shape, 型, xíng, *suffix*, L. 14, p. 150

type; style, 式, shì, *suffix*, L. 1, p. 5

typical, 典型, diǎnxíng, *adj.*, L. 27, p. 311

U

ugly, 丑, chǒu, *adj.*, L. 10, p. 107

unable; incapable, 无法, wúfǎ, *adv.*, L. 16, p. 178

unable to stand (test, trial, etc.), 禁不起, jīn.buqǐ, *v.-c.*, L. 1, p. 7

unbutton; untie, 解开, jiě//kāi, *v.-c.*, L. 27, p. 311

under ..., ...之下, zhīxià, L. 16, p. 181

under the heaven, 天下, tiānxià, *n.*, L. 9, p. 98

undergraduate, 本科, běnkē, *n.*, L. 17, p. 201

underpants; panties, 内裤, nèikù, *n.*, L. 5, p. 57

understand, 懂, dǒng, *v.*, L. 1, p. 4

understand; catch on, 明白, míng.bai, *v.*, L. 15, p. 168

understand; comprehend, understanding, 了解, liǎojiě, *v./n.*, L. 1, p. 5

understand; know, 懂得, dǒng.de, *v.*, L. 14, p. 153

understanding, 认识, rèn.shi, *n.*, L. 14, p. 151

undoubtedly, 无疑, wúyí, *adv.*, L. 19, p. 225

unexpectedly; to one's surprise, 竟然, jìngrán, *adv.*, L. 1, p. 4

unexpectedly; 竟然, 竟, jìng, *adv.*, L. 15, p. 163

unify; unite; integrate, integration; unification, 统一, tǒngyī, *v./n.*, L. 30, p. 344

unimaginable; inconceivable, 不可思议, bùkě sīyì, *idm.*, L. 8, p. 87

universities and colleges, 高校, gāoxiào, *n.*, L. 17, p. 201

University of International Trade and Economics, 对外经济贸易大学, Duìwài Jīngjì Màoyì Dàxué, *n.*, L. 18, p. 211

unless; only if, 除非, chúfēi, *conj.*, L. 8, p. 87

urge; persuade; exhort, 劝, quàn, *v.*, L. 5, p. 57

urgent, urgently, 急, jí, *adj./adv.*, L. 19, p. 224

use; employ, 使用, shǐyòng, *v.*, L. 5, p. 55

used up; with nothing left, 光, guāng, *adj.*, L. 20, p. 239

usually; commonly, general; ordinary; common, 一般, yìbān, *adv./adj.*, L. 4, p. 41

English Index

Grammar Index

语法索引

...question word..., ... question word ..., whoever; whatever; whenever, L. 15, p. 169

A

A bǐ B adj. duō.le, A 比 B adj. 多了, A is much more adj. then B, L. 2, p. 21

A bǐ B hái ..., A 比 B 还 adj., A is even more adj. than B , L. 1, p. 9

A bùrú B, A 不如 B, A cannot be compared to B; A is not as good as B, L. 5, p. 59

A .de, B .de, C .de, A 的、B 的、C 的, A ones, B ones, C ones , L. 2, p. 22

A gēn B xiāng v. , A 跟 B 相 v., L. 16 附录, p. 198

A gěi B dàilái..., A 给 B 带来..., A brings ...to B, L. 12, p. 135

A guān.xi.zhe B , A 关系着 B, affect; have a bearing on; have to do with, L. 25, p. 292

A hé B zhījiān, A 和 B 之间, between A and B , L. 10, p. 112

A shǐ B biàn.de..., A 使 B 变得..., A makes B (change to be) ..., L. 9, p. 101

A shì B .de fǎnyìng, A 是 B 的反映, A is the reflection of B , L. 15, p. 172

A yěhǎo, B yěhǎo, dōu..., A 也好，B 也好，都..., no matter whether; whether ... or ..., L. 10, p. 113

A yòu chēng B, A 又称 B, A is also called B, L. 19, p. 230

A yǔ B bèi dào ér chí, A 与 B 背道而驰, run in opposite directions; run counter to , L. 30, p. 346

adj. .de..., adj. 得..., so adj. that..., L. 23, p. 271

adj. de xiàng..., adj.得像..., as adj. as, L. 23, p. 271

adj. shì adj., jiù.shi..., adj. 是 adj.，就是..., It is indeed adj., but it's just that ... , L. 2, p. 21

adj. xiē, Adj. 些, more adj., L. 2, p. 20

adj. yú v., adj 于 v., be adj. to v., L. 26, p. 300

adj. yú, adj. 于, adj. than, L. 18, p. 218

adj.1 zé..., adj.2 zé..., adj. 1 则...，adj. 2 则... , L. 19, p. 232

àn, 按, according to , L. 31, p. 354

B

bǎ...fàng zài dìyī wèi, 把…放在第一位, put ...first, L. 18, p. 217

bǎ...lièwéi..., 把… 列为..., to list sth. as ..., L. 25, p. 291

bǎ...tuīshàng juélù, 把…推上绝路, put...to a road to ruin, L. 27, p. 313

bǎi zài....de miànqián, 摆在（人）的面前, be put in front of us; needed to be faced squarely, L. 31, p. 355

bāokuò...zàinèi, 包括…在内, including..., L. 30, p. 346

bǎozhèng, 保证, to guarantee, L. 2, p. 22

bèi...suǒ v. , 被…所 v., be v.-ed by , L. 22, p. 264

bǐqǐ...lái, 比起…来, when compared with ..., L. 21, p. 253

bìjìng, 毕竟, after all; at least, L. 28, p. 326

biǎomiànshàng..., qíshí..., 表面上...，其实..., on the surface...in fact ..., L. 7, p. 81

búbì, 不必, need not, L. 3, p. 35

búdànbù..., fǎn'ér..., 不但不...，反而..., not only...on the contrary..., L. 7, p. 80

búdào, 不到, less than; under, L. 28, p. 324

búgù, 不顾, regardless; disregard, L. 24, p. 281

búguò, 不过, merely; only, L. 6, p. 70

bújiàn.de, 不见得, not necessarily; not likely, L. 5, p. 59

búlùn A, lùn B, 不论 A，论 B , do not go by A, but rather B, L. 2, p. 24

búshì A érshì B, 不是 A，而是 B, it's not A, but B, L. 1, p. 9/L. 7, p. 81

búzhìyú, 不至于, cannot or be unlikely to go so far as to, L. 11, p. 125

bù A bù B, 不 A 不 B, not A not B; neither A nor B , L. 2, p. 23

bùchū...jiù, 不出…就..., within, L. 22, p. 262

bùdébù, 不得不, have no choice but to, L. 21, p. 254

bùdéyǐ, 不得已, to have no alternative, L. 7, p. 79

bùjǐn..., jiùlián...yě..., 不仅...，就连…也..., not only ...even..., L. 13, p. 144

fǒuzé, 否则, otherwise; if not, L. 18, p. 218

fùyǔ, 赋予, give; endow; entrust, L. 26, p. 301

fùzé, 负责, be responsible for; be in charge of, L. 3, p. 34

G

gāi v. de bù v., bù gāi v. dào v., 该 v. 的不 v., 不该 v. 倒 v., those that are supposed to *v.* do not *v.*, but, L. 12, p. 133

gànmá, 干嘛, do what? (used in a rhetorical question), L. 18, p. 216

gāng v. jiù..., 刚 v.,就..., no sooner...than..., L. 23, p. 271

gào, 告, to sue; to take (sb.) to court, L. 8, p. 90

gěi v., 给 v., L. 5, p. 59

gěi, 给, (used in a passive sentence to introduce either the doer of the action or the action itself.), L. 7, p. 79

gēnběn, 根本, at all; simply, L. 9, p. 100

gèngjiā, 更加 adj., even more adj.; more adj., L. 14, p. 156

gōngrèn, 公认, generally acknowledge, L. 24, p. 282

gòu...máng.de.le, 够（人）忙的了, enough to make sb. busy, L. 26, p. 303

gùrán..., dànshì, 固然..., 但是..., It's true that ..., but ..., L. 6, p. 69

guānyú, 关于, about; on, L. 14, p. 154

guāng...jiù..., 光...就..., only; merely, L. 26, p. 302

H

háiméi v., (jiù) ..., 还没 v., (就)..., not even v.-ed yet, ...(indicate something happens too soon), L. 23, p. 272

háobù v./adj., 毫不 v./adj., not ...at all, L. 19, p. 231

háowú n., 毫无 n., no ... at all; there is no ... at all, L. 19, p. 230

hǎoxiàng, 好像, seem to be, L. 4, p. 45

hǎozài...yào.burán, 好在..., 要不然..., luckily..., otherwise..., L. 3, p. 34

hěnhěn, 狠狠, ferociously, L. 16, p. 186

hèn.budé, 恨不得, one wishes one could; be dying to, L. 11, p. 125

huá.delái/huá.bulái, 划得来/划不来, worth it/not worth it, L. 2, p. 22

huànjùhuàshuō, 换句话说, in other words, L. 26, p. 303

huò...huò..., 或...或..., or...or..., L. 22, p. 263

J

jīběnshàng, 基本上, basically; on the whole, L. 16, p. 185

jíshǐ..., yě..., 即使..., 也..., even if ..., L. 10, p. 112

jǐyǔ, 给予 v., give (usually take abstract noun as direct object), L. 19, p. 232

jìrán..., jiù..., 既然..., 就..., since ..., then ..., L. 15, p. 173

jìrán..., wèishén.me bù/hái.ne?, 既然..., 为什么不/还...呢？, Since (it's the case that)..., why not/still...?, L. 2, p. 21

jiāqiáng, 加强, enhance; reinforce, L. 16, p. 188

..., jiā.shàng..., ..., 加上..., ..., in addition, ..., L. 3, p. 34

jiǎrú, 假如, if; supposing; in case, L. 26, p. 301

jiǎzhuāng, 假装, pretend; feign, L. 27, p. 313

jiǎnzhí, 简直, simply; at all, L. 4, p. 48

jiàn.buderén, 见不得人, not fit to be seen; shameful; cannot bear the light of the day, L. 25, p. 290

jiànyú, 鉴于, seeing that; in light of, L. 16 附录, p. 198

jiēshòu, 接受, to accept; to receive, L. 4, p. 46

jiéguǒ, 结果, result; outcome; consequence, L. 4, p. 49

jǐnguǎn, 尽管, even though; despite, L. 5, p. 60

jǐnjǐn...jiù..., 仅仅...就..., only because...; merely for..., L. 16, p. 188

jǐnkěnéng, 尽可能, as far as possible, L. 14, p. 157

jǐnliàng, 尽量, to the fullest (amount, degree, etc.), L. 1, p. 9

qiānwàn, 千万, be sure to; must, L. 3, p. 36

qiángxíng, 强行, forcefully, L. 27, p. 314

qiǎng.zhe, 抢着 v., scramble for; vie for , L. 2, p. 20

qīngxiàngyú, 倾向于, be inclined to; prefer to, L. 17, p. 204

qíngjí zhī xià, 情急之下, in a moment of desperation, L. 15, p. 169

qiúzhùyú, 求助于, turn to sb. for help, L. 20, p. 243

qǔdài, 取代, to replace; to supersede, L. 4, p. 48

R

rán'ér, 然而, however; nevertheless; but, L. 15, p. 171

rèzhōngyú, 热衷于, be fond of; be keen on, L. 18, p. 218

rìyì v./adj., 日益 v./adj., v./adj. day by day, L. 14, p. 157

rú, 如, for example; such as, L. 17, p. 205

rúguǒ/yào.shì..., (nà) jiù..., 如果/要是..., （那）就..., if..., then ..., L. 4, p. 46

rútóng...yíyàng, 如同...一样 (+ adj.) , like; similar to; , L. 20, p. 243

S

S. nǎr v., S. 哪儿 v. !, (rhetorical question), L. 10, p. 111

S.1 zài v., S.2 jiù..., S.1 再 v., S.2 就..., If S.1 goes on v.-ing, S.2 would ..., L. 16, p. 186

shànzì, 擅自, (do sth.) without authorization, L. 26, p. 300

shéi yě bù v. shéi, 谁也不 v.谁, neither of them v. one another, L. 22, p. 263

shéi zhī.dào, 谁知道..., who knows that...; no one expects that ..., L. 15, p. 172

shènzhì, 甚至, even (to the point of); so much so that, L. 6, p. 71

shènzhì(yú), 甚至（于）, even; even to the point that; so much so that, L. 5, p. 61

shíjìshàng, 实际上, actually; in reality; in actual fact, L. 5, p. 62

shǐzhōng, 始终, from beginning to end; all along, L. 32, p. 364

shìfǒu, 是否, whether or not; whether; if, L. 19, p. 231

shì.shi, 试试, to give it a try, L. 2, p. 24

shǒuxiān..., qícì..., 首先..., 其次... , first ... , second ..., L. 19, p. 231

shǔyú, 属于, be part of; fall into the category of ..., L. 18, p. 216

shuō.budìng, 说不定, perhaps; maybe , L. 12, p. 135

shuōmíng, 说明, to show; to illustrate; to explain, L. 4, p. 48

suíshí suídì, 随时随地都···, at any time and at any place, L. 12, p. 134

suí.zhe, 随着, along with..., L. 20, p. 244

suǒwèi.de, 所谓的 n. , the so-called n., L. 7, p. 80

T

tígāo duì....de rènshí, 提高对... 的认识, be more aware of, L. 29, p. 337

tíqián, 提前, shift to an earlier date/time; in advance; ahead of time, L. 29, p. 336

tīngshuō, 听说, to hear that; be told, L. 6, p. 69

Time duration + v. xià.lai, Time duration + v. 下来, after v.-ing for ... , L. 2, p. 24

Time duration + xià.lai, Time duration + 下来, after + time duration, L. 5, p. 60

tōngguò, 通过, through; by means of, L. 13, p. 144

tú, 图, seek; pursue, L. 22, p. 262

V

v. bùchū o. lái, v. 不出 o. 来, unable to v. – o., L. 10, p. 111

v./adj. dào...dìbù, v./adj. 到...地步, v./adj. to the extent of ..., L. 12, p. 134

v. diào, V. 掉, v. away, L. 4, p. 47

v. guāng, v. 光, v. it all up; consumed completely, L. 20, p. 242

yìxīn yíyì, 一心一意, wholeheartedly, L. 32, p. 365

yīncǐ, 因此, therefore; hence; consequently , L. 9, p. 101

yǐnqǐ, 引起, lead up to; give rise to, L. 14, p. 156

yìng v., 硬 v., v. obstinately, L. 28, p. 325

yòng…lái v., 用…来 v., use …to…, L. 18, p. 216

yóu, 由, by means of; be v-ed by sb./sth., L. 26, p. 303

yóu…v., 由…v., v. from , L. 31, p. 354

yóucǐ, 由此 , from this; by this, L. 20, p. 242

…, yóuqíshì, …, 尤其是…, …, especially …, L. 4, p. 47

yóuyú, 由于, due to; owing to, L. 14, p. 155

yóuyù, 犹豫, hesitate; hesitant, L. 22, p. 262

yǒu….de, yǒu….de, 有…的, 有…的, some …, some …, L. 15, p. 171

yǒuquán v., 有权 v., have the right to, L. 21, p. 253

yǒushén.me hǎo v. .de.ne?, 有什么好 v. 的呢? , What is there to v. ? , L. 12, p. 134

yǒusuǒ v., 有所 v., have v-ed to some extent, L. 20, p. 242

yǒuyìyú, 有益于, to do good to; to benefit, L. 14, p. 157

yǒuzhùyú, 有助于, help to; contribute to, L. 14, p. 156

yòu, 又, on top of sth.; in addition to sth., L. 23, p. 271

yòu…, yòu…, hái…, 又…, 又…, 还…, both … and …, in addition, …, L. 2, p. 23

yúshì, 于是, consequently; hence; thereupon, L. 8, p. 89

yǔ…xiāngbǐ, 与…相比, compared with, L. 29, p. 336

yǔqí A, bùrú B, 与其 A, 不如 B, rather then A, it would be better B , L. 11, p. 125

Z

zài…dāngzhōng, 在…当中, among; in the middle of , L. 21, p. 252

zài….de tóngshí, 在…的同时, while doing…, L. 25, p. 291

zài…guòchéng zhōng, 在…过程中, in the course of …, L. 31, p. 354

zài…kànlái, 在 sb. 看来, in sb.'s view, L. 7, p. 80

zài…nèi, （在） time duration 内, in (certain) time, L. 31, p. 355

zài…shàng, 在…上, in terms of, L. 5, p. 61

zài…xià…, 在…下, under, L. 7, p. 81

zài…zhōng suǒ zhàn .de fènliàng, 在…中所占的分量, the influential role played in …, L. 22, p. 263

zàicì, 再次, once more; the second time; once again, L. 16, p. 186

zài.hu, 在乎, care about; mind, L. 11, p. 124

zàishuō, 再说, moreover; furthermore, L. 10, p. 112

zǎojiù v. .le, 早就 v. 了, has v.-ed a long time ago, L. 12, p. 134

zǎoyǐ, 早已, long since, L. 24, p. 281

zǎozài…jiù v., 早在… 就 v., have v.-ed as early as, L. 18, p. 217

zé, 则, (a conjunction used in second sentence or clause meaning "however."), L. 15, p. 172

zěn.me v. yě bù…, 怎么 v.也不…, no matter how…, still can not…, L. 23, p. 272

zhàn, 占, make up …, L. 17, p. 204

zhǎo, 找, to call on (sb.); to seek (the help of sb.), L. 8, p. 90

zhàocháng, 照常, as usual; as before, L. 16, p. 188

zhàoyàng, 照样, same as before, L. 23, p. 272

zhèiyàng xià.qu, 这样下去, go on like this, L. 12, p. 135

zhènjīng, 震惊, shock; astonish, L. 16, p. 187

zhèngmíng, 证明, proof; prove, L. 12, p. 133

…zhījí, …之极, extremely, L. 24, p. 282

…zhīzhì, …之至 , extremely, L. 24, p. 282

zhí.de v., 值得 v., deserve to be v.-ed ; worth v.-ing, L. 4, p. 46